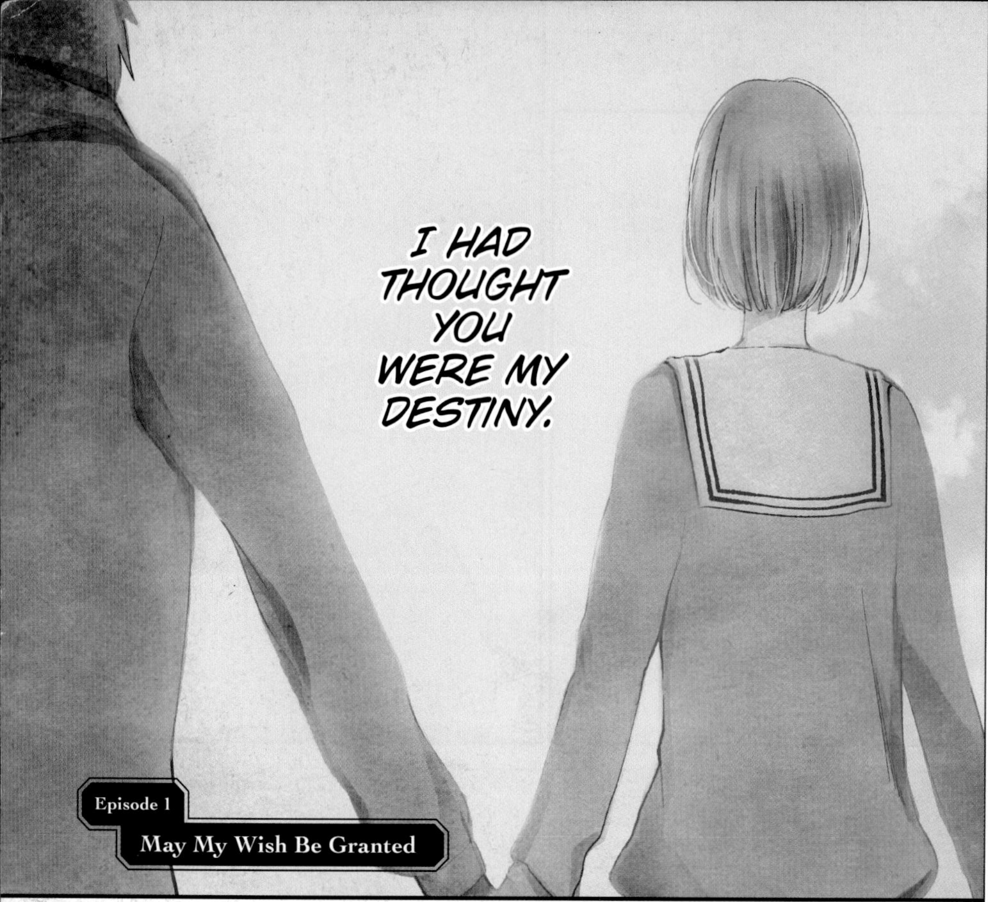
I HAD THOUGHT YOU WERE MY DESTINY.
Episode 1
May My Wish Be Granted

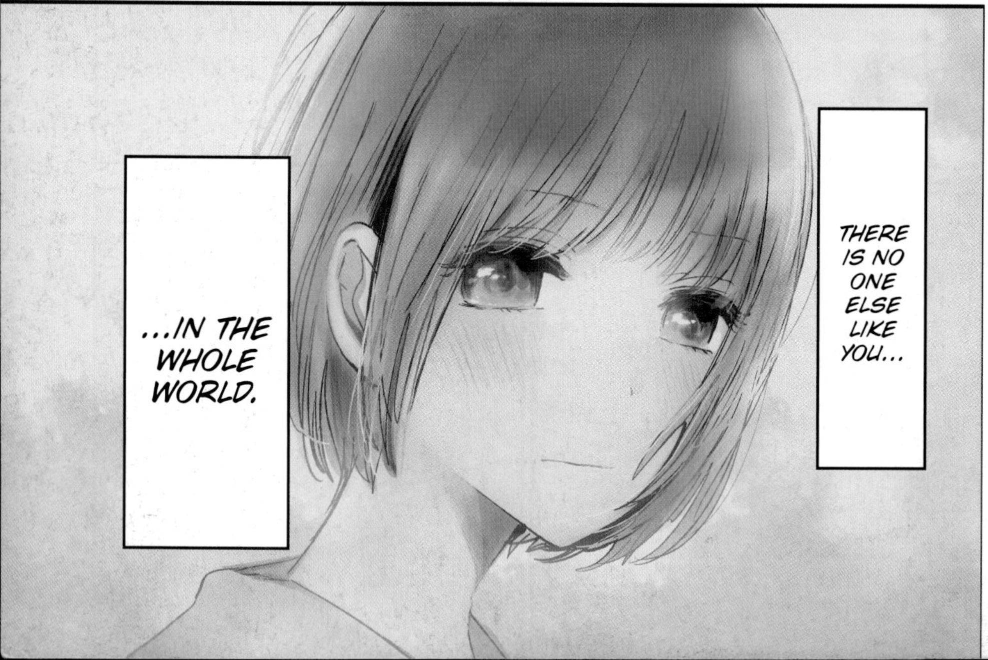
THERE IS NO ONE ELSE LIKE YOU...
...IN THE WHOLE WORLD.

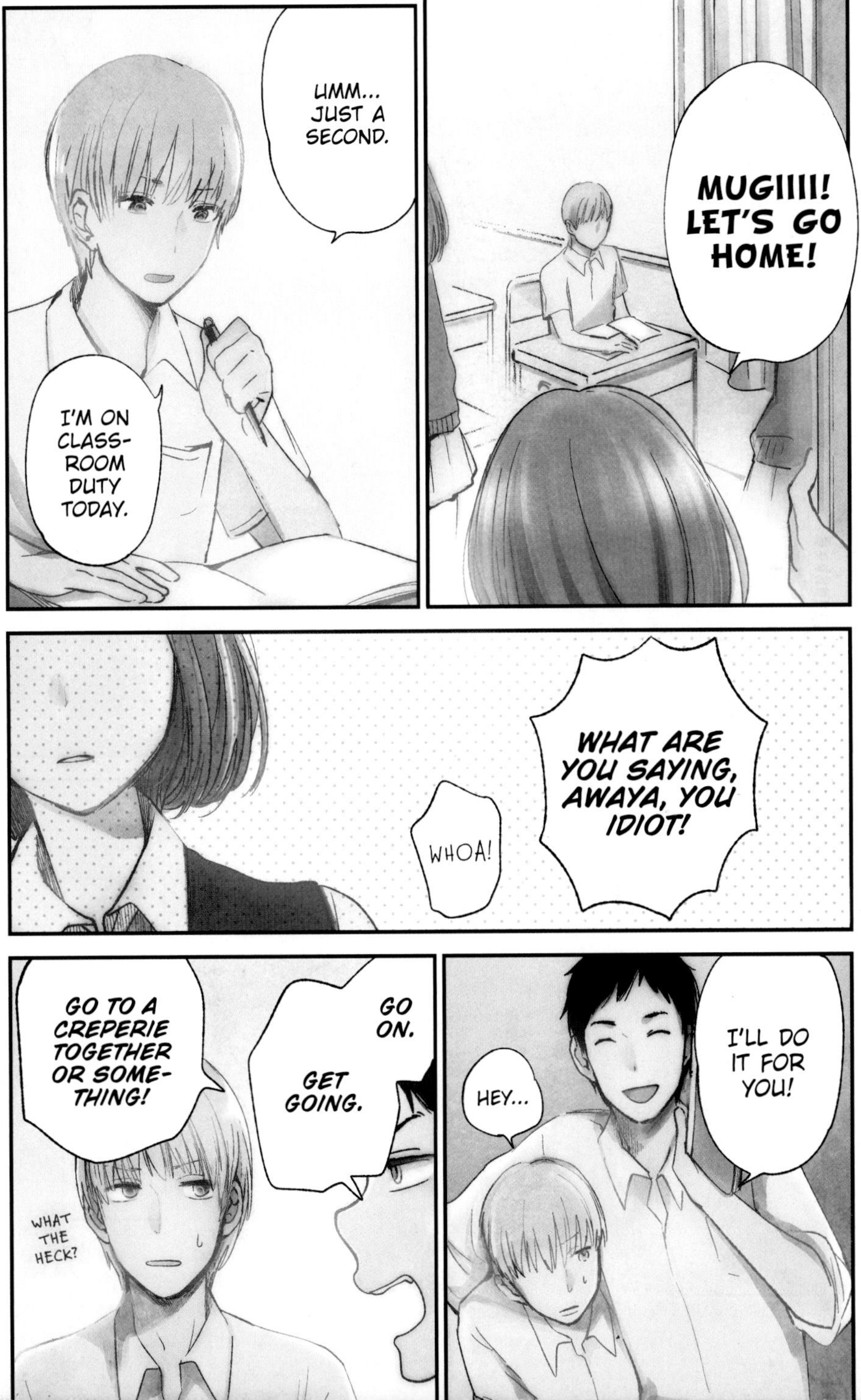
MUGIIII! LET'S GO HOME!
UMM... JUST A SECOND.
I'M ON CLASS-ROOM DUTY TODAY.
WHAT ARE YOU SAYING, AWAYA, YOU IDIOT!
WHOA!
I'LL DO IT FOR YOU!
HEY...
GO ON.
GET GOING.
GO TO A CREPERIE TOGETHER OR SOME-THING!
WHAT THE HECK?

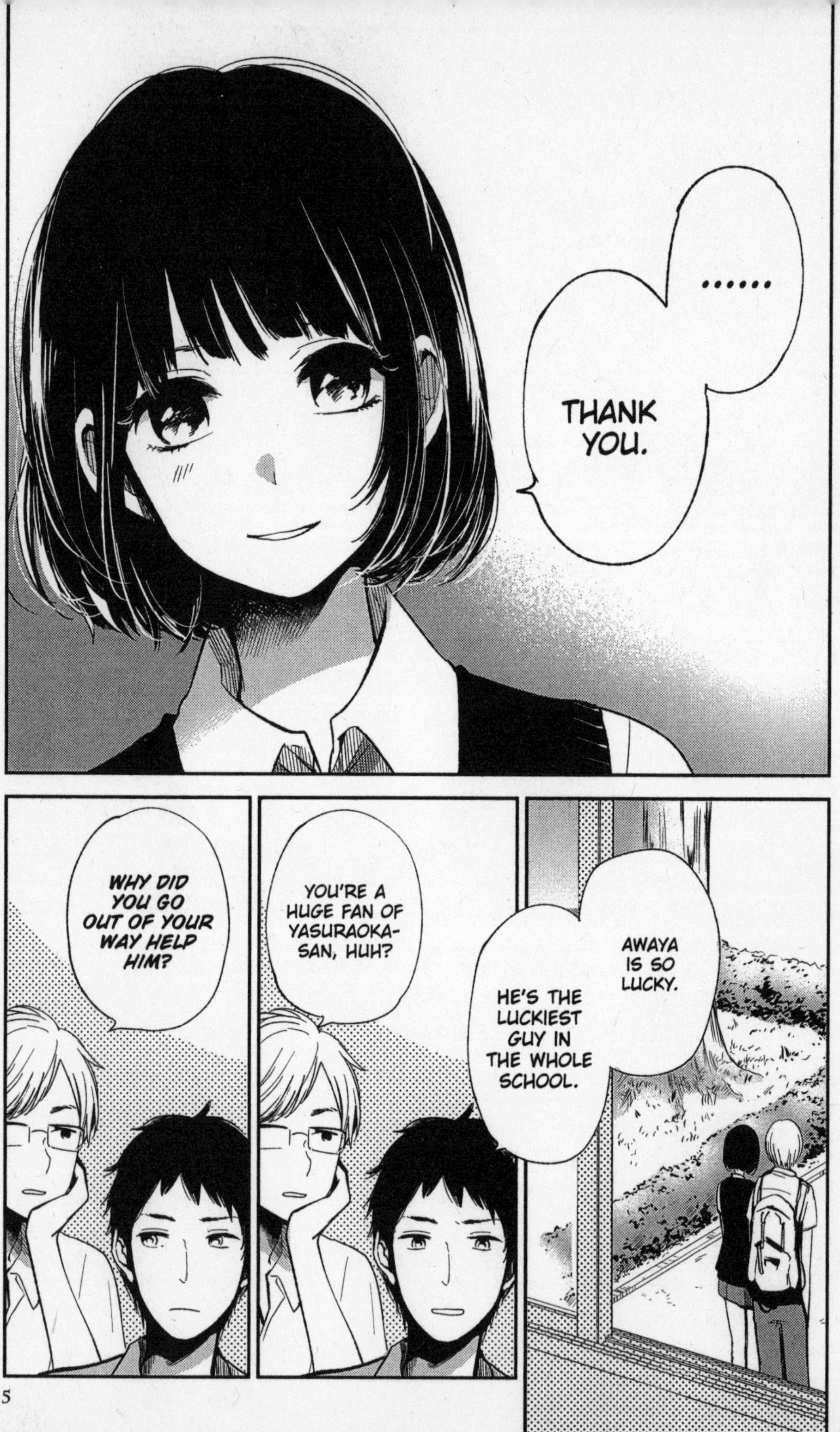
......
THANK YOU.
AWAYA IS SO LUCKY.
HE'S THE LUCKIEST GUY IN THE WHOLE SCHOOL.
YOU'RE A HUGE FAN OF YASURAOKA-SAN, HUH?
WHY DID YOU GO OUT OF YOUR WAY HELP HIM?

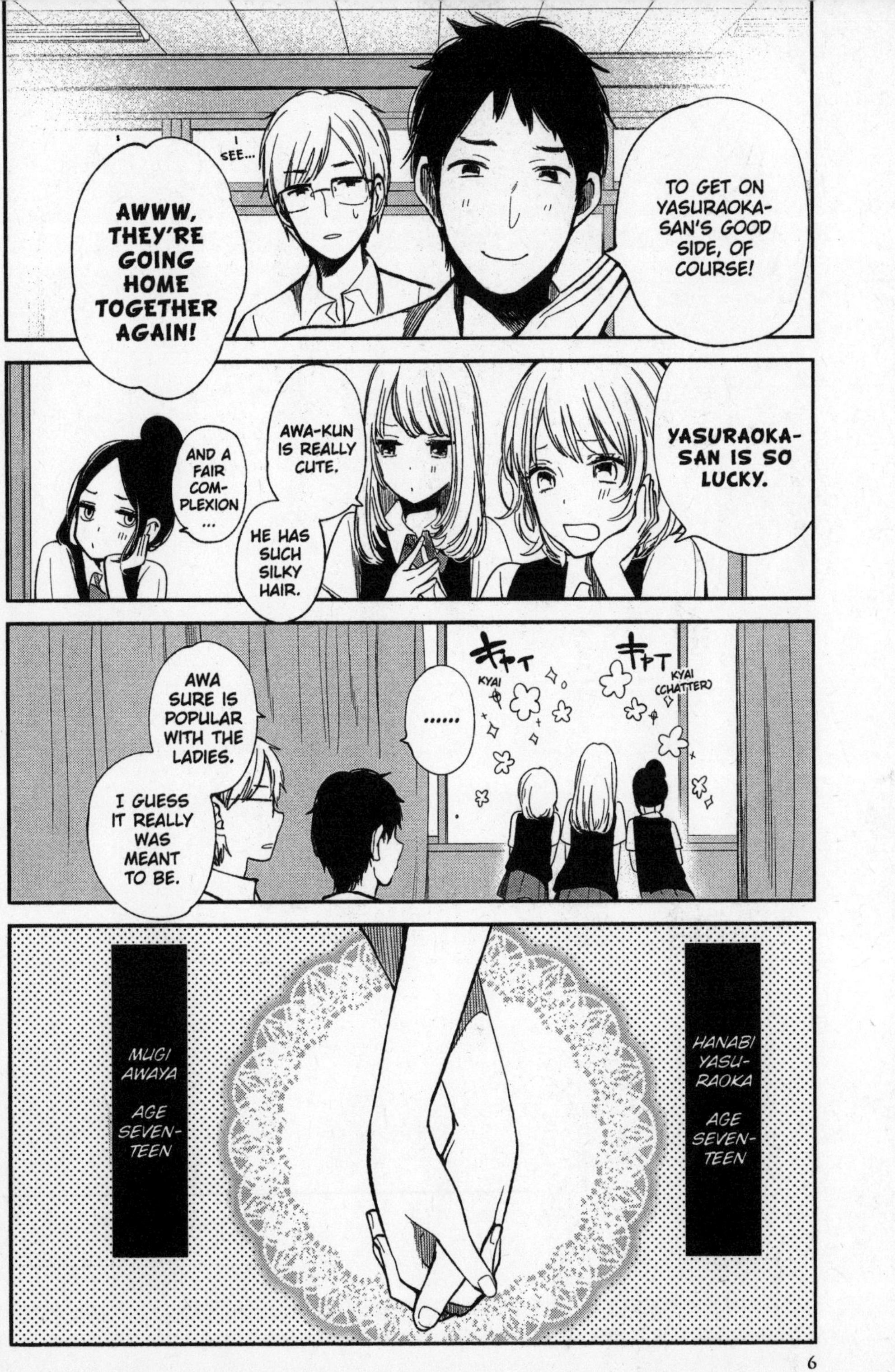
TO GET ON YASURAOKA-SAN'S GOOD SIDE, OF COURSE!
I SEE...
AWWW, THEY'RE GOING HOME TOGETHER AGAIN!
YASURAOKA-SAN IS SO LUCKY.
AWA-KUN IS REALLY CUTE.
HE HAS SUCH SILKY HAIR.
AND A FAIR COMPLEXION...
KYAI (CHATTER)
KYAI
......
AWA SURE IS POPULAR WITH THE LADIES.
I GUESS IT REALLY WAS MEANT TO BE.
HANABI YASURAOKA AGE SEVENTEEN
MUGI AWAYA AGE SEVENTEEN

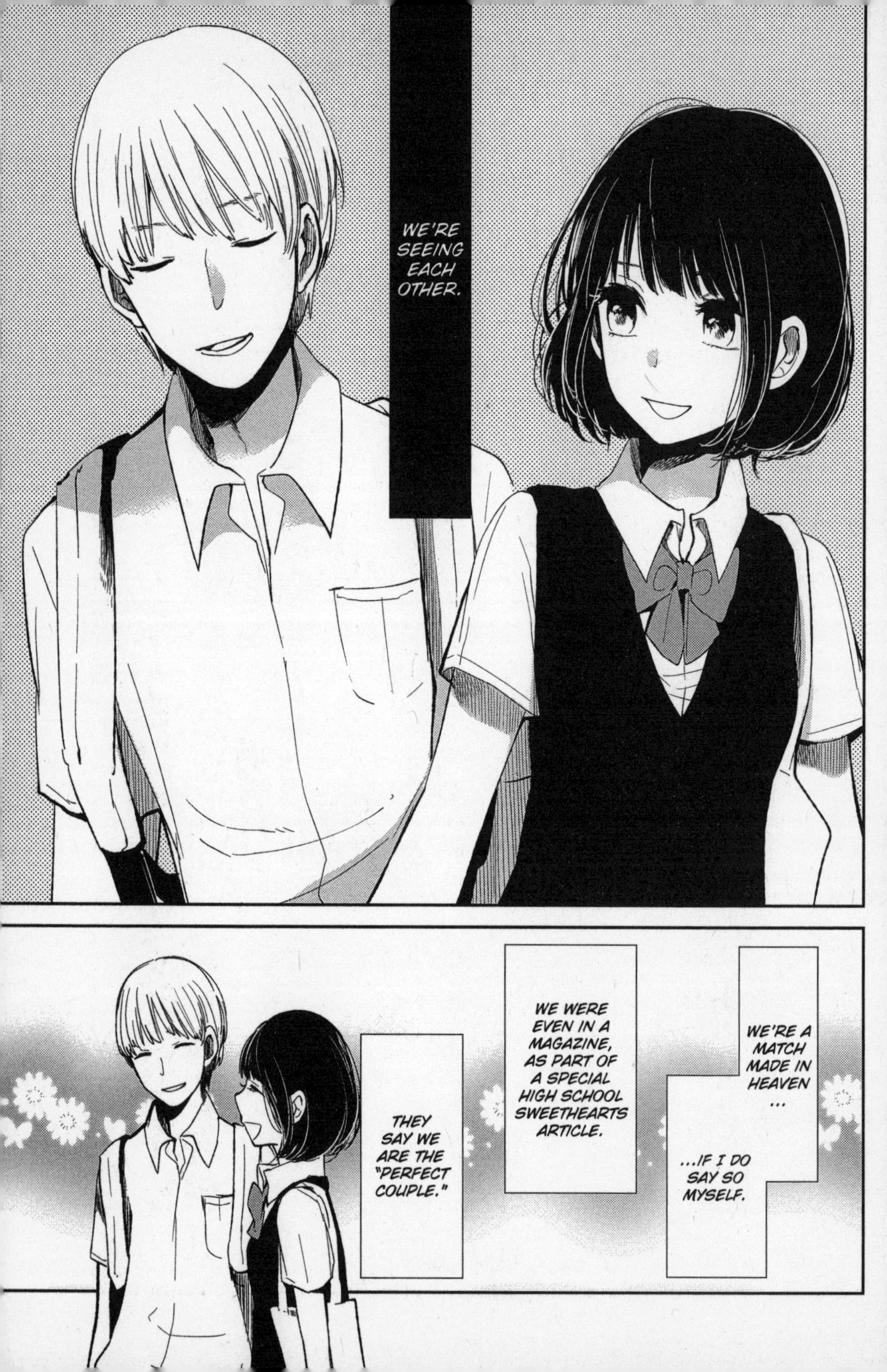
WE'RE SEEING EACH OTHER.
WE'RE A MATCH MADE IN HEAVEN...
...IF I DO SAY SO MYSELF.
WE WERE EVEN IN A MAGAZINE, AS PART OF A SPECIAL HIGH SCHOOL SWEETHEARTS ARTICLE.
THEY SAY WE ARE THE "PERFECT COUPLE."

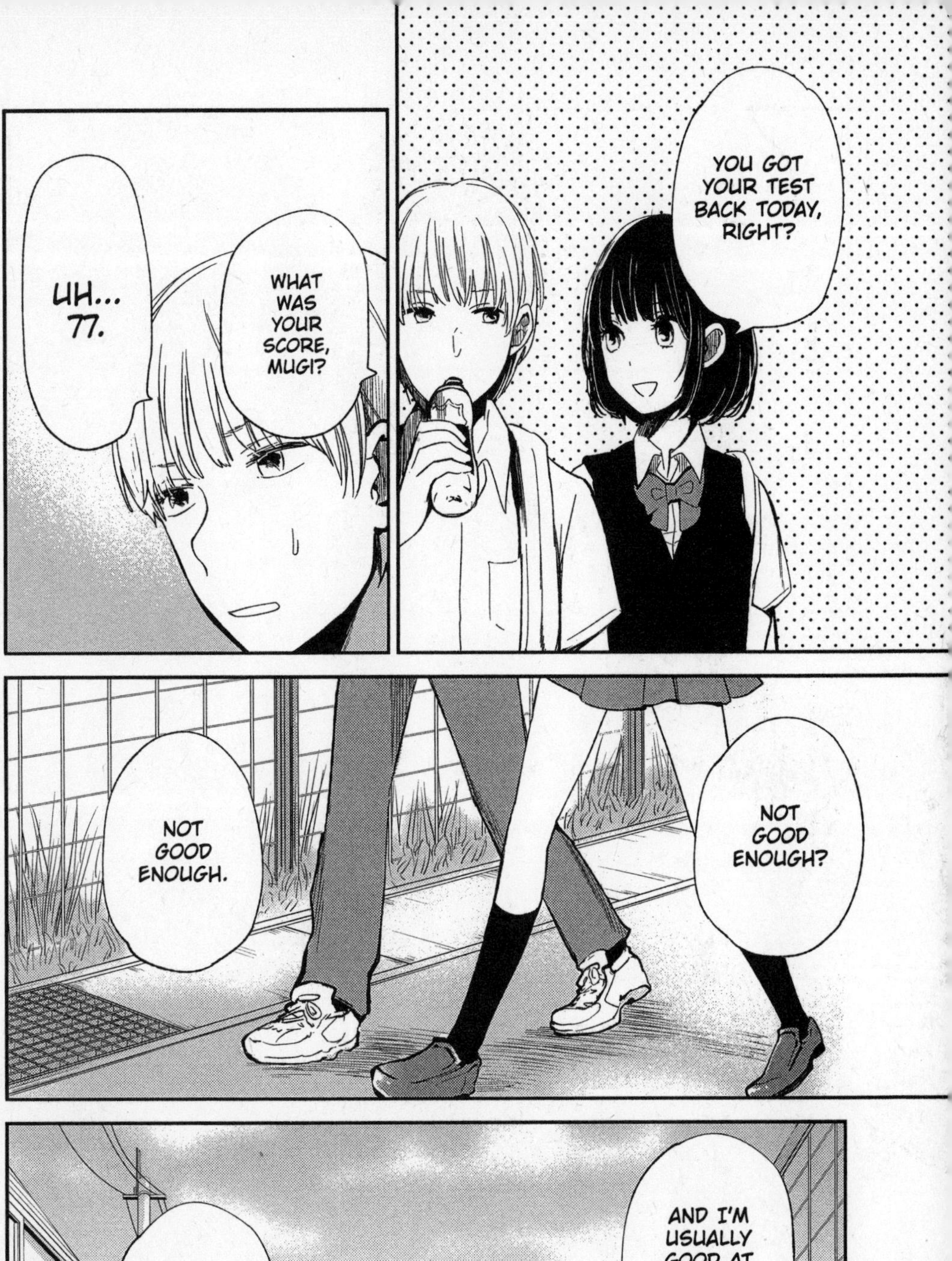
YOU GOT YOUR TEST BACK TODAY, RIGHT?
WHAT WAS YOUR SCORE, MUGI?
UH... 77.
NOT GOOD ENOUGH?
NOT GOOD ENOUGH.
AND I'M USUALLY GOOD AT CLASSICS...
THAT'S TOO BAD.

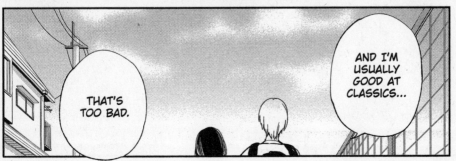

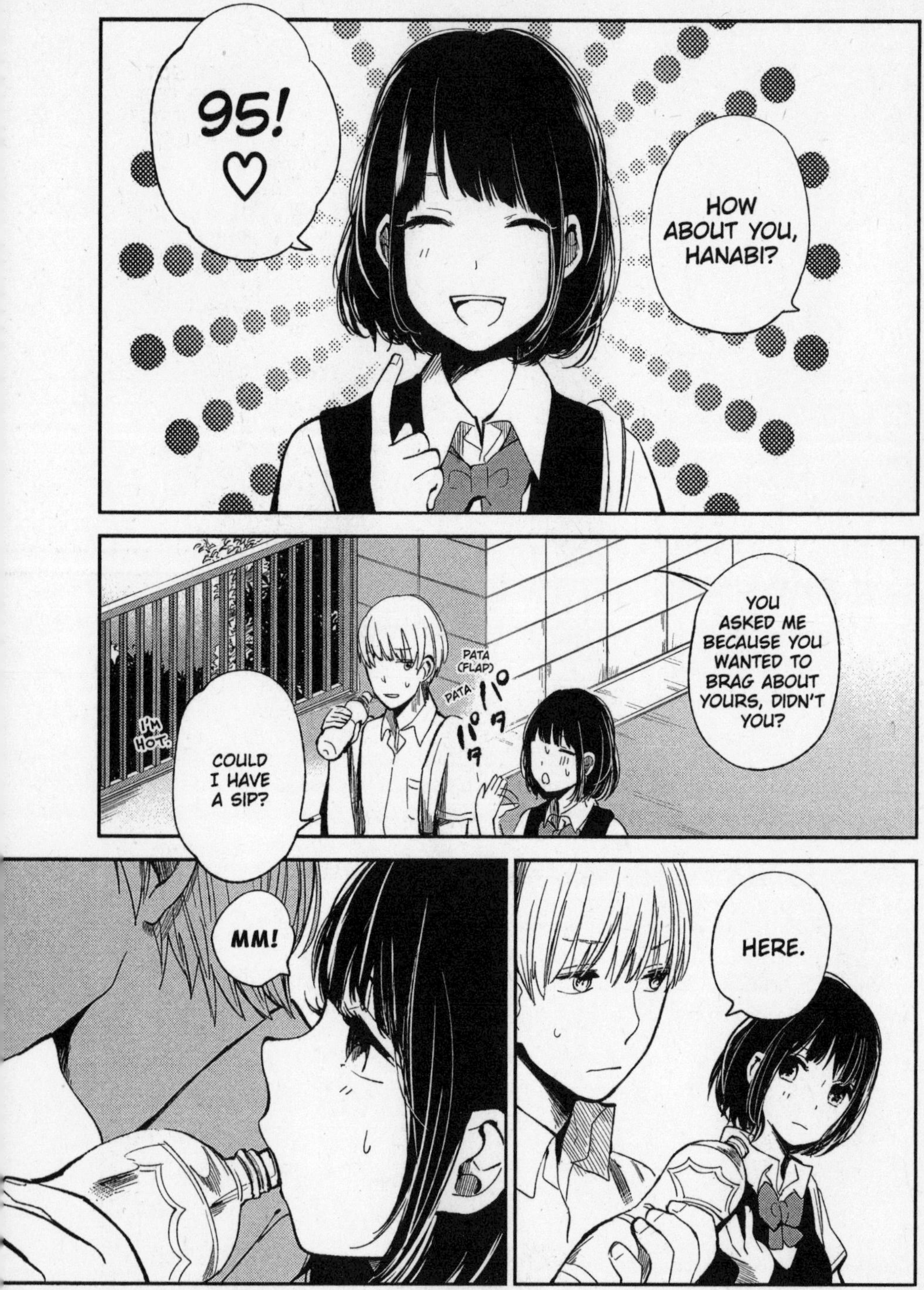
HOW ABOUT YOU, HANABI?
95! ♡
YOU ASKED ME BECAUSE YOU WANTED TO BRAG ABOUT YOURS, DIDN'T YOU?
PATA (FLAP)
PATA
パタパタ
I'M HOT.
COULD I HAVE A SIP?
HERE.
MM!

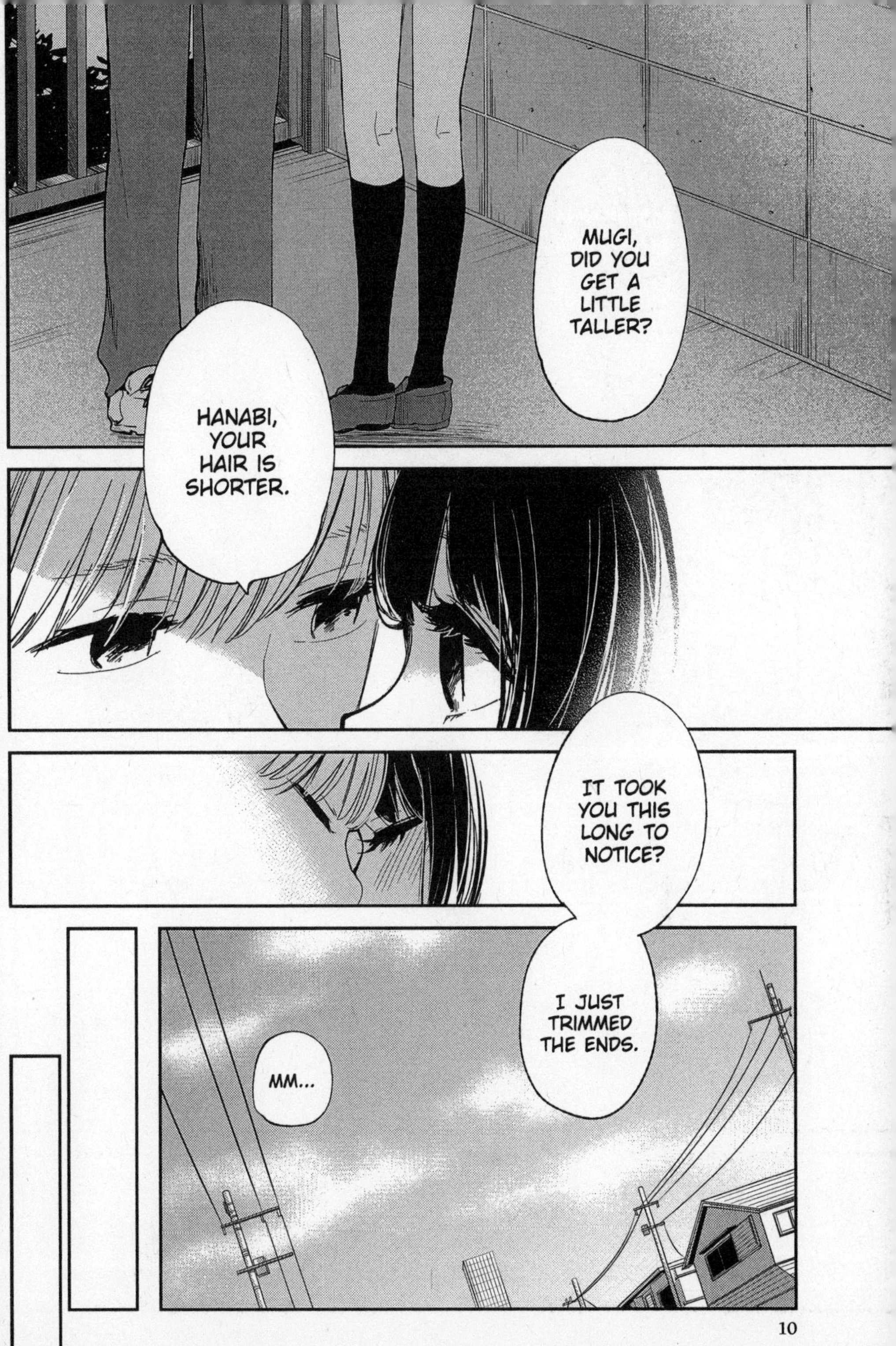
MUGI, DID YOU GET A LITTLE TALLER?
HANABI, YOUR HAIR IS SHORTER.
IT TOOK YOU THIS LONG TO NOTICE?
I JUST TRIMMED THE ENDS.
MM...

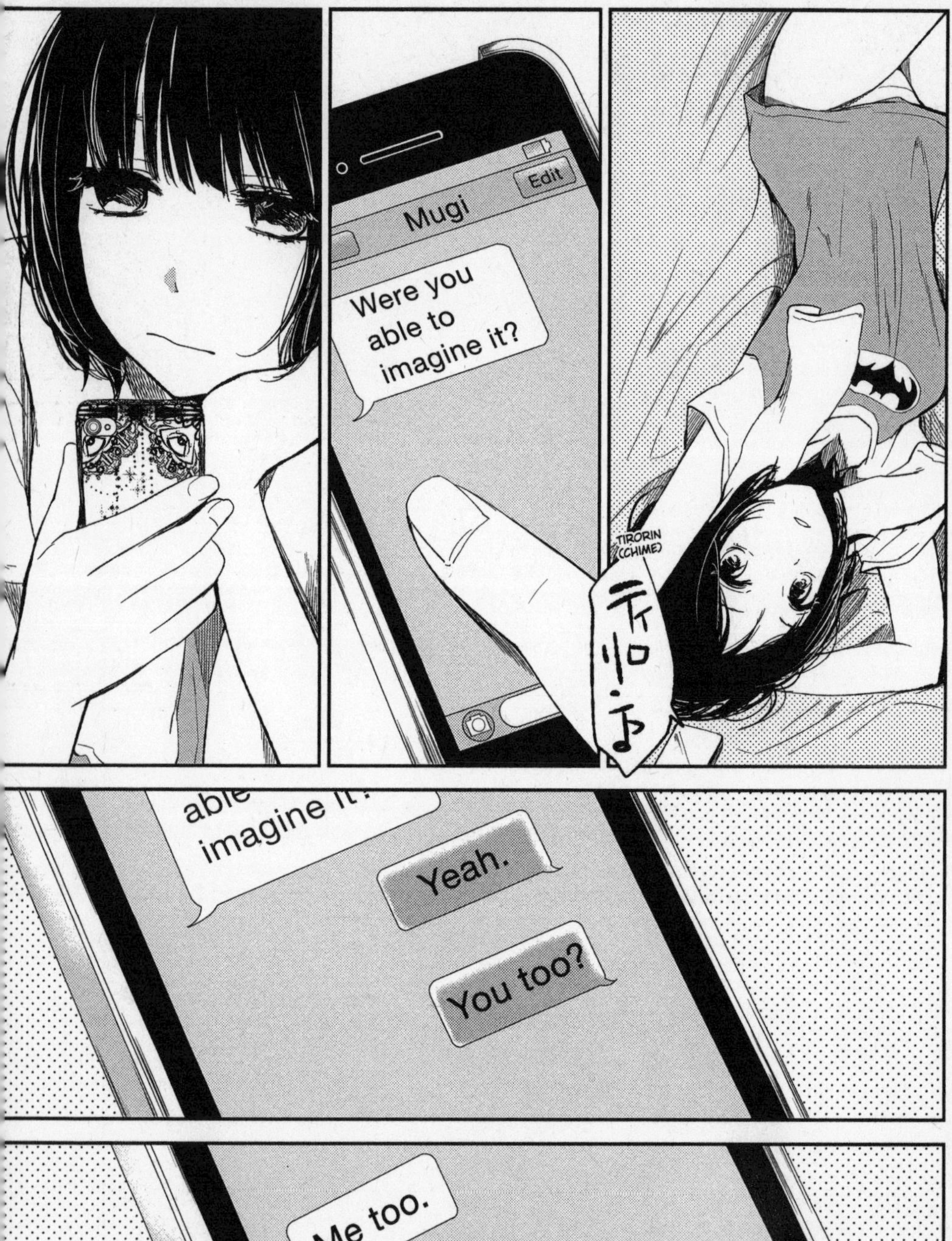
TIRORIN (CHIME)
Edit
Mugi
Were you able to imagine it?
able
imagine it
Yeah.
You too?
Me too.

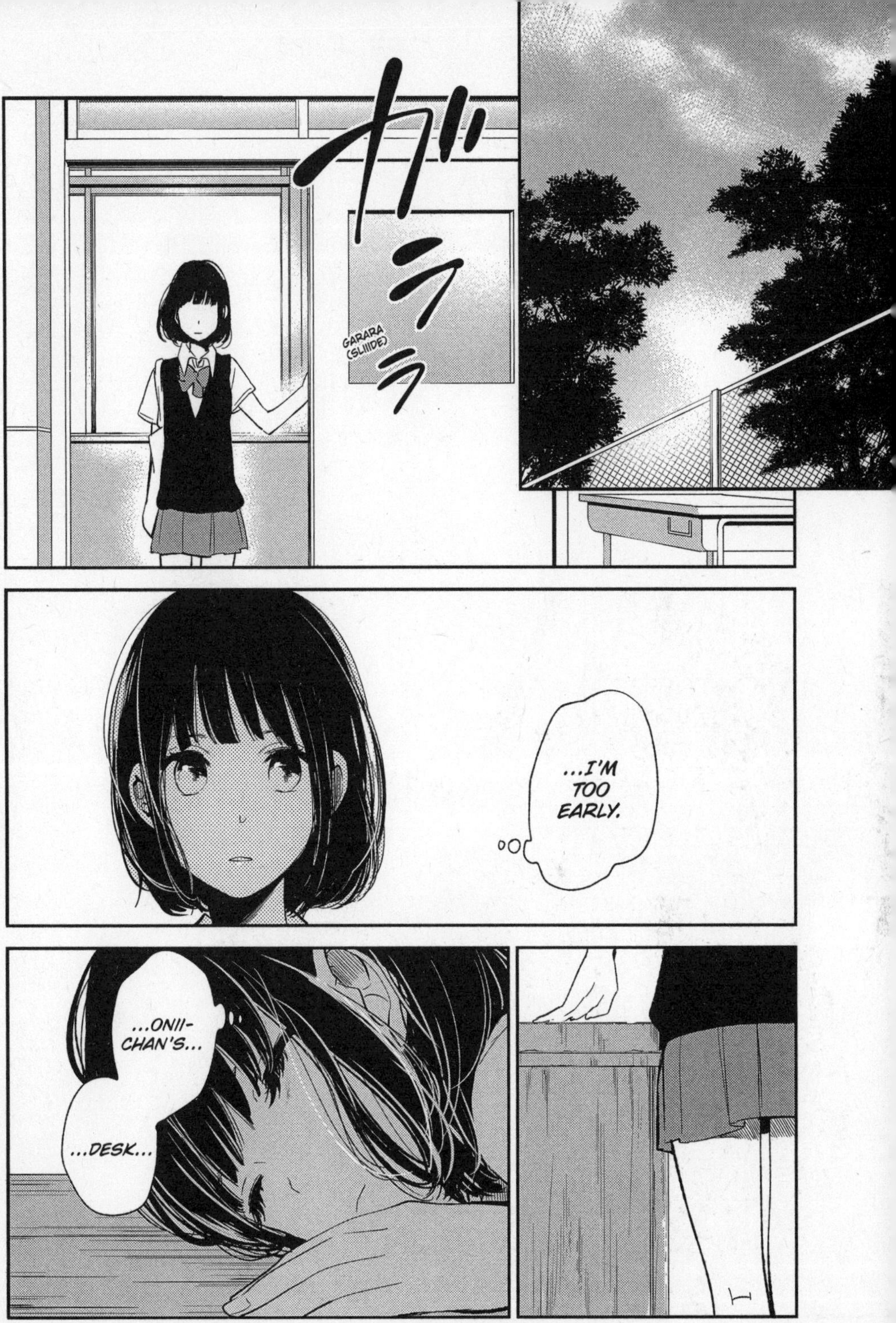
ガララ
GARARA (SLIIIDE)
...I'M TOO EARLY.
...ONII-CHAN'S...
...DESK...

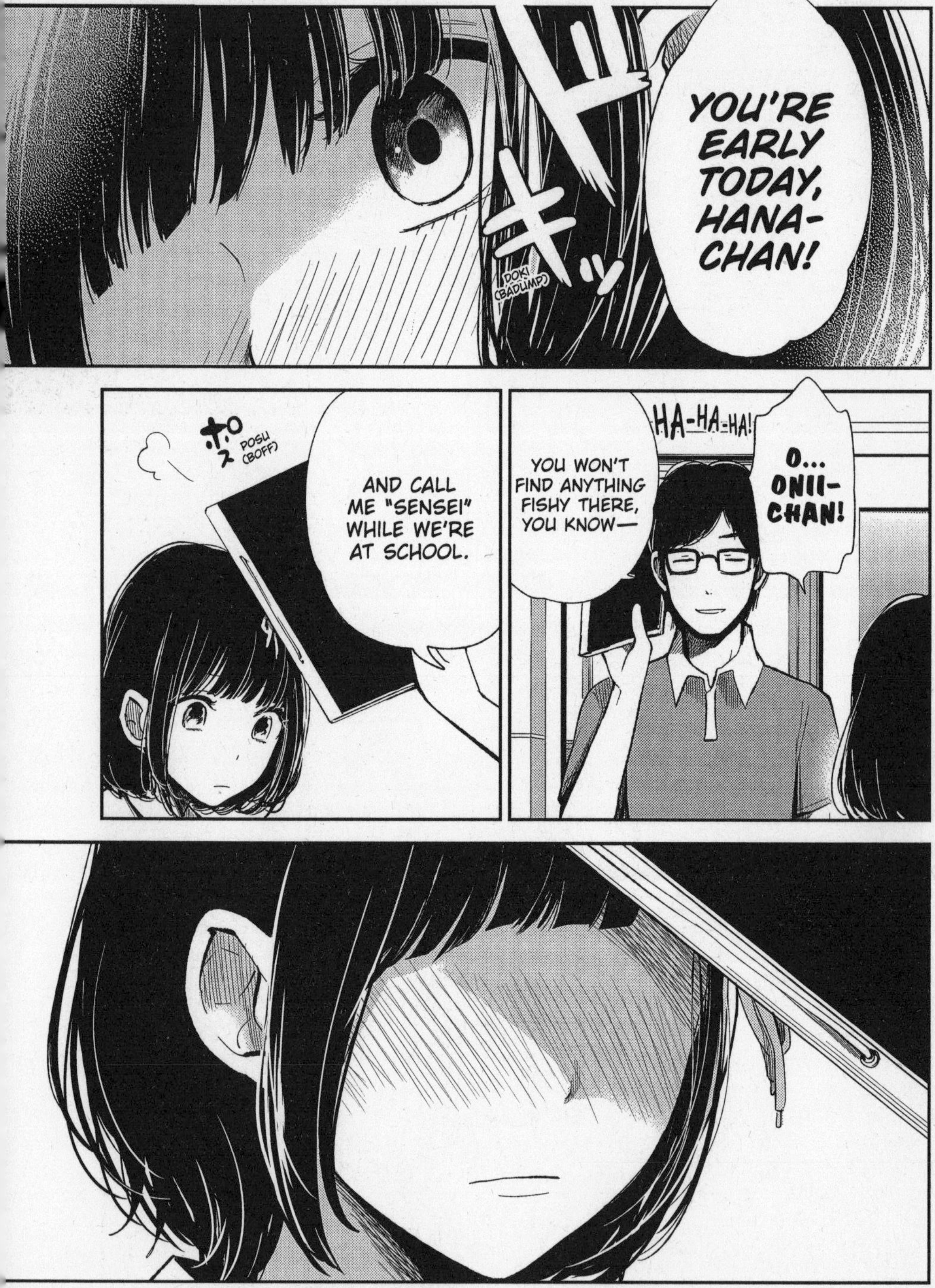
YOU'RE EARLY TODAY, HANA-CHAN!
DOKI (BADUMP)
O... ONII-CHAN!
HA-HA-HA!
YOU WON'T FIND ANYTHING FISHY THERE, YOU KNOW—
AND CALL ME "SENSEI" WHILE WE'RE AT SCHOOL.
POSU (BOFF)

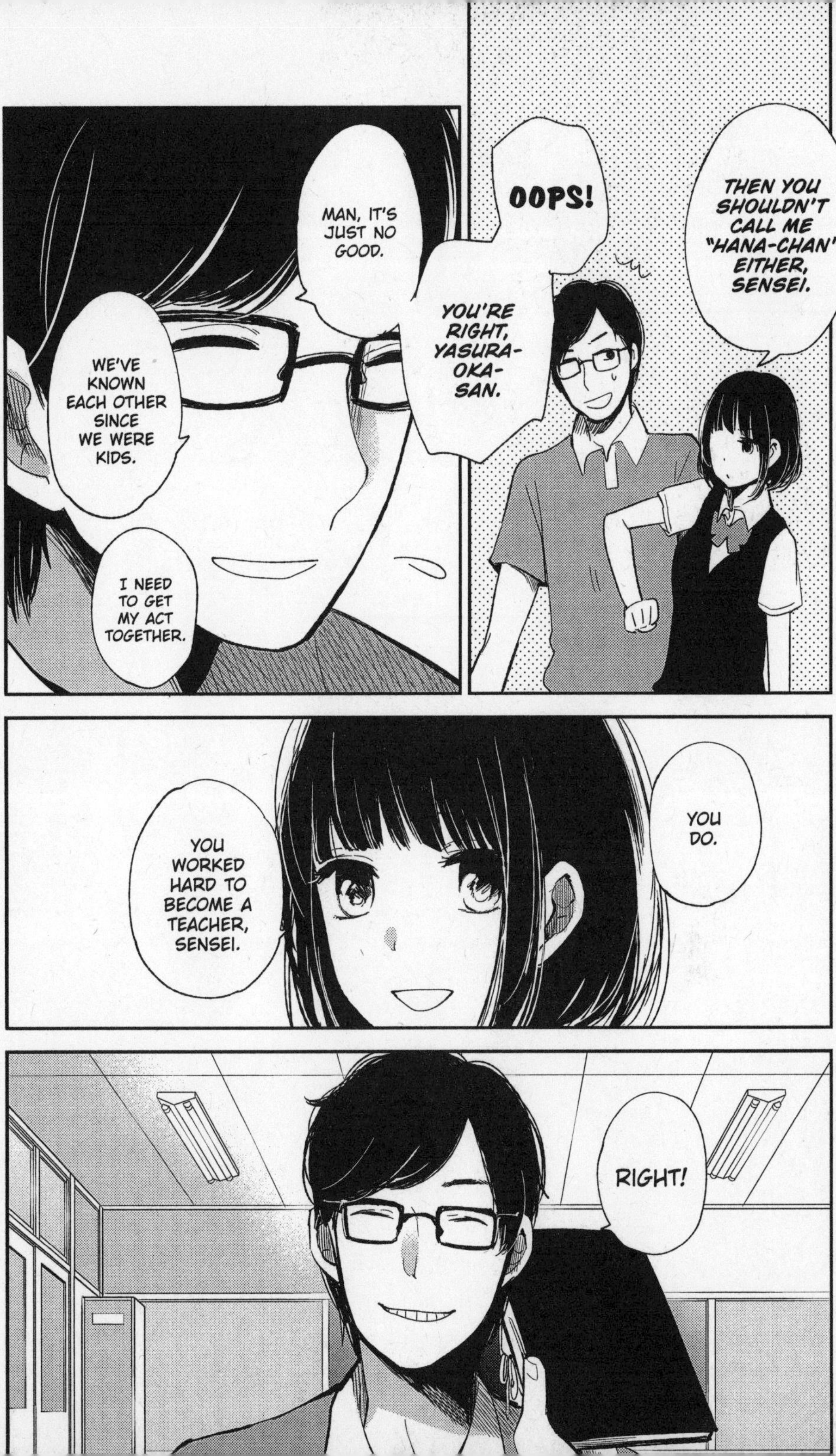
THEN YOU SHOULDN'T CALL ME "HANA-CHAN" EITHER, SENSEI.
OOPS!
YOU'RE RIGHT, YASURA-OKA-SAN.
MAN, IT'S JUST NO GOOD.
WE'VE KNOWN EACH OTHER SINCE WE WERE KIDS.
I NEED TO GET MY ACT TOGETHER.
YOU DO.
YOU WORKED HARD TO BECOME A TEACHER, SENSEI.
RIGHT!

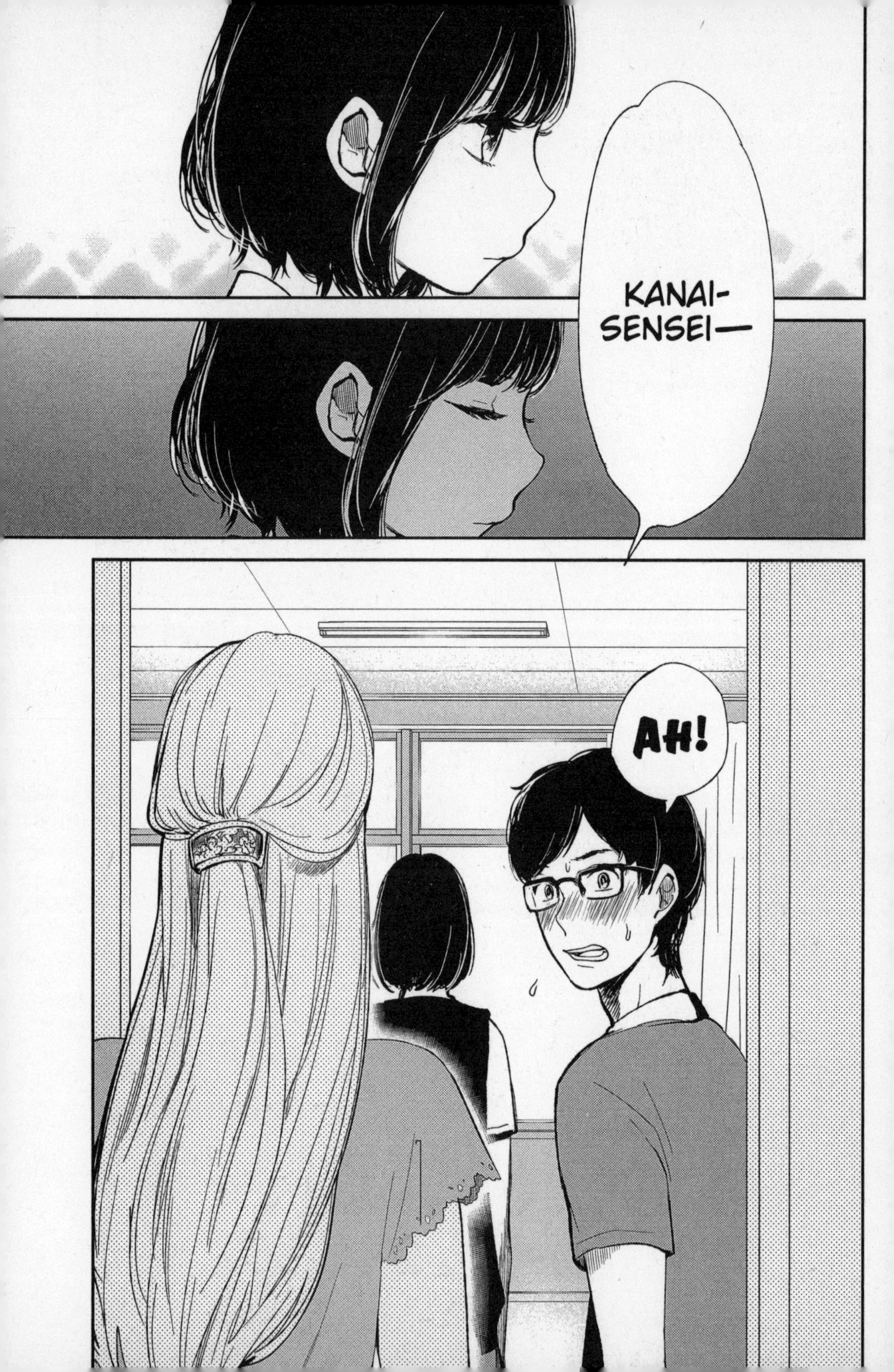
KANAI-SENSEI—
AH!

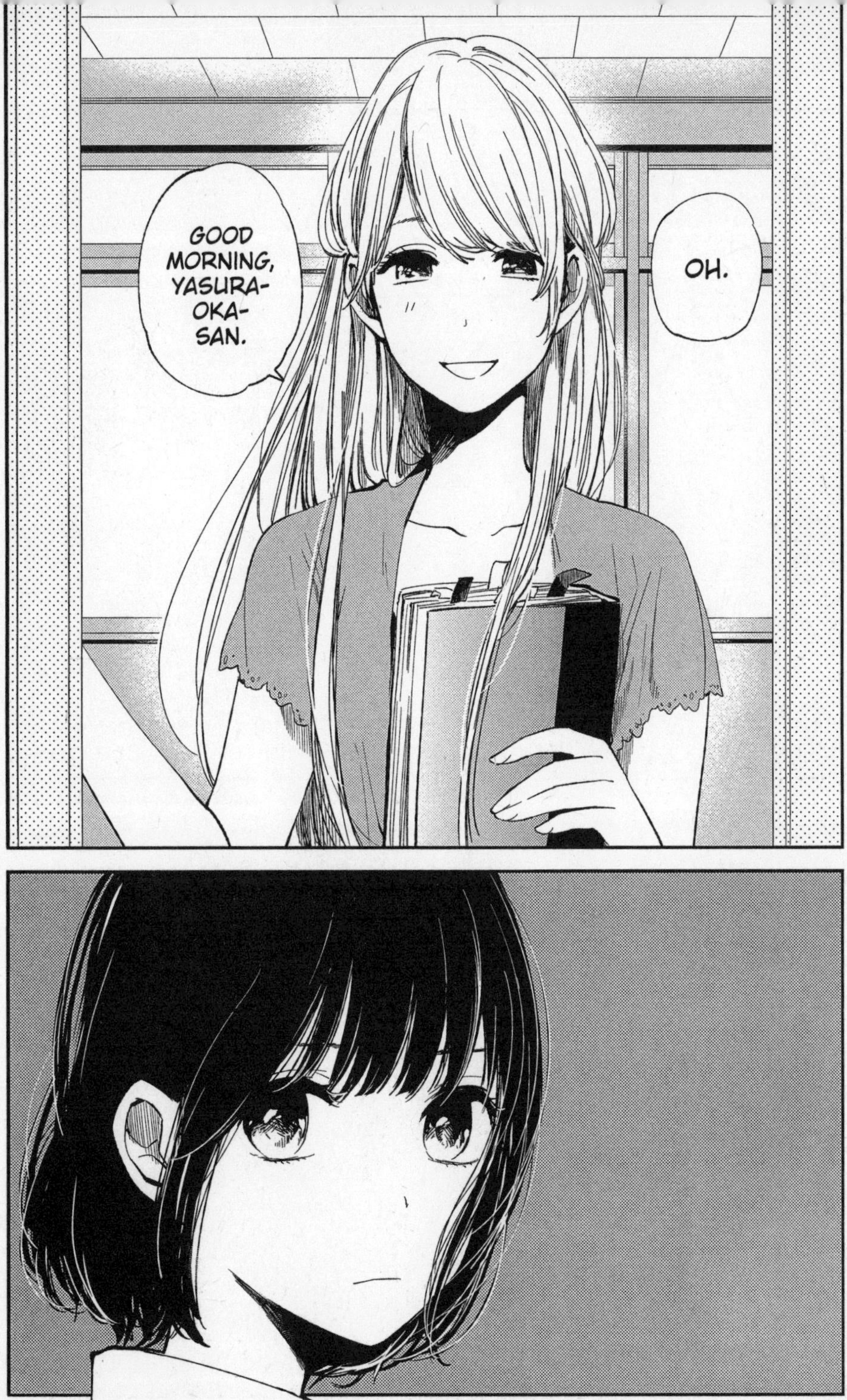
OH.
GOOD MORNING, YASURA-OKA-SAN.

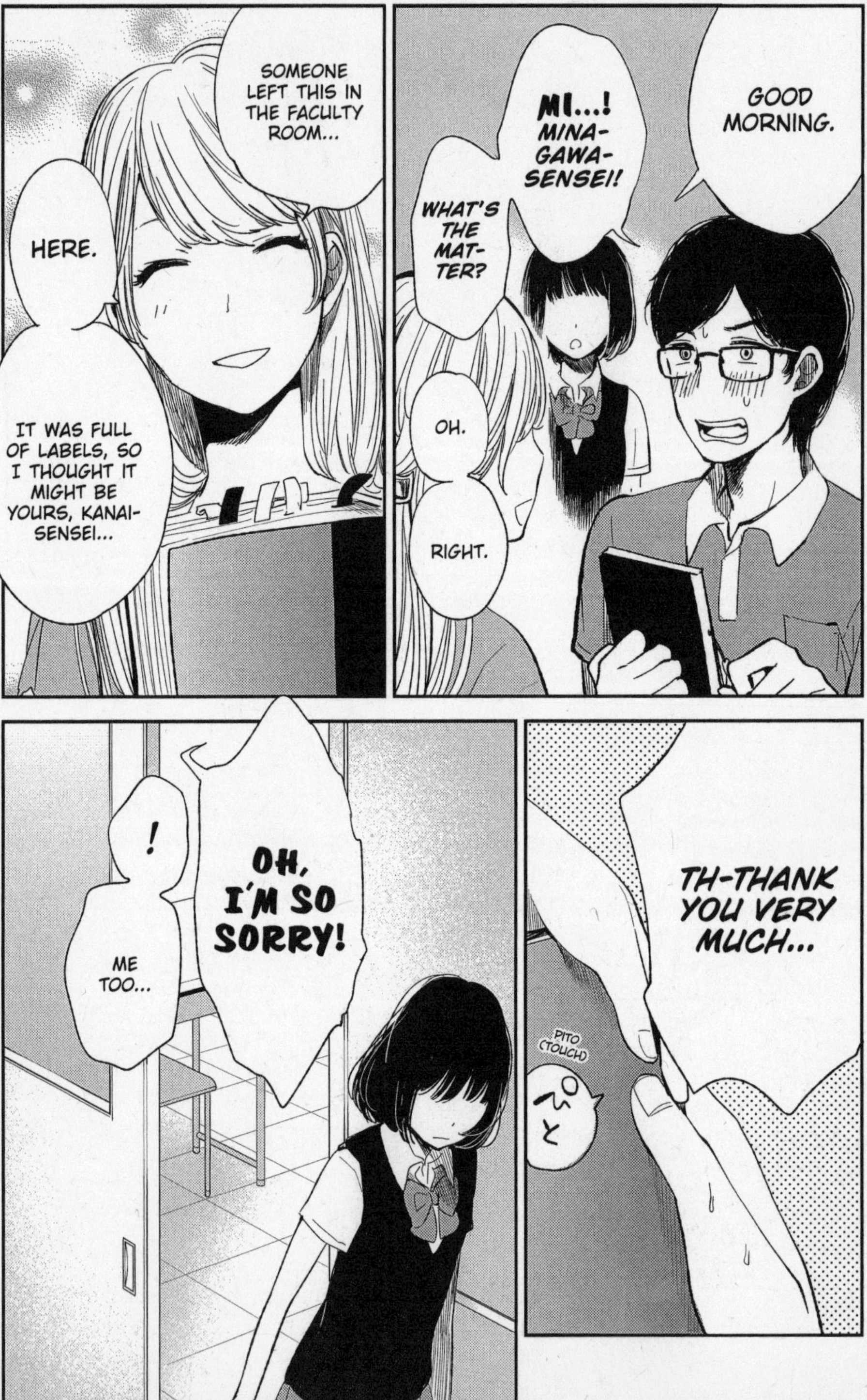
GOOD MORNING.
MI...! MINA-GAWA-SENSEI!
WHAT'S THE MAT-TER?
OH.
RIGHT.
SOMEONE LEFT THIS IN THE FACULTY ROOM...
HERE.
IT WAS FULL OF LABELS, SO I THOUGHT IT MIGHT BE YOURS, KANAI-SENSEI...
TH-THANK YOU VERY MUCH...
PITO (TOUCH)
ぴと
OH, I'M SO SORRY!
!
ME TOO...

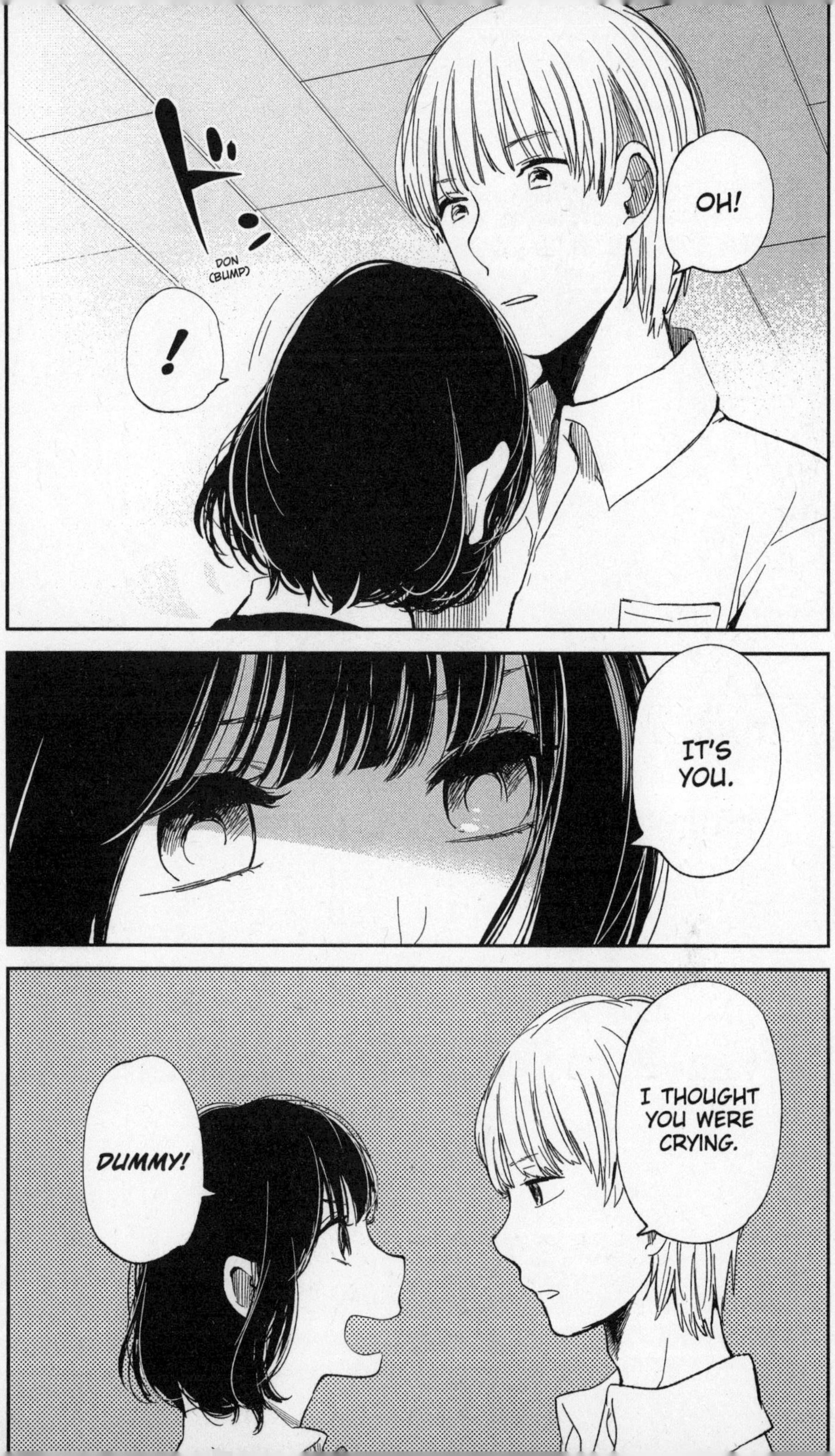
OH!
ドン
DON (BUMP)
!
IT'S YOU.
I THOUGHT YOU WERE CRYING.
DUMMY!

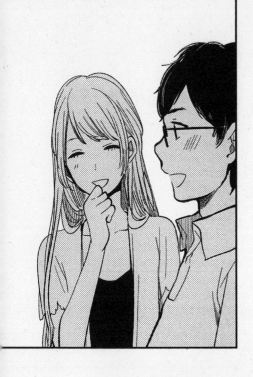

FRUITLESS
LOVE...

PAINFUL
LOVE....

UNREQUITED
LOVE...

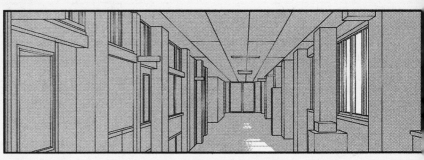

IS THERE BEAUTY
IN THOSE FEELINGS?

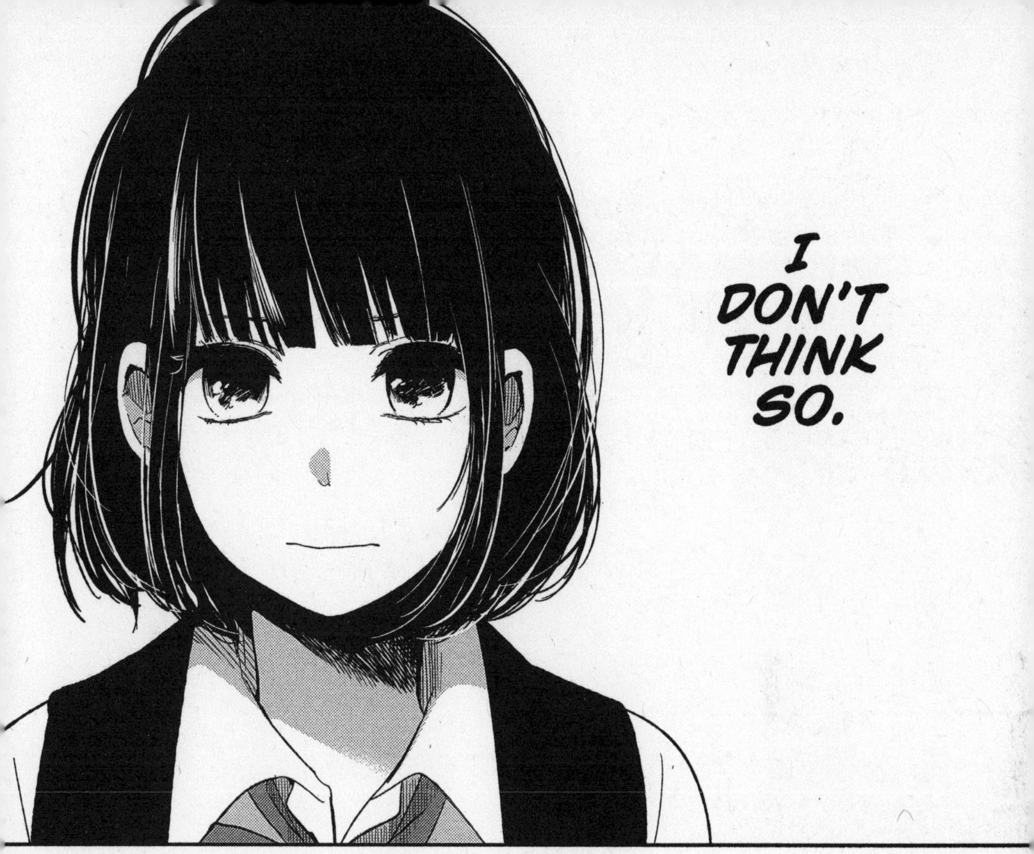
I DON'T THINK SO.
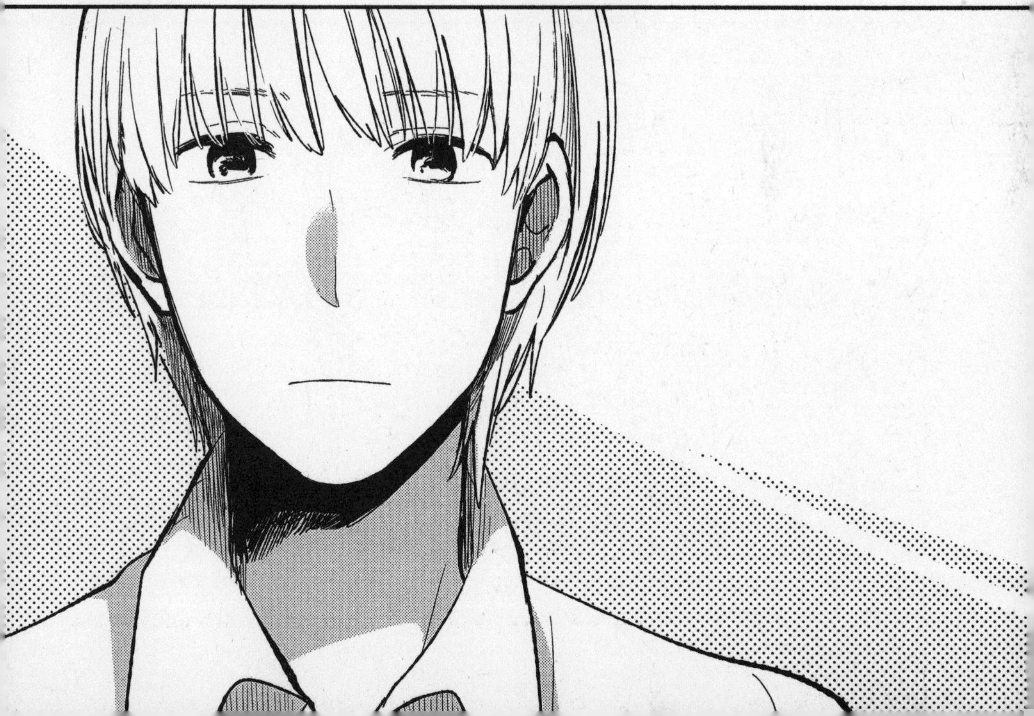

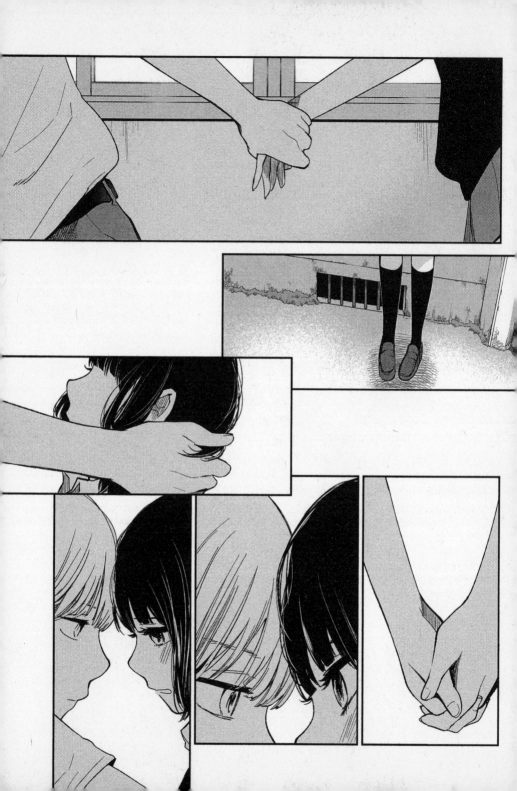

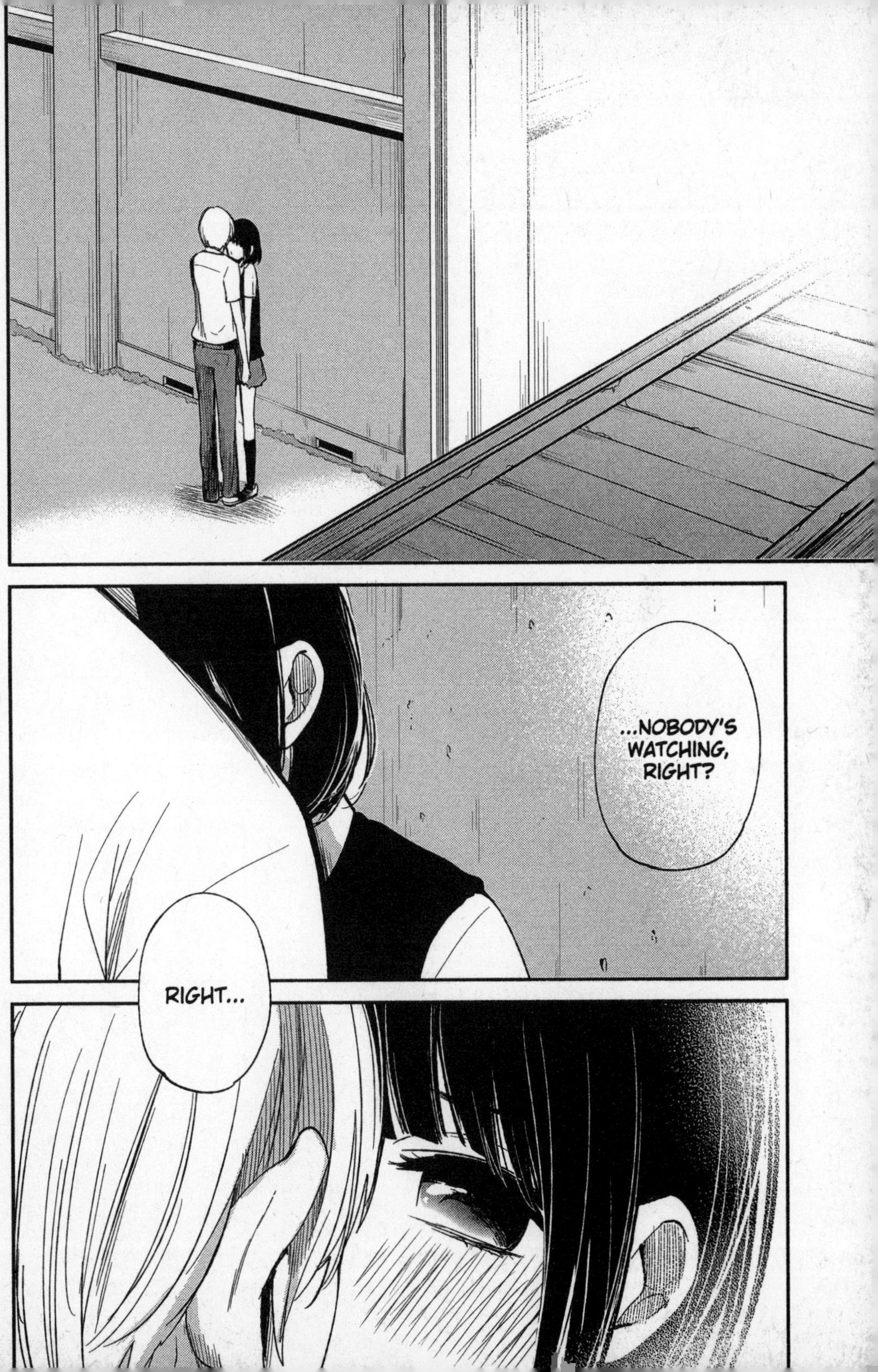
...NOBODY'S WATCHING, RIGHT?
RIGHT...

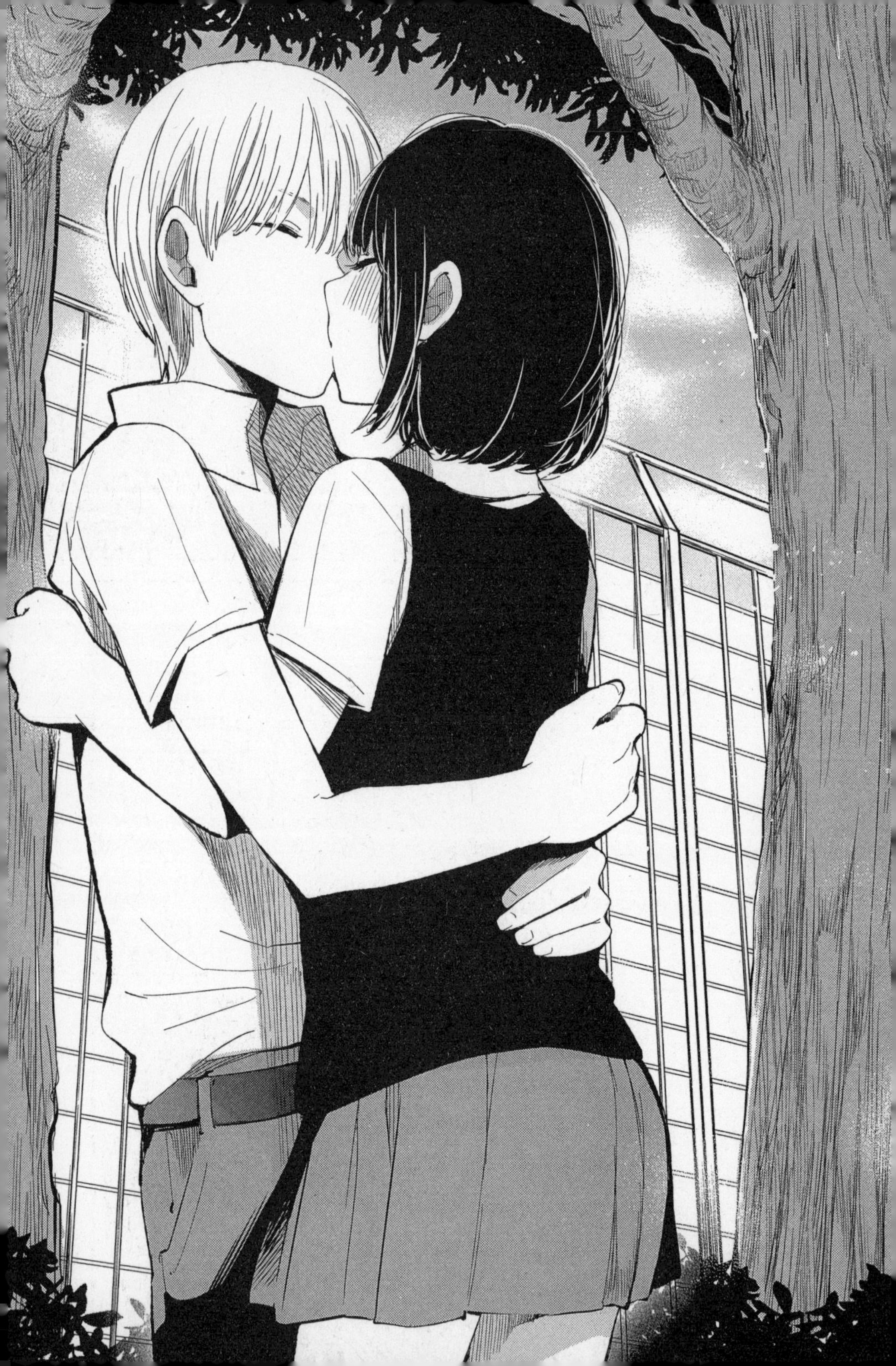

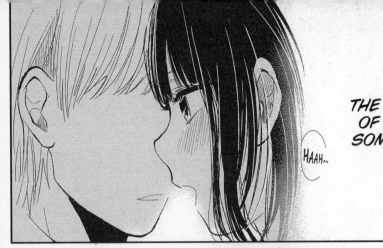

THE FEELING
OF LOVING
SOMEONE...

HAAH...

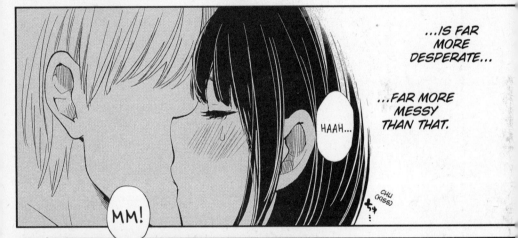

...IS FAR
MORE
DESPERATE...

...FAR MORE
MESSY
THAN THAT.

HAAH...

ちゅ
CHU
(KISS)

MM!

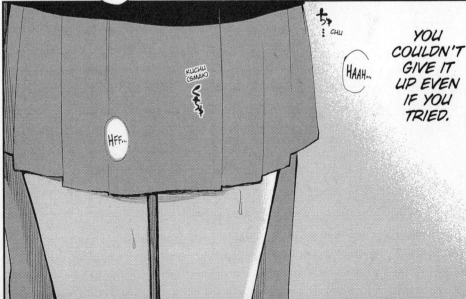

ちゅ
CHU

HAAH...

YOU
COULDN'T
GIVE IT
UP EVEN
IF YOU
TRIED.

KUCHU
(SMAK)

HFF...

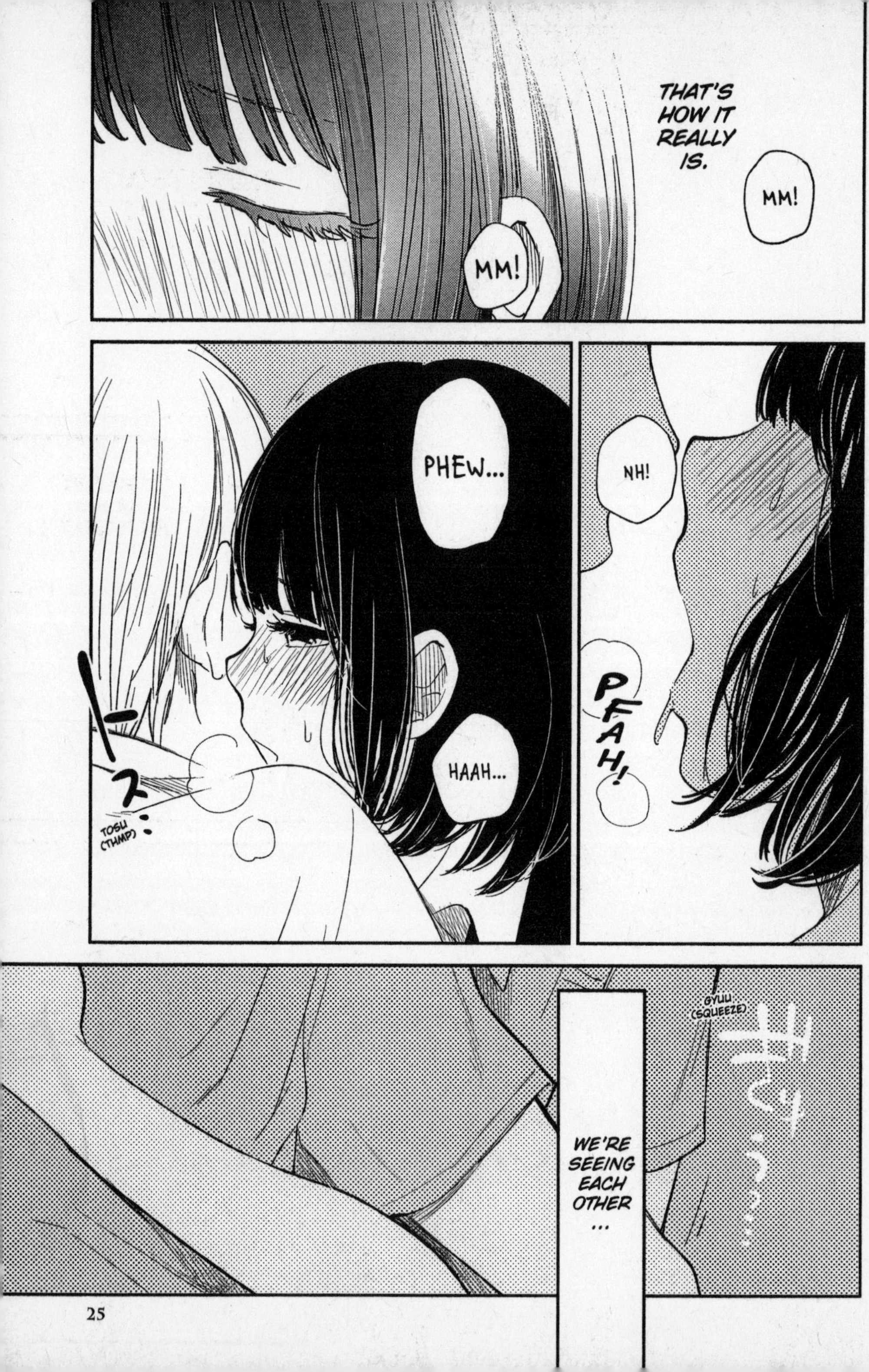
THAT'S HOW IT REALLY IS.
MM!
MM!
NH!
PFAH!
PHEW...
HAAH...
TOSU (THMP)
GYUU (SQUEEZE)
WE'RE SEEING EACH OTHER ...

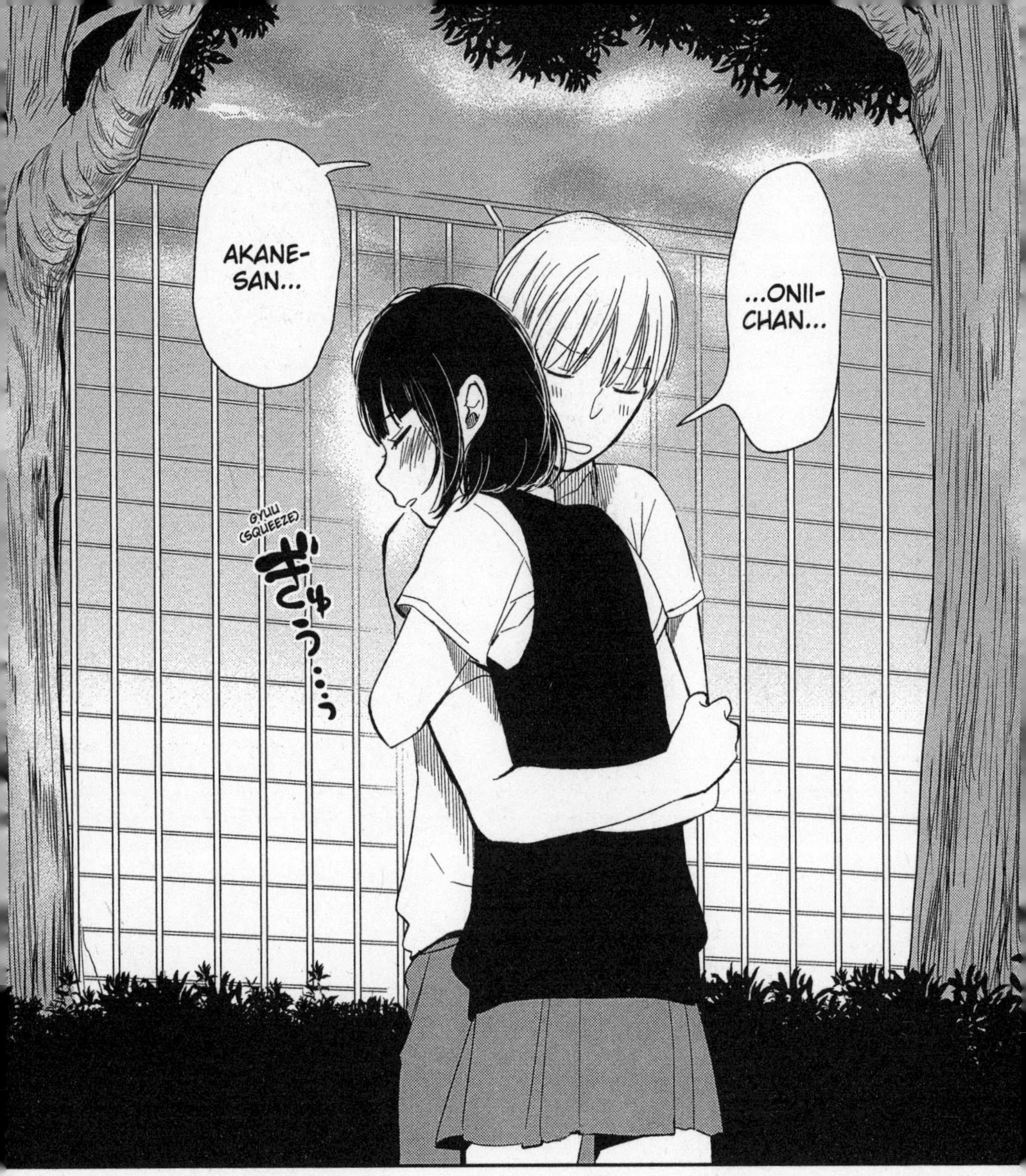
...ONII-CHAN...
AKANE-SAN...
GYUU (SQUEEZE)
ぎゅう…

...BUT WE BOTH HAVE SOMEONE ELSE WE LOVE.

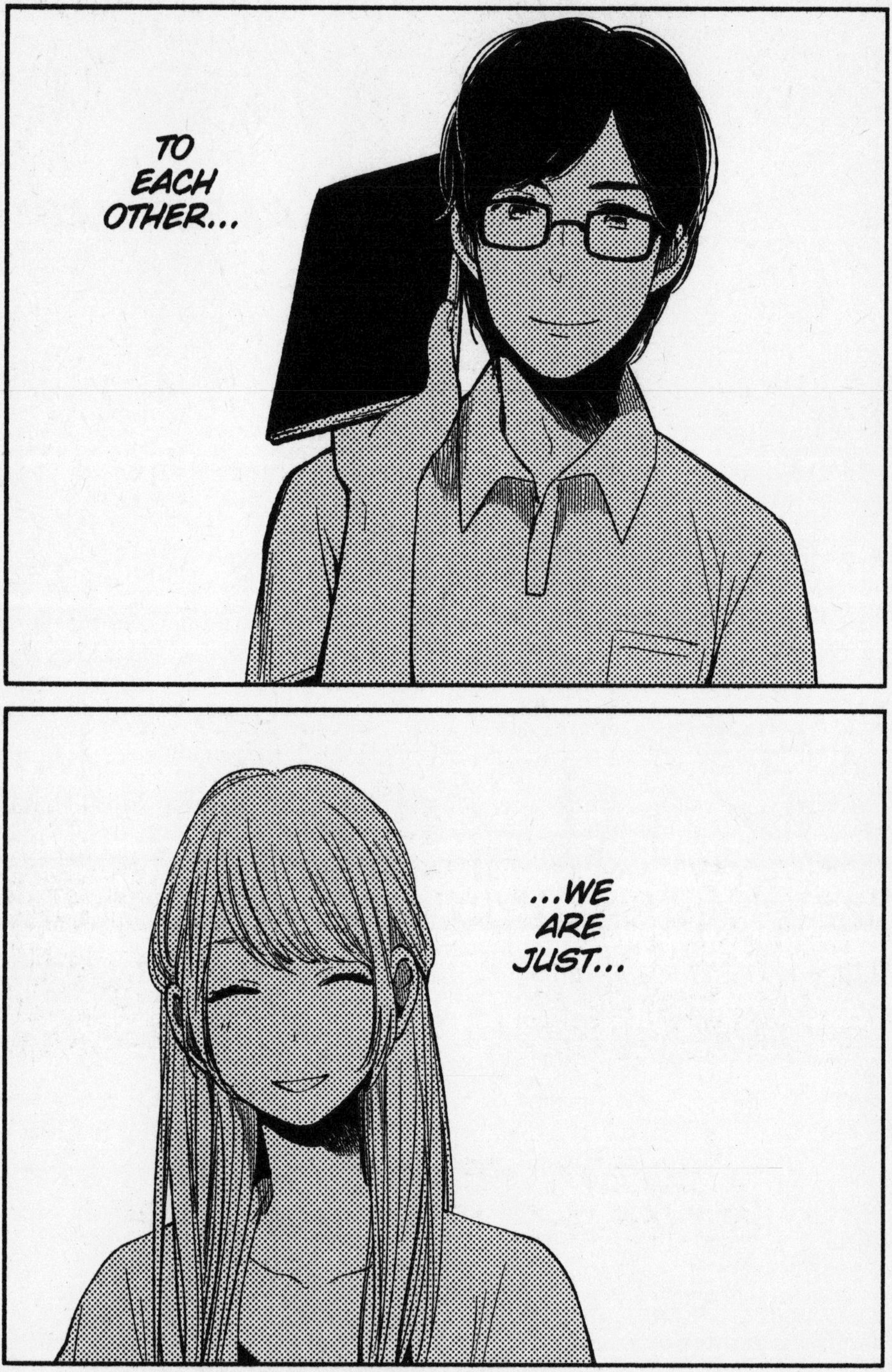
TO EACH OTHER...
...WE ARE JUST...

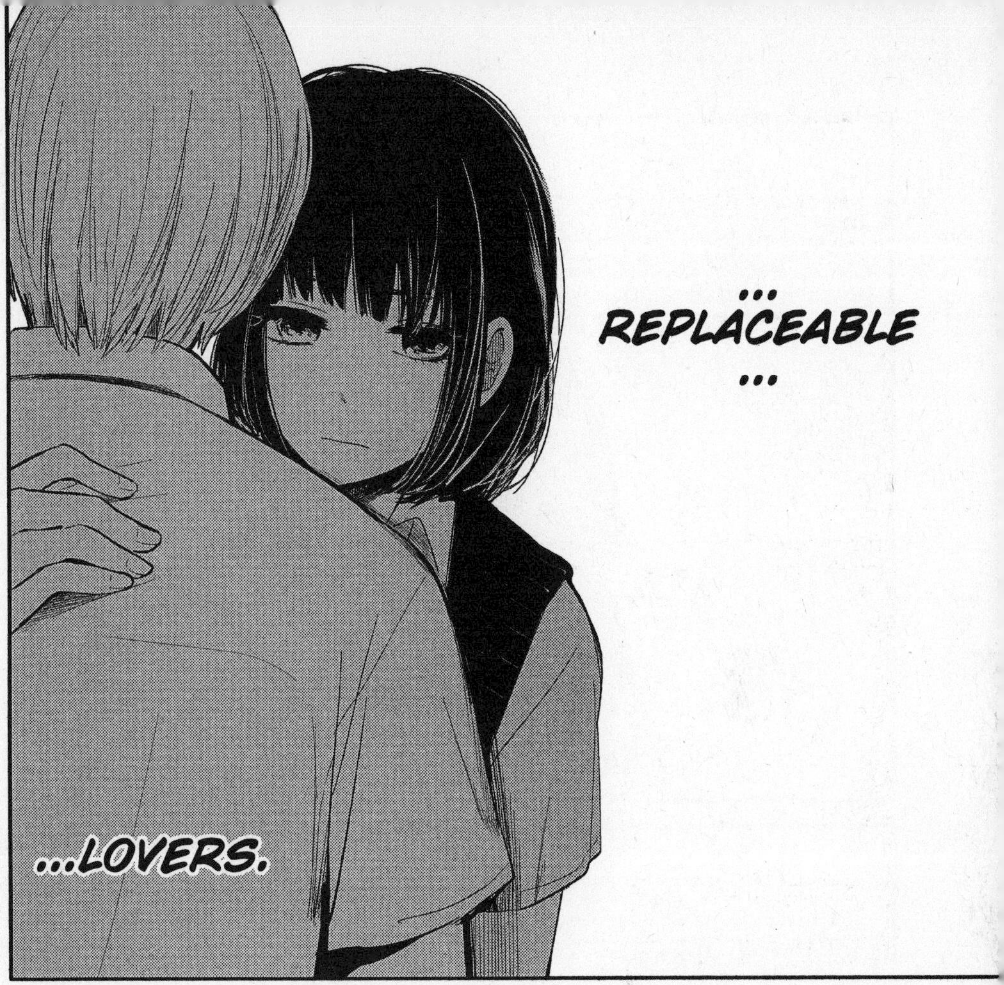
...REPLACEABLE...
...LOVERS.
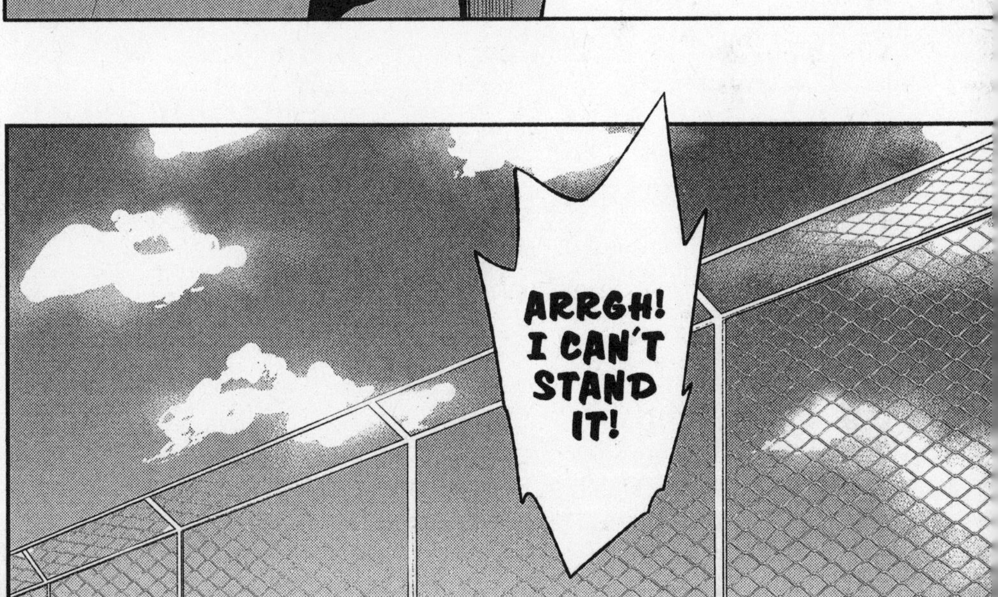
ARRGH! I CAN'T STAND IT!

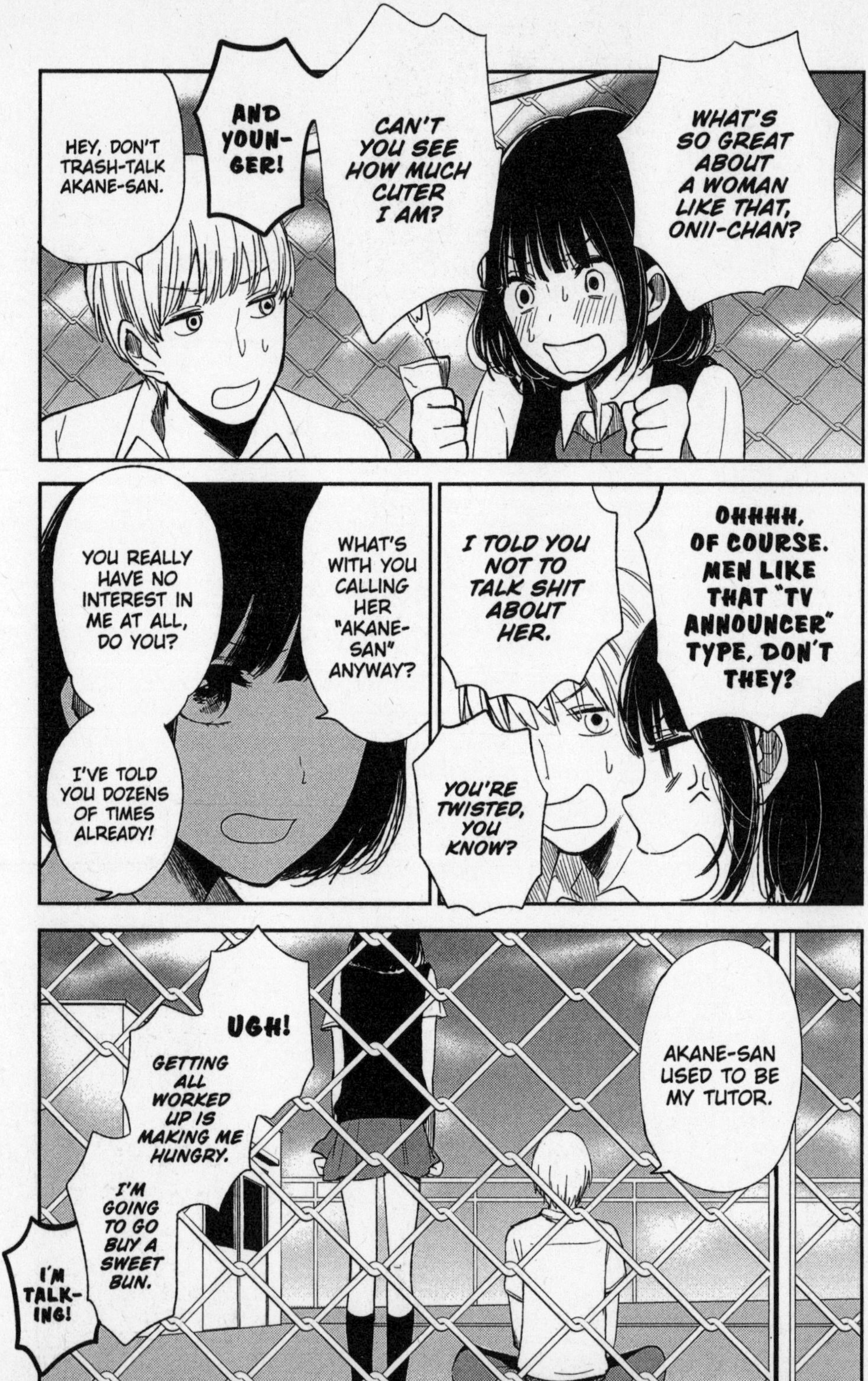
WHAT'S SO GREAT ABOUT A WOMAN LIKE THAT, ONII-CHAN?
CAN'T YOU SEE HOW MUCH CUTER I AM?
AND YOUNGER!
HEY, DON'T TRASH-TALK AKANE-SAN.
OHHHHH, OF COURSE. MEN LIKE THAT "TV ANNOUNCER" TYPE, DON'T THEY?
I TOLD YOU NOT TO TALK SHIT ABOUT HER.
YOU'RE TWISTED, YOU KNOW?
WHAT'S WITH YOU CALLING HER "AKANE-SAN" ANYWAY?
YOU REALLY HAVE NO INTEREST IN ME AT ALL, DO YOU?
I'VE TOLD YOU DOZENS OF TIMES ALREADY!
AKANE-SAN USED TO BE MY TUTOR.
UGH!
GETTING ALL WORKED UP IS MAKING ME HUNGRY.
I'M GOING TO GO BUY A SWEET BUN.
I'M TALKING!

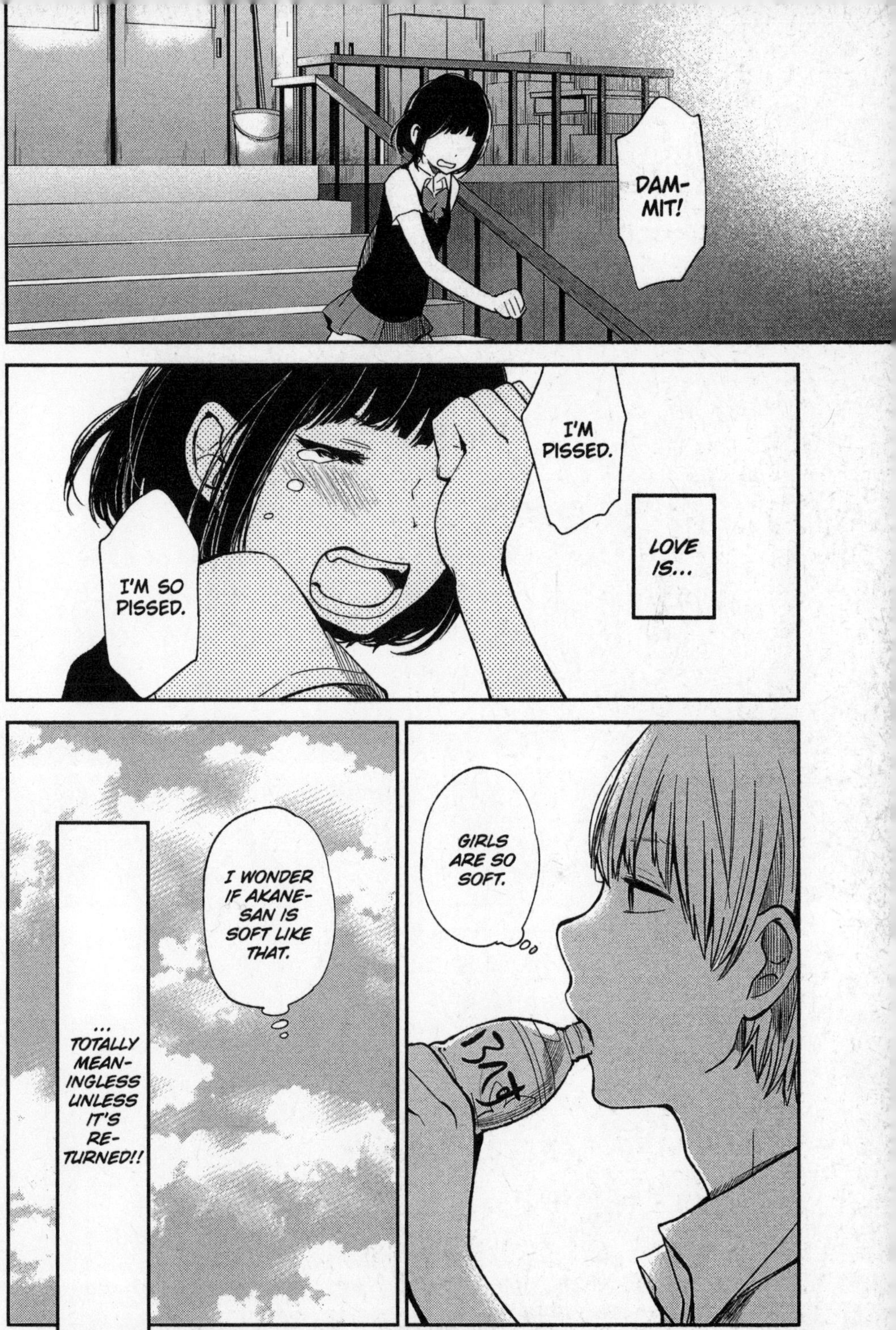
DAM-MIT!
I'M PISSED.
LOVE IS...
I'M SO PISSED.
GIRLS ARE SO SOFT.
I WONDER IF AKANE-SAN IS SOFT LIKE THAT.
...TOTALLY MEAN-INGLESS UNLESS IT'S RE-TURNED!!

LABEL: SPARKLING WATER

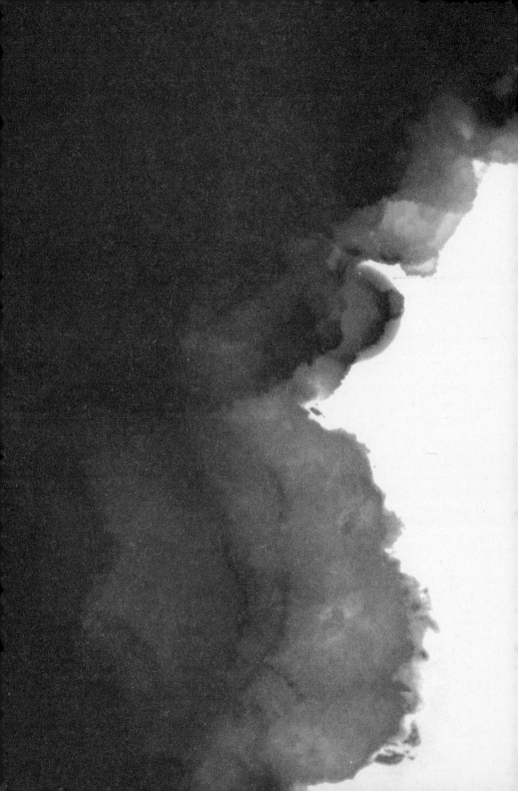

Scum's Wish

Episode 2

Only One

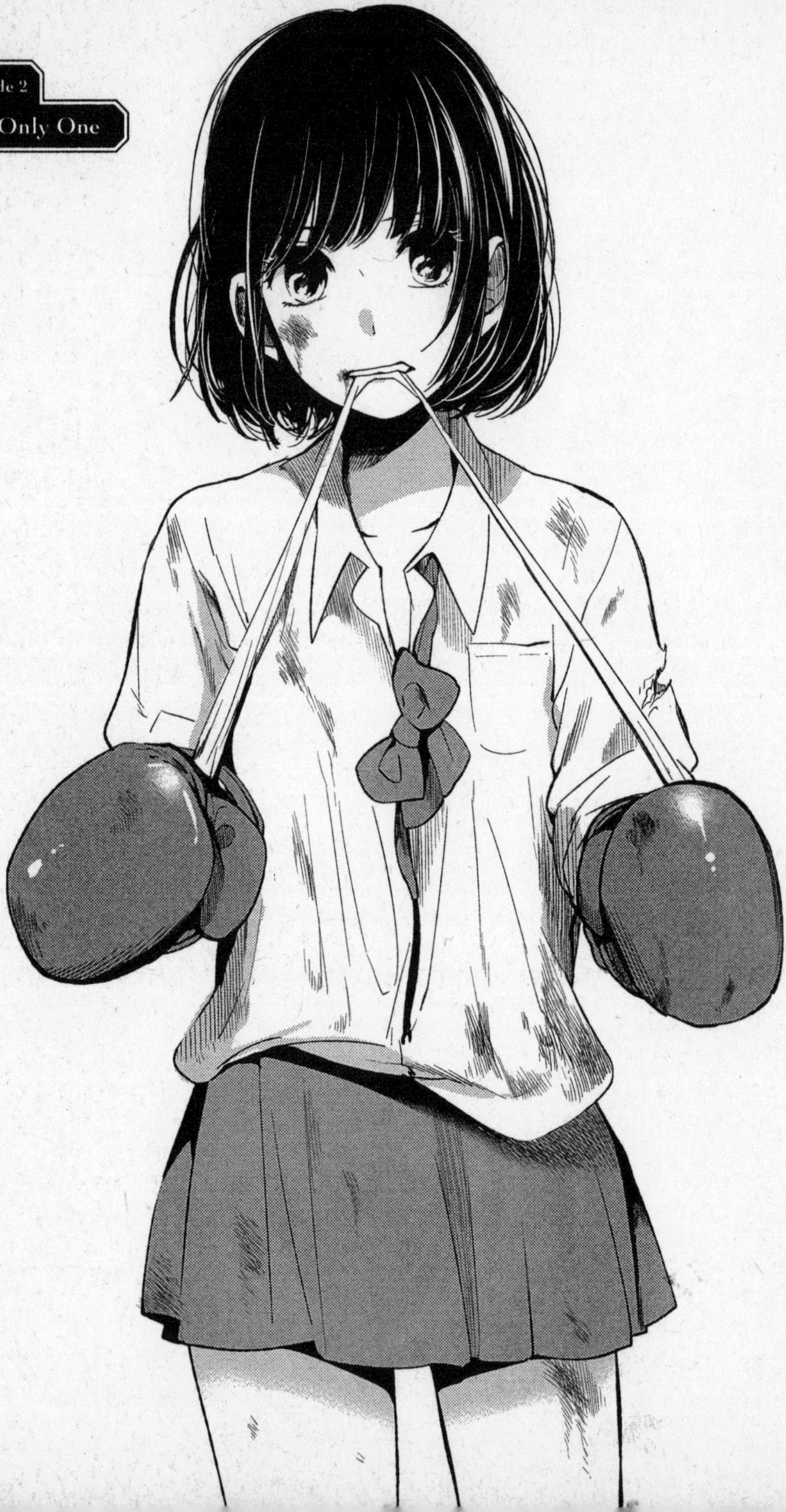

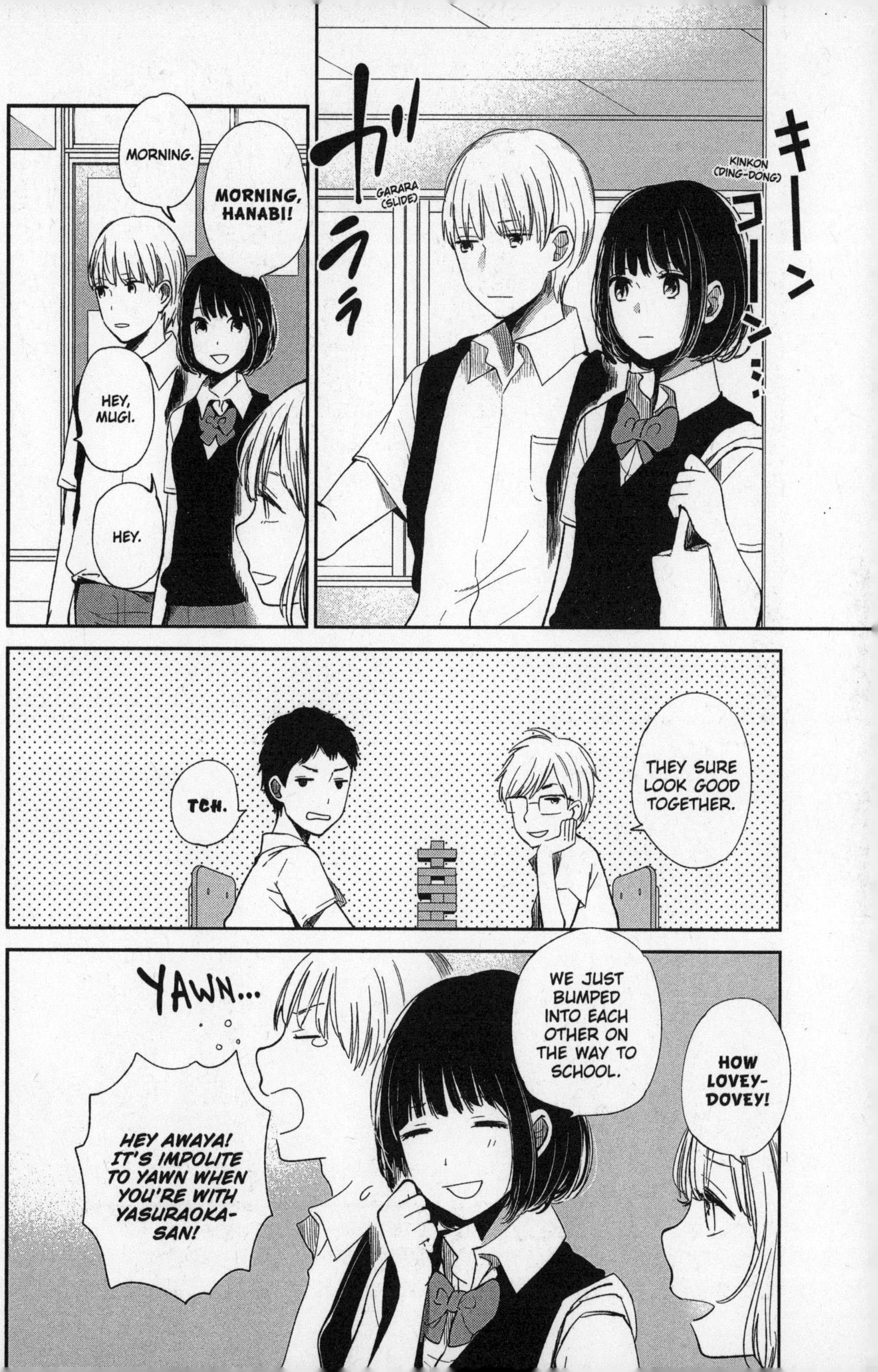
キーンコーン
KINKON (DING-DONG)
ガラ
GARARA (SLIDE)
MORNING, HANABI!
MORNING.
HEY, MUGI.
HEY.
THEY SURE LOOK GOOD TOGETHER.
TCH.
HOW LOVEY-DOVEY!
WE JUST BUMPED INTO EACH OTHER ON THE WAY TO SCHOOL.
YAWN...
HEY AWAYA! IT'S IMPOLITE TO YAWN WHEN YOU'RE WITH YASURAOKA-SAN!

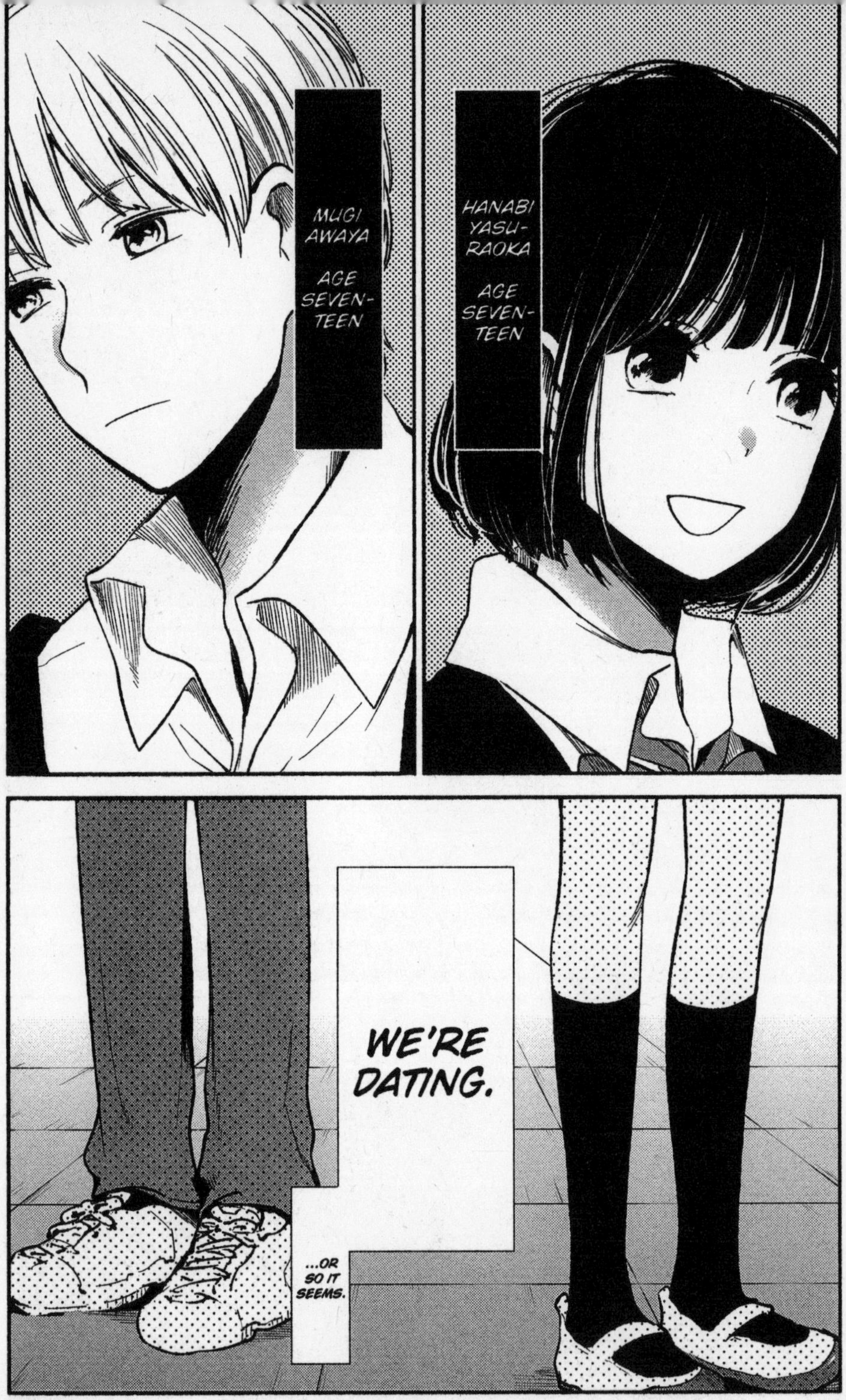
HANABI YASU-RAOKA
AGE SEVEN-TEEN
MUGI AWAYA
AGE SEVEN-TEEN
WE'RE DATING.
...OR SO IT SEEMS.

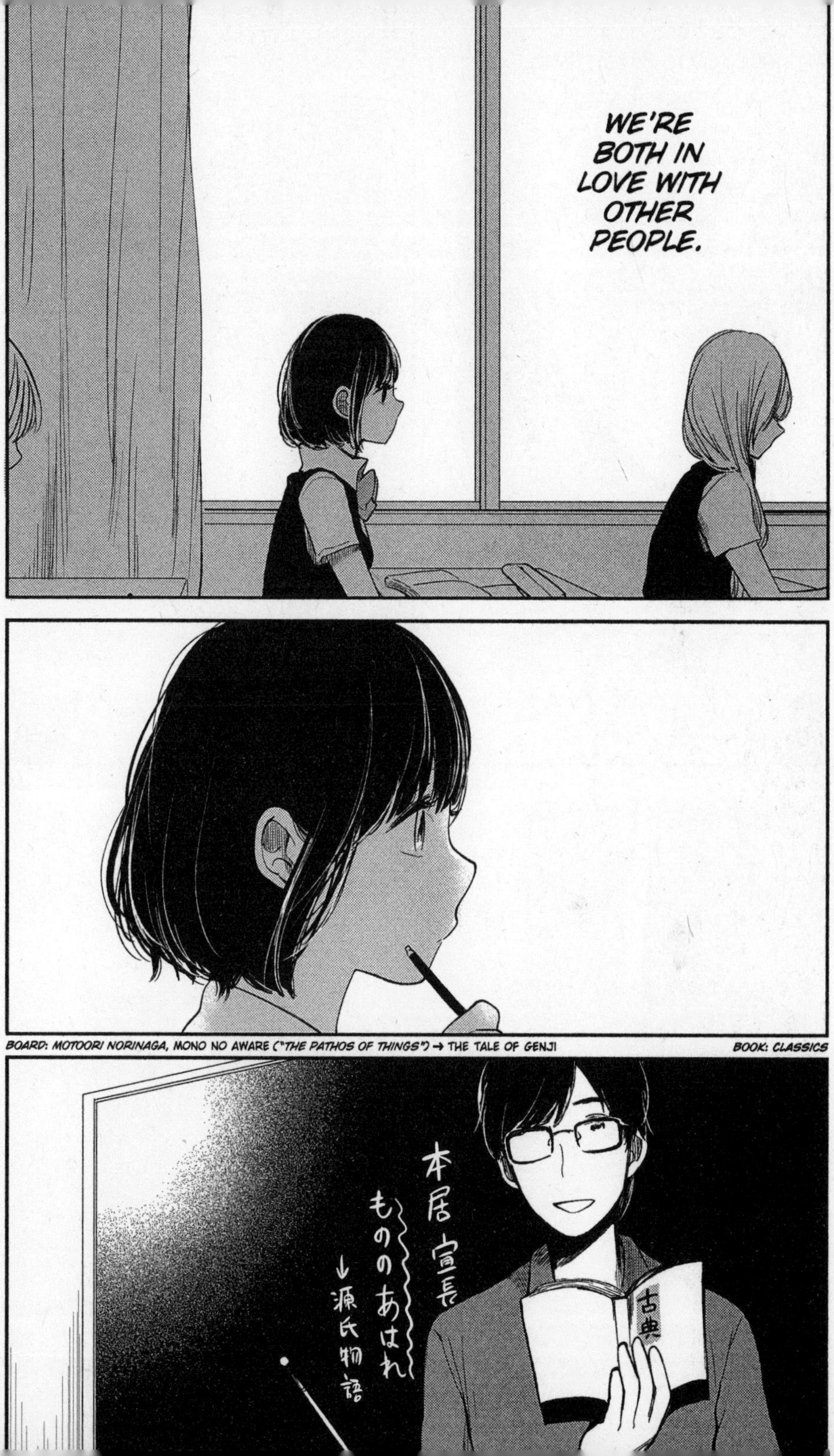
WE'RE BOTH IN LOVE WITH OTHER PEOPLE.
BOARD: MOTOORI NORINAGA, MONO NO AWARE ("THE PATHOS OF THINGS") → THE TALE OF GENJI
BOOK: CLASSICS
本居宣長
もののあはれ
↓源氏物語
古典

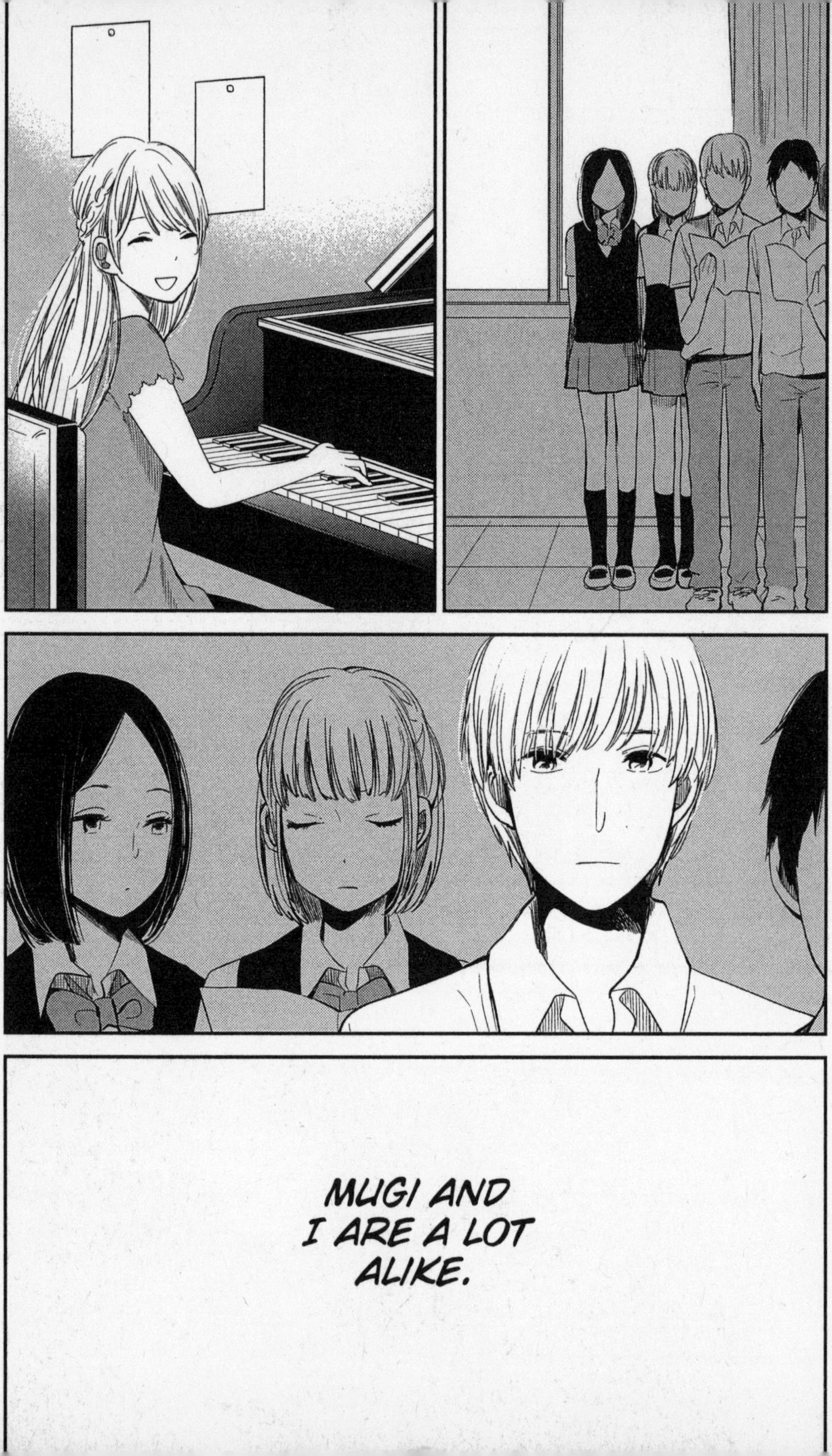
MUGI AND I ARE A LOT ALIKE.

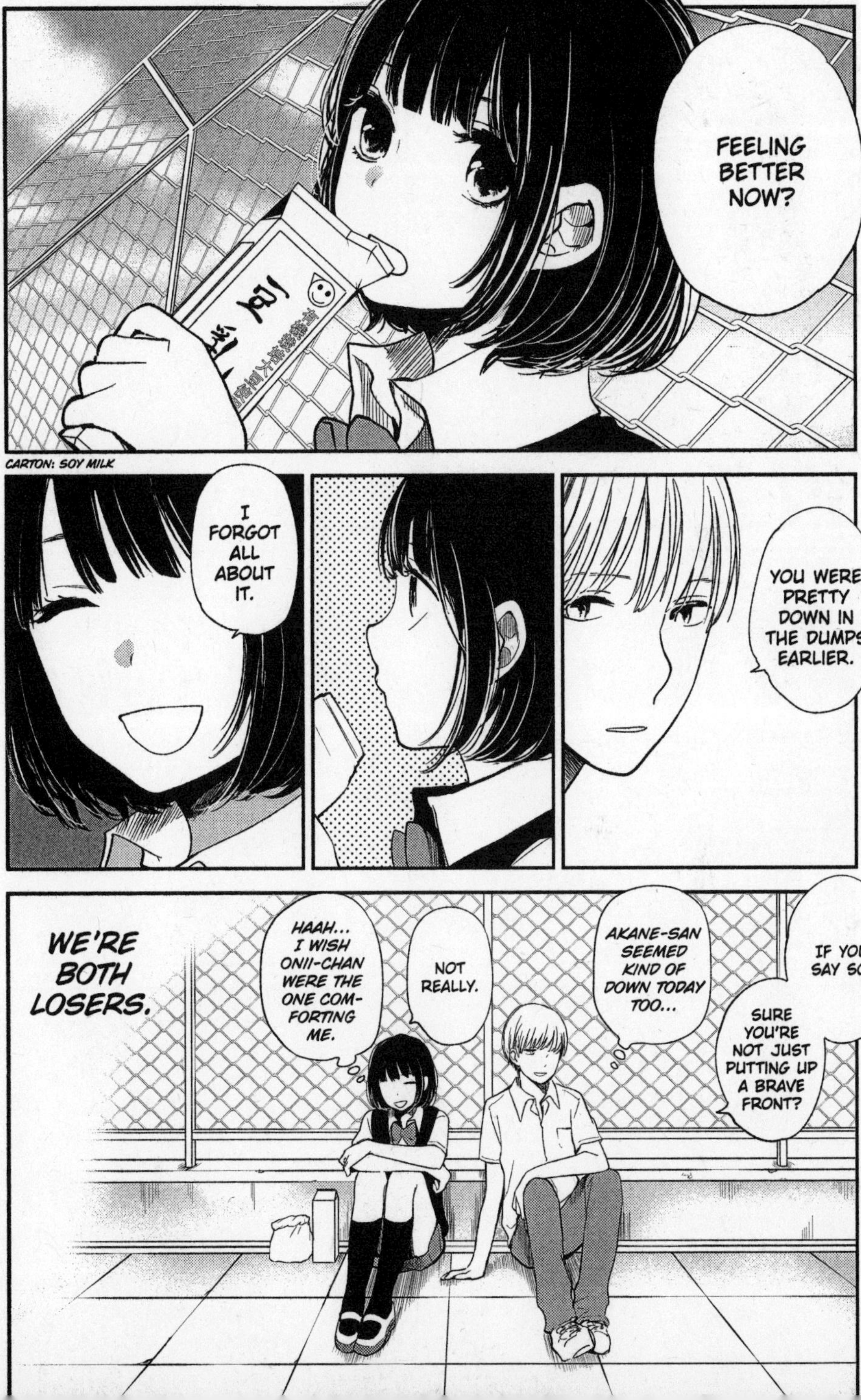
FEELING BETTER NOW?
CARTON: SOY MILK
YOU WERE PRETTY DOWN IN THE DUMPS EARLIER.
I FORGOT ALL ABOUT IT.
IF YOU SAY SO.
SURE YOU'RE NOT JUST PUTTING UP A BRAVE FRONT?
AKANE-SAN SEEMED KIND OF DOWN TODAY TOO...
NOT REALLY.
HAAH... I WISH ONII-CHAN WERE THE ONE COM-FORTING ME.
WE'RE BOTH LOSERS.

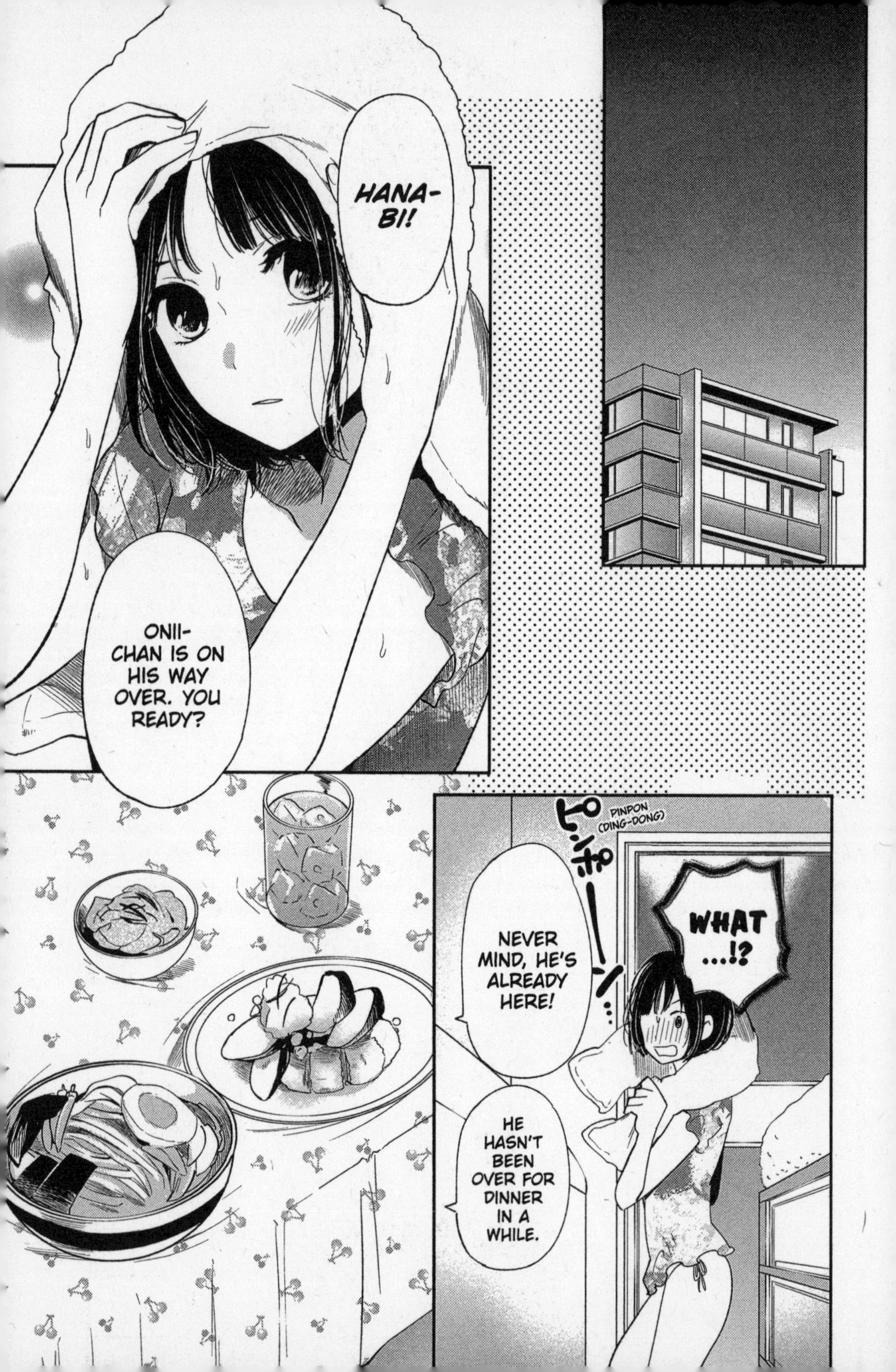
HANA-BI!
ONII-CHAN IS ON HIS WAY OVER. YOU READY?
ピンポーン
PINPON (DING-DONG)
WHAT ...!?
NEVER MIND, HE'S ALREADY HERE!
HE HASN'T BEEN OVER FOR DINNER IN A WHILE.

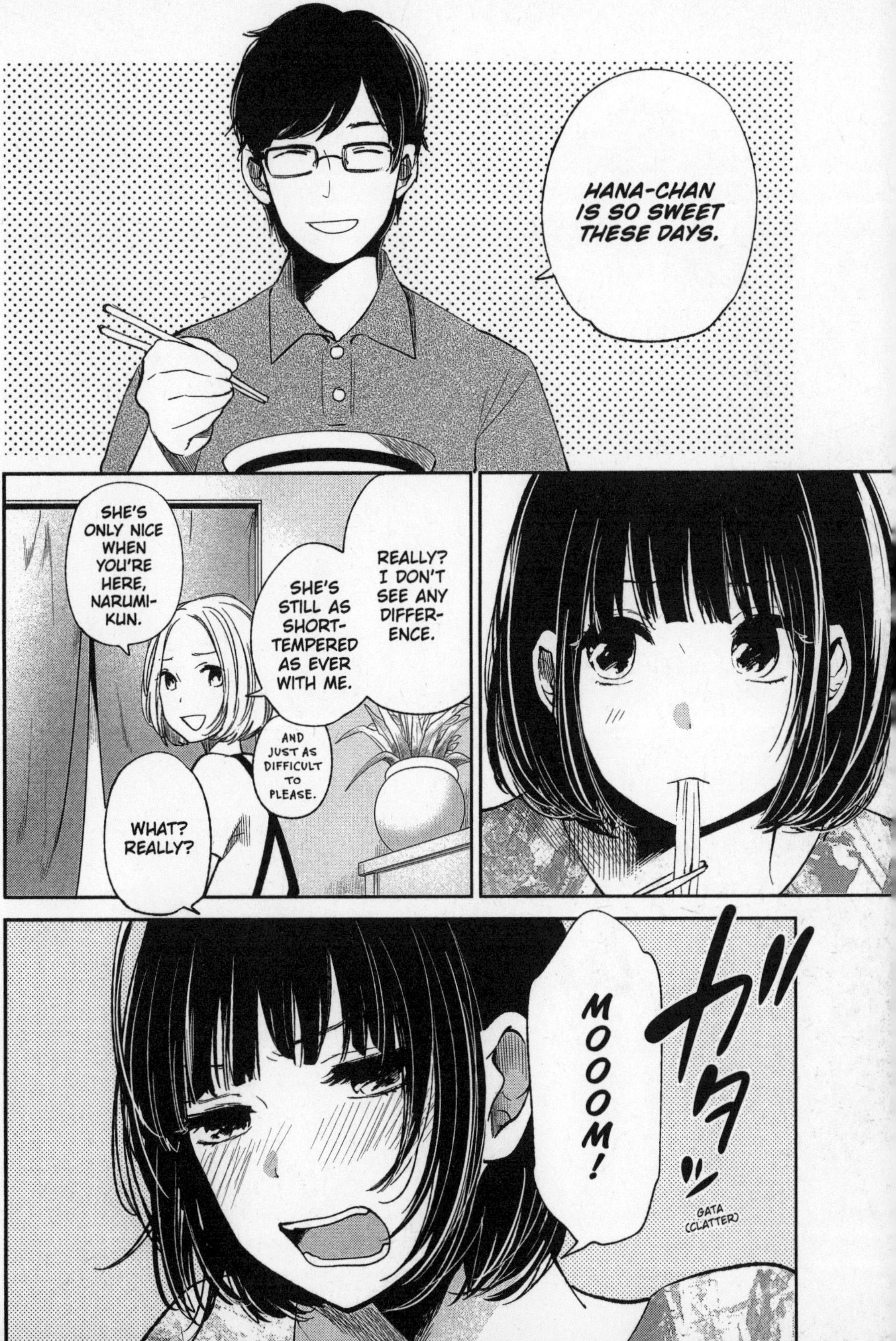
HANA-CHAN IS SO SWEET THESE DAYS.
REALLY? I DON'T SEE ANY DIFFER-ENCE.
SHE'S STILL AS SHORT-TEMPERED AS EVER WITH ME.
AND JUST AS DIFFICULT TO PLEASE.
SHE'S ONLY NICE WHEN YOU'RE HERE, NARUMI-KUN.
WHAT? REALLY?
ガタッ
GATA (CLATTER)
MOOOM!

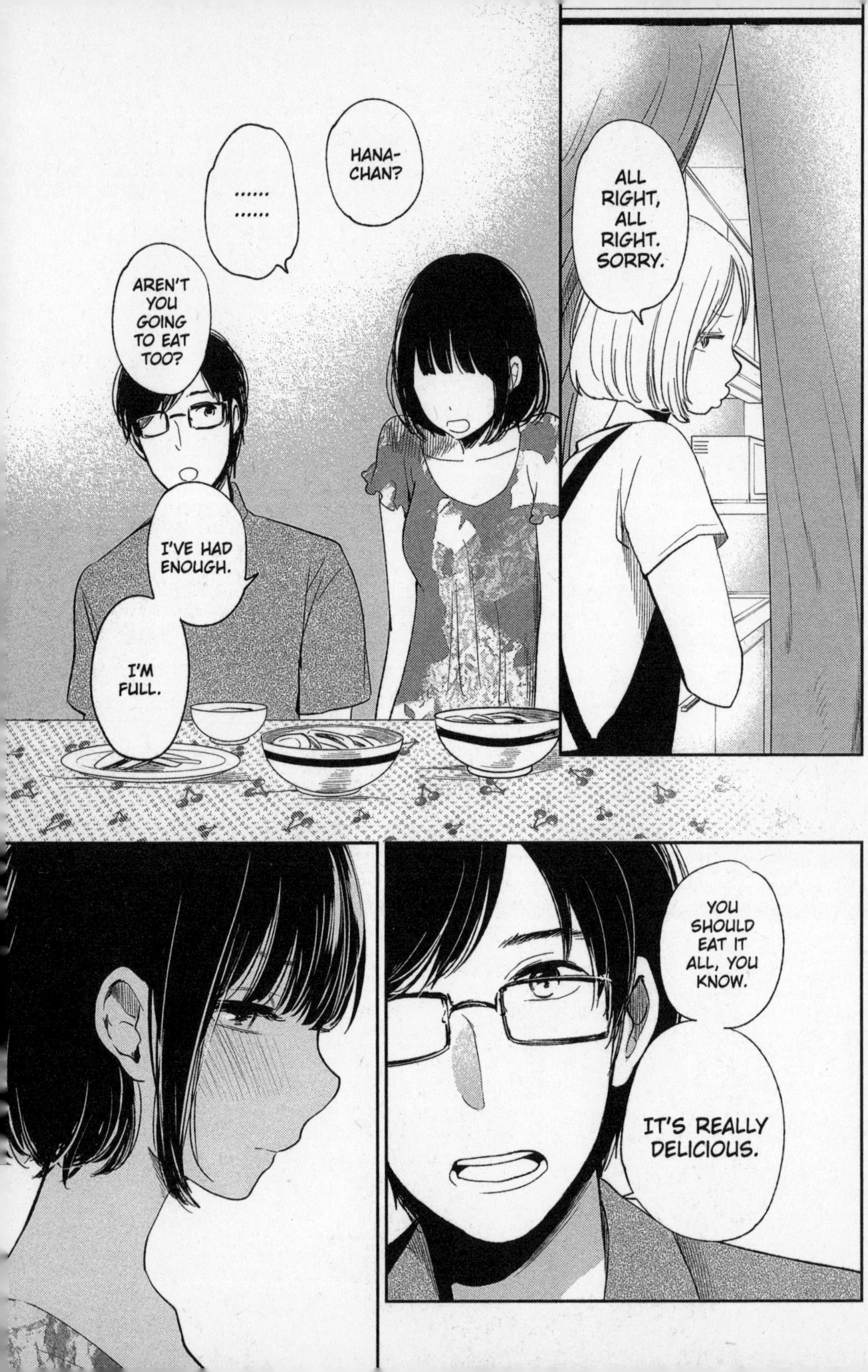
ALL RIGHT, ALL RIGHT. SORRY.
HANA-CHAN?
....
AREN'T YOU GOING TO EAT TOO?
I'VE HAD ENOUGH.
I'M FULL.
YOU SHOULD EAT IT ALL, YOU KNOW.
IT'S REALLY DELICIOUS.

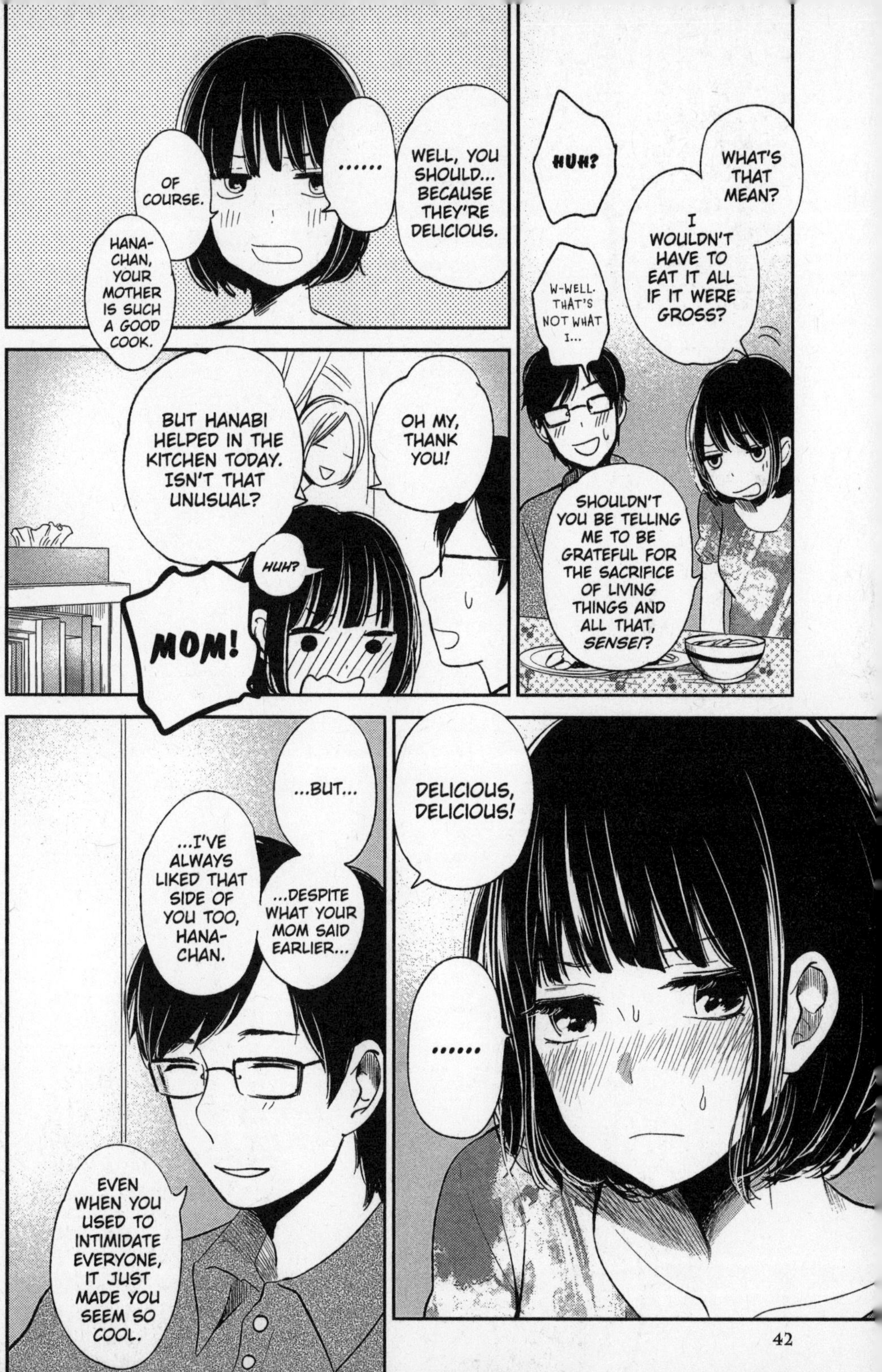
WHAT'S THAT MEAN?
HUH?
I WOULDN'T HAVE TO EAT IT ALL IF IT WERE GROSS?
W-WELL. THAT'S NOT WHAT I...
SHOULDN'T YOU BE TELLING ME TO BE GRATEFUL FOR THE SACRIFICE OF LIVING THINGS AND ALL THAT, *SENSEI*?
WELL, YOU SHOULD... BECAUSE THEY'RE DELICIOUS.
......
OF COURSE.
HANA-CHAN, YOUR MOTHER IS SUCH A GOOD COOK.
OH MY, THANK YOU!
BUT HANABI HELPED IN THE KITCHEN TODAY. ISN'T THAT UNUSUAL?
HUH?
MOM!
DELICIOUS, DELICIOUS!
......
...BUT...
...DESPITE WHAT YOUR MOM SAID EARLIER...
...I'VE ALWAYS LIKED THAT SIDE OF YOU TOO, HANA-CHAN.
EVEN WHEN YOU USED TO INTIMIDATE EVERYONE, IT JUST MADE YOU SEEM SO COOL.

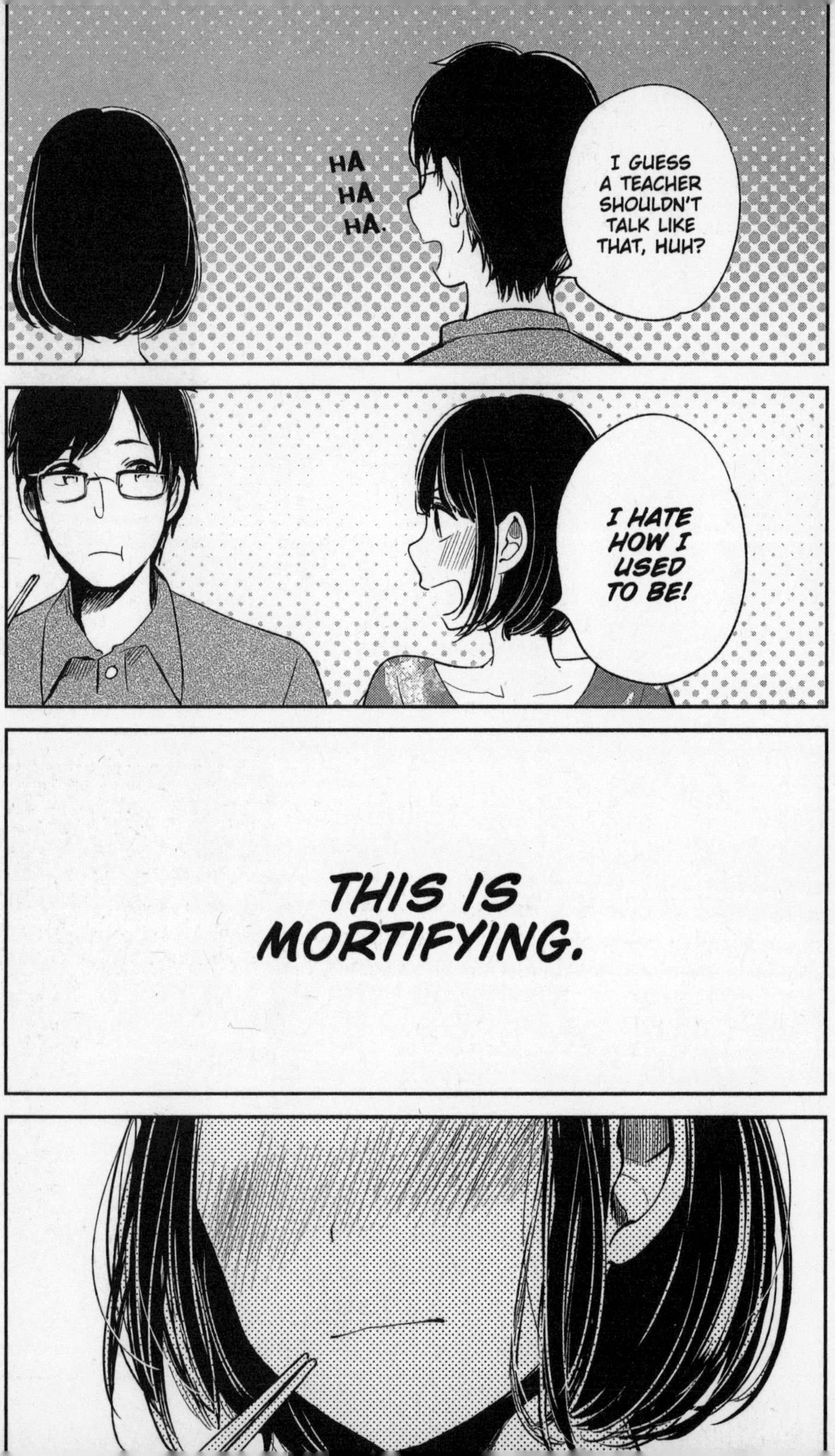
I GUESS A TEACHER SHOULDN'T TALK LIKE THAT, HUH?
HA HA HA.
I HATE HOW I USED TO BE!
THIS IS MORTIFYING.

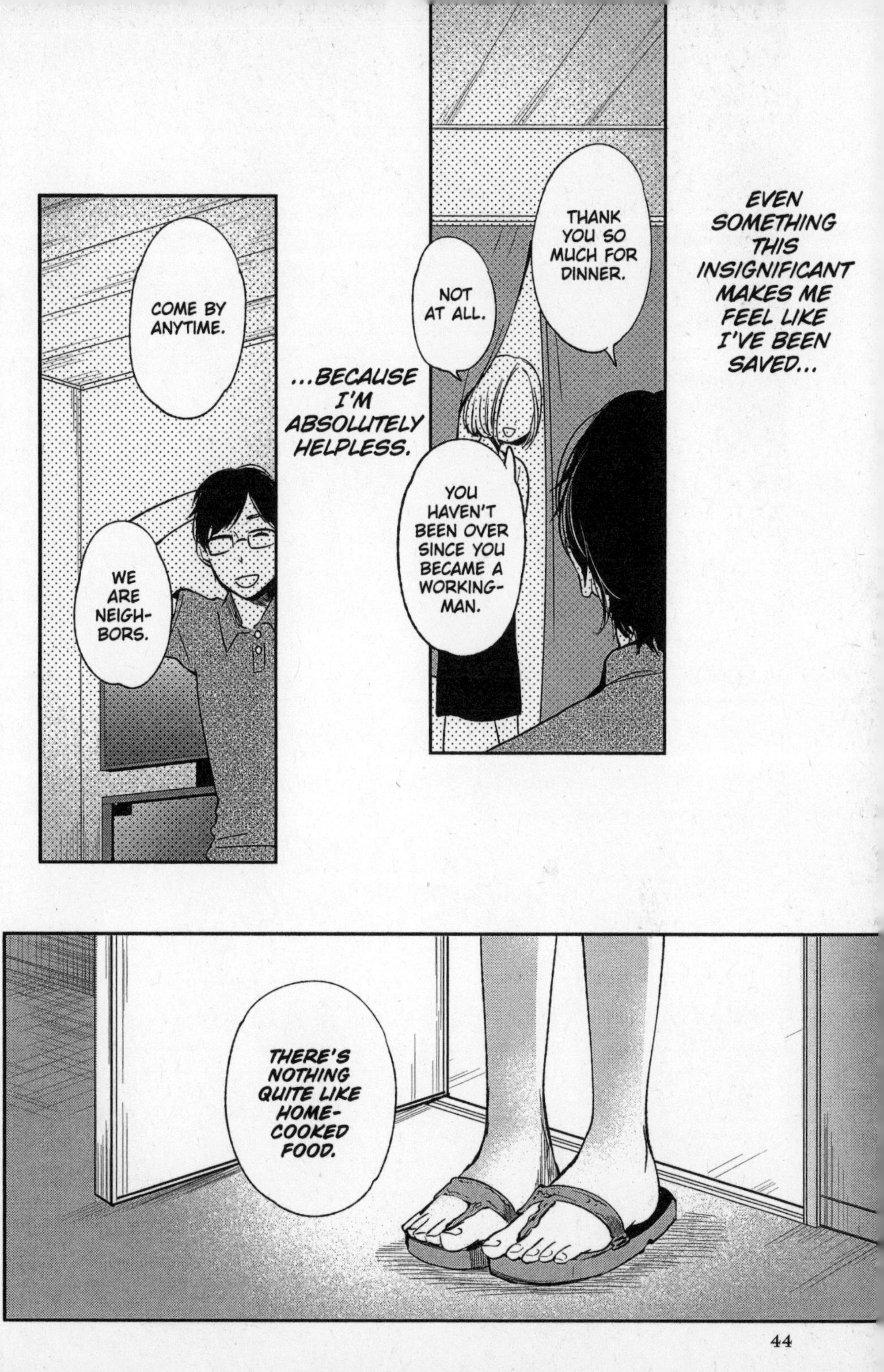
EVEN SOMETHING THIS INSIGNIFICANT MAKES ME FEEL LIKE I'VE BEEN SAVED...
THANK YOU SO MUCH FOR DINNER.
NOT AT ALL.
YOU HAVEN'T BEEN OVER SINCE YOU BECAME A WORKING-MAN.
...BECAUSE I'M ABSOLUTELY HELPLESS.
COME BY ANYTIME.
WE ARE NEIGH-BORS.
THERE'S NOTHING QUITE LIKE HOME-COOKED FOOD.

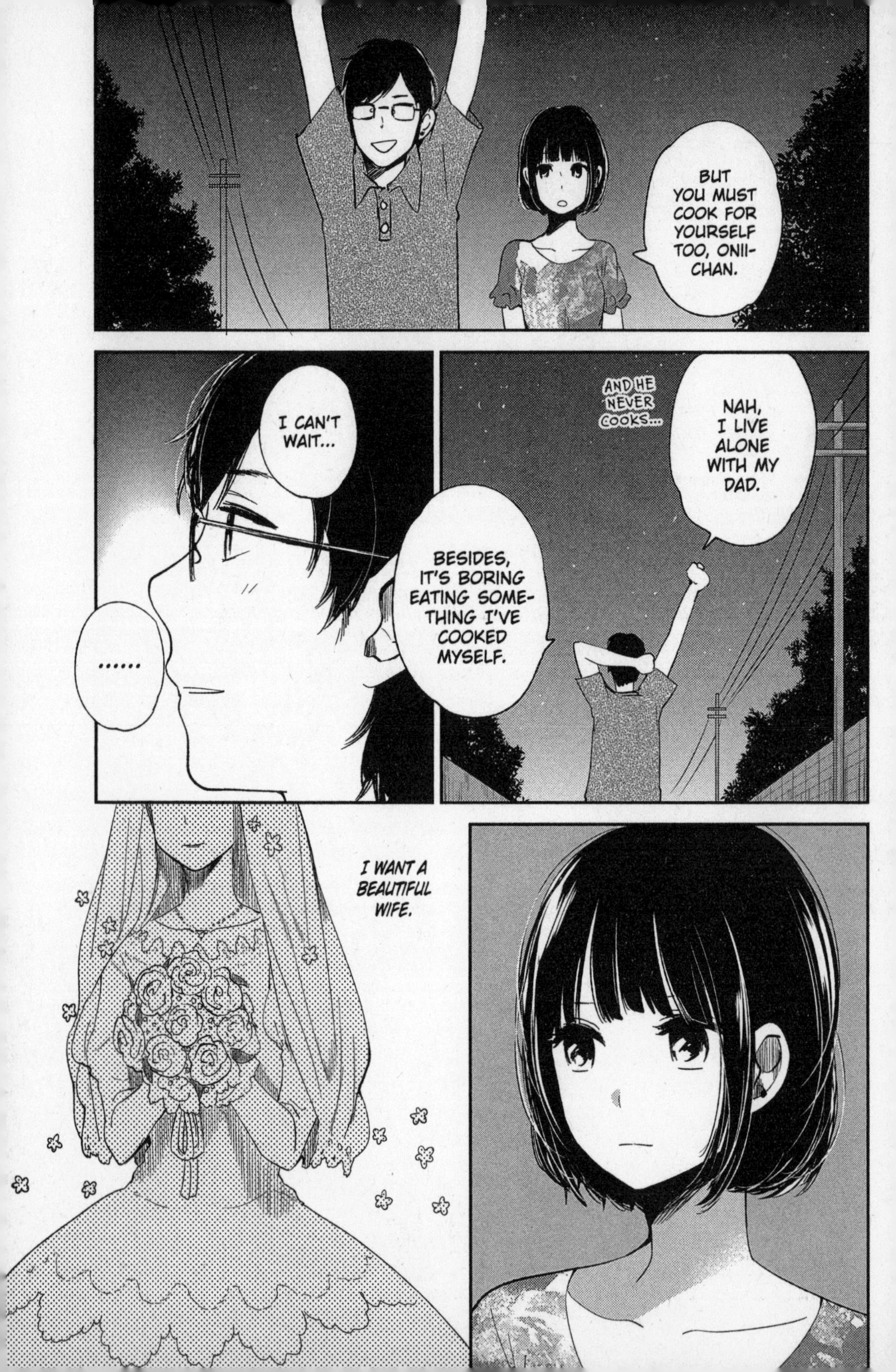
BUT YOU MUST COOK FOR YOURSELF TOO, ONII-CHAN.
NAH, I LIVE ALONE WITH MY DAD.
AND HE NEVER COOKS...
BESIDES, IT'S BORING EATING SOMETHING I'VE COOKED MYSELF.
I CAN'T WAIT...
......
I WANT A BEAUTIFUL WIFE.

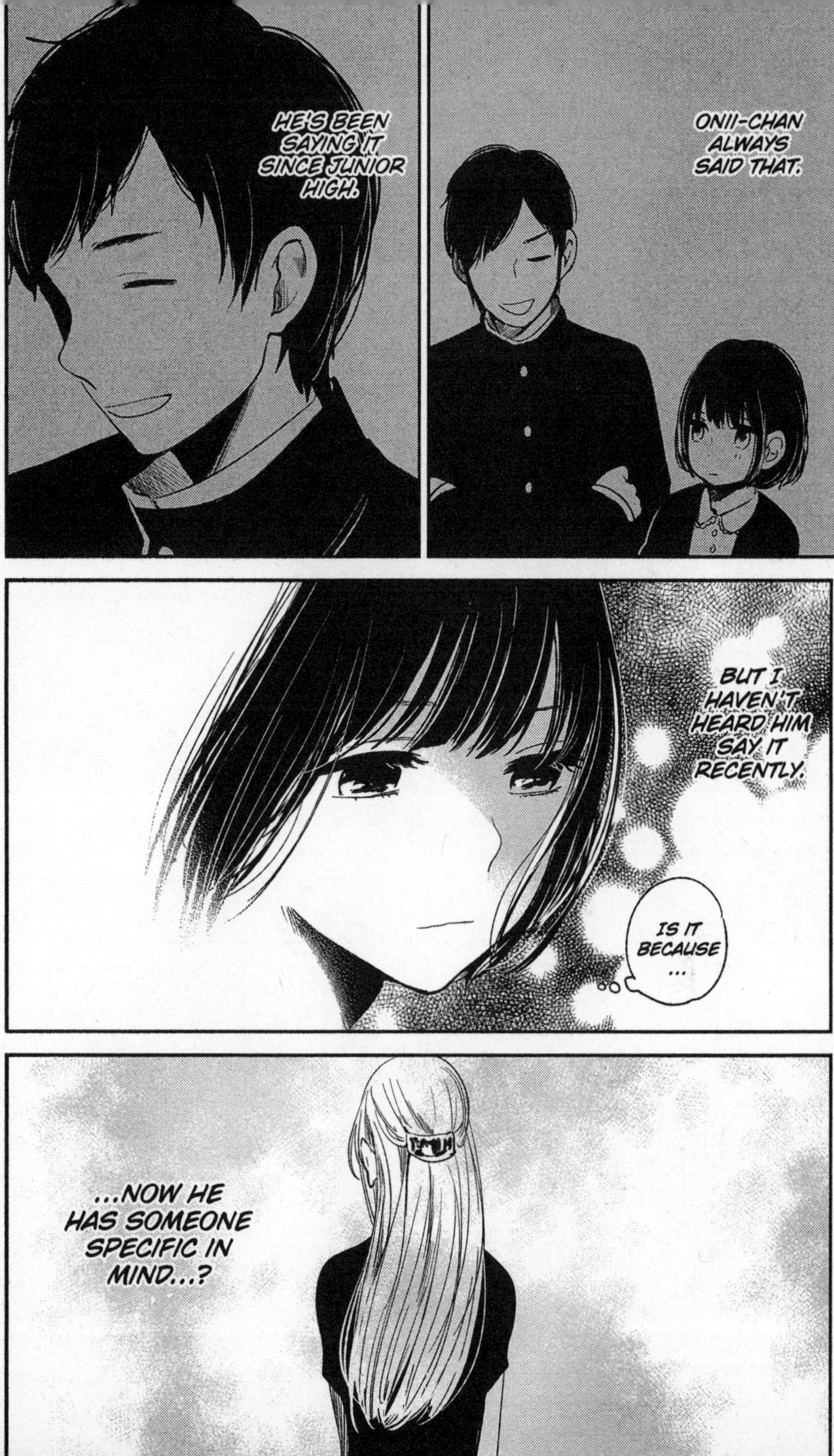
ONII-CHAN ALWAYS SAID THAT.
HE'S BEEN SAYING IT SINCE JUNIOR HIGH.
BUT I HAVEN'T HEARD HIM SAY IT RECENTLY.
IS IT BECAUSE ...
...NOW HE HAS SOMEONE SPECIFIC IN MIND...?

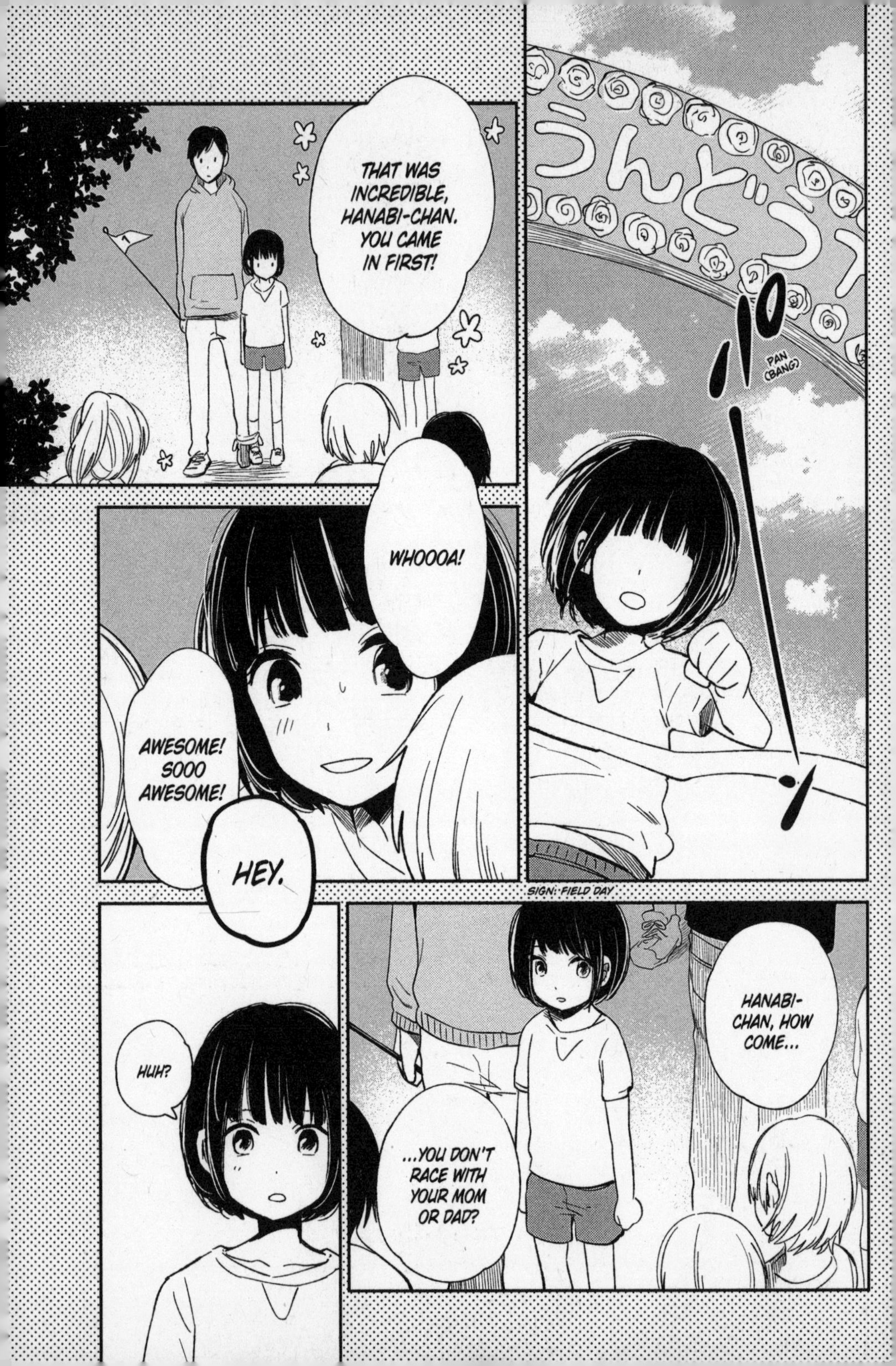
うんど
PAN (BANG)
THAT WAS INCREDIBLE, HANABI-CHAN. YOU CAME IN FIRST!
WHOOOA!
AWESOME! SOOO AWESOME!
HEY.
SIGN: FIELD DAY
HANABI-CHAN, HOW COME...
...YOU DON'T RACE WITH YOUR MOM OR DAD?
HUH?

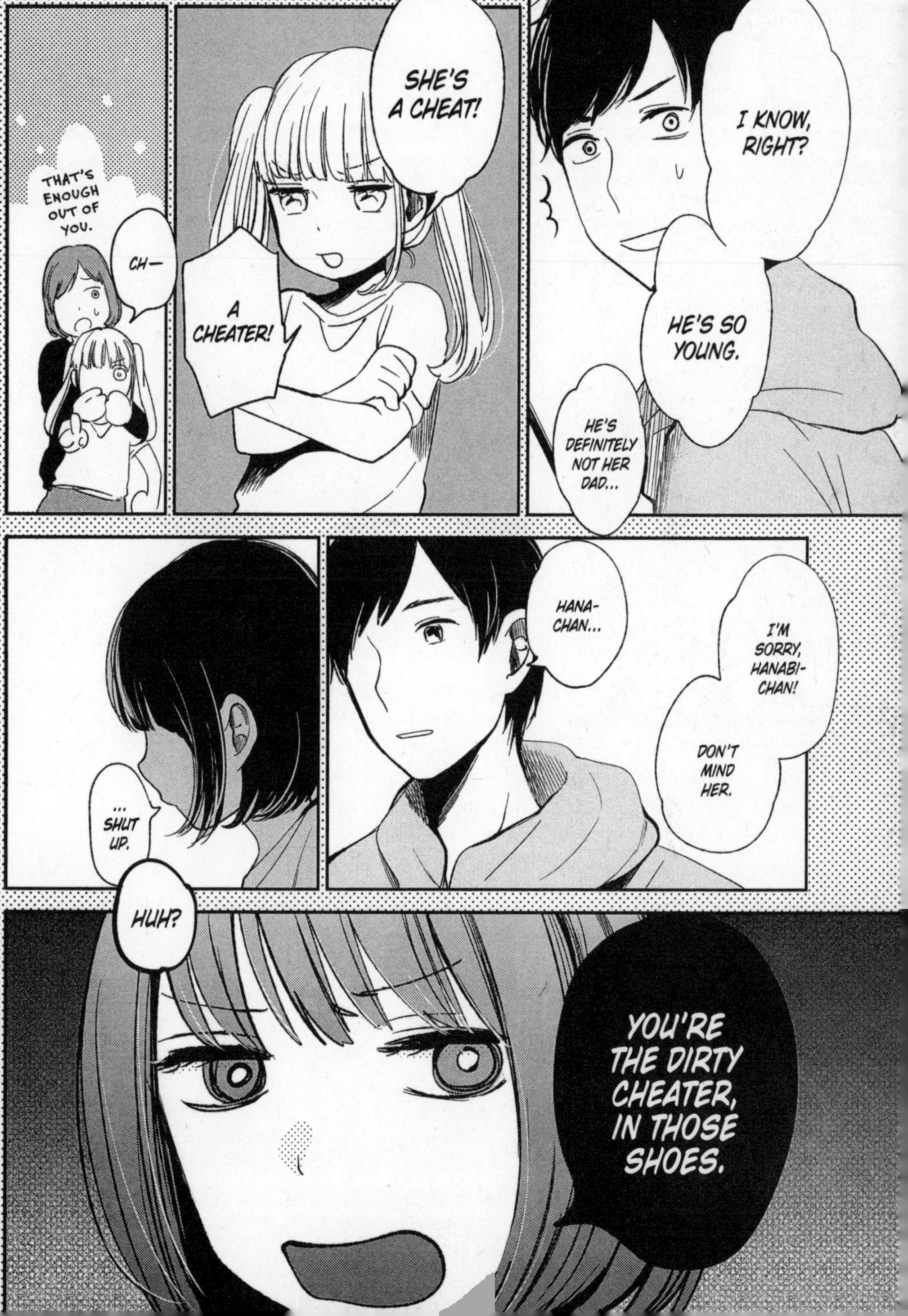
I KNOW, RIGHT?
HE'S SO YOUNG.
HE'S DEFINITELY NOT HER DAD...
SHE'S A CHEAT!
A CHEATER!
THAT'S ENOUGH OUT OF YOU.
CH—
HANA-CHAN...
I'M SORRY, HANABI-CHAN!
DON'T MIND HER.
...SHUT UP.
HUH?
YOU'RE THE DIRTY CHEATER, IN THOSE SHOES.

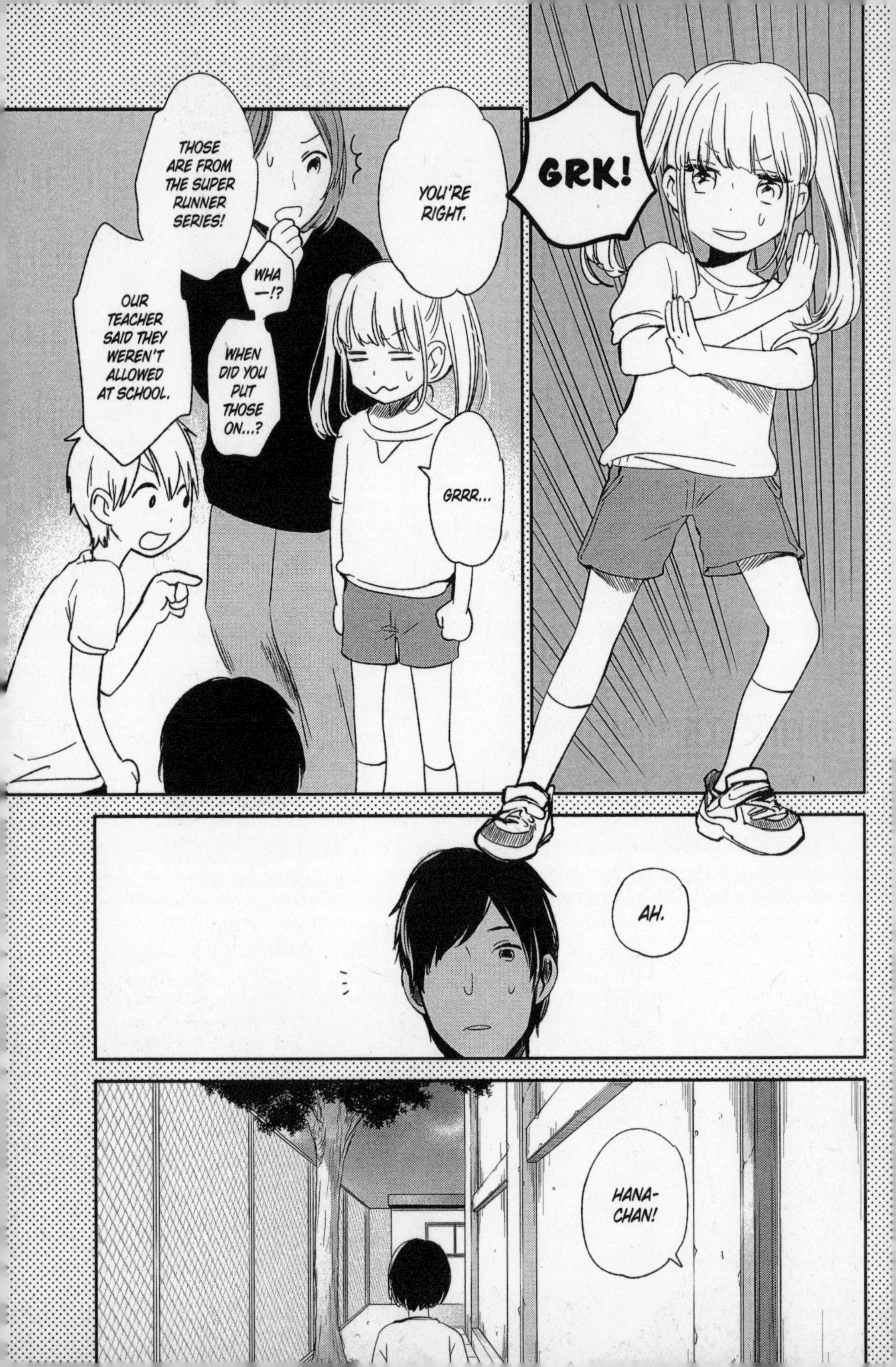
GRK!
YOU'RE RIGHT.
THOSE ARE FROM THE SUPER RUNNER SERIES!
WHA—!?
WHEN DID YOU PUT THOSE ON...?
OUR TEACHER SAID THEY WEREN'T ALLOWED AT SCHOOL.
GRRR...
AH.
HANA-CHAN!

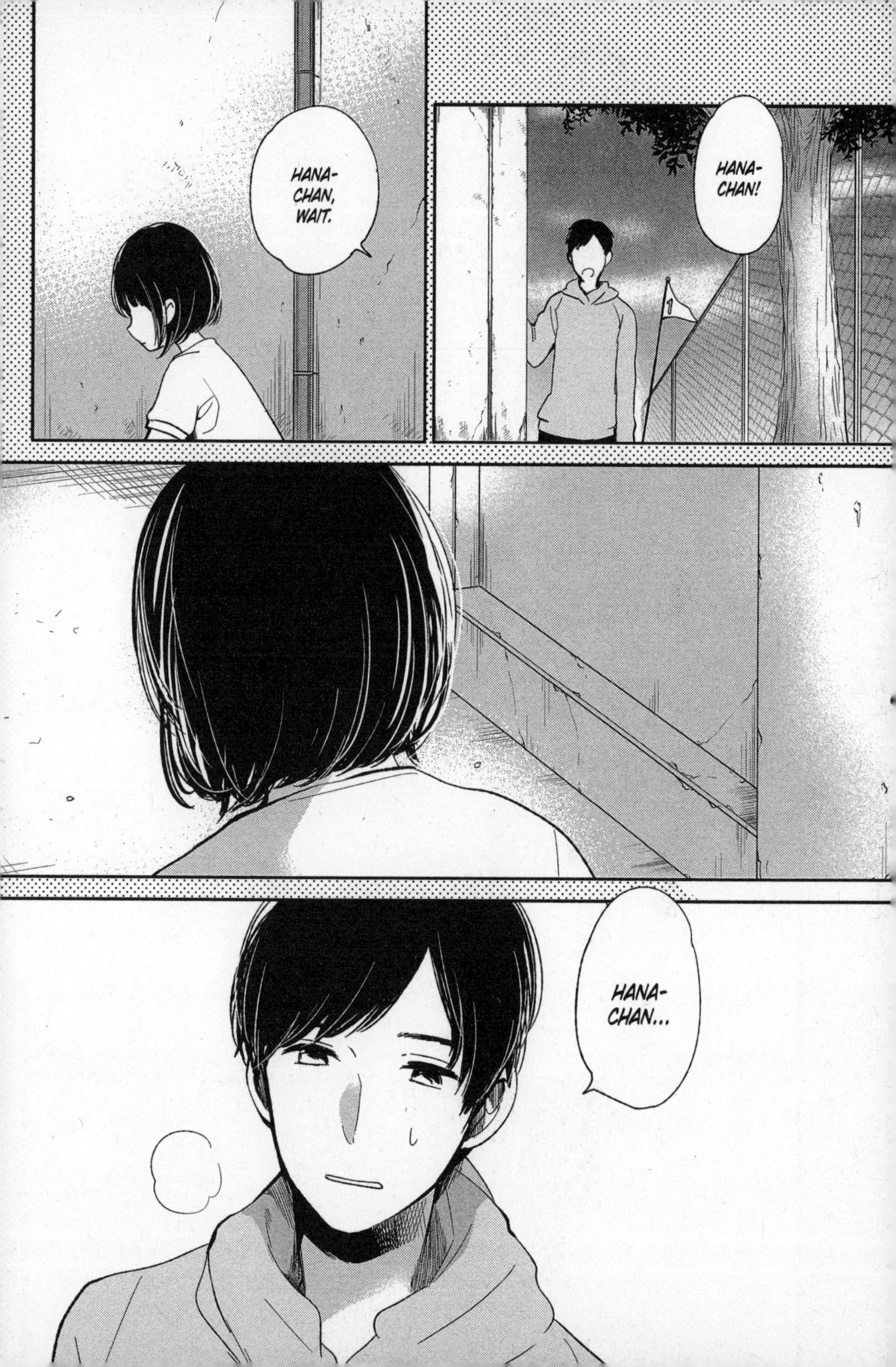
HANA-CHAN!
HANA-CHAN, WAIT.
HANA-CHAN...

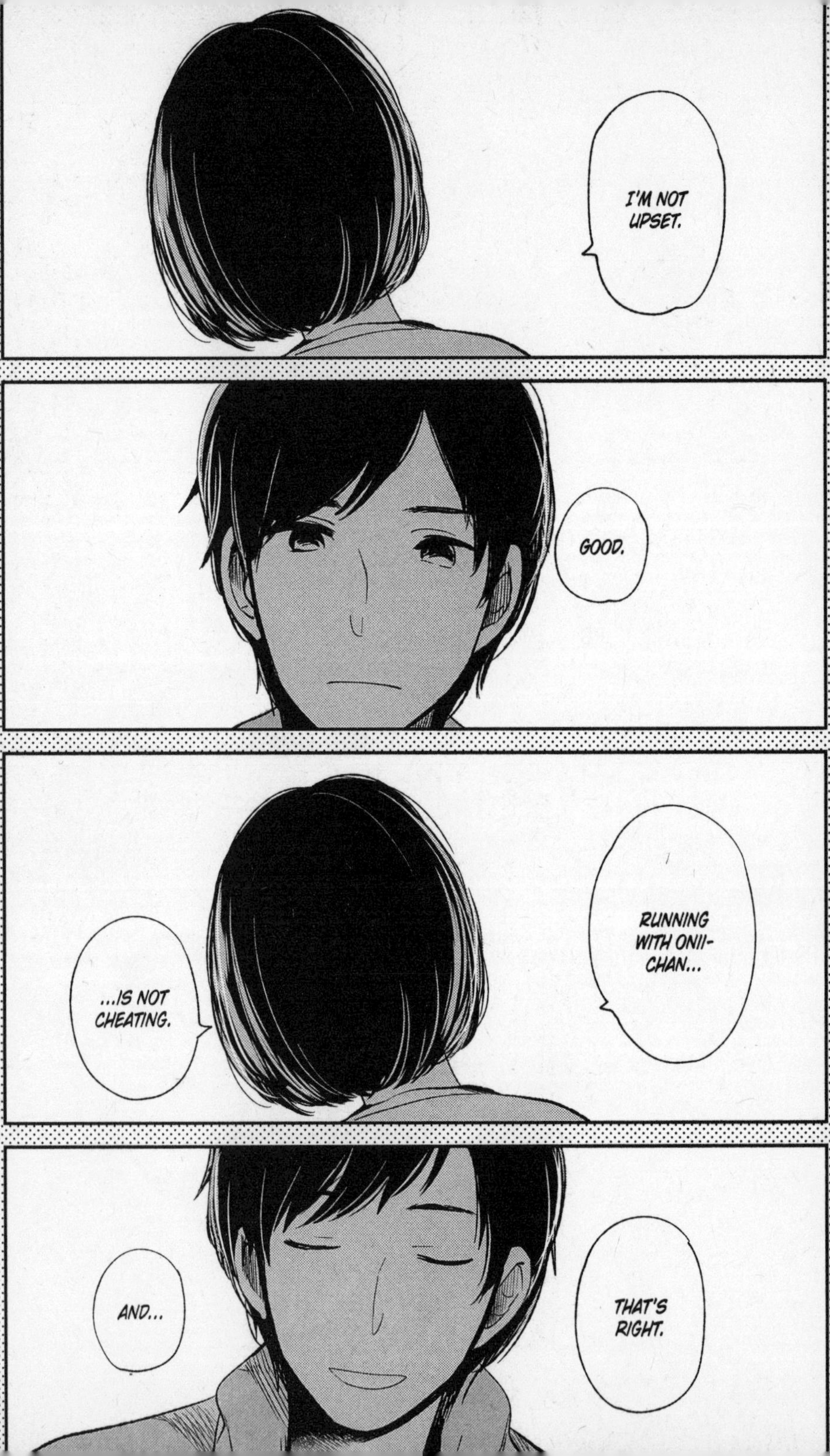
I'M NOT UPSET.
GOOD.
RUNNING WITH ONII-CHAN...
...IS NOT CHEATING.
THAT'S RIGHT.
AND...

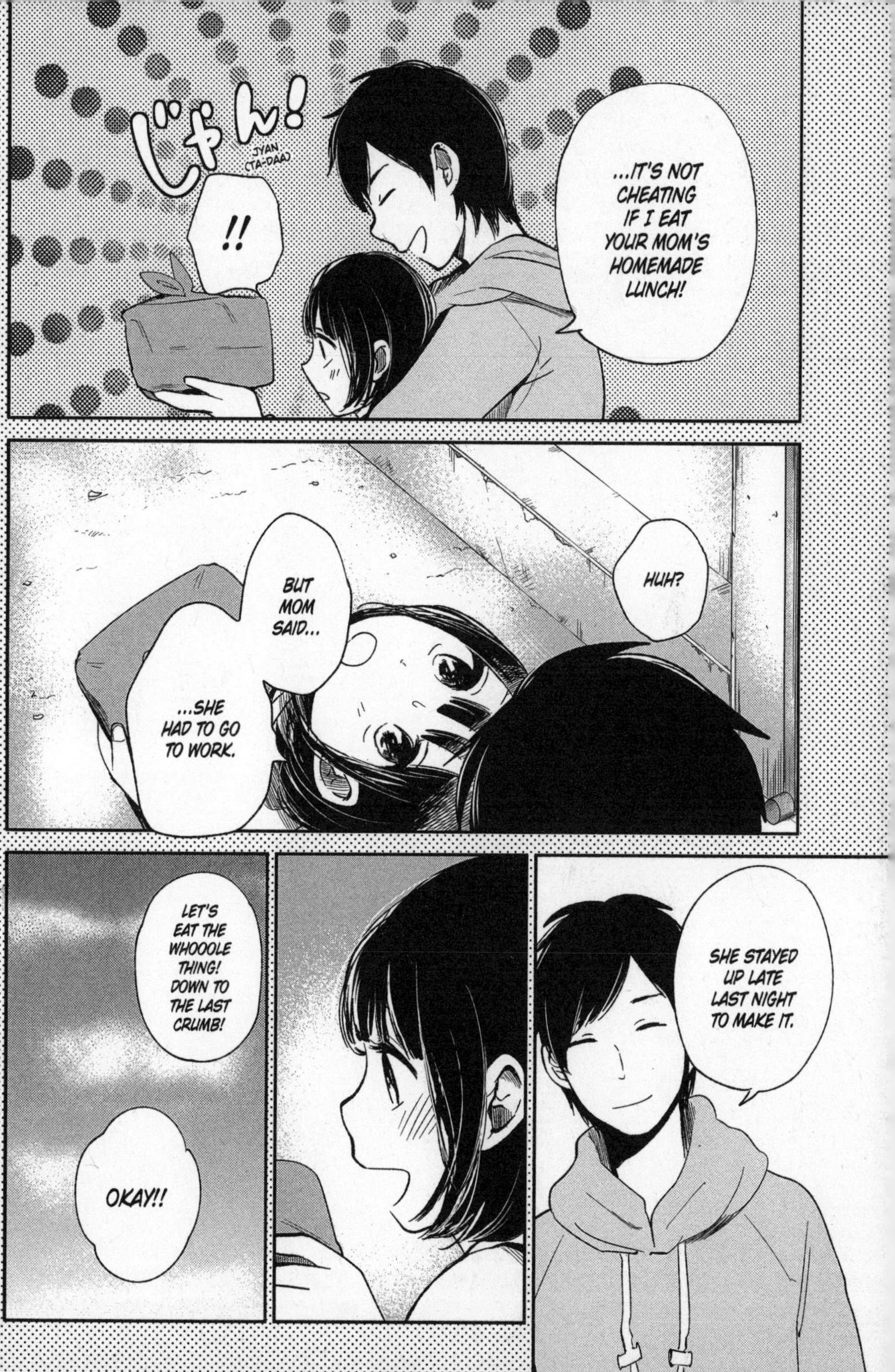
...IT'S NOT CHEATING IF I EAT YOUR MOM'S HOMEMADE LUNCH!
じゃん!
JYAN (TA-DAA)
!!
HUH?
BUT MOM SAID...
...SHE HAD TO GO TO WORK.
SHE STAYED UP LATE LAST NIGHT TO MAKE IT.
LET'S EAT THE WHOOOLE THING! DOWN TO THE LAST CRUMB!
OKAY!!

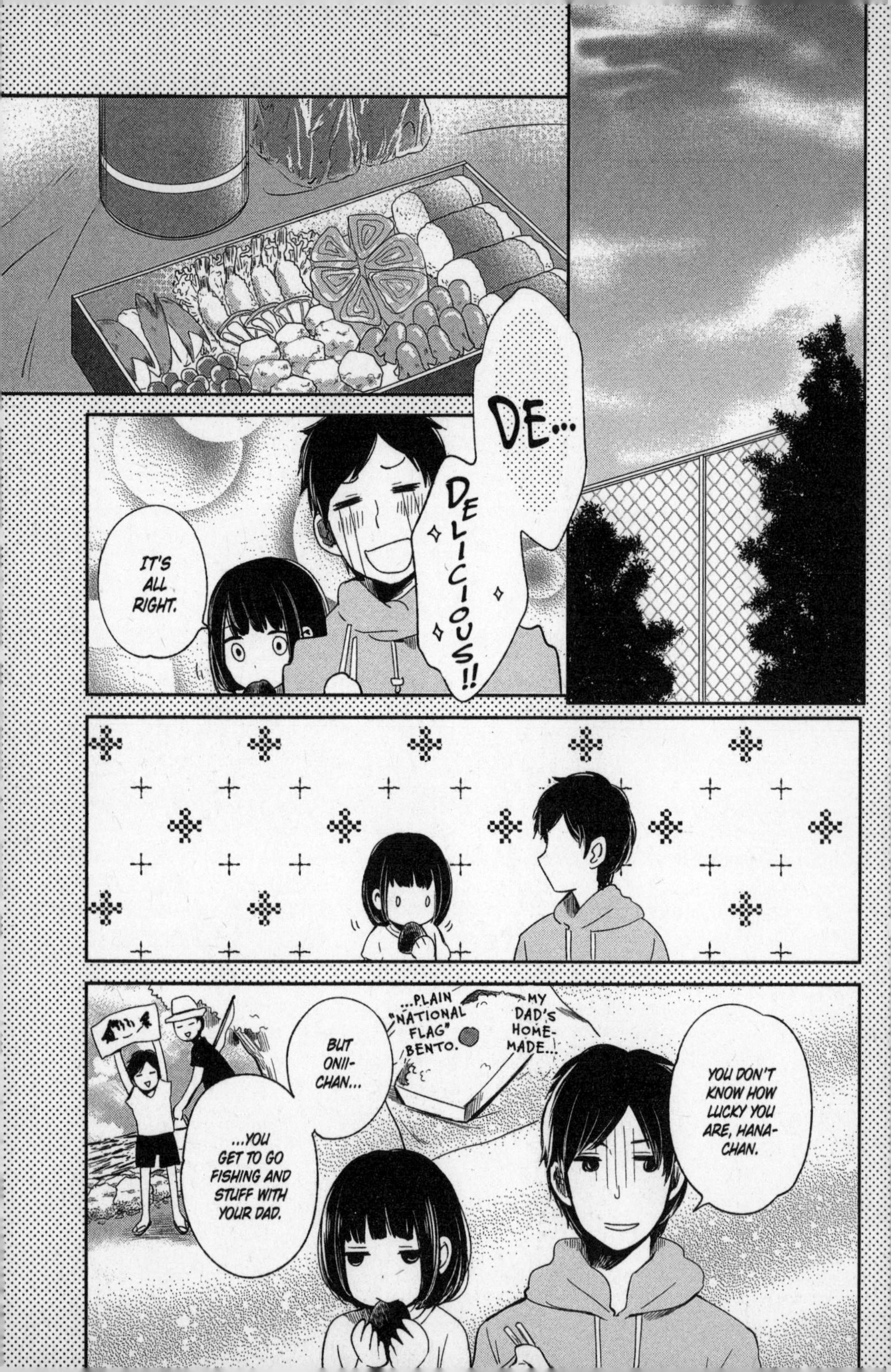
DE...
DELICIOUS!!
IT'S ALL RIGHT.
YOU DON'T KNOW HOW LUCKY YOU ARE, HANA-CHAN.
MY DAD'S HOME-MADE...
...PLAIN "NATIONAL FLAG" BENTO.
BUT ONII-CHAN...
...YOU GET TO GO FISHING AND STUFF WITH YOUR DAD.

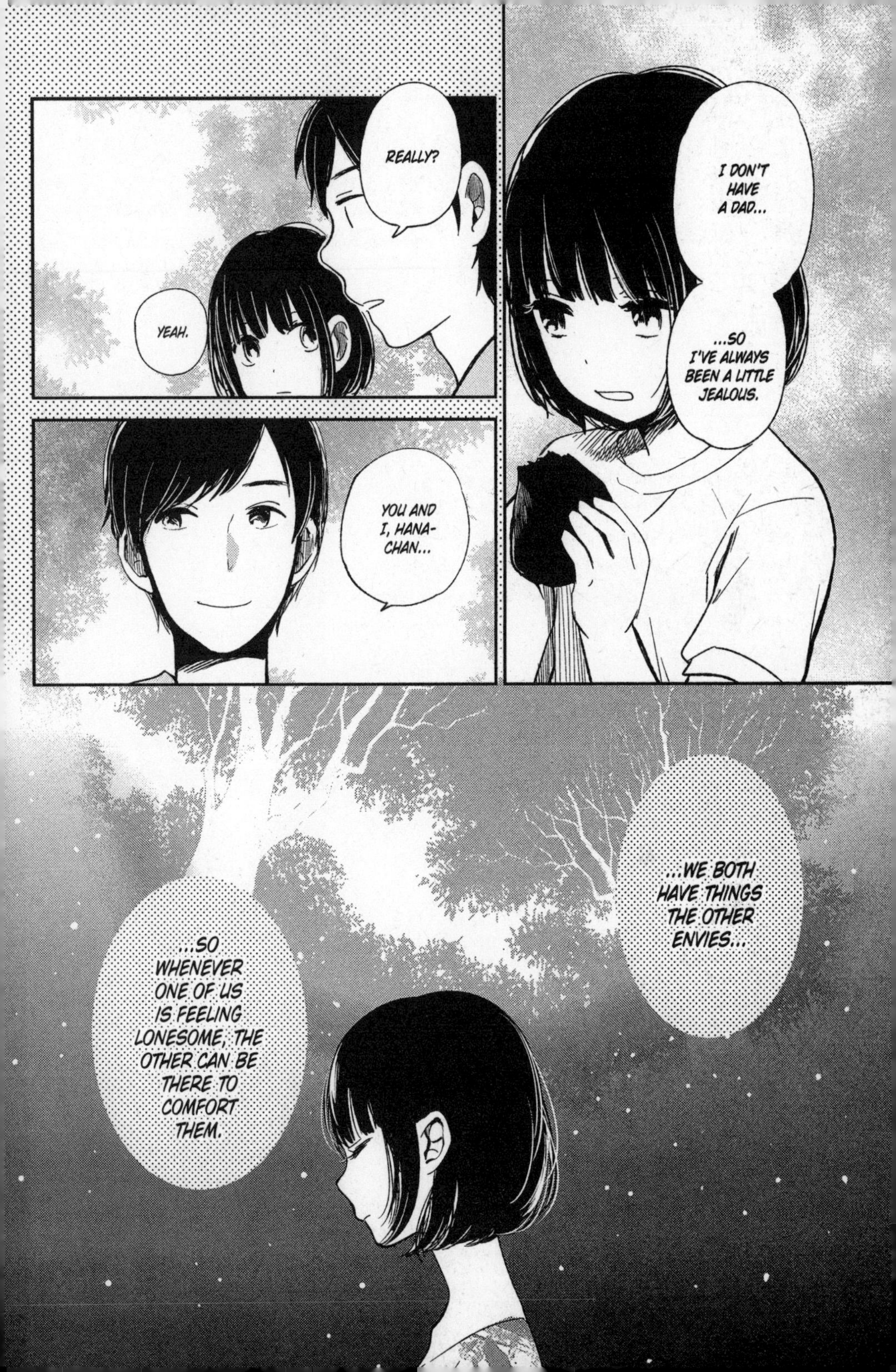
I DON'T HAVE A DAD...
...SO I'VE ALWAYS BEEN A LITTLE JEALOUS.
REALLY?
YEAH.
YOU AND I, HANA-CHAN...
...WE BOTH HAVE THINGS THE OTHER ENVIES...
...SO WHENEVER ONE OF US IS FEELING LONESOME, THE OTHER CAN BE THERE TO COMFORT THEM.

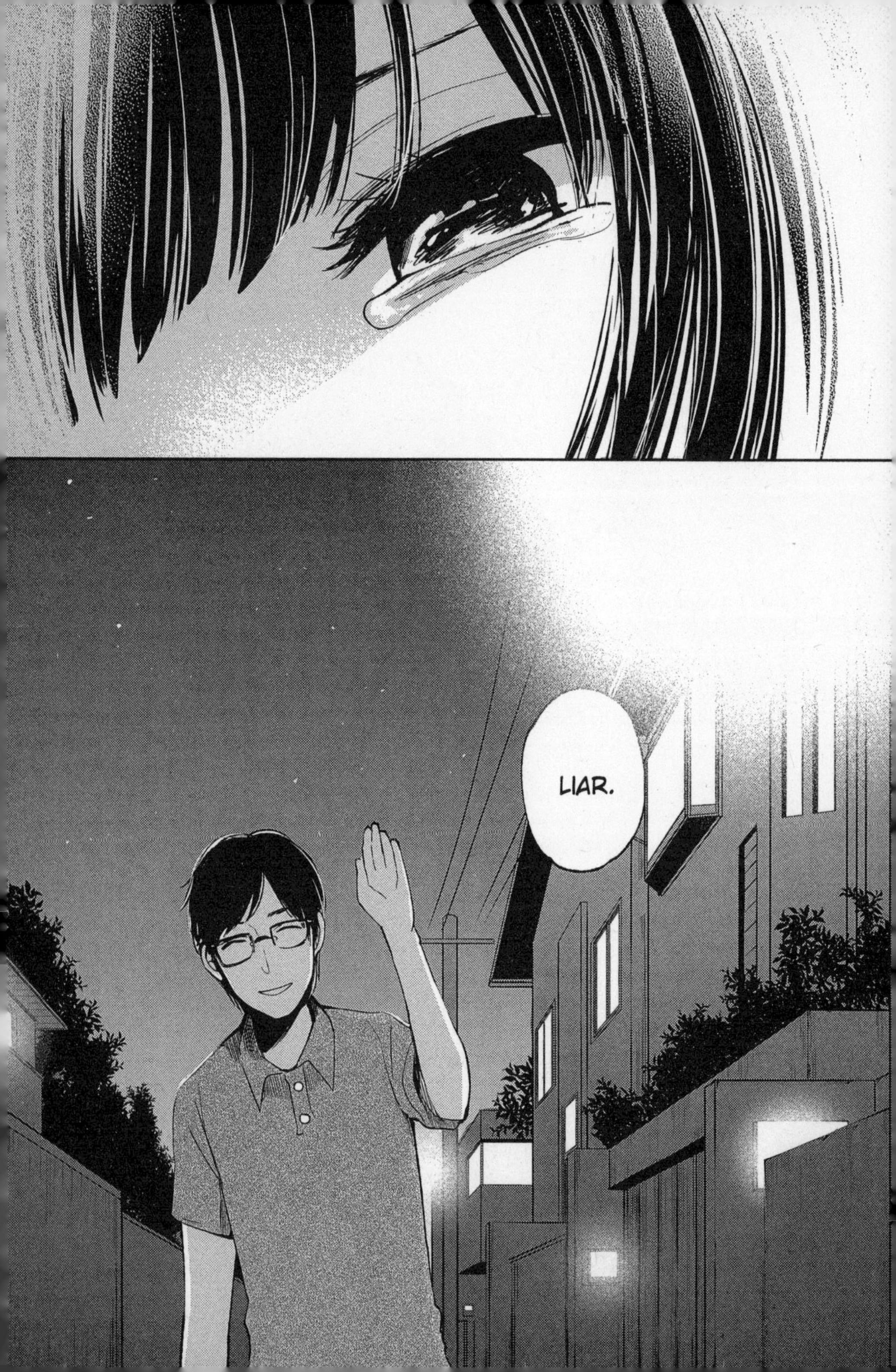
LIAR.

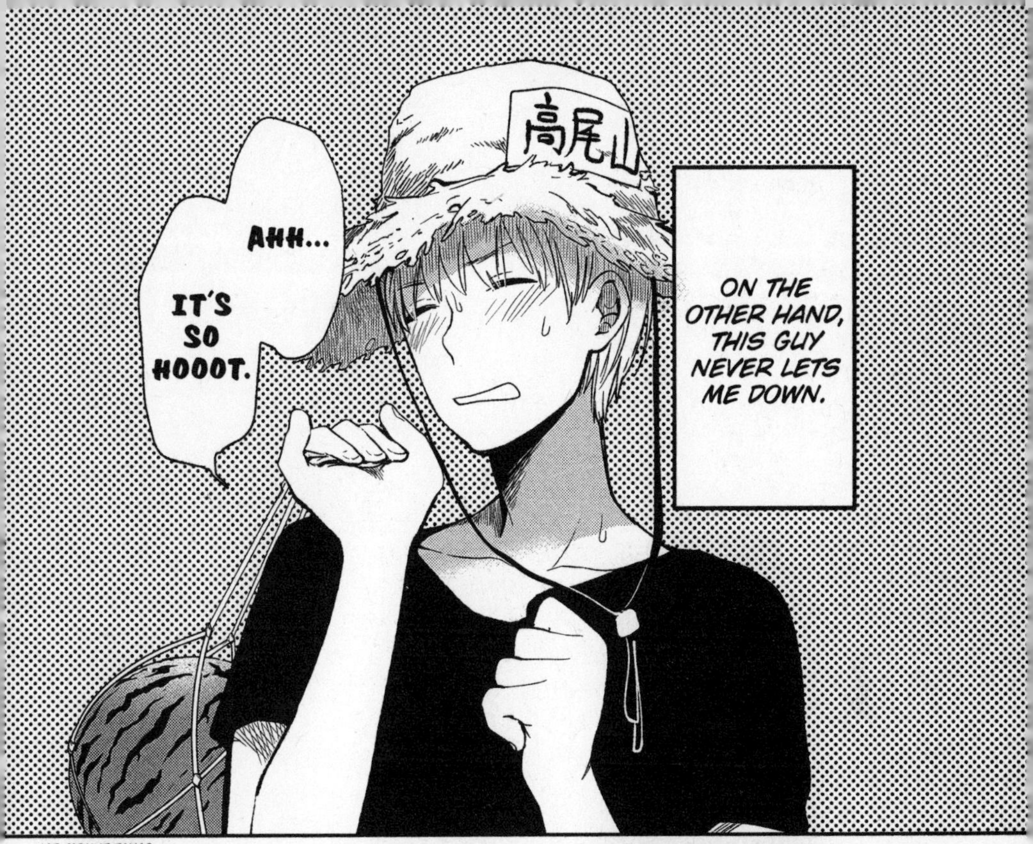
ON THE OTHER HAND, THIS GUY NEVER LETS ME DOWN.
高尾山
AHH...
IT'S SO HOOOT.

HAT: MOUNT TAKAO

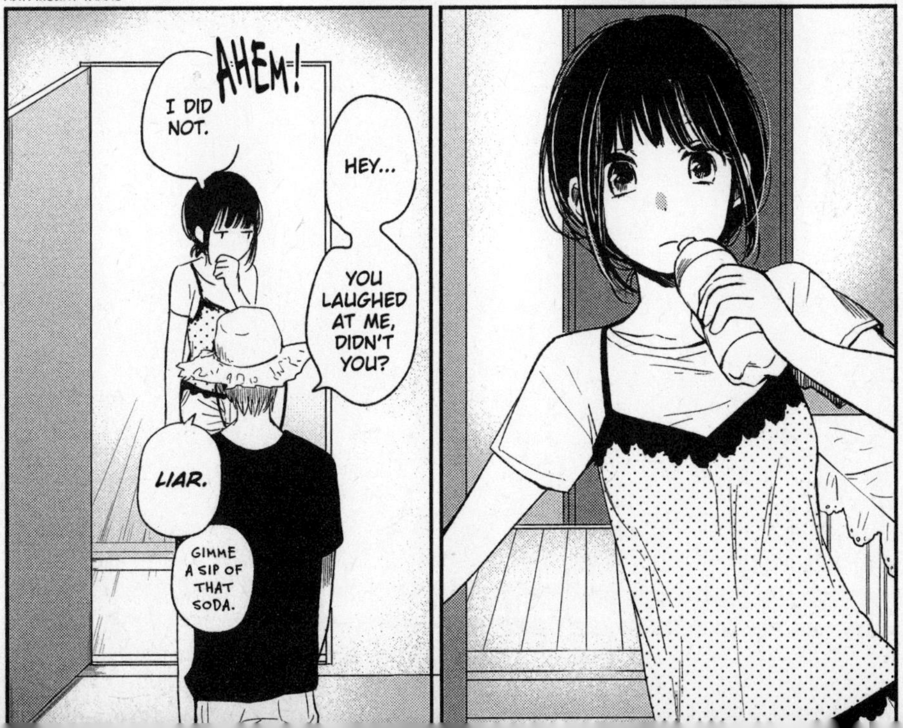
HEY...
YOU LAUGHED AT ME, DIDN'T YOU?
AHEM!
I DID NOT.
LIAR.
GIMME A SIP OF THAT SODA.

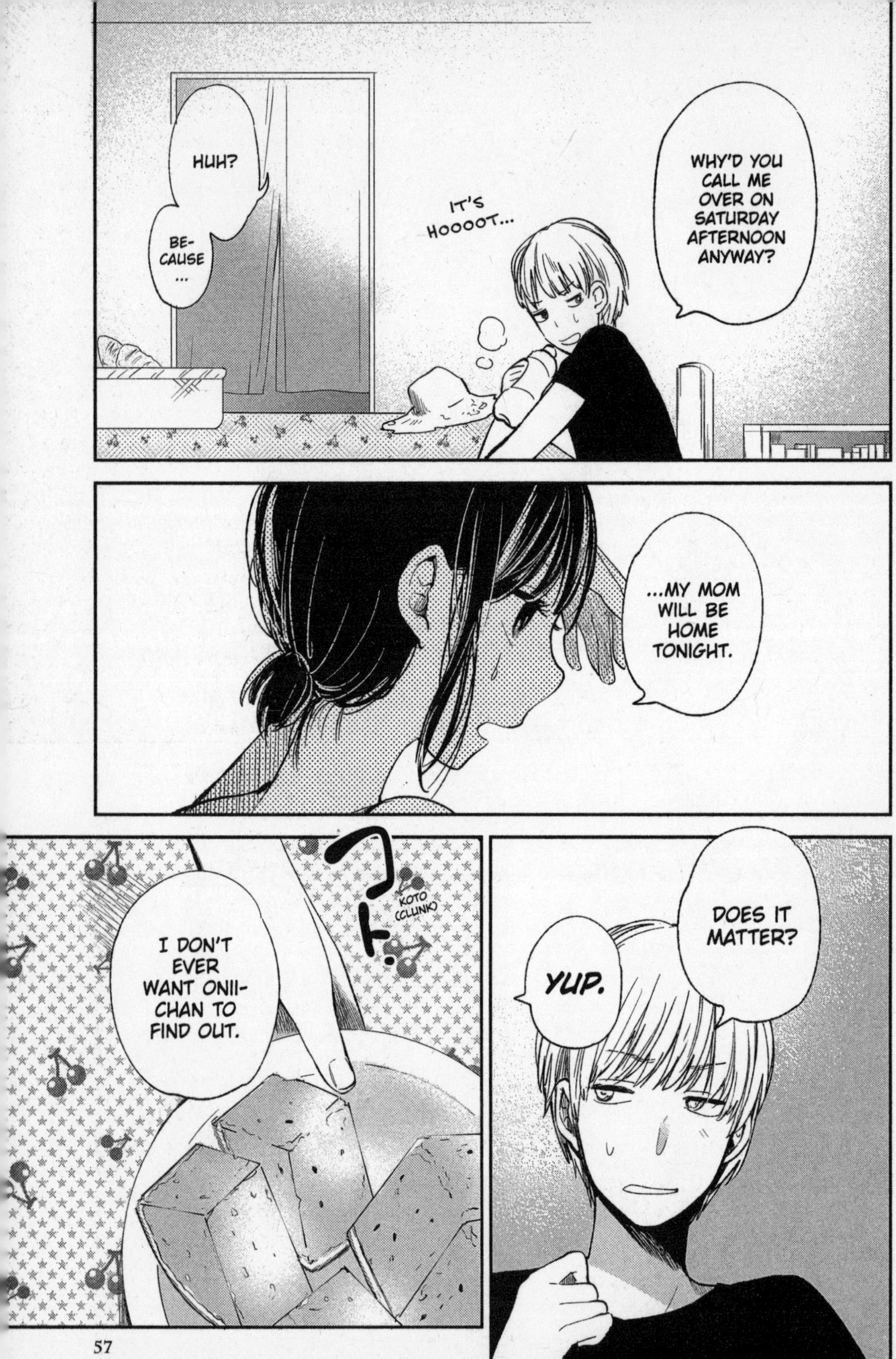
WHY'D YOU CALL ME OVER ON SATURDAY AFTERNOON ANYWAY?
IT'S HOOOOT...
HUH?
BE-CAUSE ...
...MY MOM WILL BE HOME TONIGHT.
DOES IT MATTER?
YUP.
KOTO (CLUNK)
I DON'T EVER WANT ONII-CHAN TO FIND OUT.

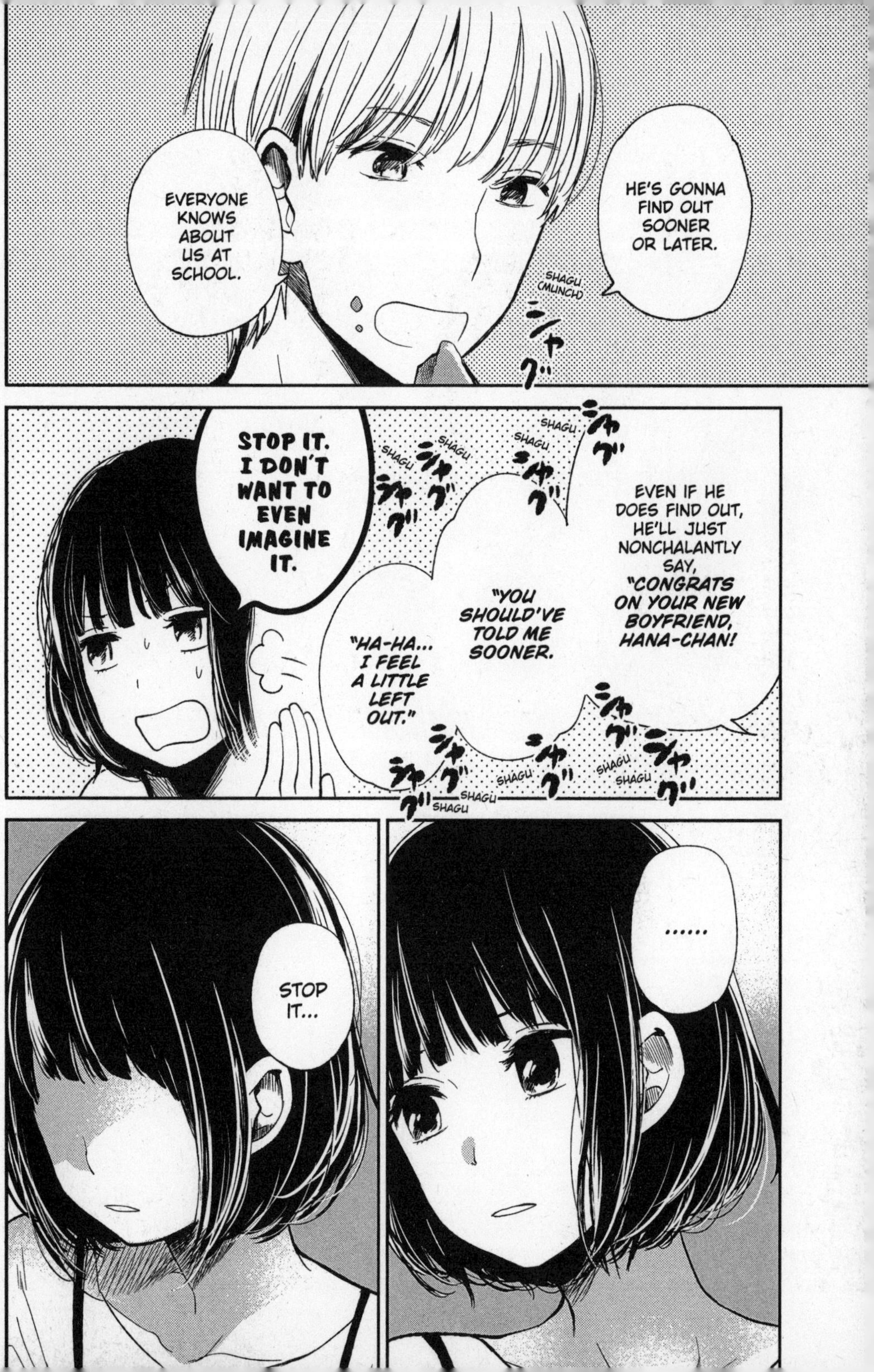
HE'S GONNA FIND OUT SOONER OR LATER.
SHAGU (MUNCH)
EVERYONE KNOWS ABOUT US AT SCHOOL.
SHAGU
SHAGU
SHAGU
SHAGU
EVEN IF HE DOES FIND OUT, HE'LL JUST NONCHALANTLY SAY, "CONGRATS ON YOUR NEW BOYFRIEND, HANA-CHAN!
"YOU SHOULD'VE TOLD ME SOONER.
"HA-HA... I FEEL A LITTLE LEFT OUT."
STOP IT. I DON'T WANT TO EVEN IMAGINE IT.
SHAGU
SHAGU
SHAGU
SHAGU
SHAGU
......
STOP IT...

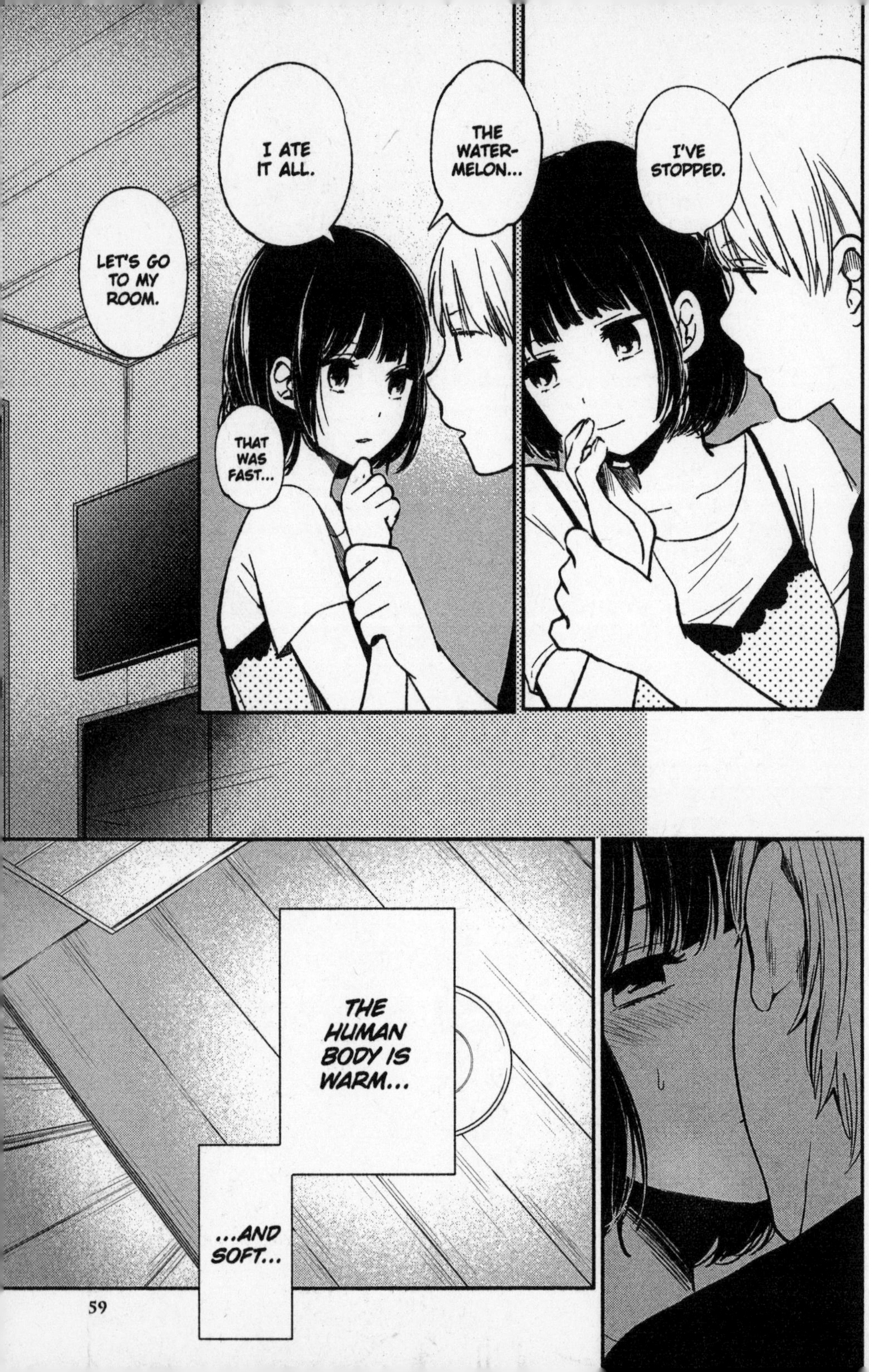
I'VE STOPPED.
THE WATER-MELON...
I ATE IT ALL.
THAT WAS FAST...
LET'S GO TO MY ROOM.
THE HUMAN BODY IS WARM...
...AND SOFT...

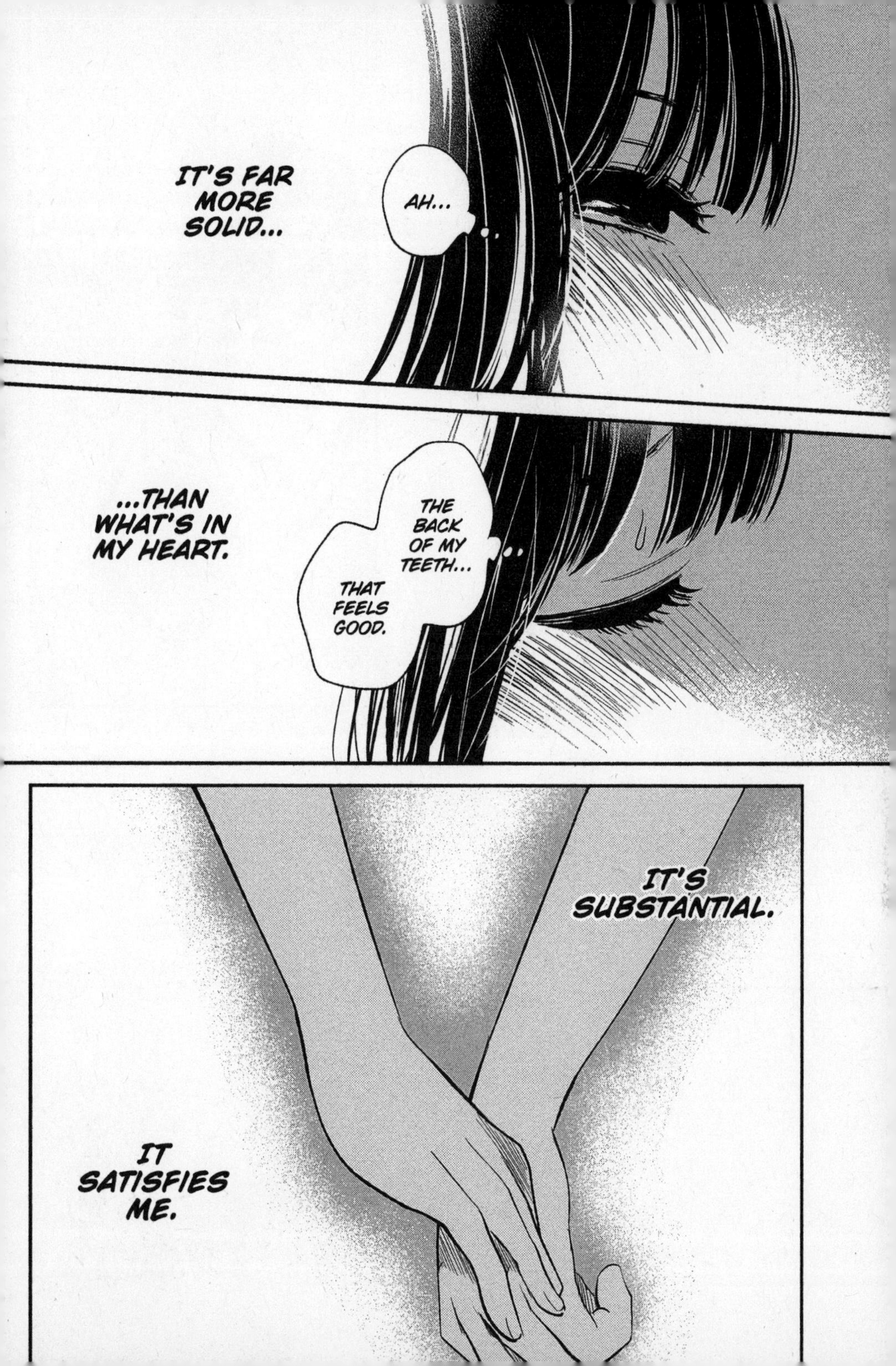
AH...
IT'S FAR MORE SOLID...
THE BACK OF MY TEETH...
THAT FEELS GOOD.
...THAN WHAT'S IN MY HEART.
IT'S SUBSTANTIAL.
IT SATISFIES ME.

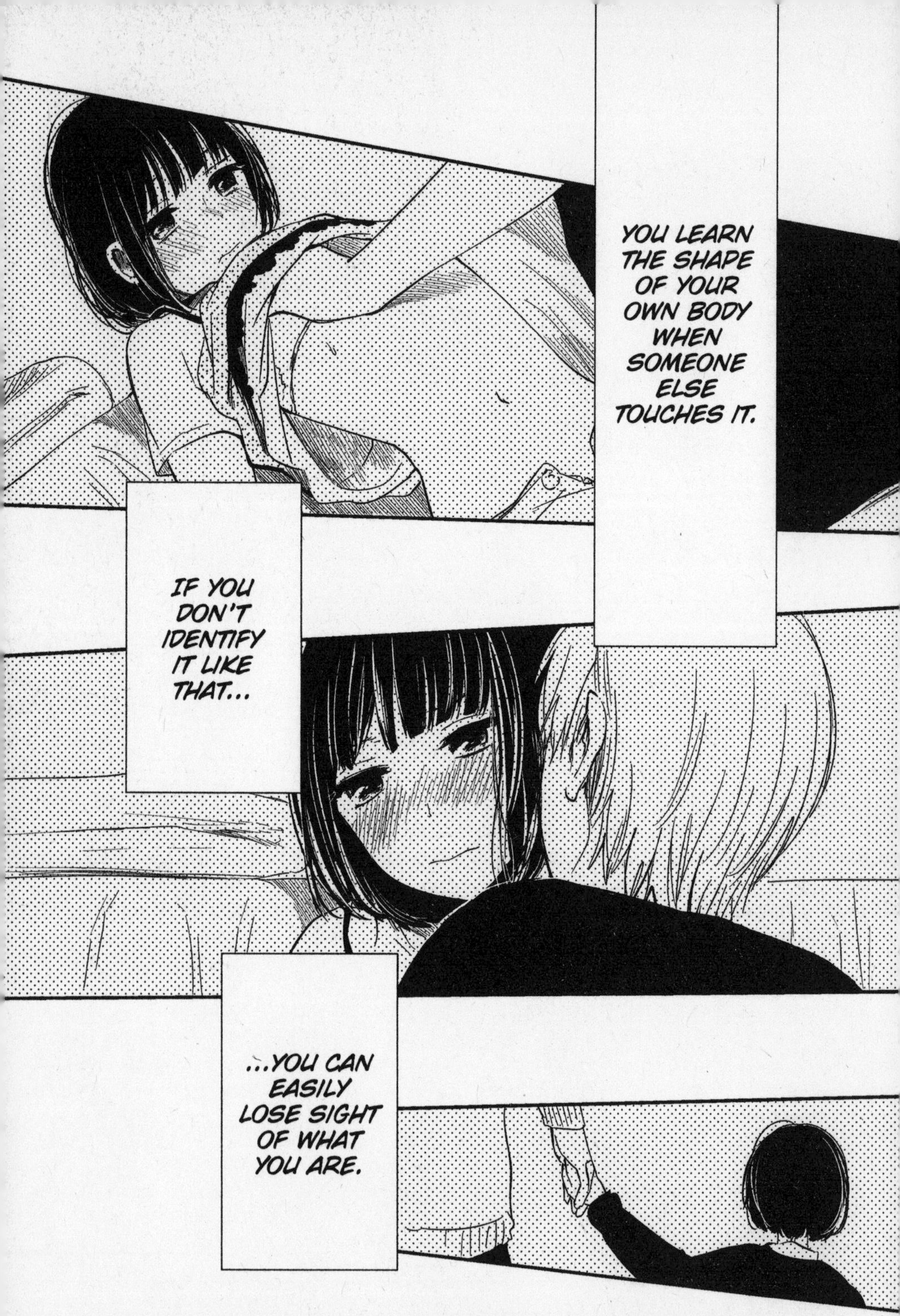
YOU LEARN THE SHAPE OF YOUR OWN BODY WHEN SOMEONE ELSE TOUCHES IT.
IF YOU DON'T IDENTIFY IT LIKE THAT...
...YOU CAN EASILY LOSE SIGHT OF WHAT YOU ARE.

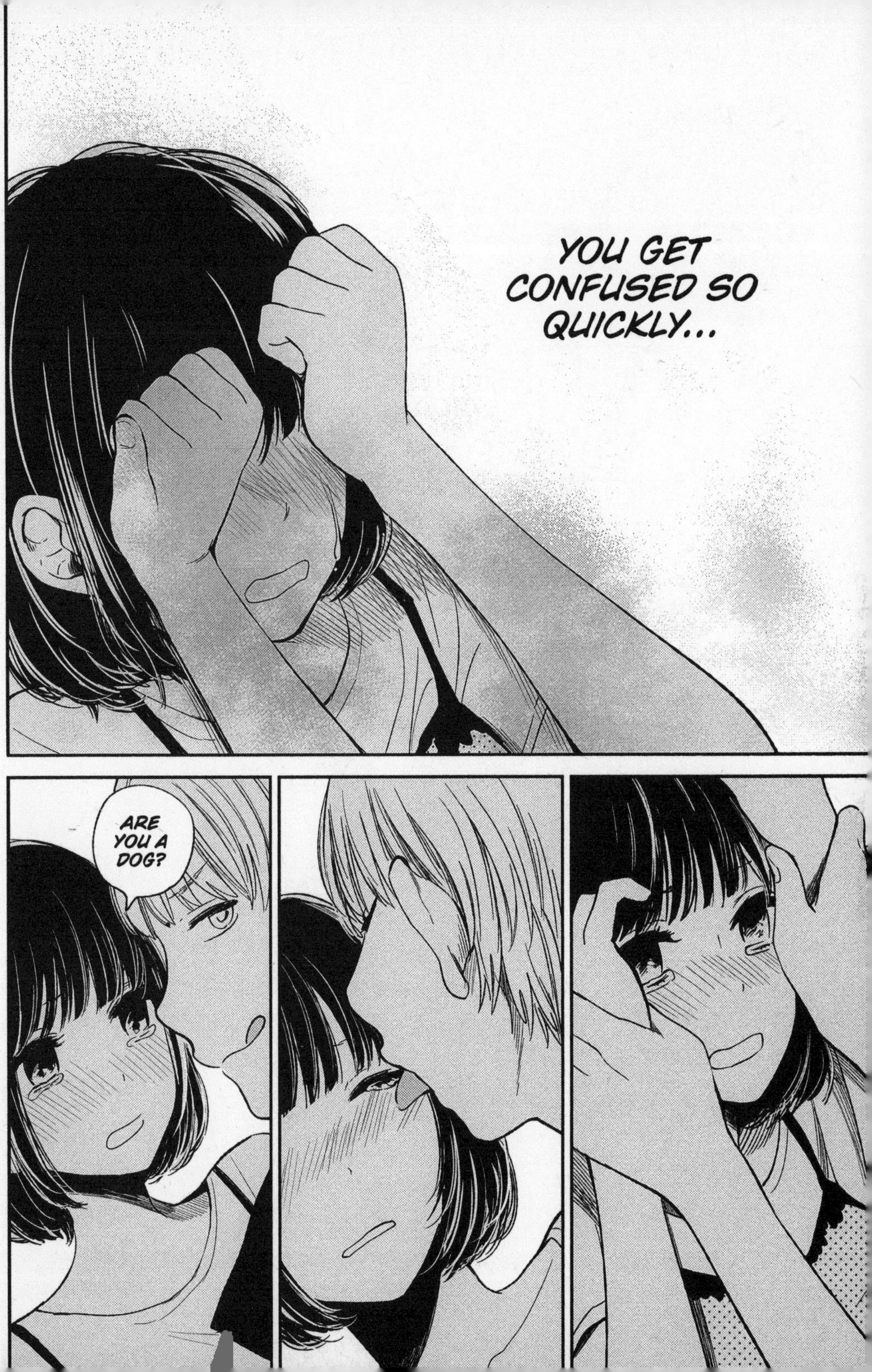
YOU GET CONFUSED SO QUICKLY...
ARE YOU A DOG?

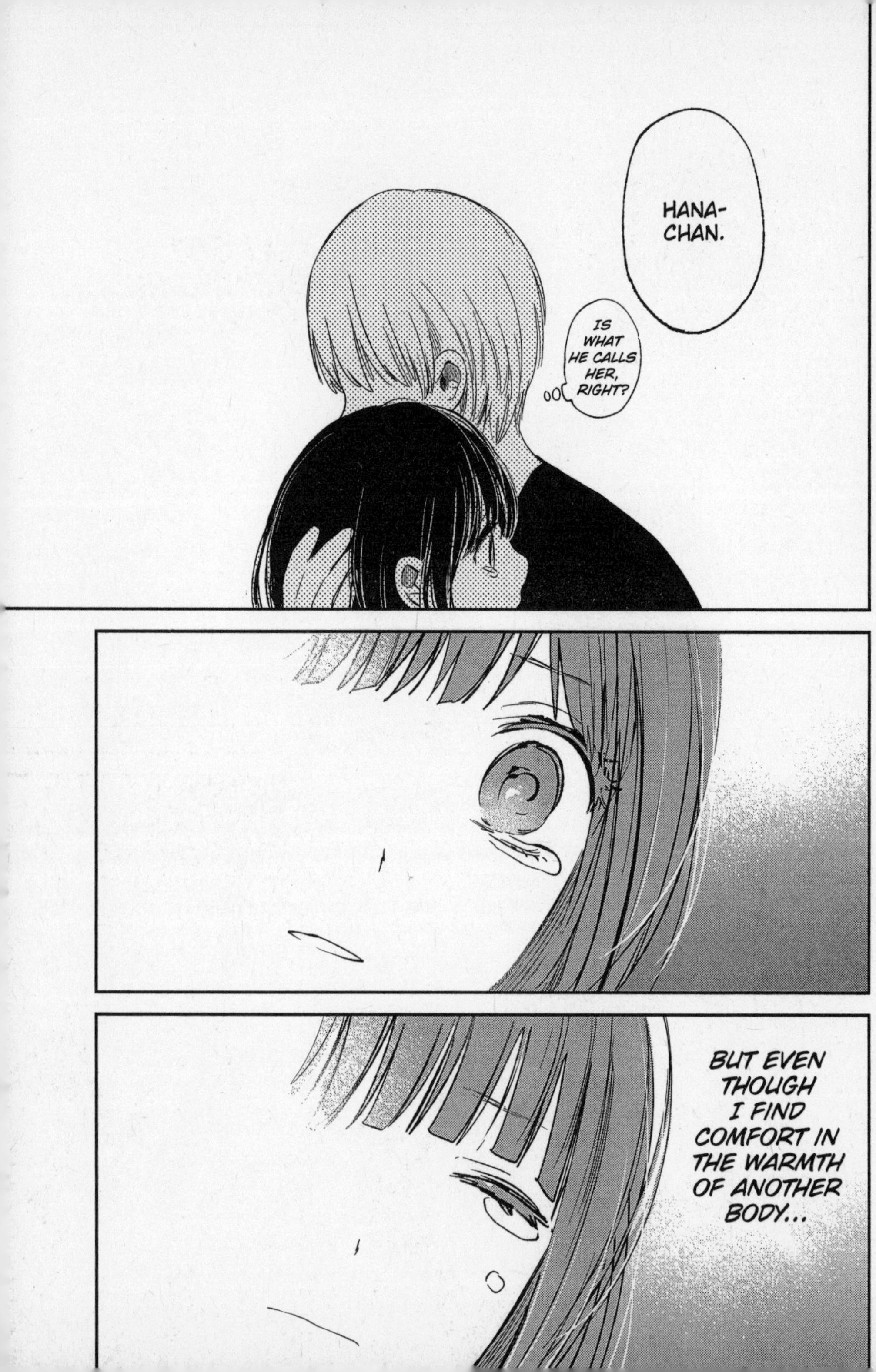
HANA-CHAN.
IS WHAT HE CALLS HER, RIGHT?
BUT EVEN THOUGH I FIND COMFORT IN THE WARMTH OF ANOTHER BODY...

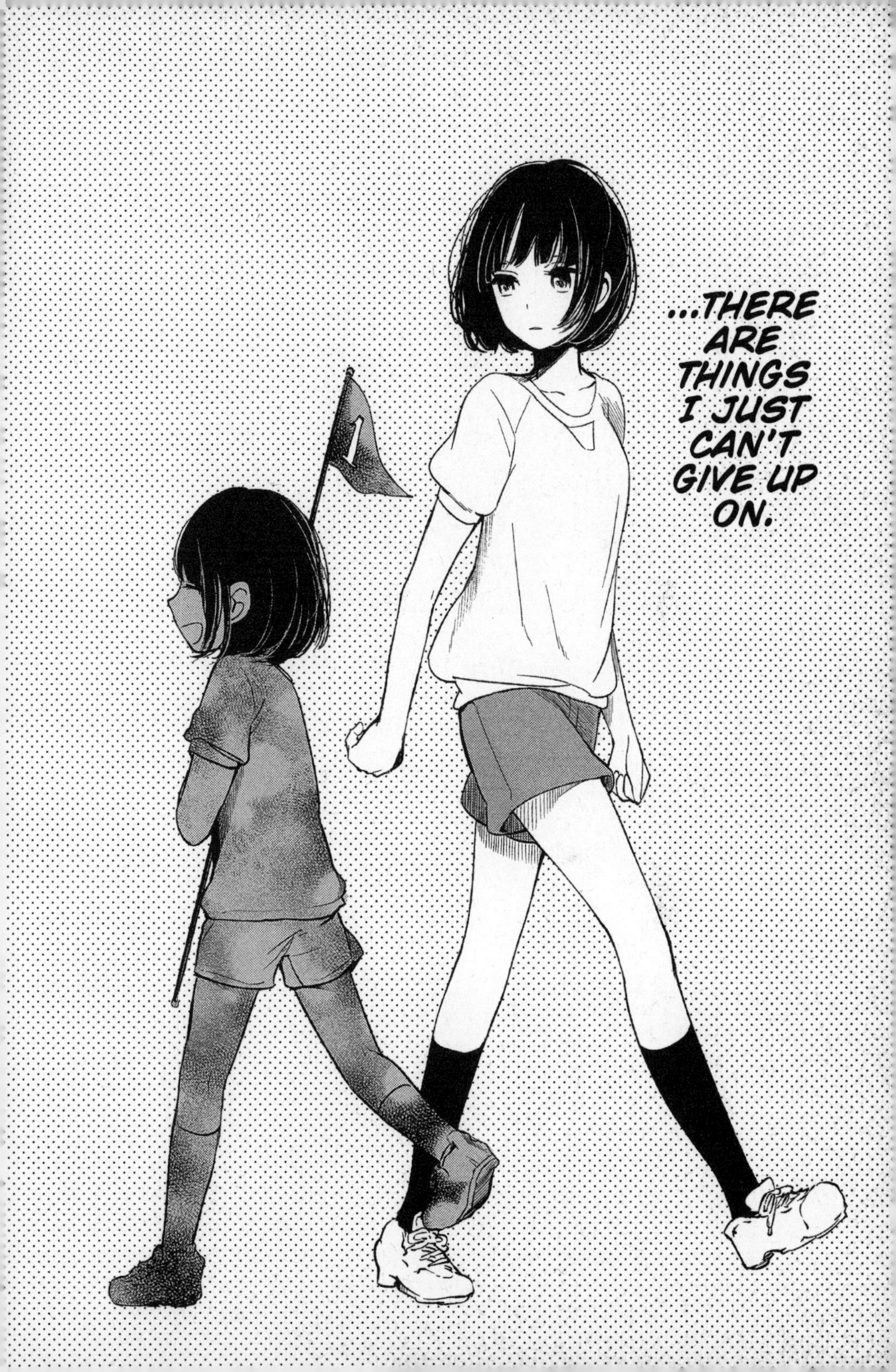
...THERE ARE THINGS I JUST CAN'T GIVE UP ON.

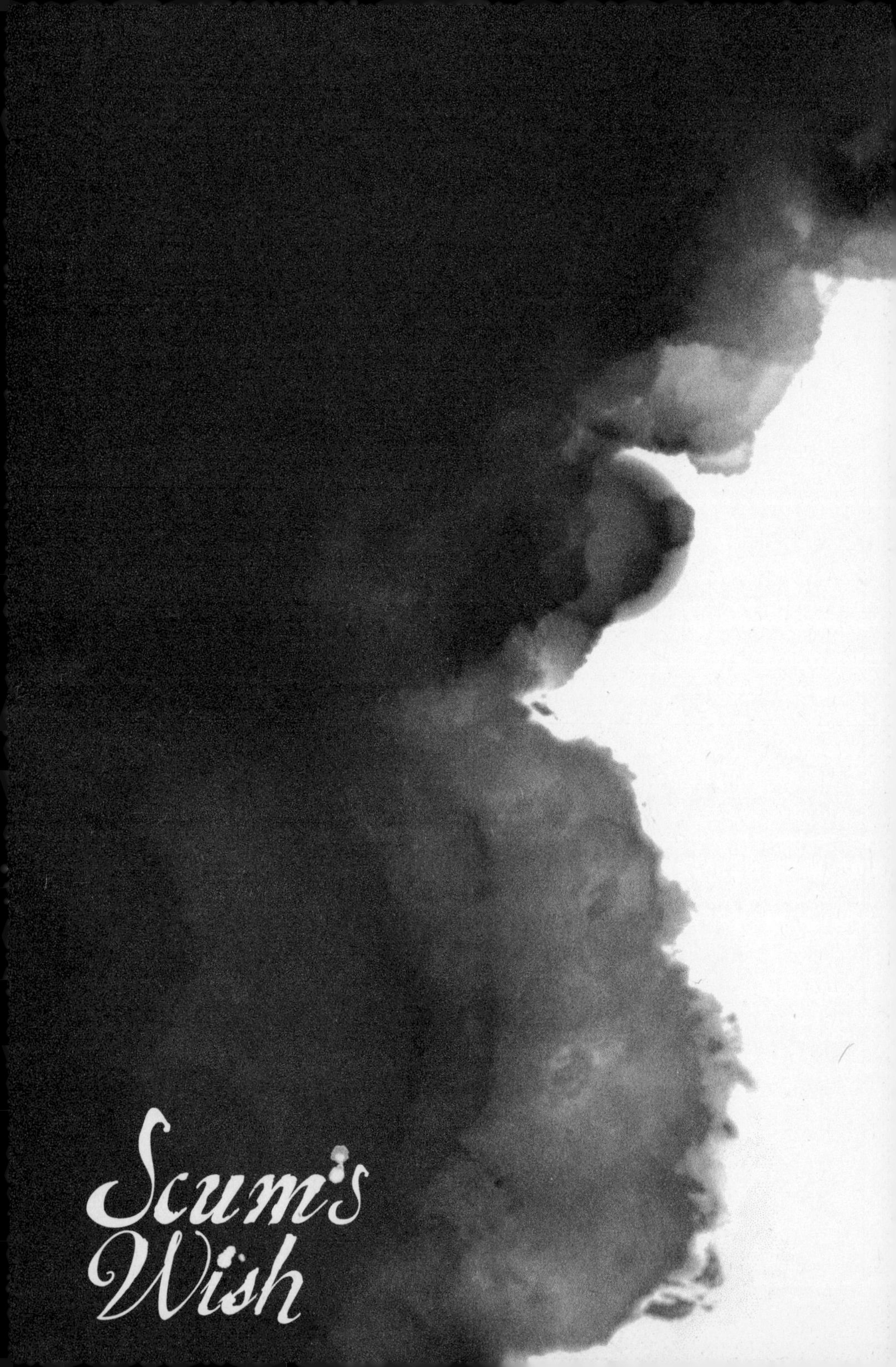
Scum's
Wish

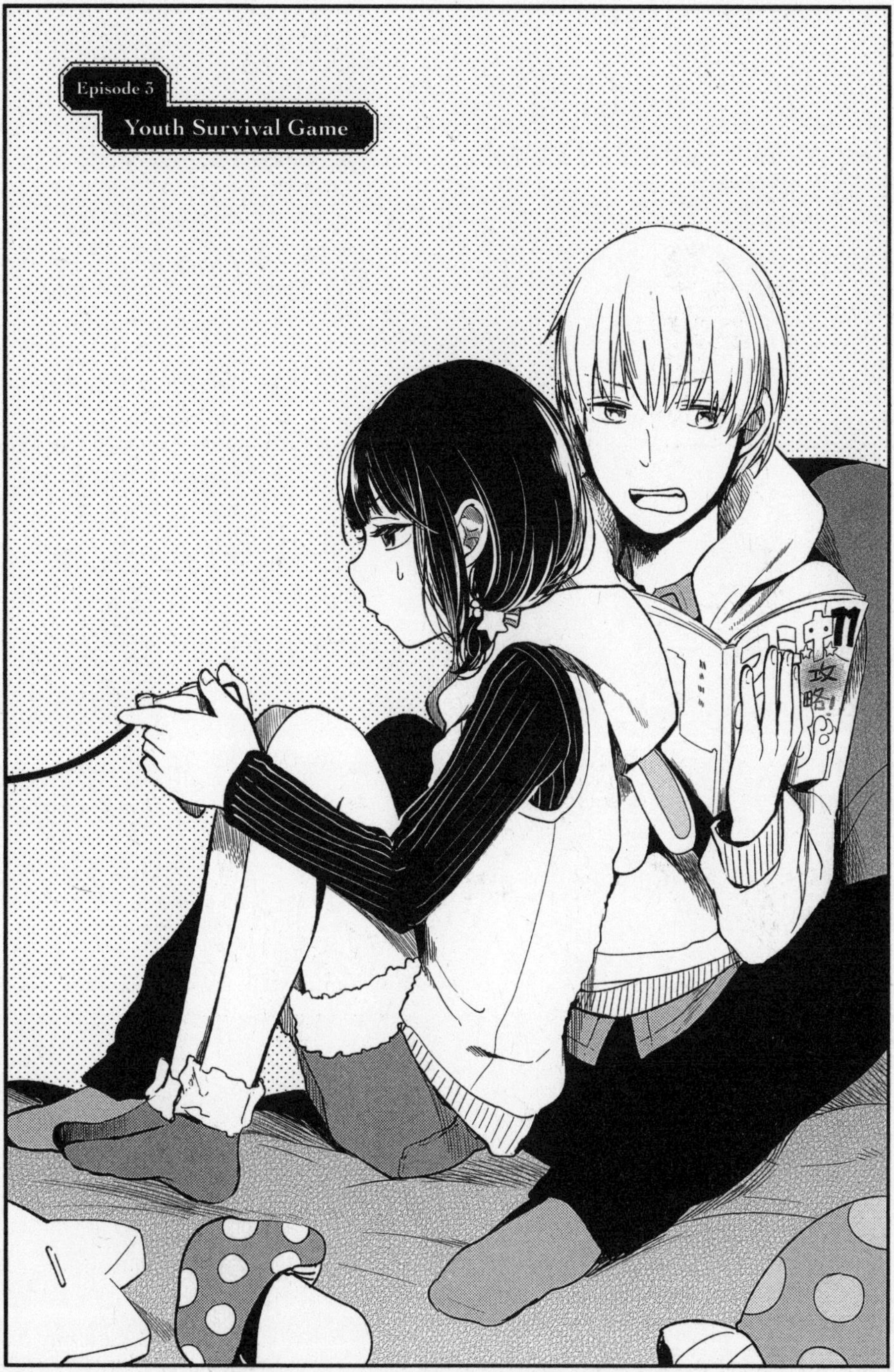
Episode 3
Youth Survival Game

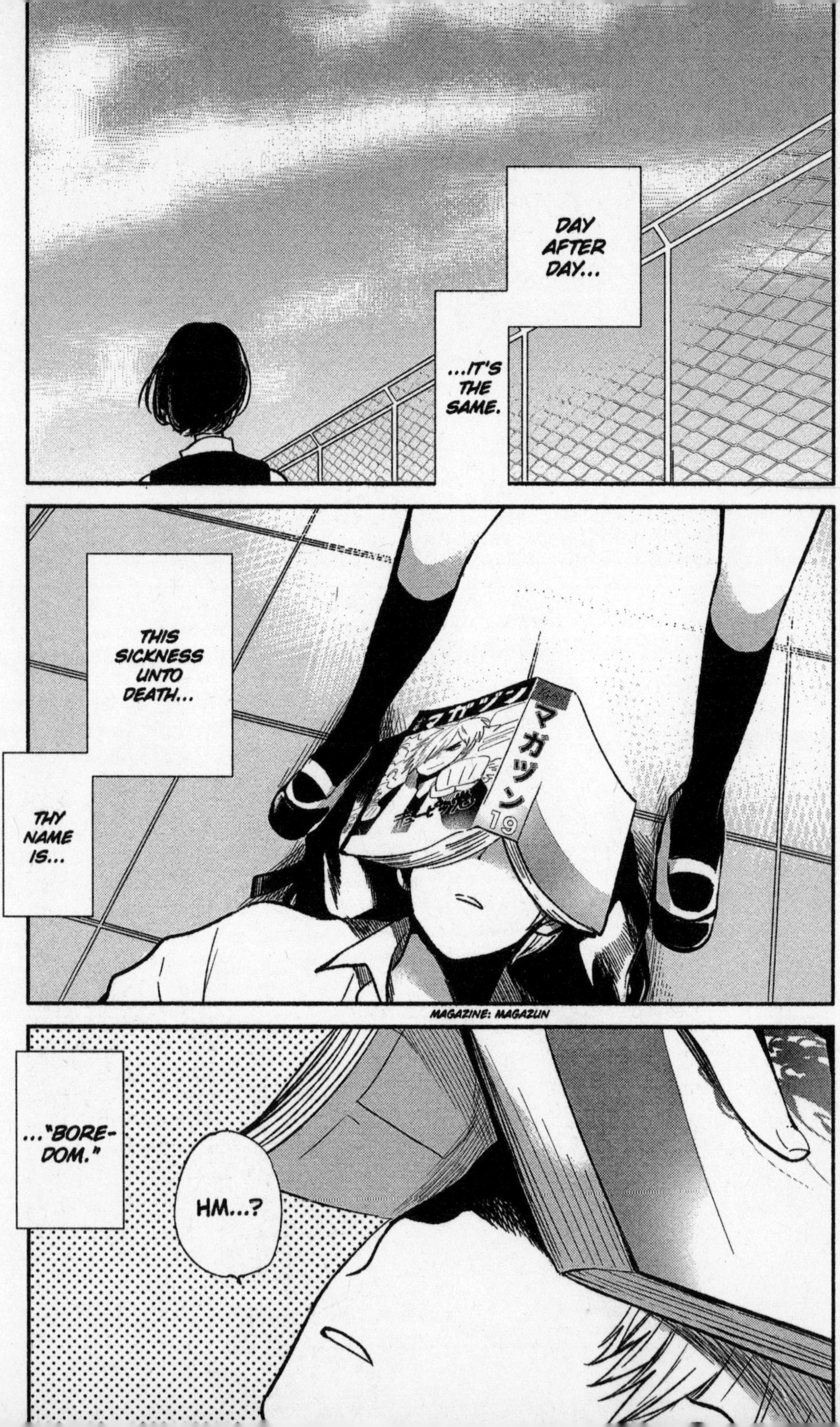
DAY AFTER DAY...
...IT'S THE SAME.
THIS SICKNESS UNTO DEATH...
THY NAME IS...
マガヅン
19
MAGAZINE: MAGAZUN
..."BORE-DOM."
HM...?

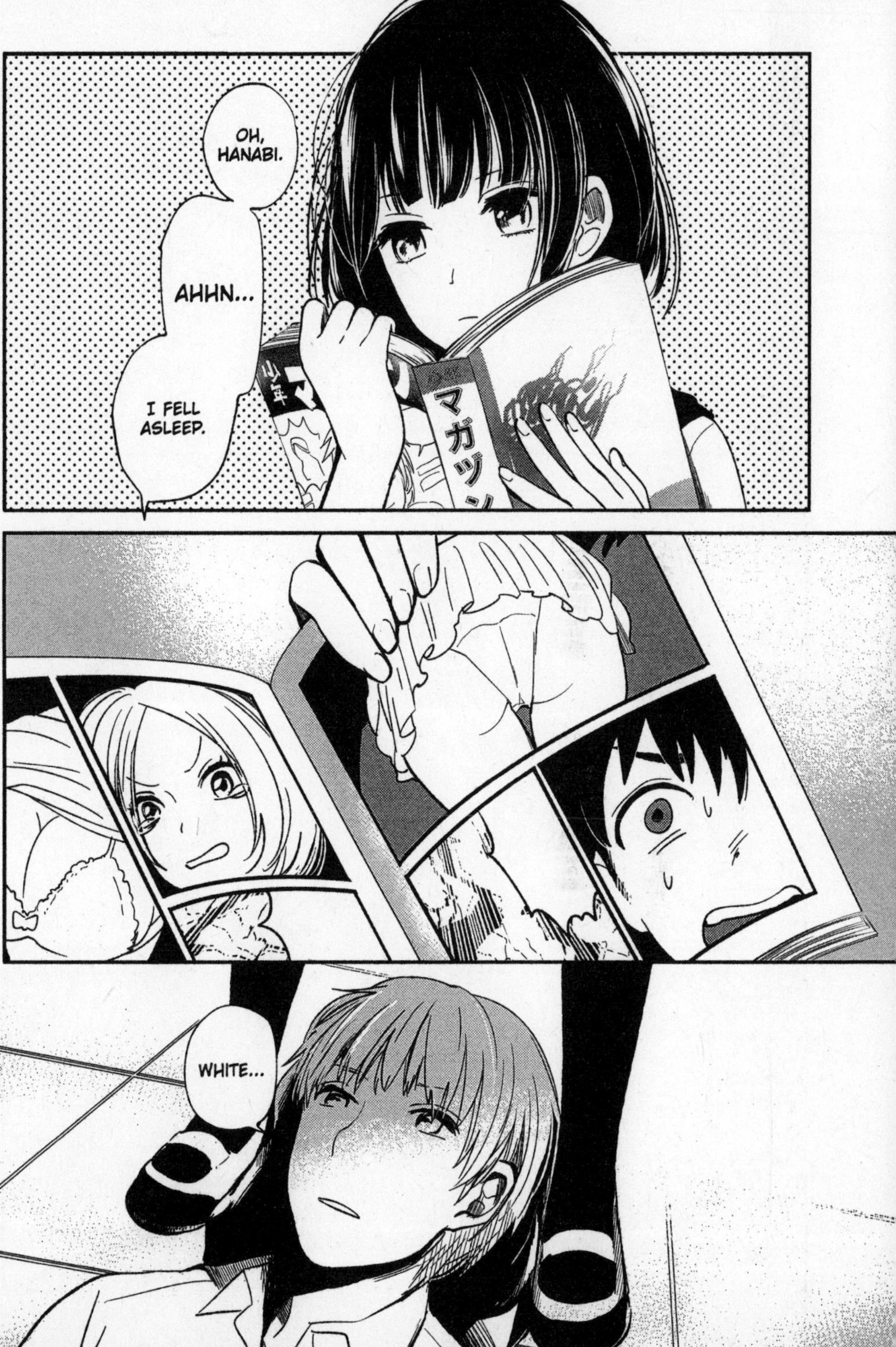
OH, HANABI.
AHHN...
I FELL ASLEEP.
WHITE...

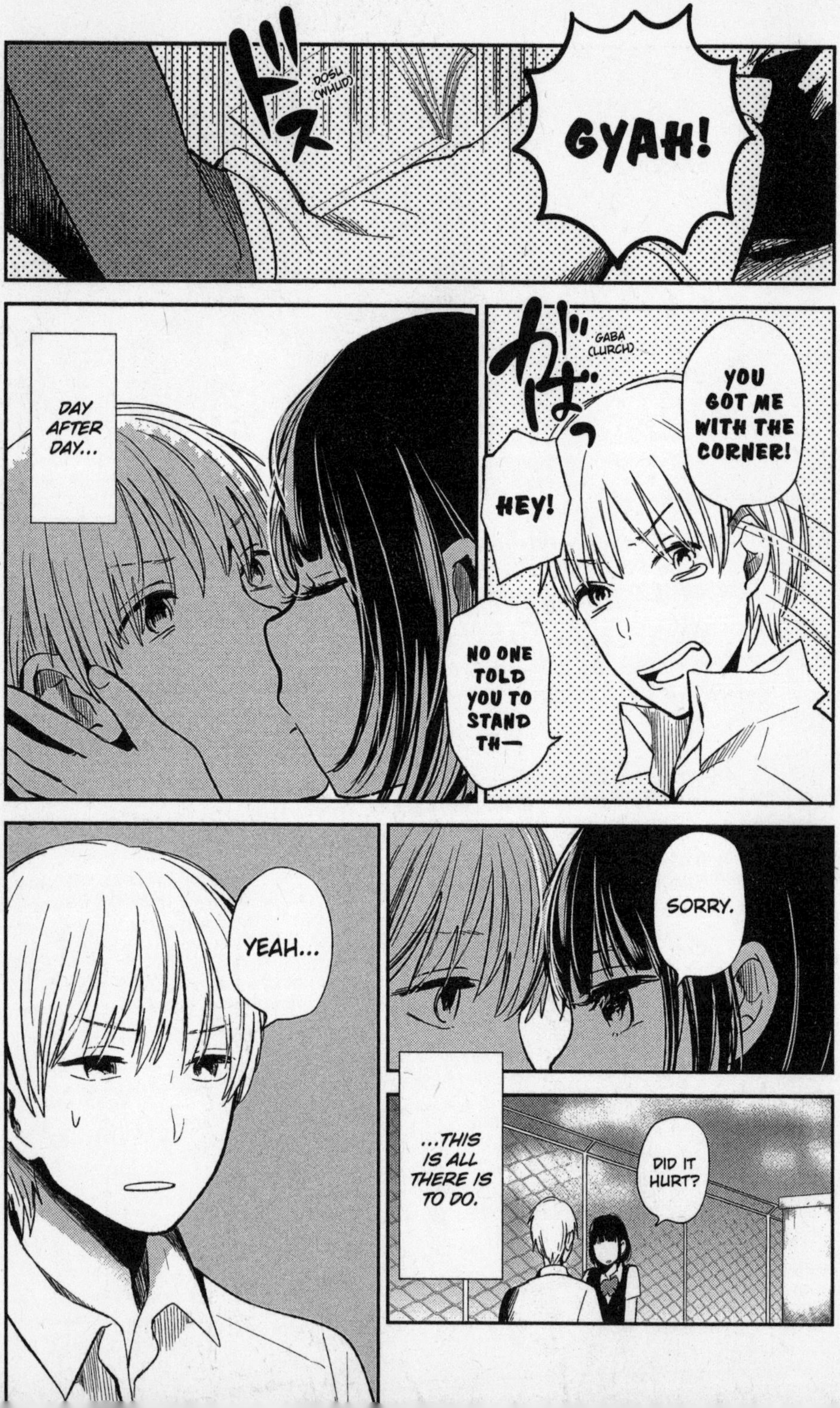
GYAH!
ドス
DOSU (WHUD)
がばっ
GABA (LURCH)
YOU GOT ME WITH THE CORNER!
HEY!
NO ONE TOLD YOU TO STAND TH—
DAY AFTER DAY...
SORRY.
DID IT HURT?
...THIS IS ALL THERE IS TO DO.
YEAH...

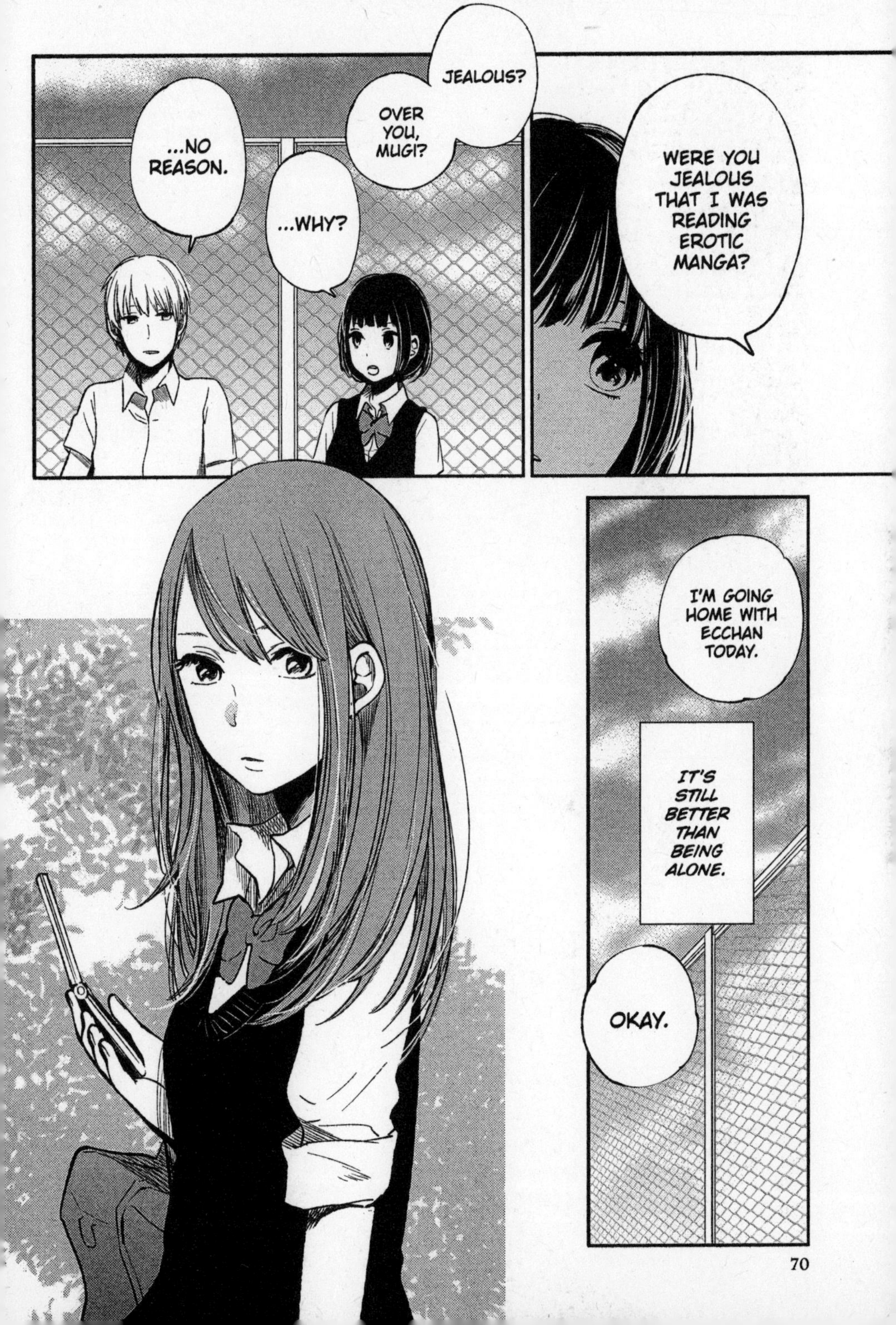
WERE YOU JEALOUS THAT I WAS READING EROTIC MANGA?
JEALOUS?
OVER YOU, MUGI?
...WHY?
...NO REASON.
I'M GOING HOME WITH ECCHAN TODAY.
IT'S STILL BETTER THAN BEING ALONE.
OKAY.

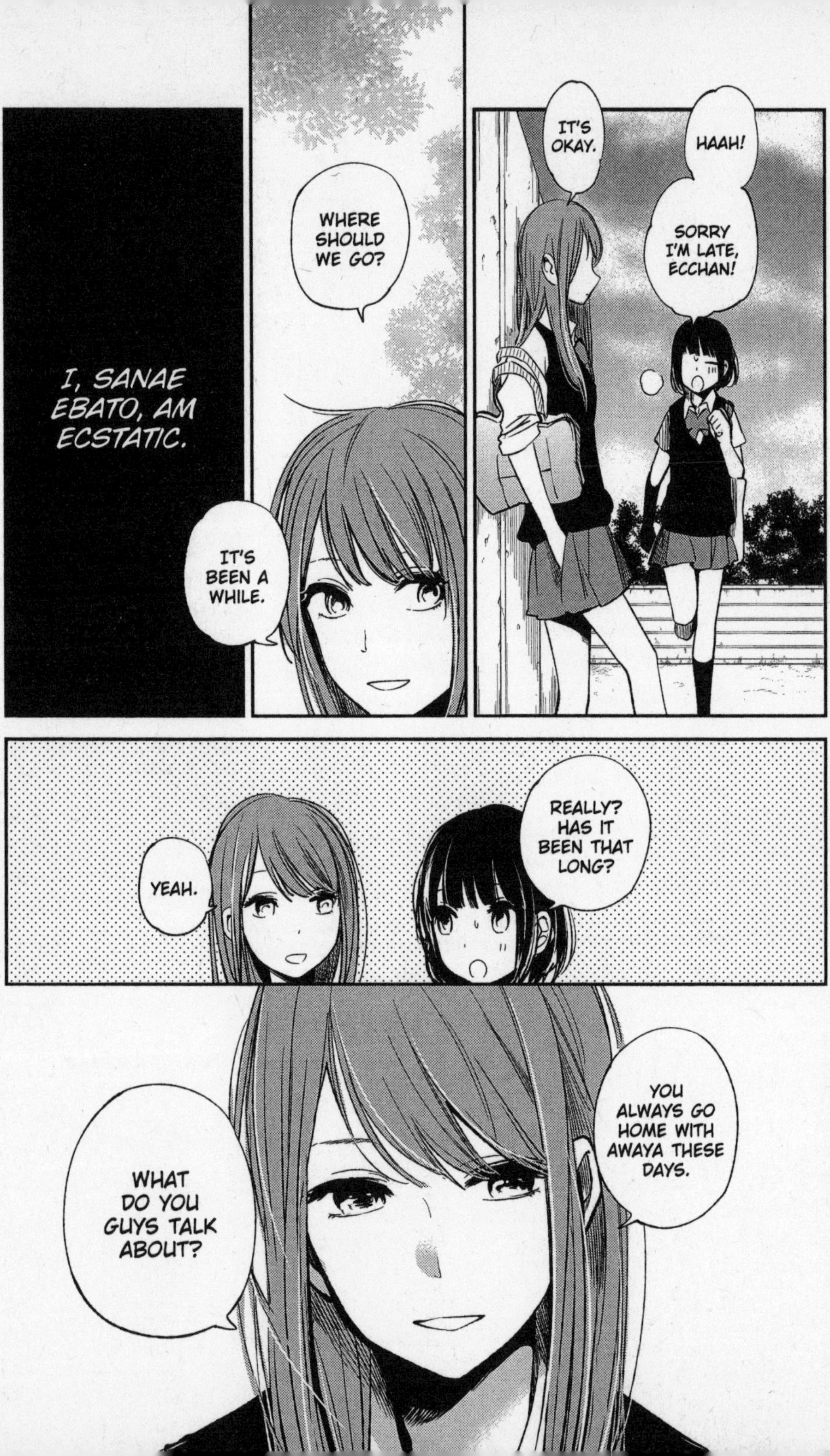
HAAH!
SORRY I'M LATE, ECCHAN!
IT'S OKAY.
WHERE SHOULD WE GO?
IT'S BEEN A WHILE.
I, SANAE EBATO, AM ECSTATIC.
REALLY? HAS IT BEEN THAT LONG?
YEAH.
YOU ALWAYS GO HOME WITH AWAYA THESE DAYS.
WHAT DO YOU GUYS TALK ABOUT?

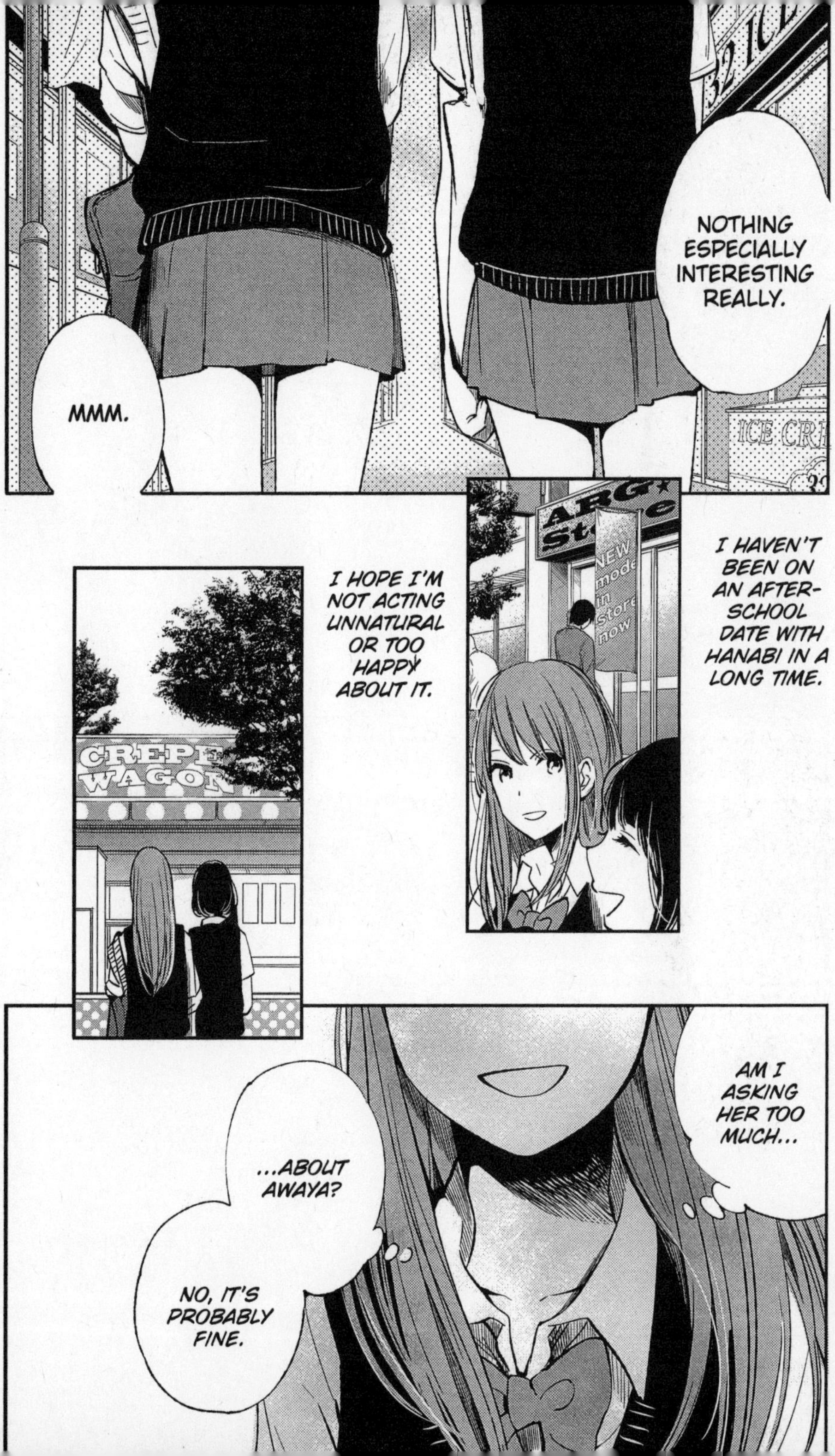
NOTHING ESPECIALLY INTERESTING REALLY.
MMM.
I HAVEN'T BEEN ON AN AFTER-SCHOOL DATE WITH HANABI IN A LONG TIME.
I HOPE I'M NOT ACTING UNNATURAL OR TOO HAPPY ABOUT IT.
CREPE WAGON
AM I ASKING HER TOO MUCH...
...ABOUT AWAYA?
NO, IT'S PROBABLY FINE.

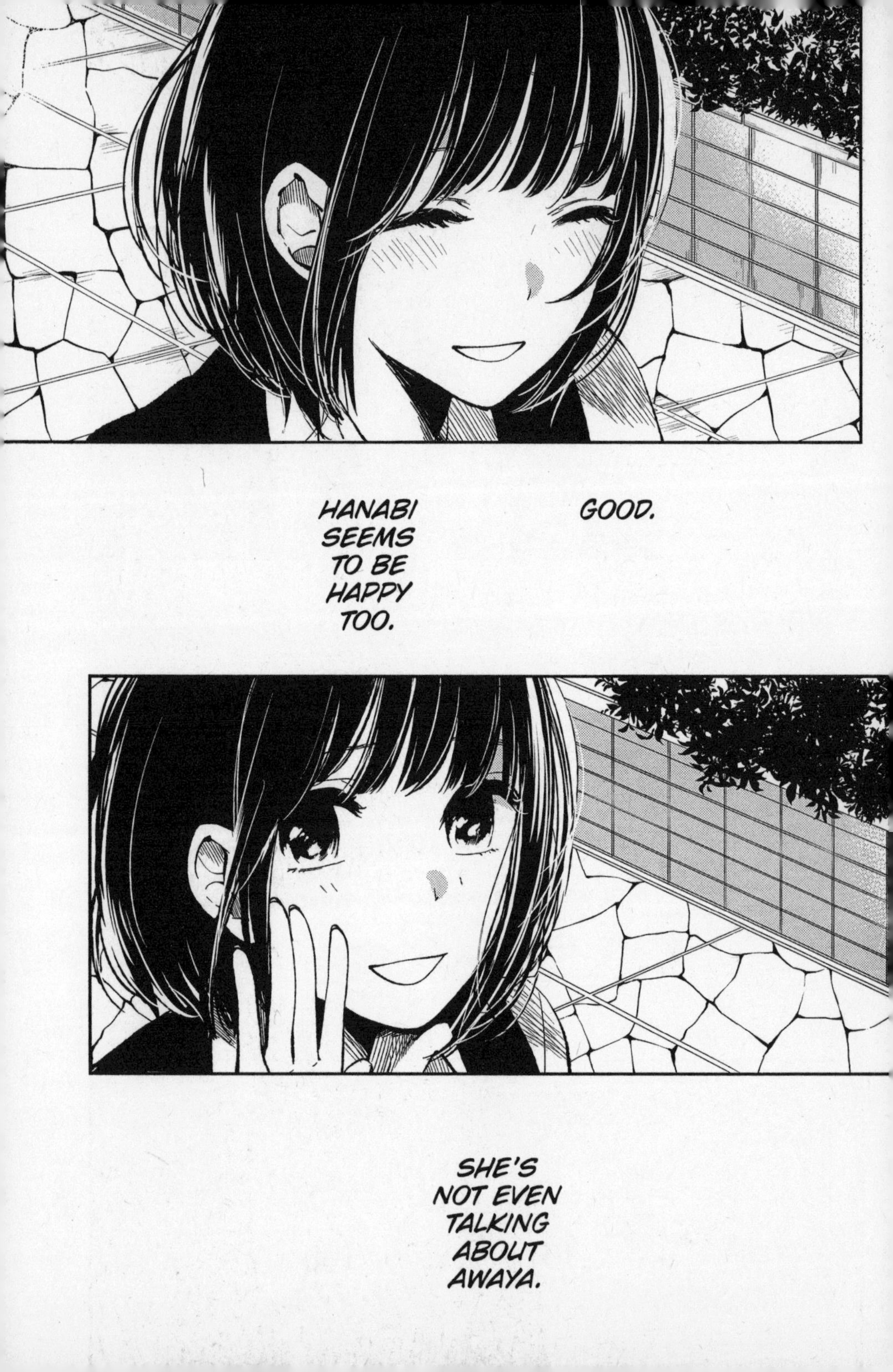
GOOD.
HANABI SEEMS TO BE HAPPY TOO.
SHE'S NOT EVEN TALKING ABOUT AWAYA.

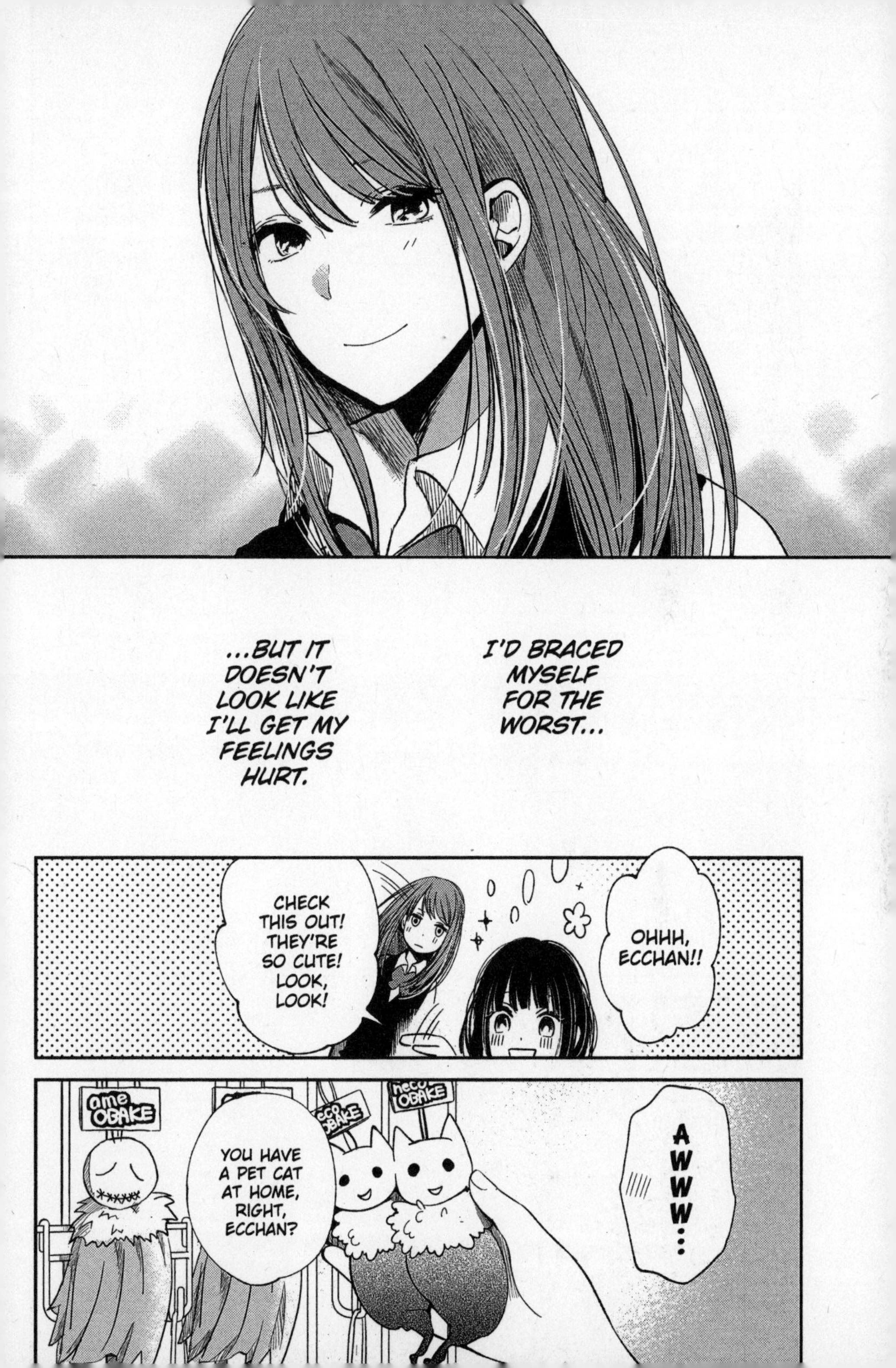
I'D BRACED MYSELF FOR THE WORST...
...BUT IT DOESN'T LOOK LIKE I'LL GET MY FEELINGS HURT.
OHHH, ECCHAN!!
CHECK THIS OUT! THEY'RE SO CUTE! LOOK, LOOK!
AWWW...
neco OBAKE
neco OBAKE
YOU HAVE A PET CAT AT HOME, RIGHT, ECCHAN?
ame OBAKE

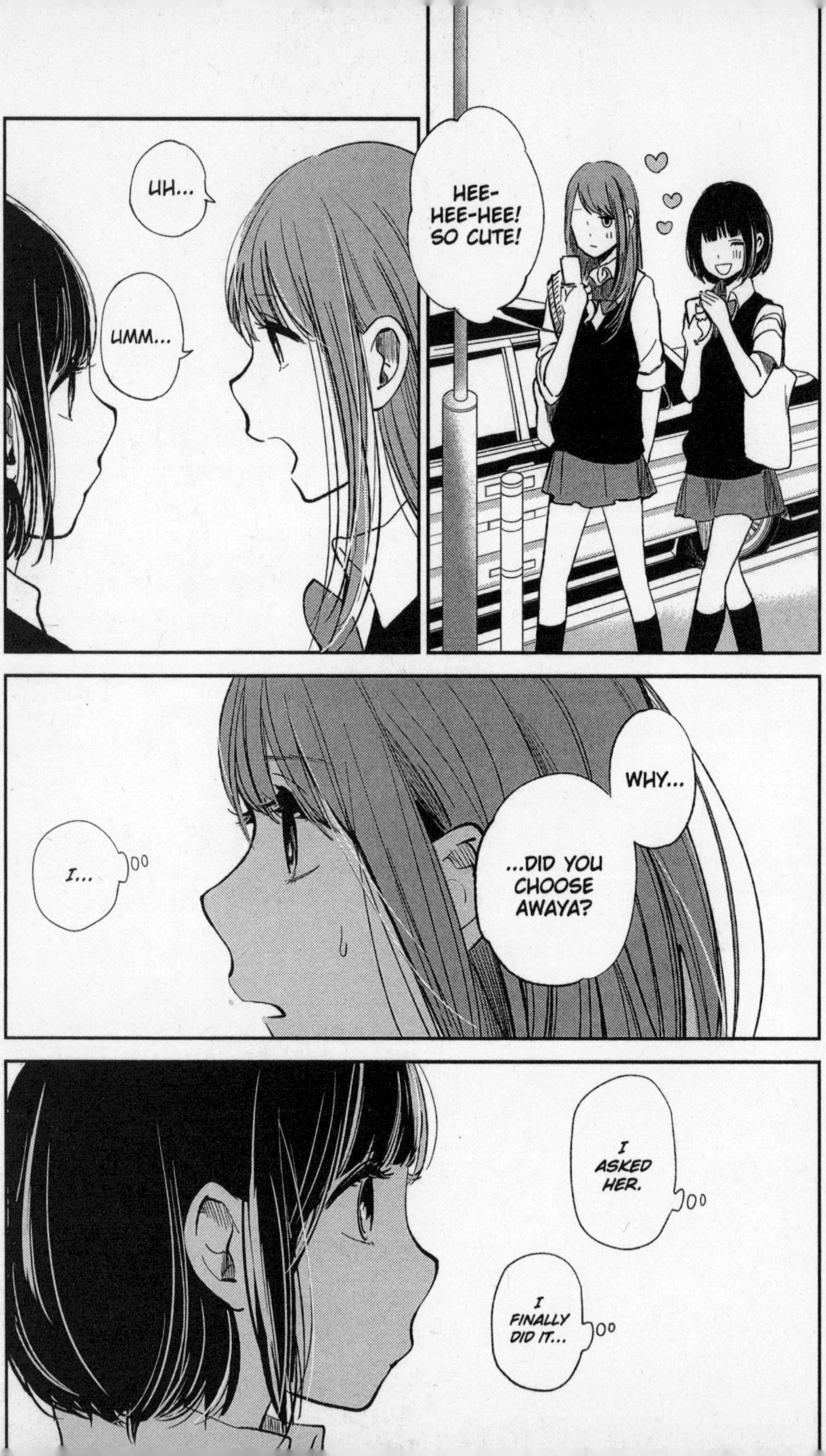
HEE-HEE-HEE! SO CUTE!
UH...
UMM...
WHY...
...DID YOU CHOOSE AWAYA?
I...
I ASKED HER.
I FINALLY DID IT...

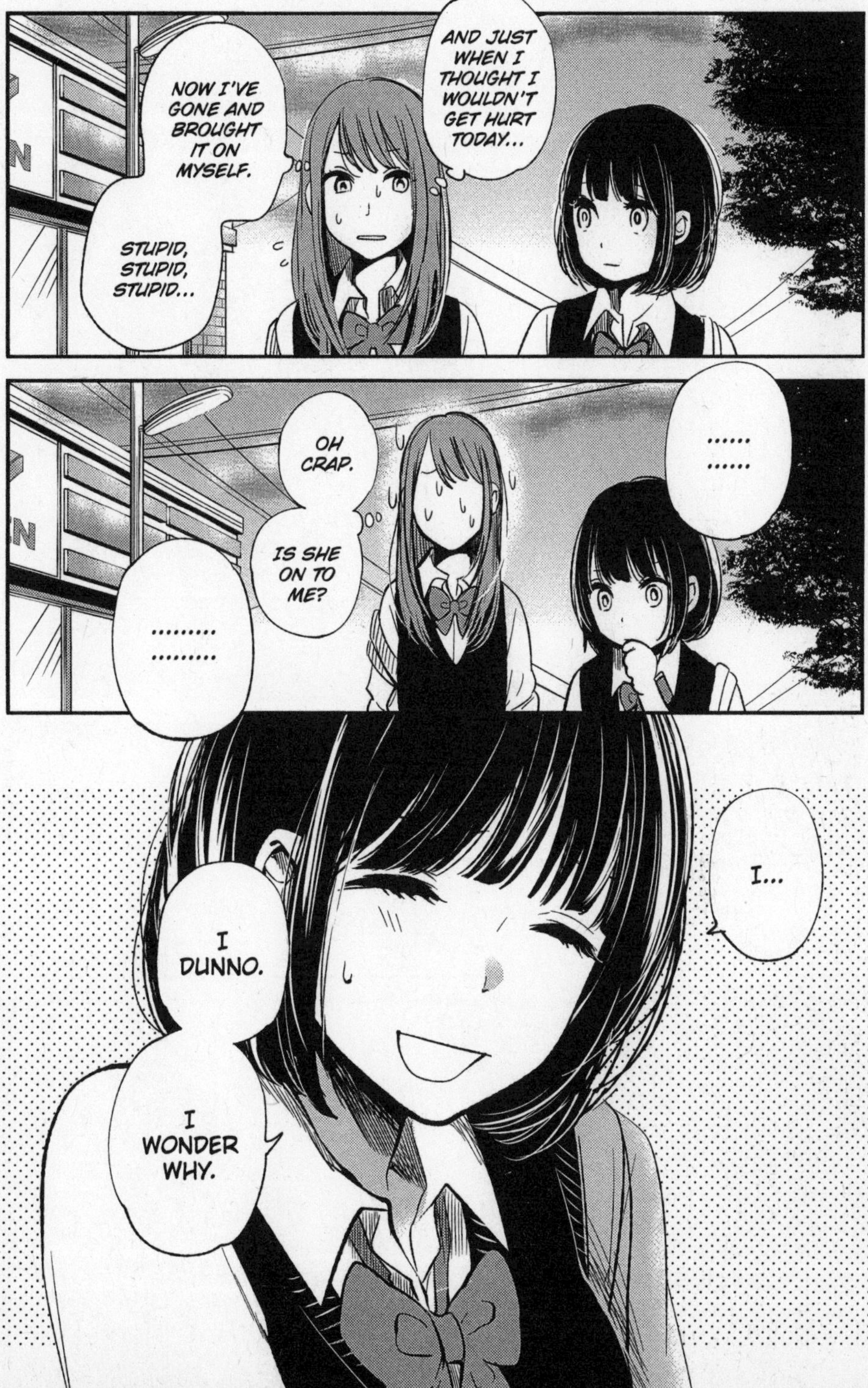
AND JUST WHEN I THOUGHT I WOULDN'T GET HURT TODAY...
NOW I'VE GONE AND BROUGHT IT ON MYSELF.
STUPID, STUPID, STUPID...
....
OH CRAP.
IS SHE ON TO ME?
....
I...
I DUNNO.
I WONDER WHY.

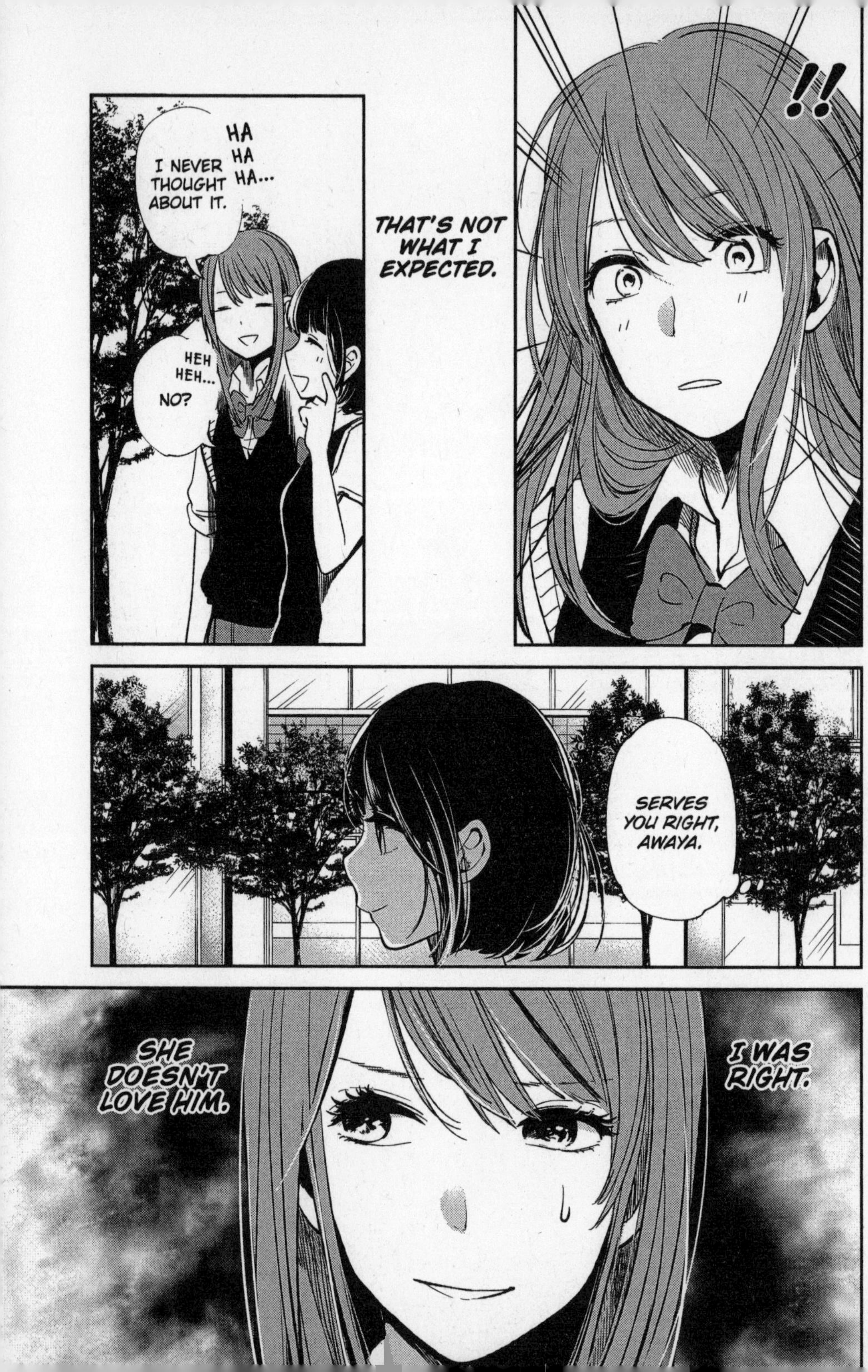
!!
THAT'S NOT WHAT I EXPECTED.
HA HA HA...
I NEVER THOUGHT ABOUT IT.
HEH HEH... NO?
SERVES YOU RIGHT, AWAYA.
I WAS RIGHT.
SHE DOESN'T LOVE HIM.

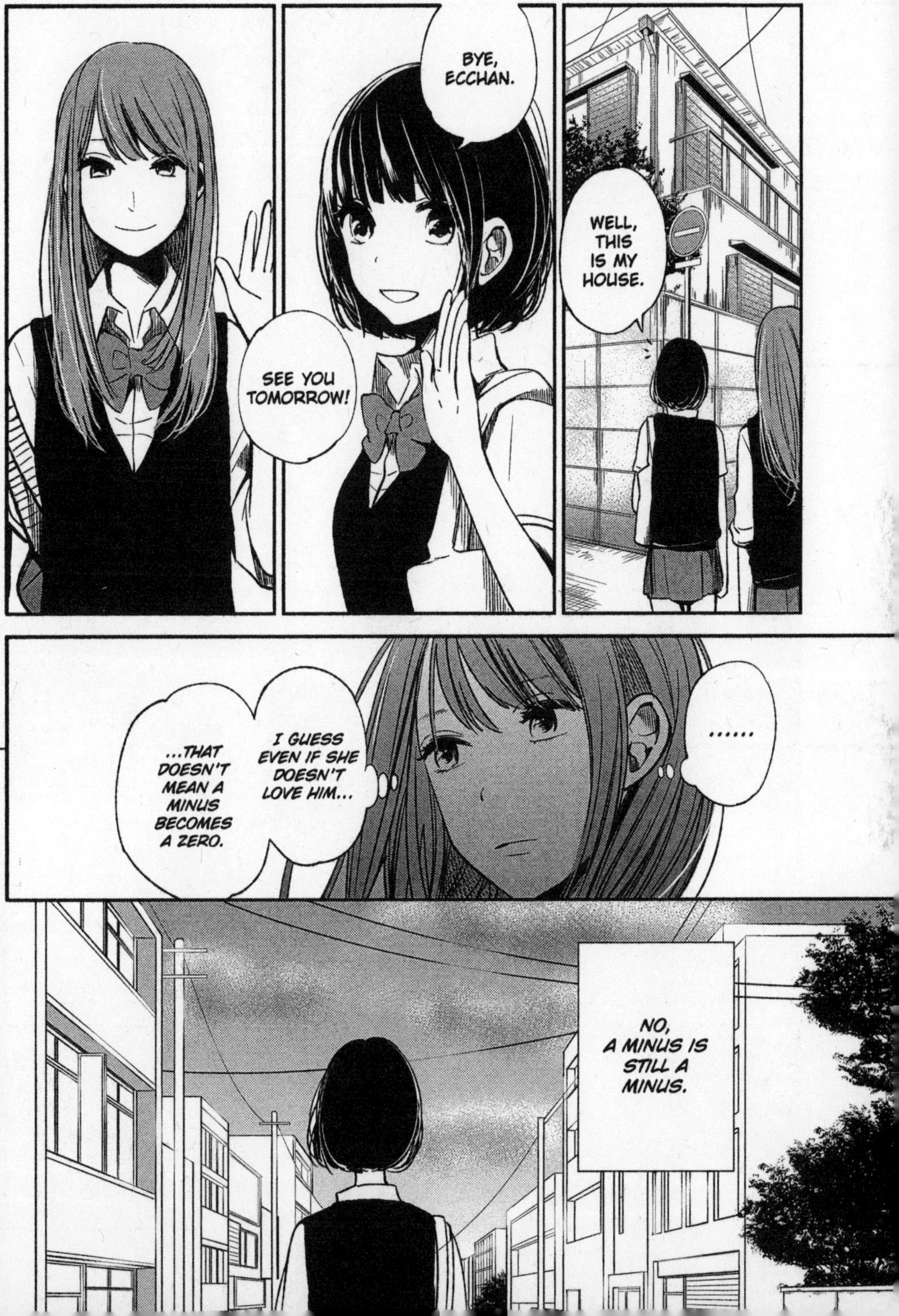
WELL, THIS IS MY HOUSE.
BYE, ECCHAN.
SEE YOU TOMORROW!
......
I GUESS EVEN IF SHE DOESN'T LOVE HIM...
...THAT DOESN'T MEAN A MINUS BECOMES A ZERO.
NO, A MINUS IS STILL A MINUS.

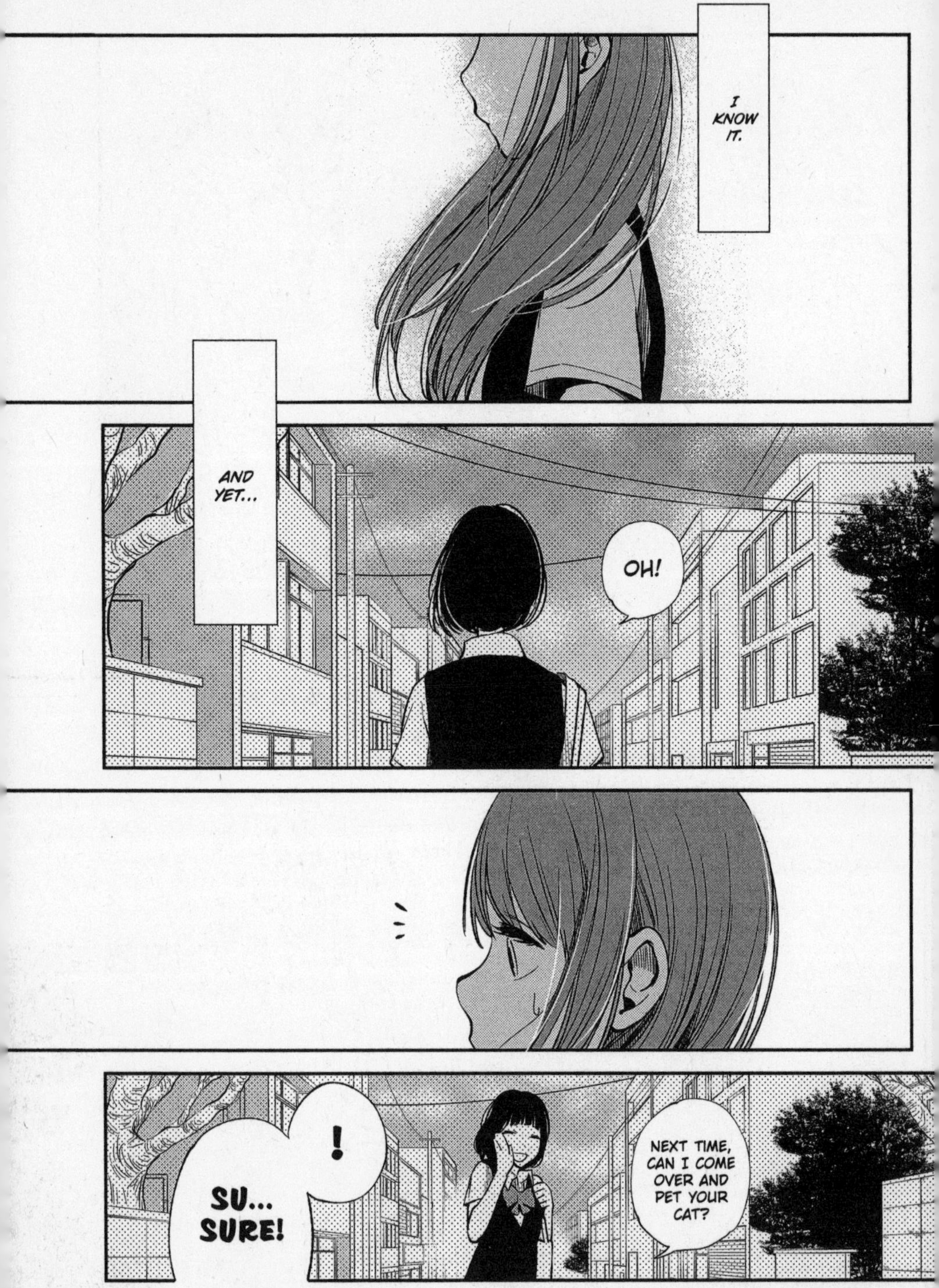
I KNOW IT.
AND YET...
OH!
NEXT TIME, CAN I COME OVER AND PET YOUR CAT?
!
SU... SURE!

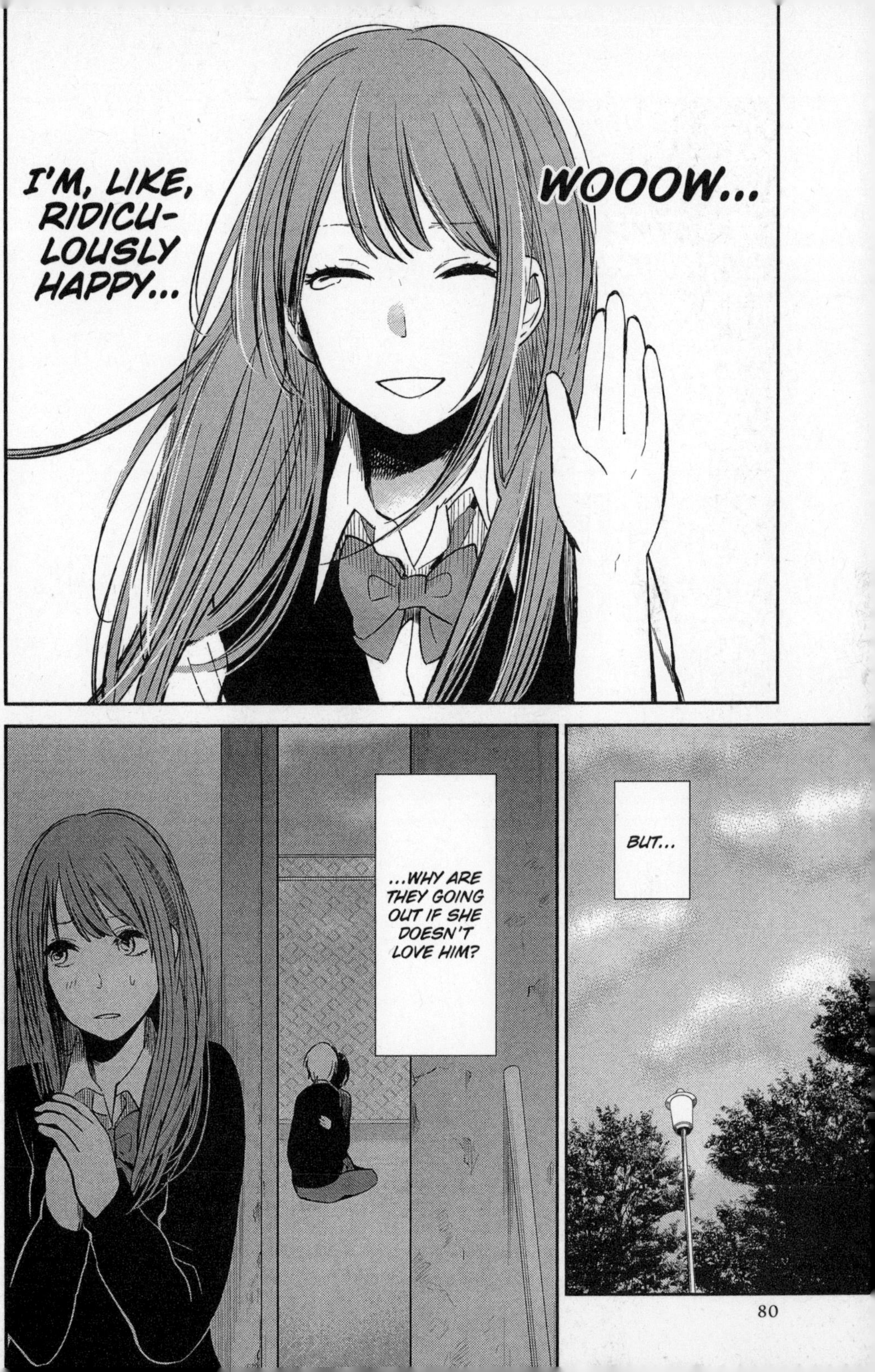
WOOOW...
I'M, LIKE, RIDICU-LOUSLY HAPPY...
BUT...
...WHY ARE THEY GOING OUT IF SHE DOESN'T LOVE HIM?

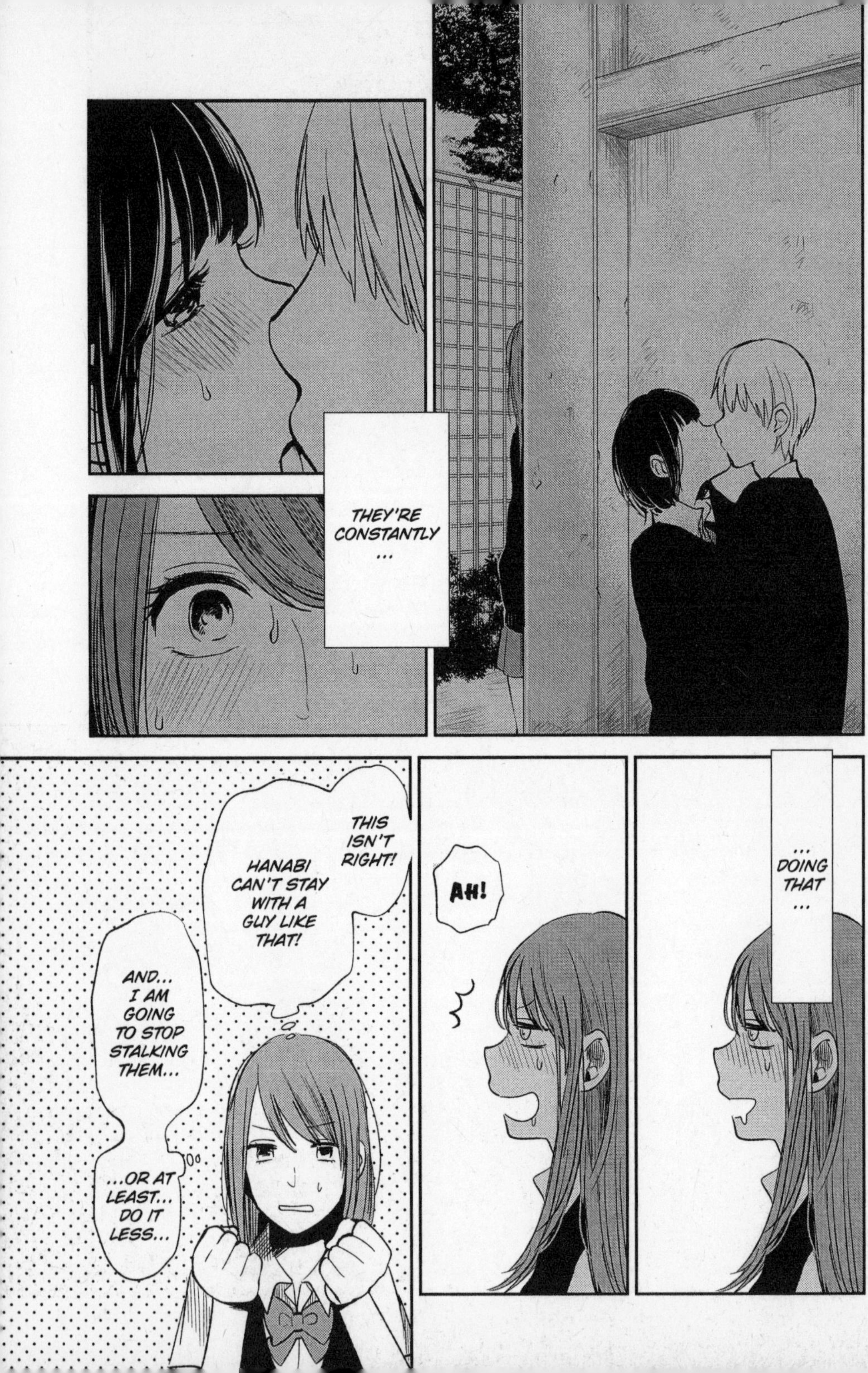
THEY'RE CONSTANTLY ...
... DOING THAT ...
AH!
THIS ISN'T RIGHT!
HANABI CAN'T STAY WITH A GUY LIKE THAT!
AND... I AM GOING TO STOP STALKING THEM...
...OR AT LEAST... DO IT LESS...

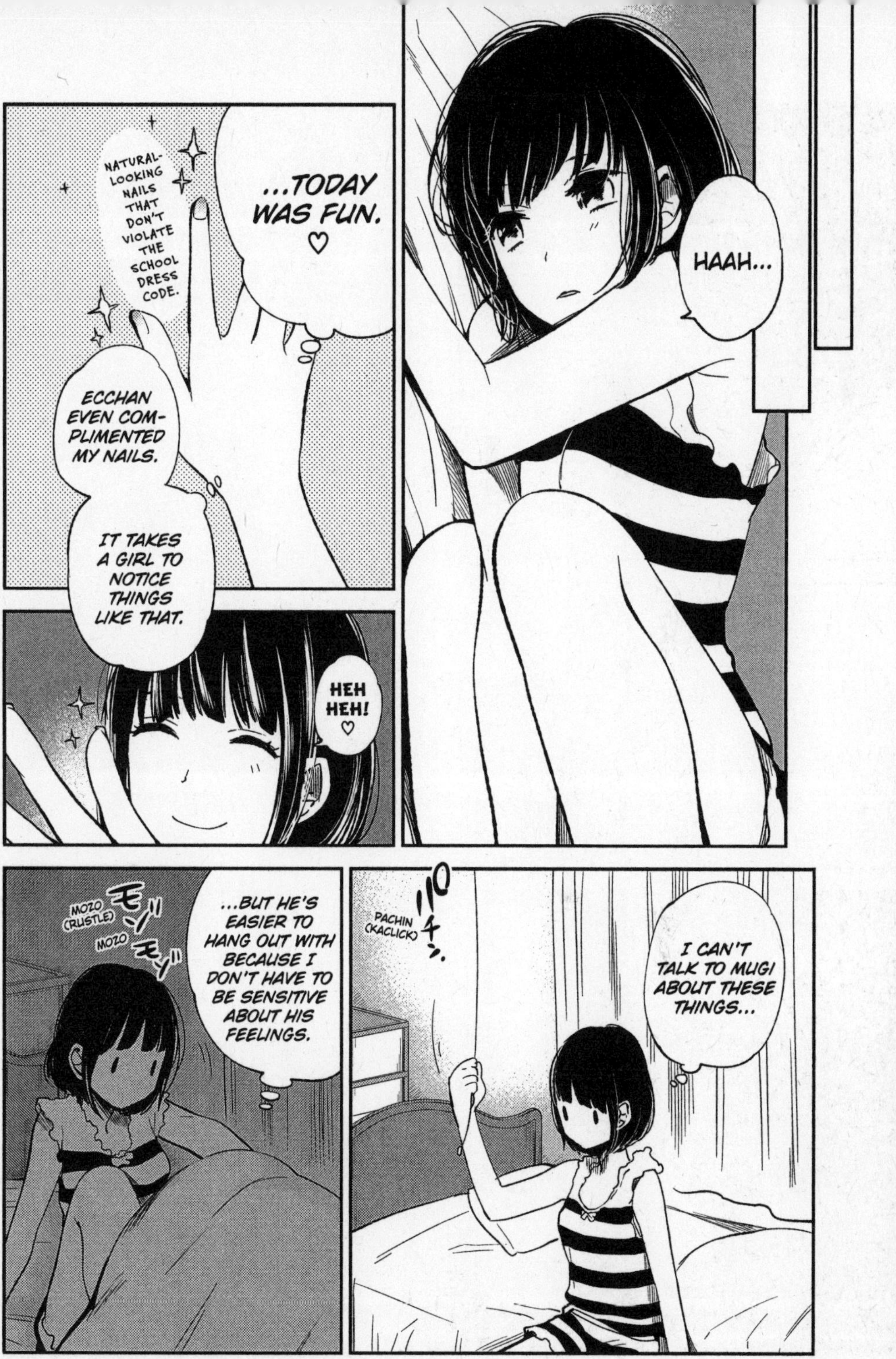
HAAH...
...TODAY WAS FUN. ♡
NATURAL-LOOKING NAILS THAT DON'T VIOLATE THE SCHOOL DRESS CODE.
ECCHAN EVEN COMPLIMENTED MY NAILS.
IT TAKES A GIRL TO NOTICE THINGS LIKE THAT.
HEH HEH! ♡
PACHIN (KACLICK)
I CAN'T TALK TO MUGI ABOUT THESE THINGS...
...BUT HE'S EASIER TO HANG OUT WITH BECAUSE I DON'T HAVE TO BE SENSITIVE ABOUT HIS FEELINGS.
MOZO (RUSTLE)
MOZO

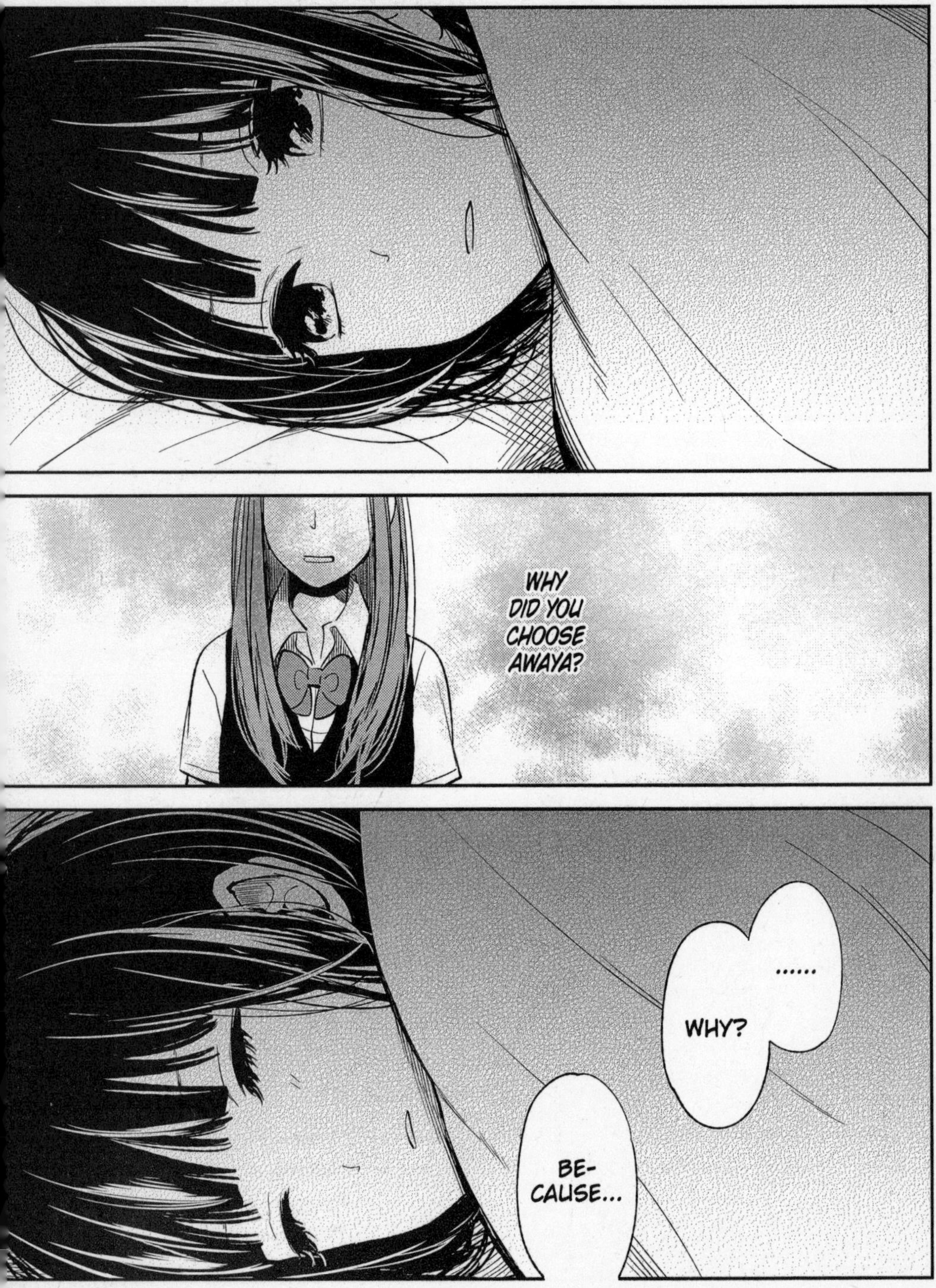
WHY DID YOU CHOOSE AWAYA?
...... WHY?
BE-CAUSE...

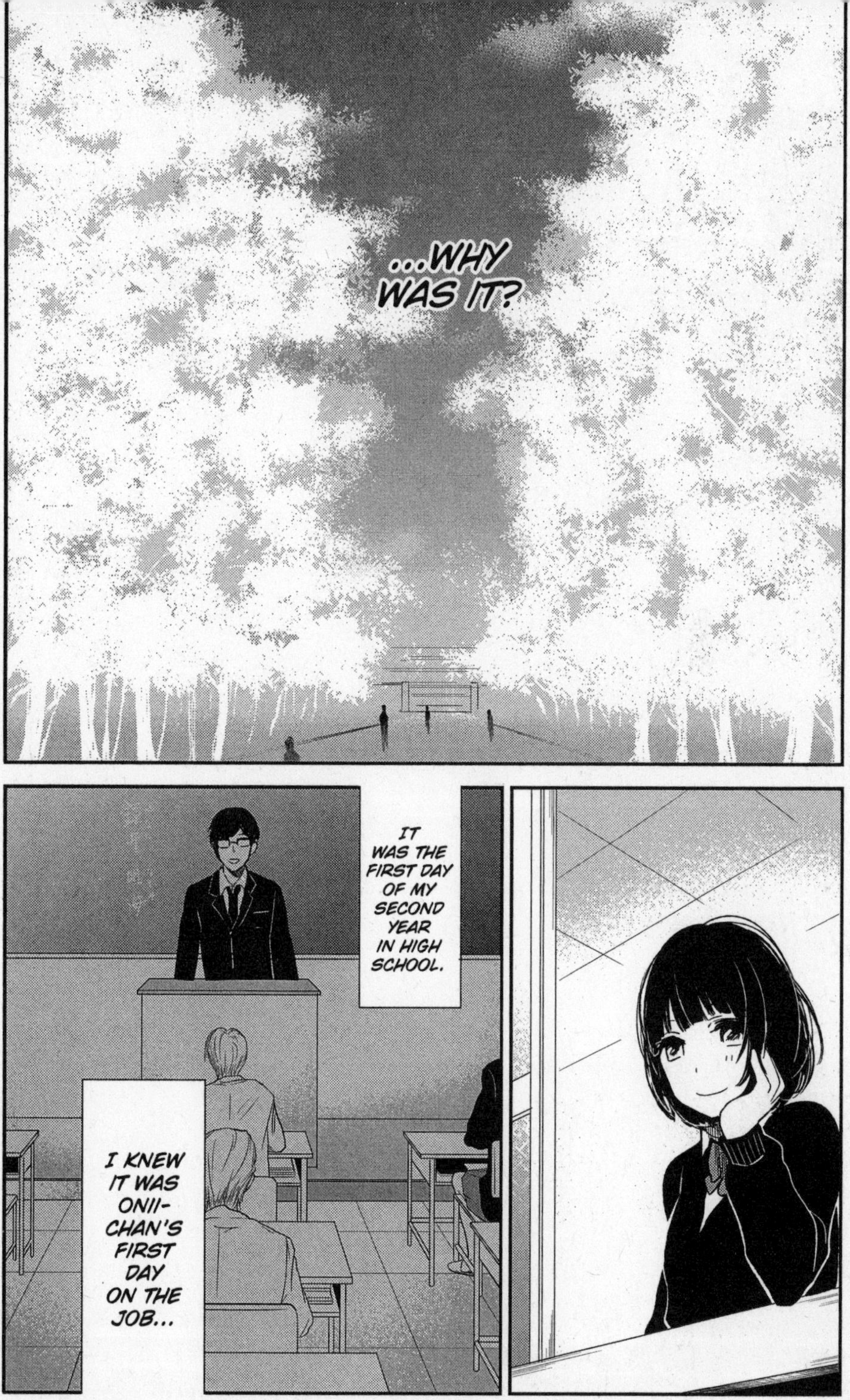
...WHY WAS IT?
IT WAS THE FIRST DAY OF MY SECOND YEAR IN HIGH SCHOOL.
I KNEW IT WAS ONII-CHAN'S FIRST DAY ON THE JOB...

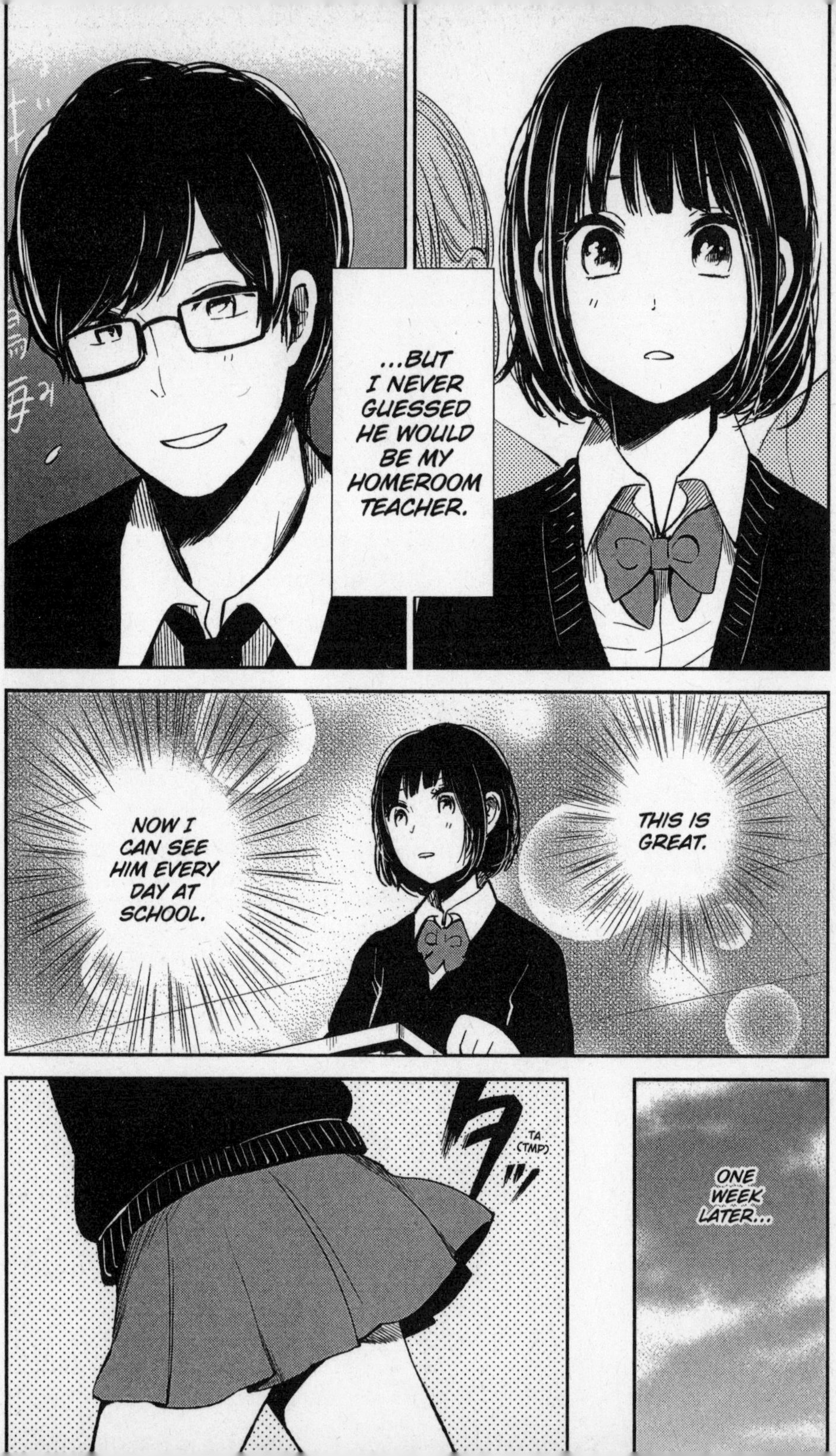
...BUT I NEVER GUESSED HE WOULD BE MY HOMEROOM TEACHER.
THIS IS GREAT.
NOW I CAN SEE HIM EVERY DAY AT SCHOOL.
ONE WEEK LATER...
TA (TMP)

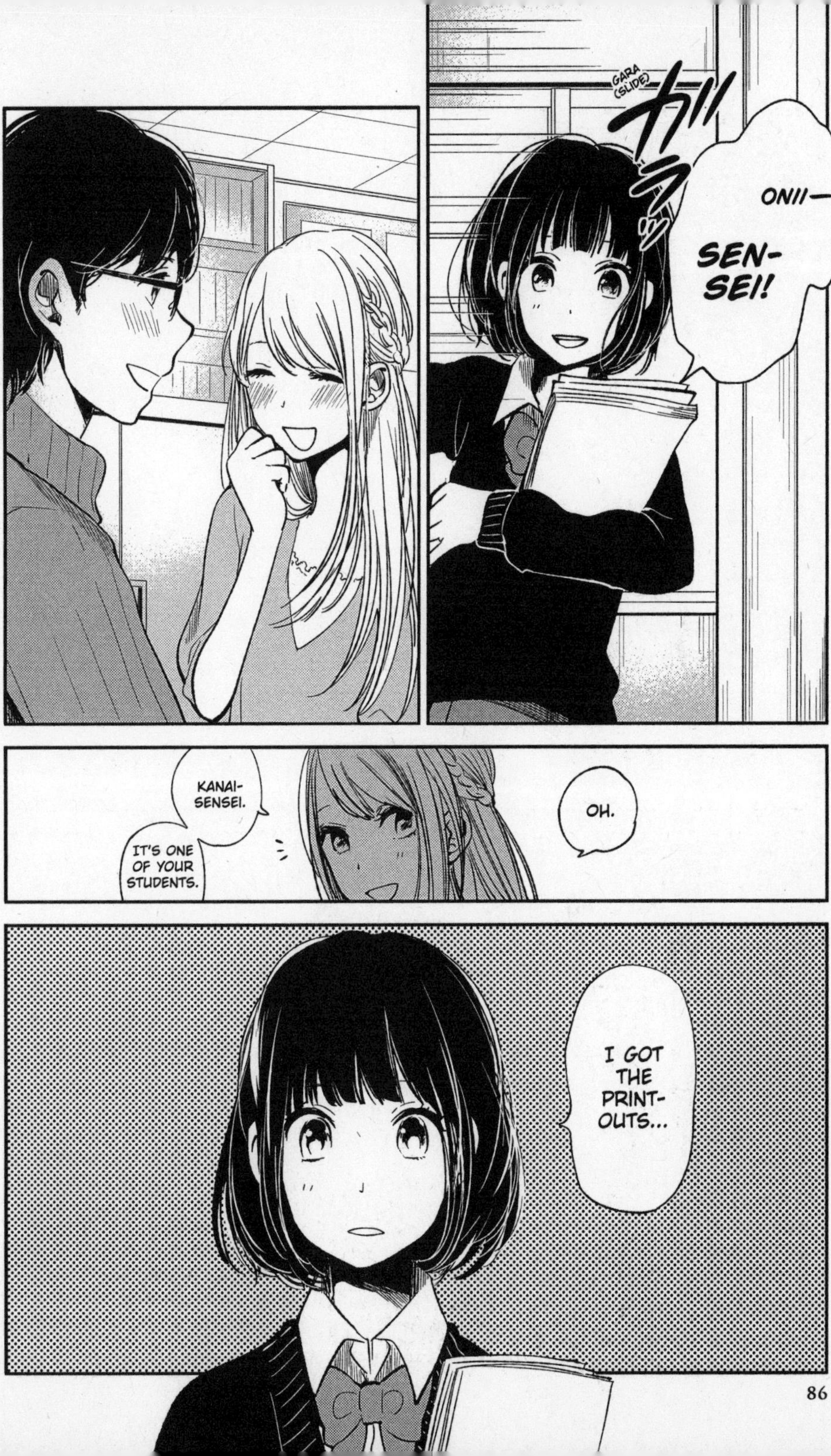
GARA (SLIDE)
ONII— SEN-SEI!
OH.
KANAI-SENSEI.
IT'S ONE OF YOUR STUDENTS.
I GOT THE PRINT-OUTS...

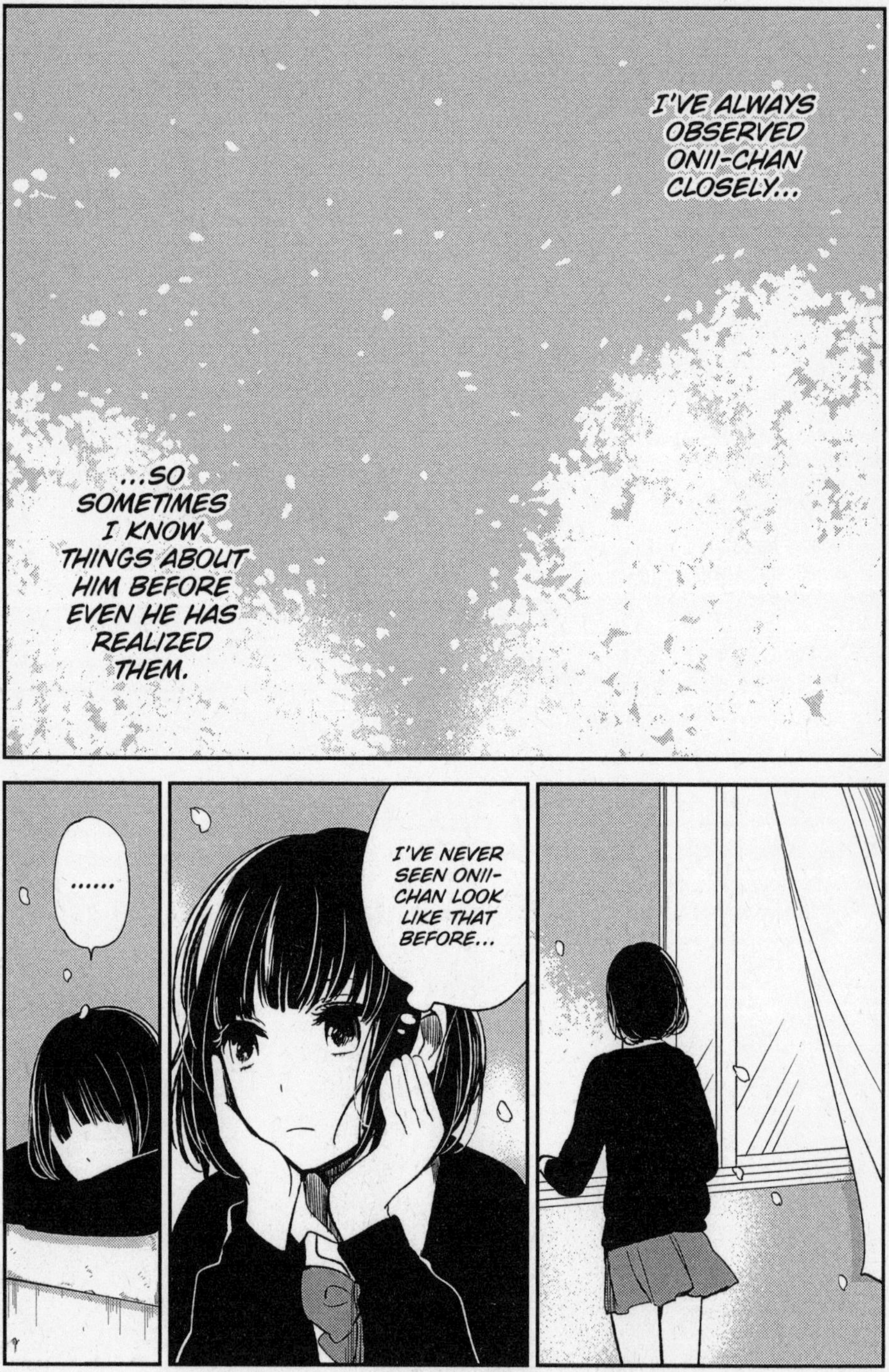
I'VE ALWAYS OBSERVED ONII-CHAN CLOSELY...
...SO SOMETIMES I KNOW THINGS ABOUT HIM BEFORE EVEN HE HAS REALIZED THEM.
I'VE NEVER SEEN ONII-CHAN LOOK LIKE THAT BEFORE...
......

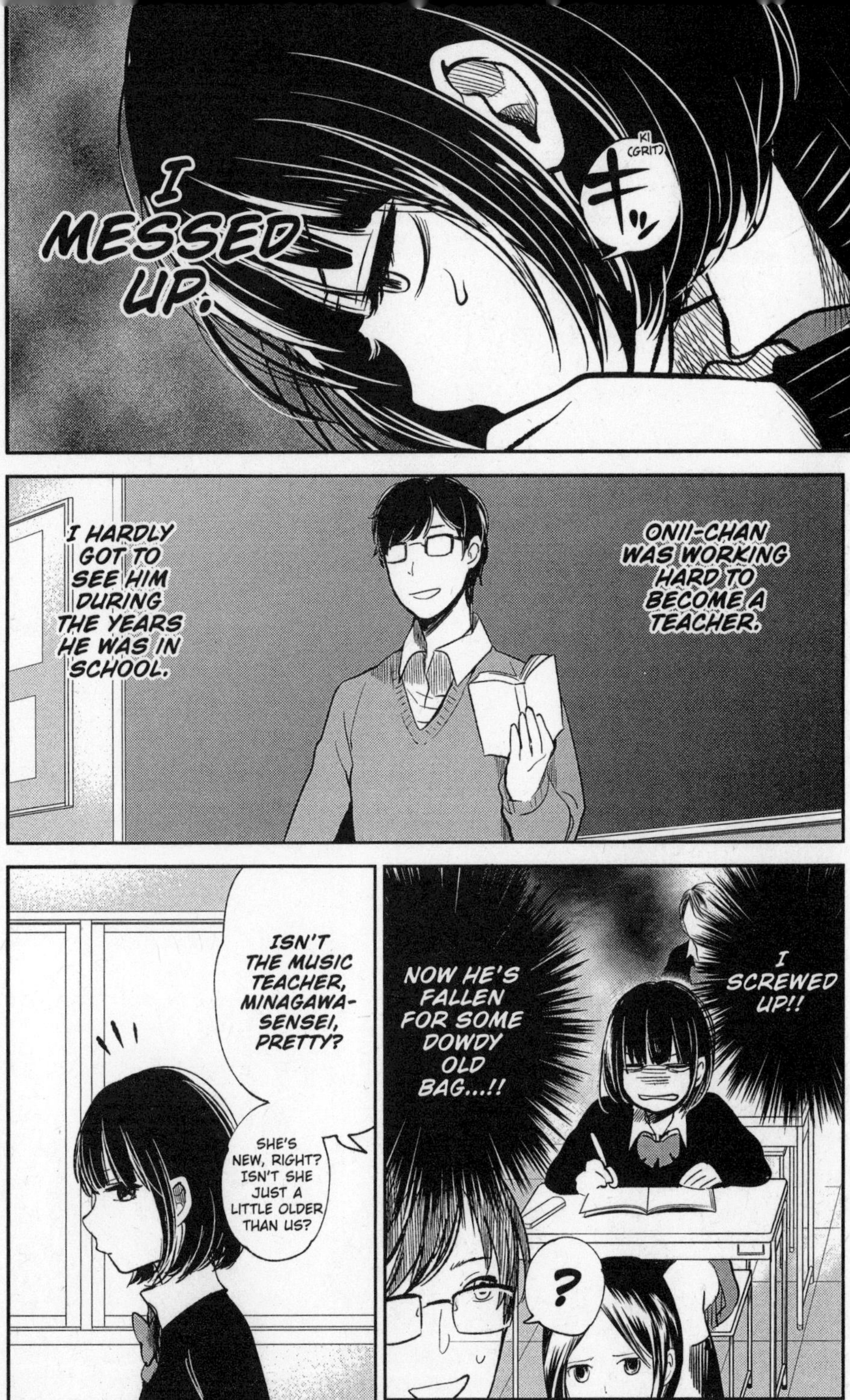
KI (GRIT)
I MESSED UP.
ONII-CHAN WAS WORKING HARD TO BECOME A TEACHER.
I HARDLY GOT TO SEE HIM DURING THE YEARS HE WAS IN SCHOOL.
I SCREWED UP!!
NOW HE'S FALLEN FOR SOME DOWDY OLD BAG...!!
?
ISN'T THE MUSIC TEACHER, MINAGAWA-SENSEI, PRETTY?
SHE'S NEW, RIGHT? ISN'T SHE JUST A LITTLE OLDER THAN US?

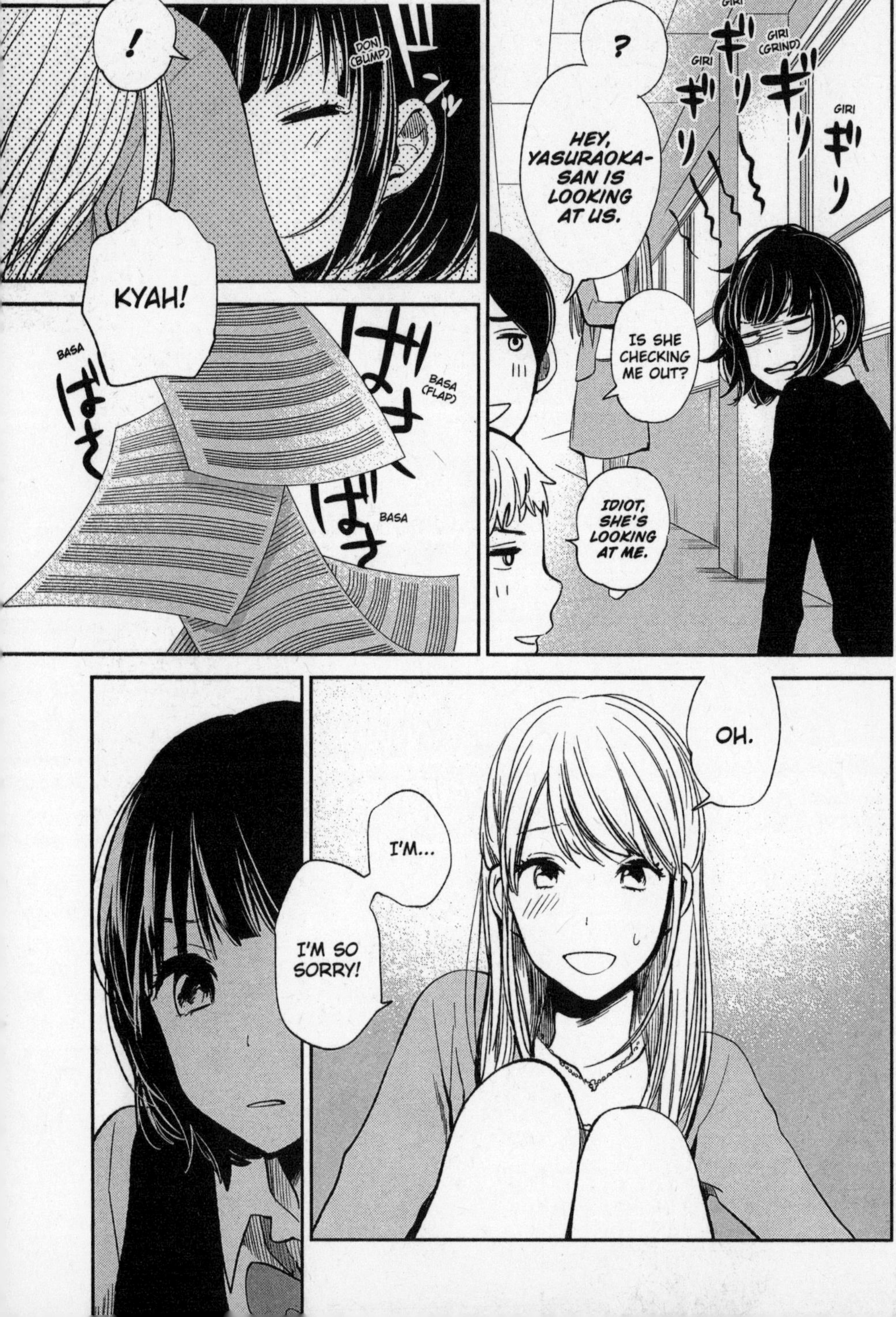
GIRI
GIRI (GRIND)
GIRI
GIRI
?
HEY, YASURAOKA-SAN IS LOOKING AT US.
IS SHE CHECKING ME OUT?
IDIOT, SHE'S LOOKING AT ME.
!
DON (BUMP)
KYAH!
BASA (FLAP)
BASA
BASA
OH.
I'M...
I'M SO SORRY!

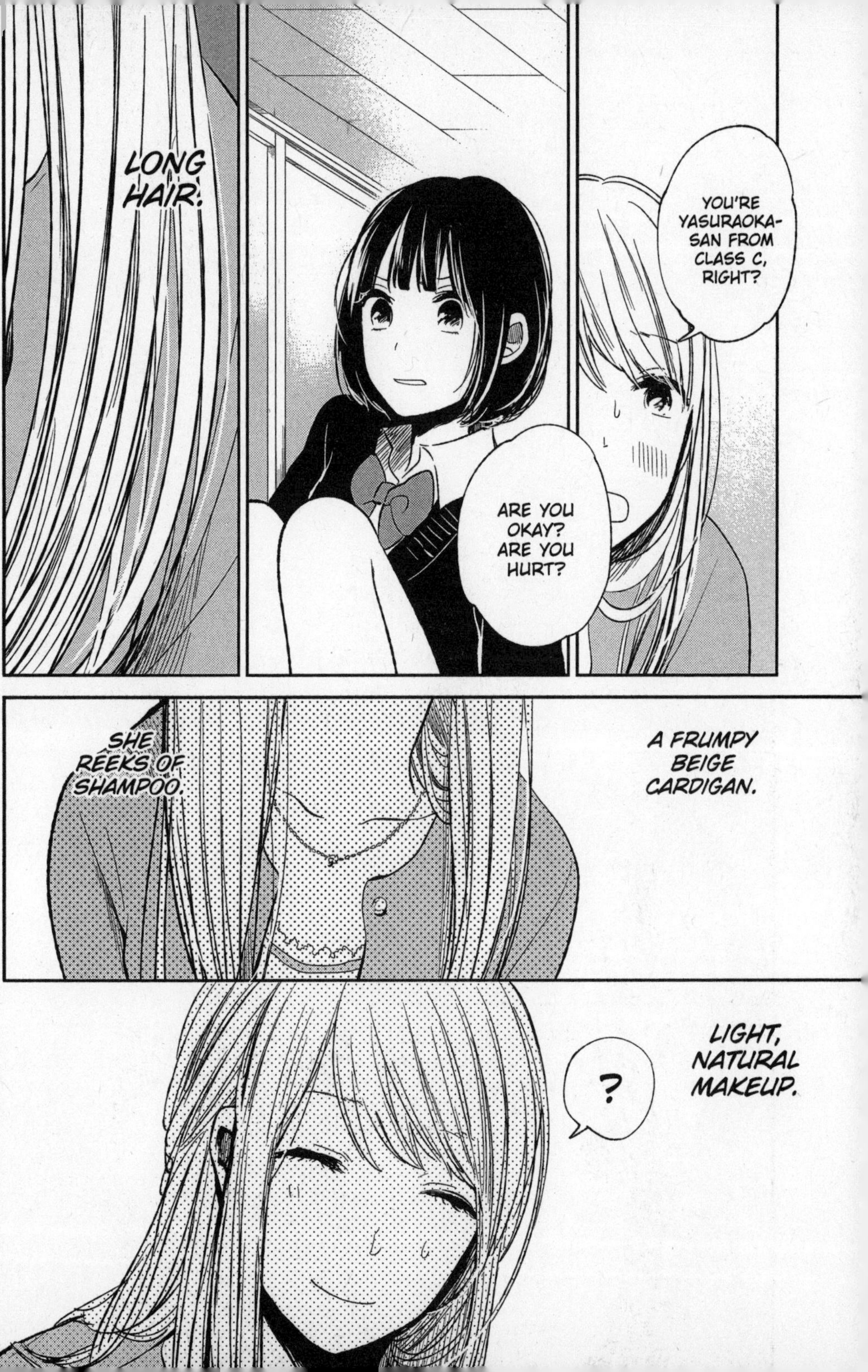
YOU'RE YASURAOKA-SAN FROM CLASS C, RIGHT?
ARE YOU OKAY? ARE YOU HURT?
LONG HAIR.
A FRUMPY BEIGE CARDIGAN.
SHE REEKS OF SHAMPOO.
LIGHT, NATURAL MAKEUP.
?

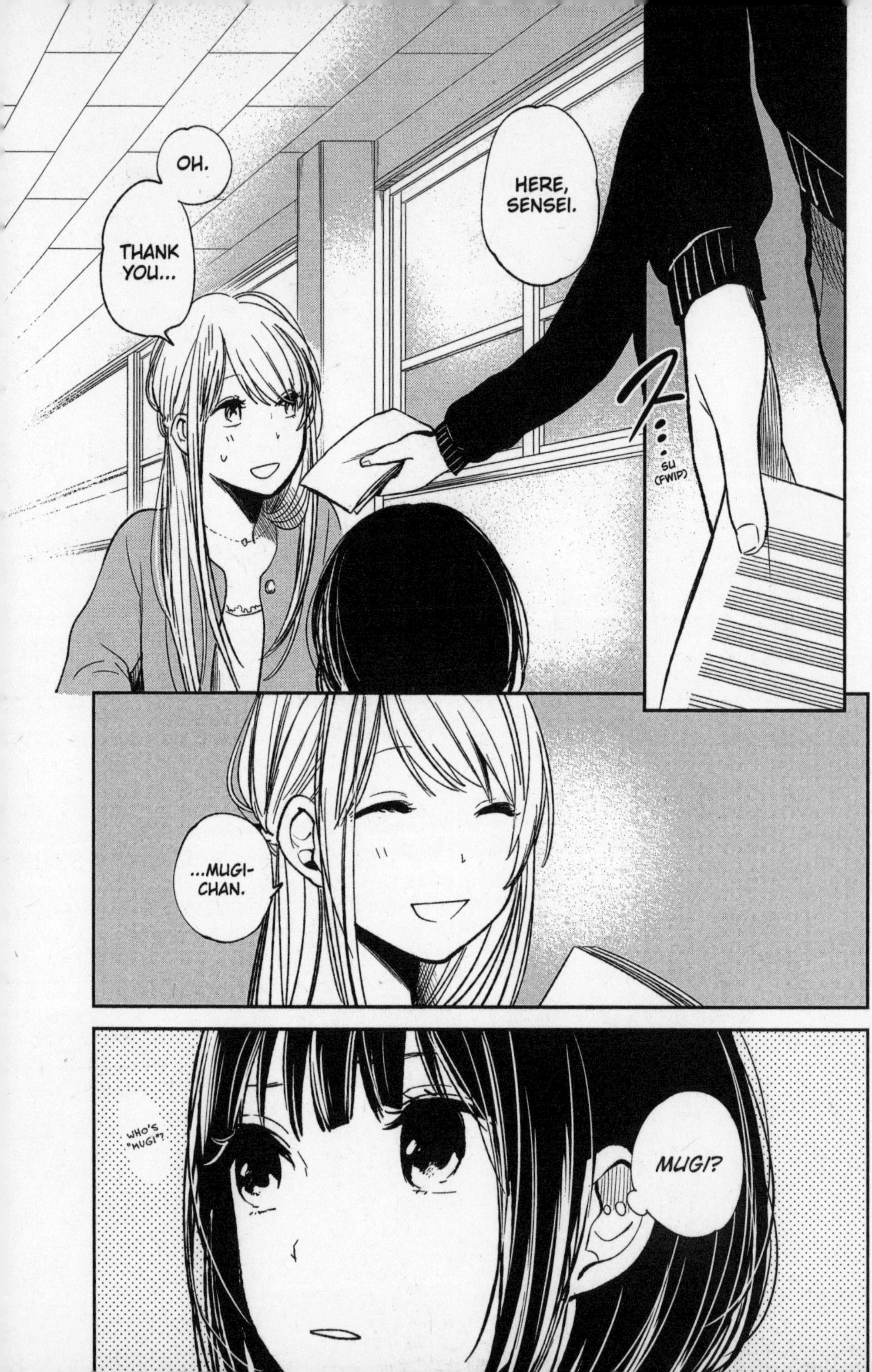
HERE, SENSEI.
SU (FWIP)
OH.
THANK YOU...
...MUGI-CHAN.
MUGI?
WHO'S "MUGI"?

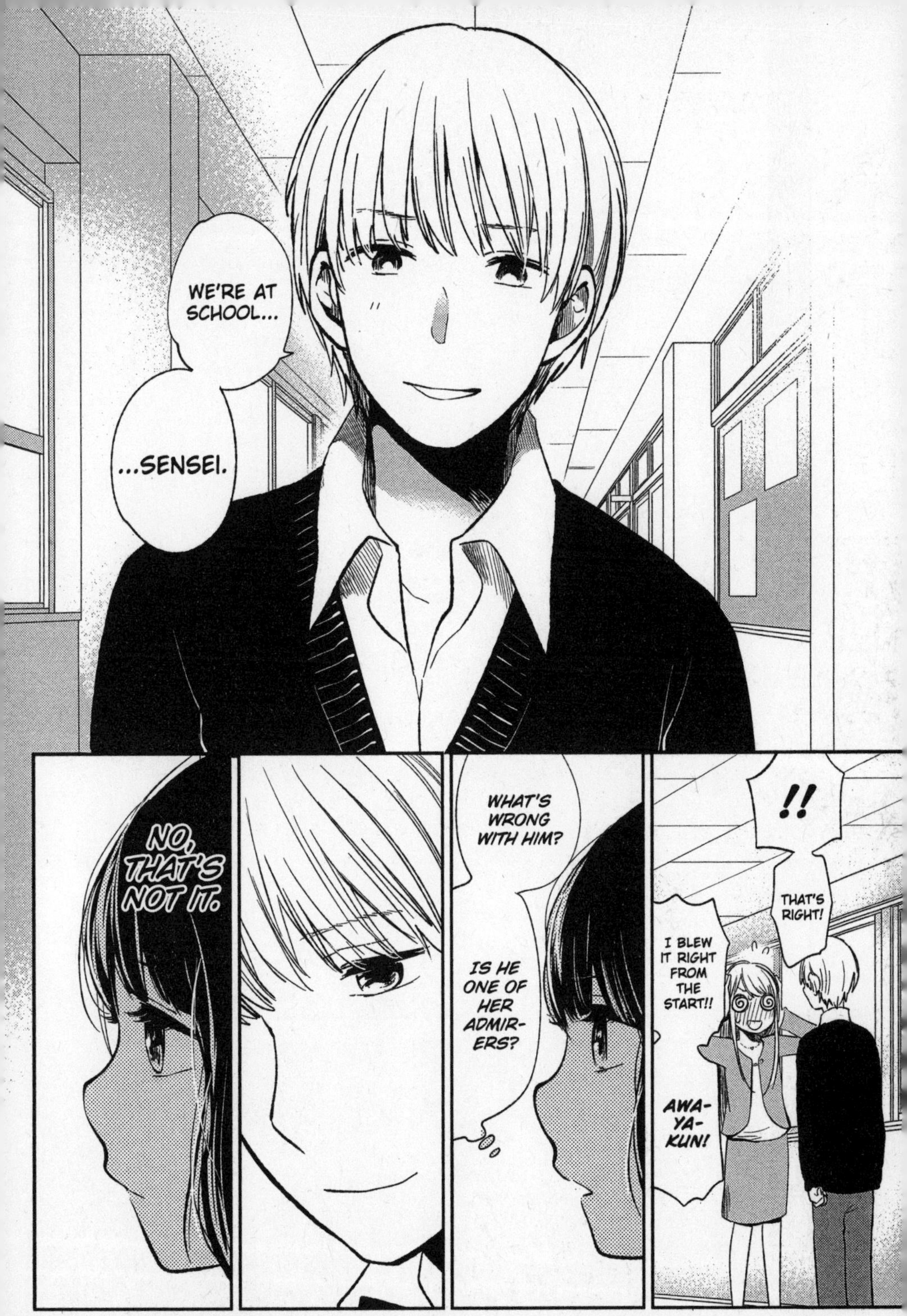
WE'RE AT SCHOOL...
...SENSEI.
!!
THAT'S RIGHT!
I BLEW IT RIGHT FROM THE START!!
AWA-YA-KUN!
WHAT'S WRONG WITH HIM?
IS HE ONE OF HER ADMIR-ERS?
NO, THAT'S NOT IT.

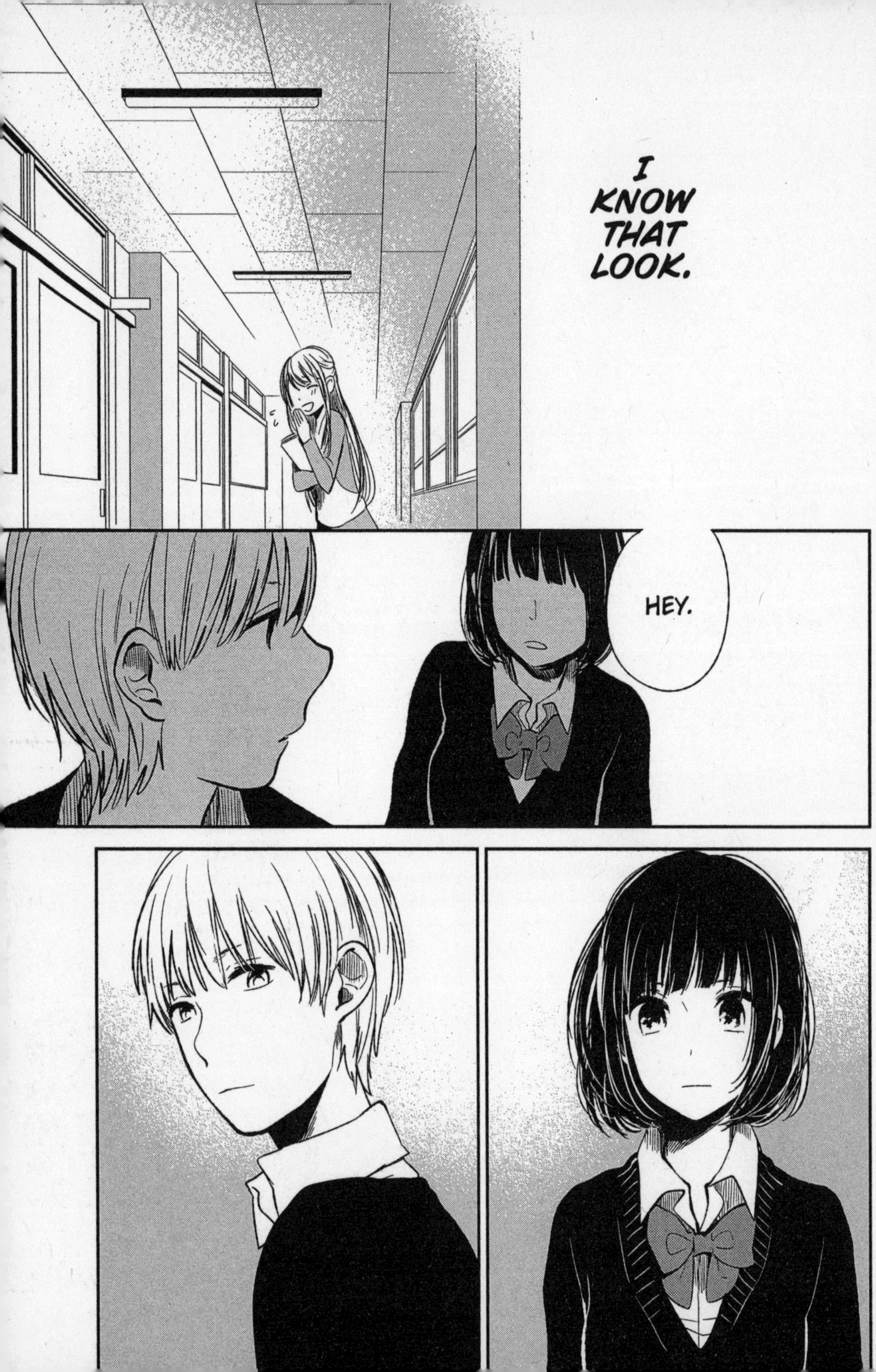
I KNOW THAT LOOK.
HEY.

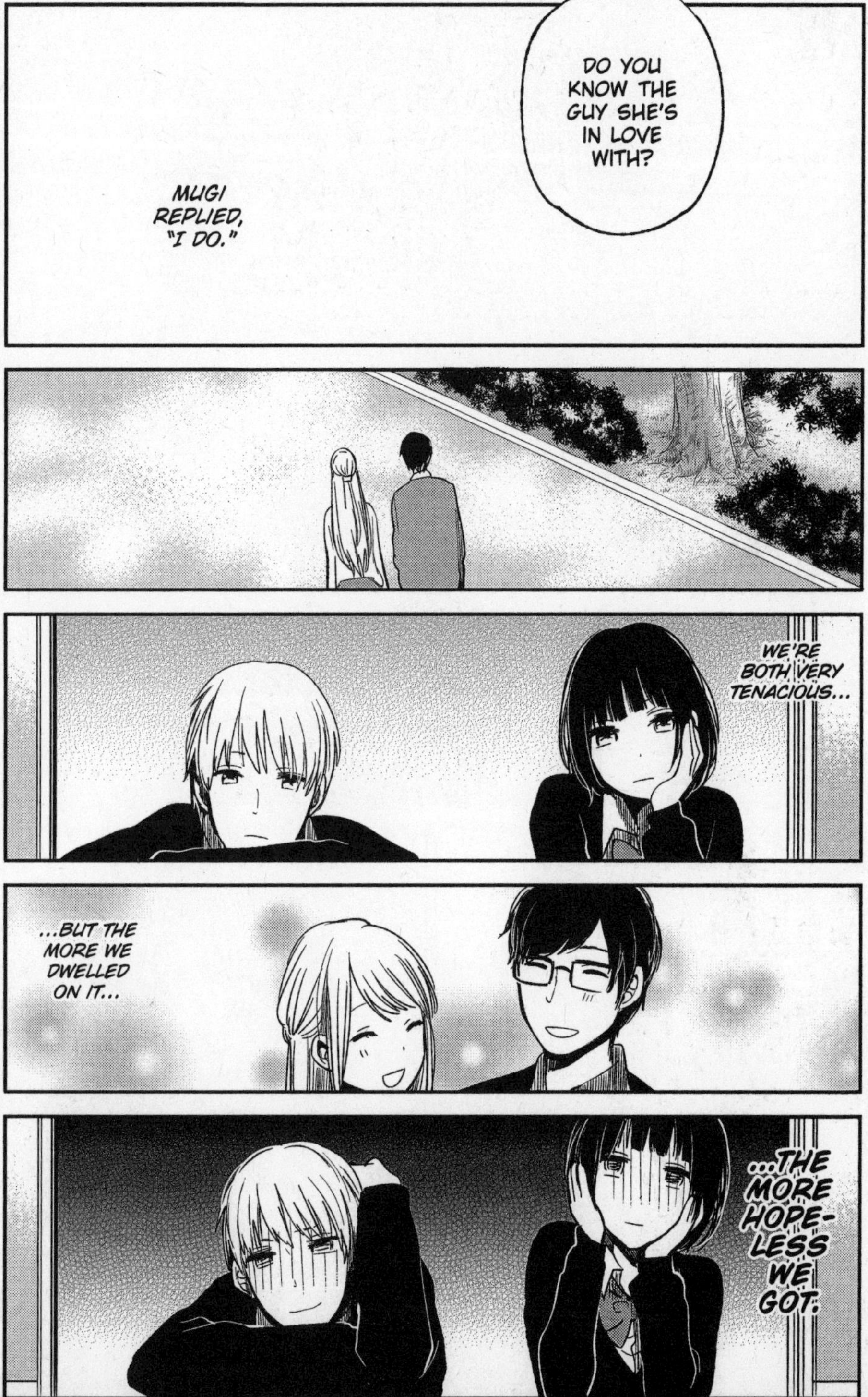
DO YOU KNOW THE GUY SHE'S IN LOVE WITH?
MUGI REPLIED, "I DO."
WE'RE BOTH VERY TENACIOUS...
...BUT THE MORE WE DWELLED ON IT...
...THE MORE HOPE-LESS WE GOT.

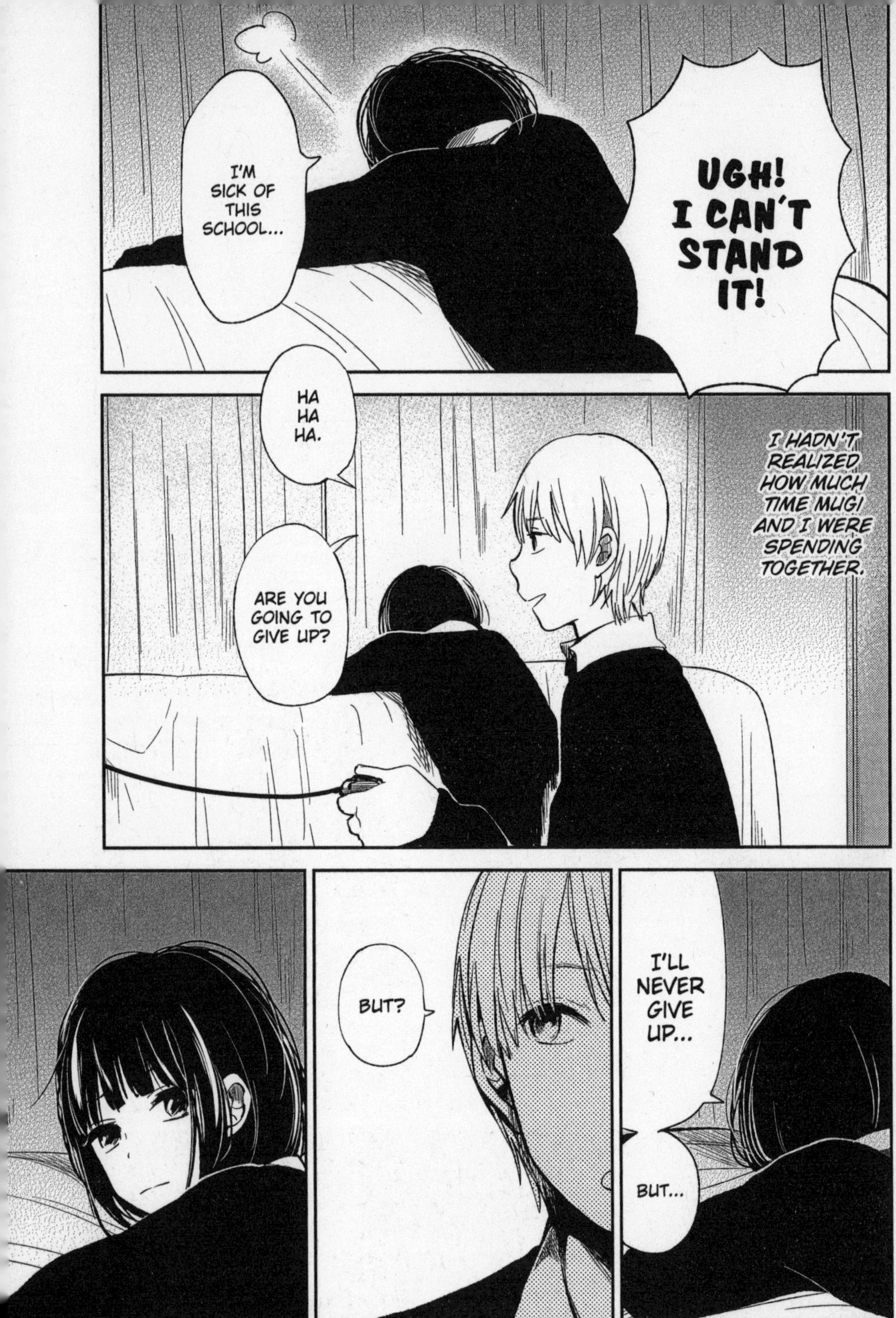
UGH! I CAN'T STAND IT!
I'M SICK OF THIS SCHOOL...
I HADN'T REALIZED HOW MUCH TIME MUGI AND I WERE SPENDING TOGETHER.
HA HA HA.
ARE YOU GOING TO GIVE UP?
I'LL NEVER GIVE UP...
BUT...
BUT?

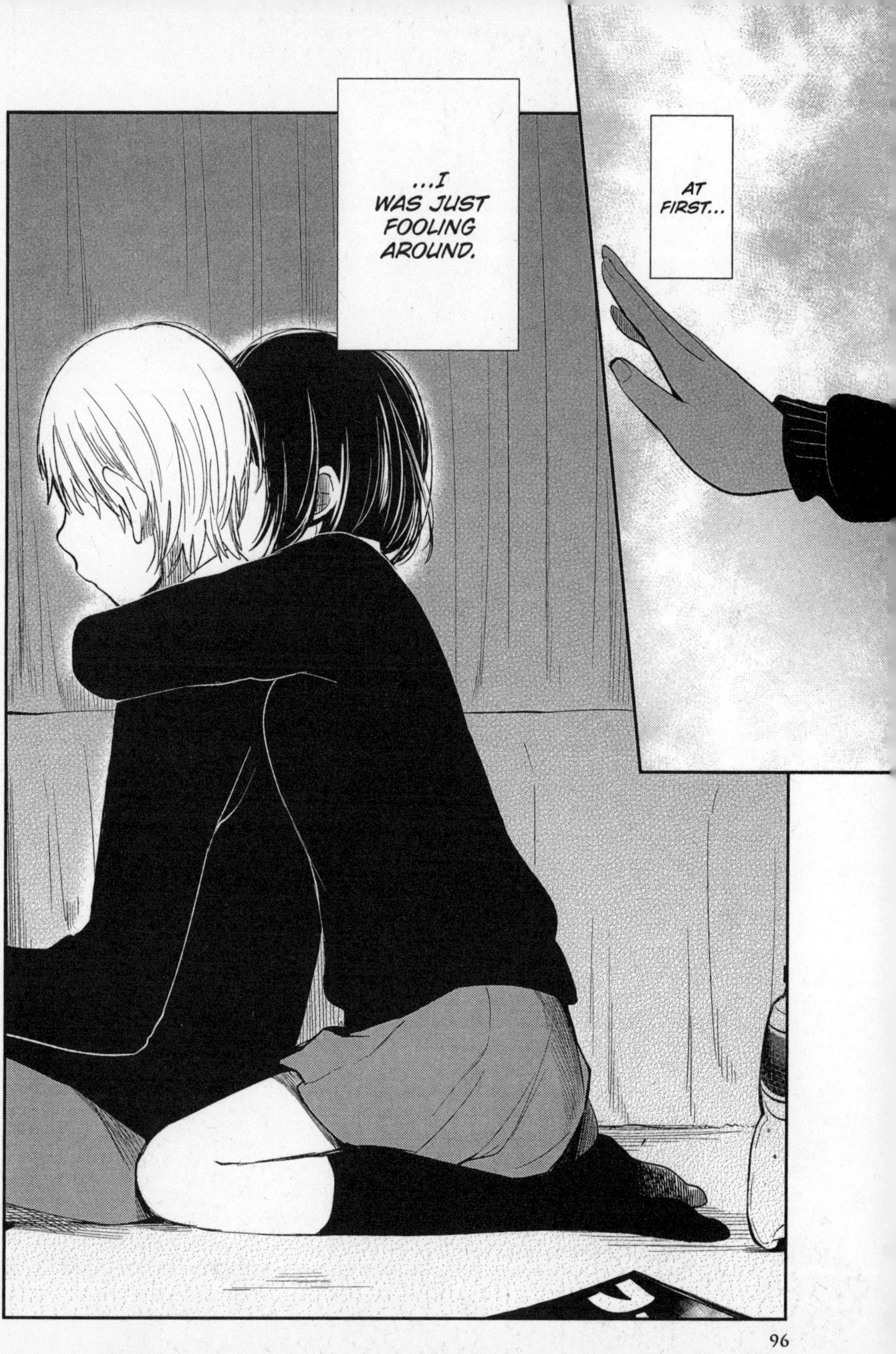
AT FIRST...
...I WAS JUST FOOLING AROUND.

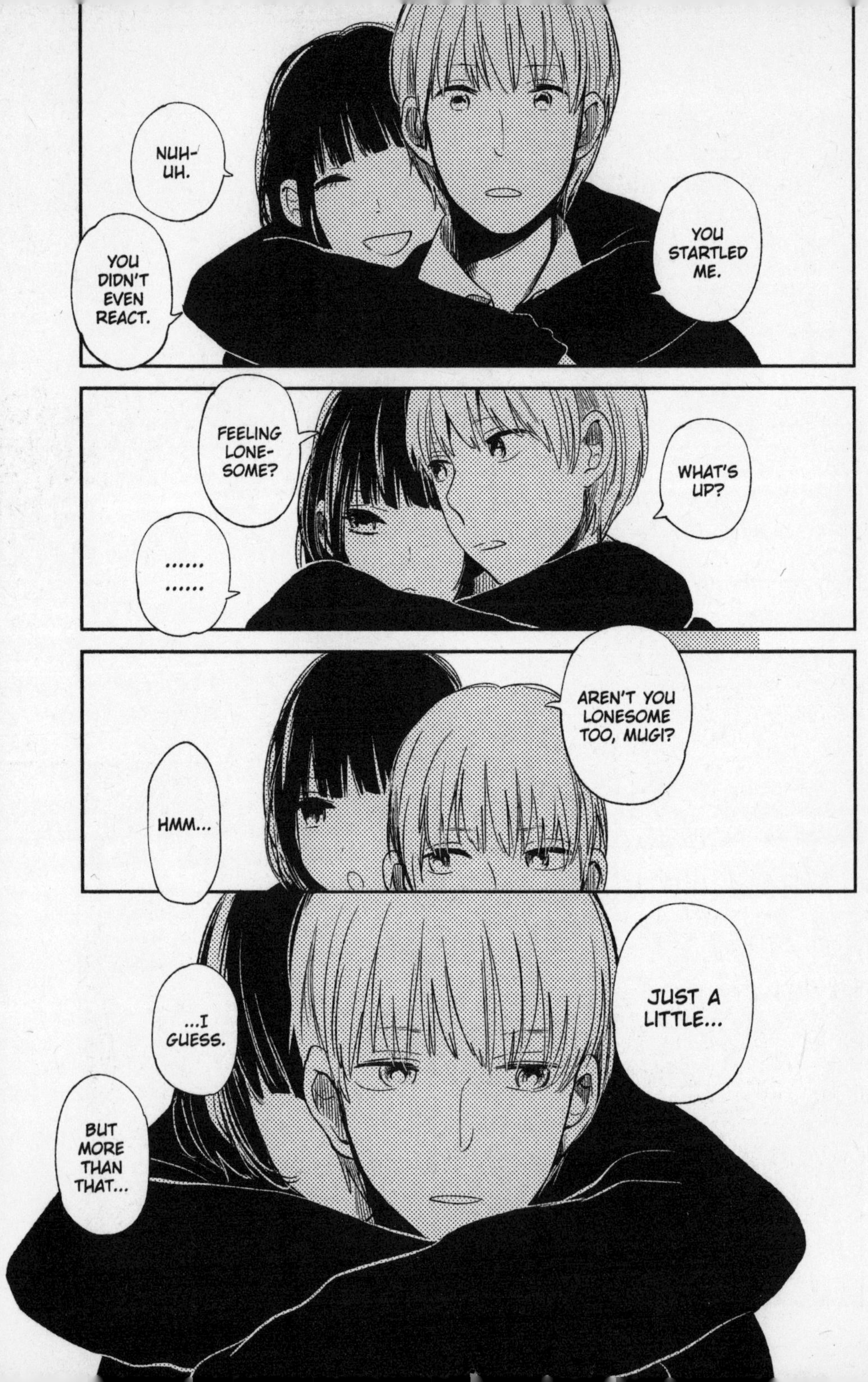
YOU STARTLED ME.
NUH-UH.
YOU DIDN'T EVEN REACT.
WHAT'S UP?
FEELING LONESOME?
......
......
AREN'T YOU LONESOME TOO, MUGI?
HMM...
JUST A LITTLE...
...I GUESS.
BUT MORE THAN THAT...

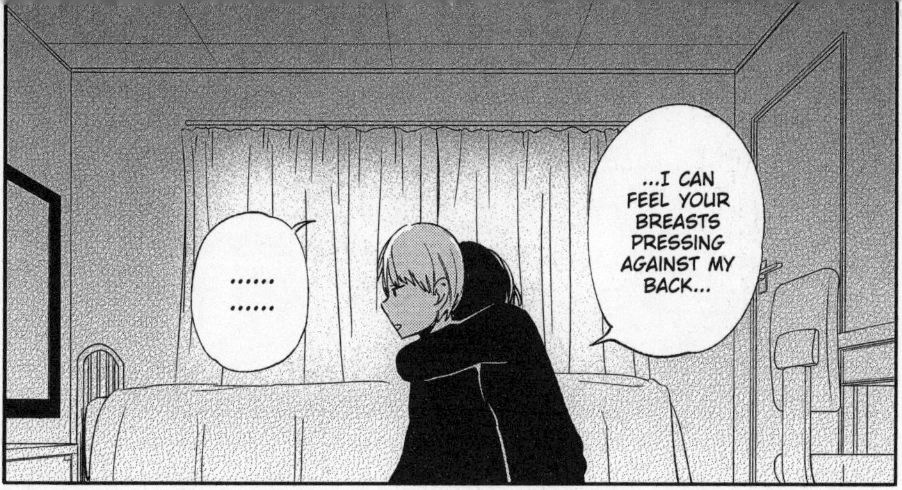
...I CAN FEEL YOUR BREASTS PRESSING AGAINST MY BACK...
......
......

AT THAT VERY MOMENT, I'M SURE WE WERE THINKING THE SAME THING.

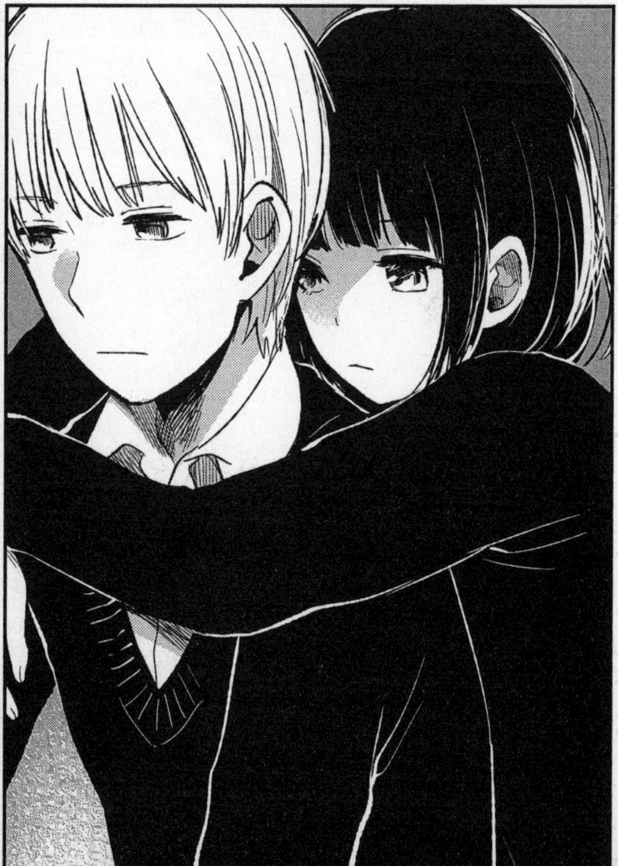

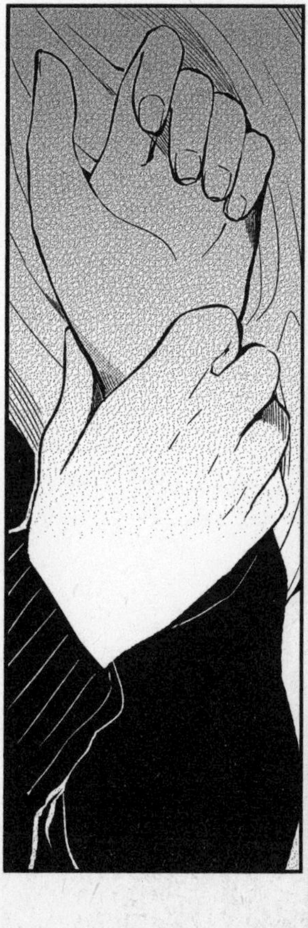

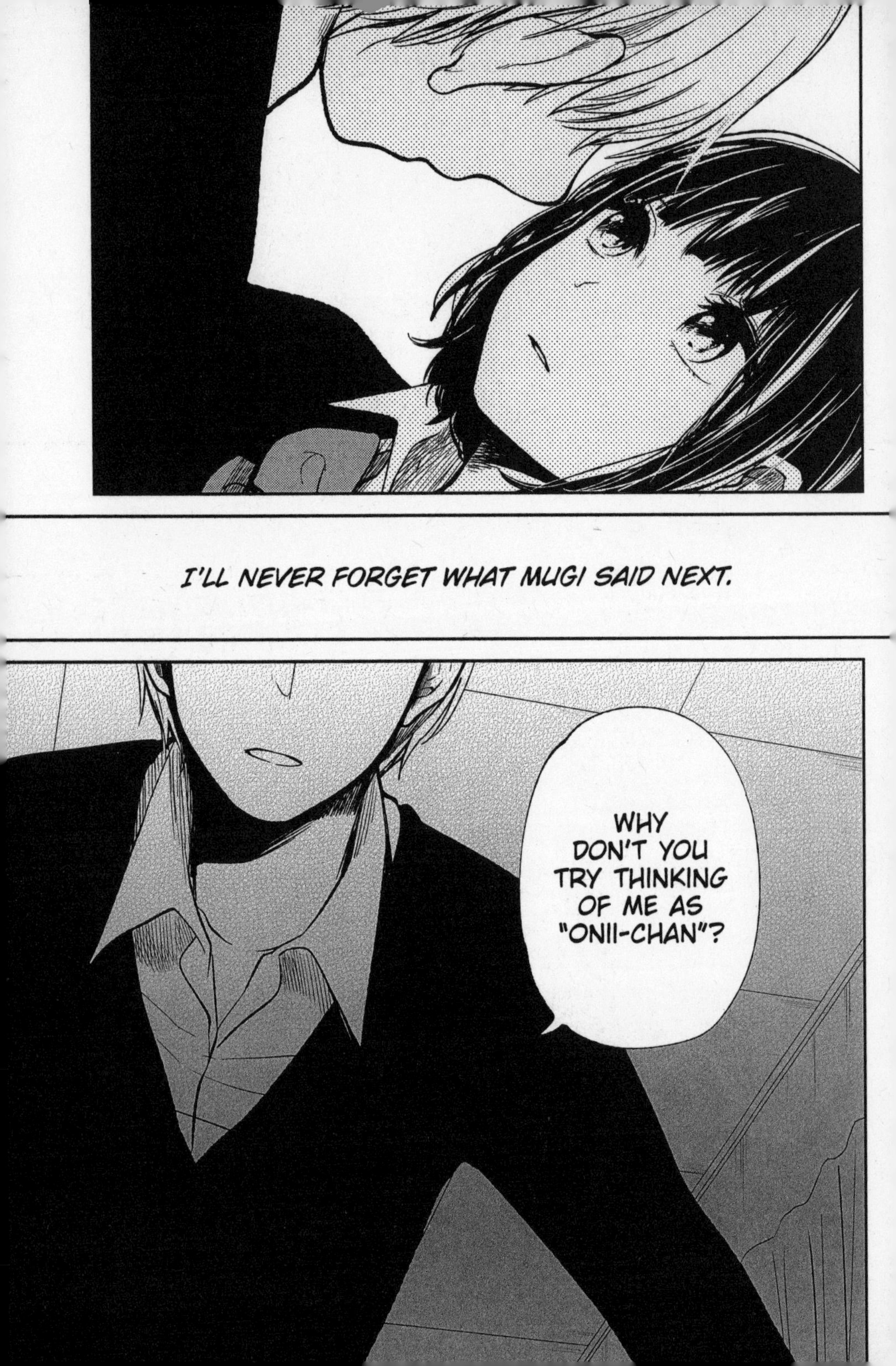
I'LL NEVER FORGET WHAT MUGI SAID NEXT.
WHY DON'T YOU TRY THINKING OF ME AS "ONII-CHAN"?

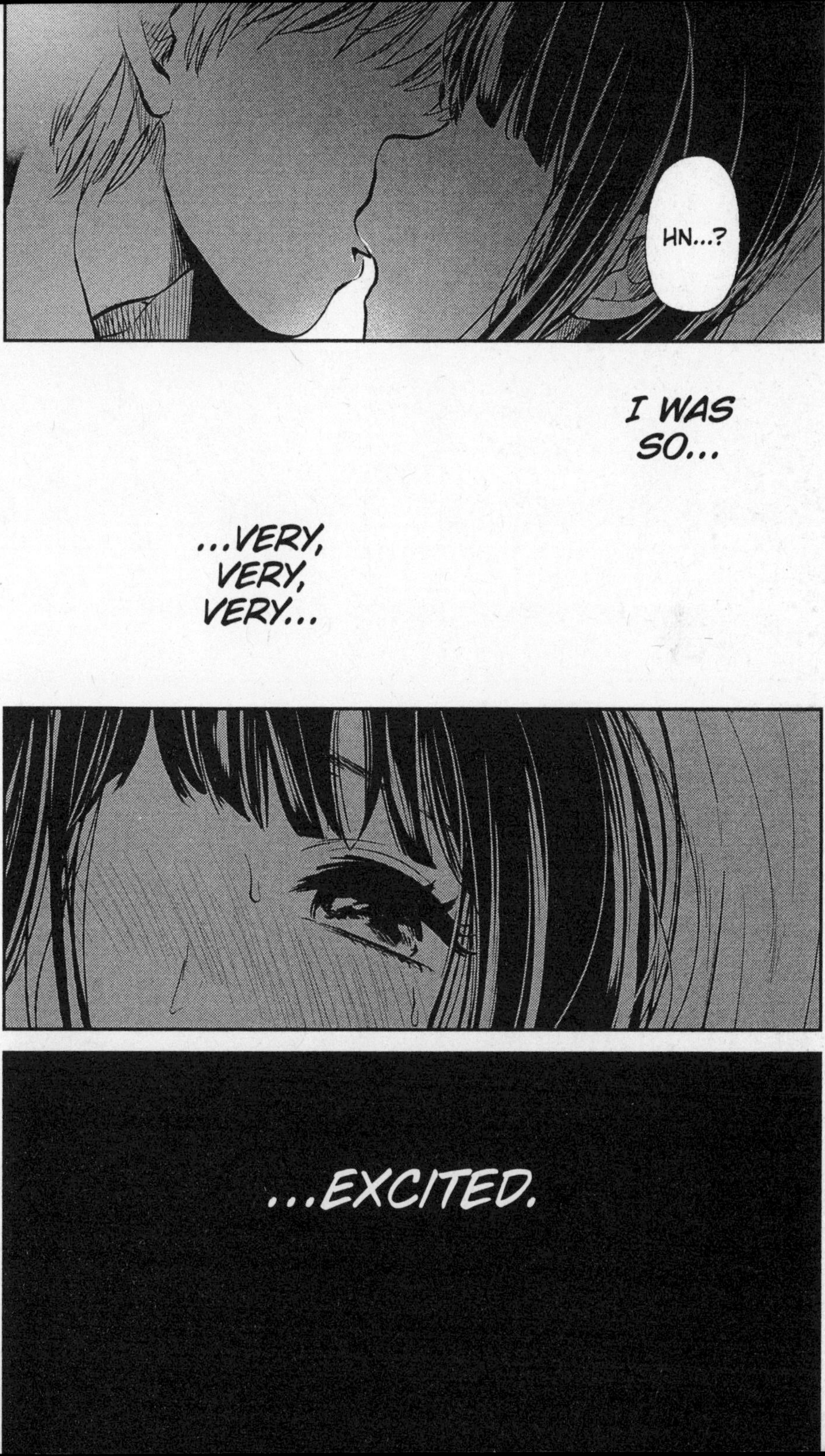
HN...?
I WAS SO...
...VERY, VERY, VERY...
...EXCITED.

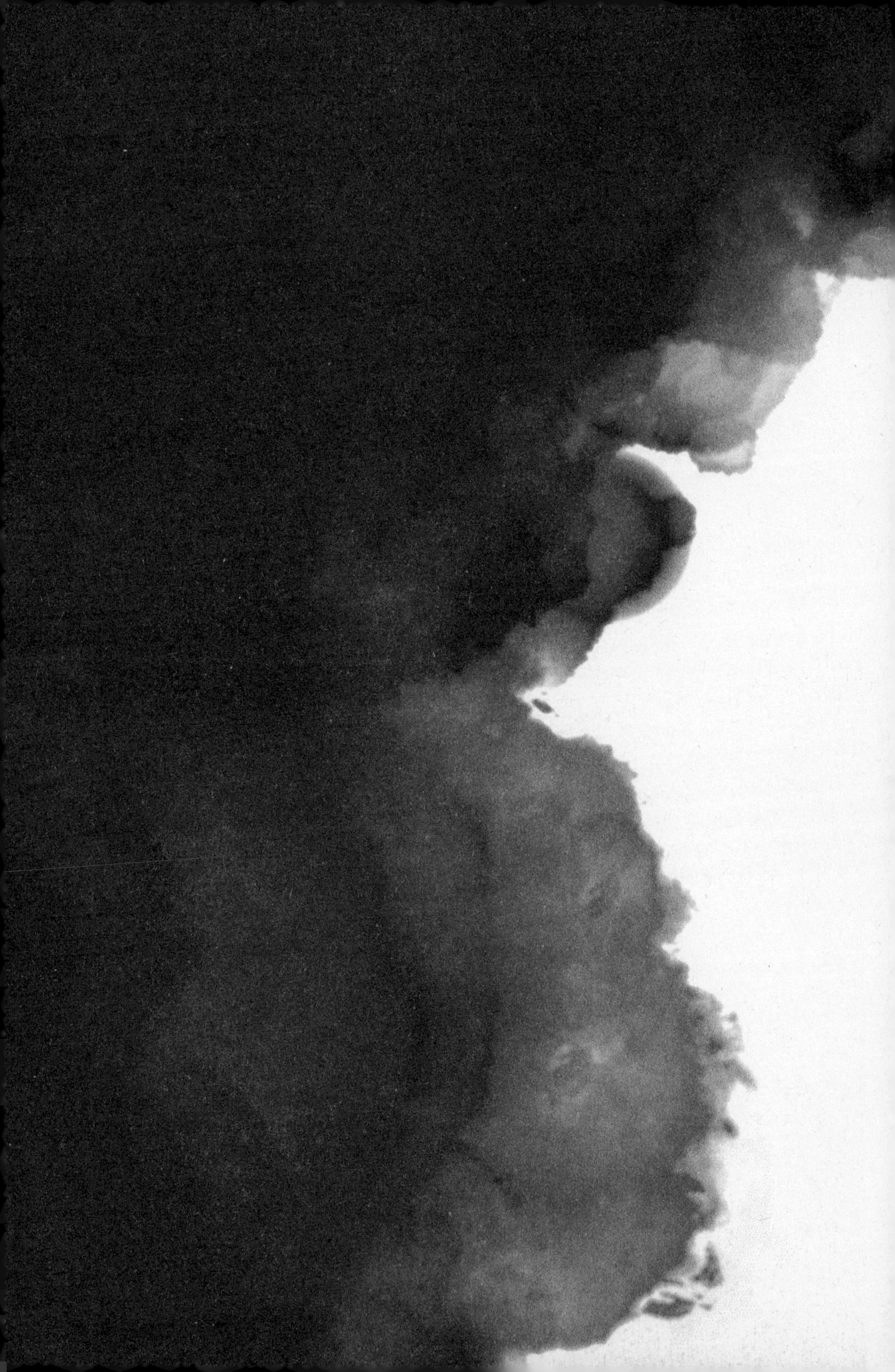

Scum's Wish

Episode 4
High School Girl Lullaby

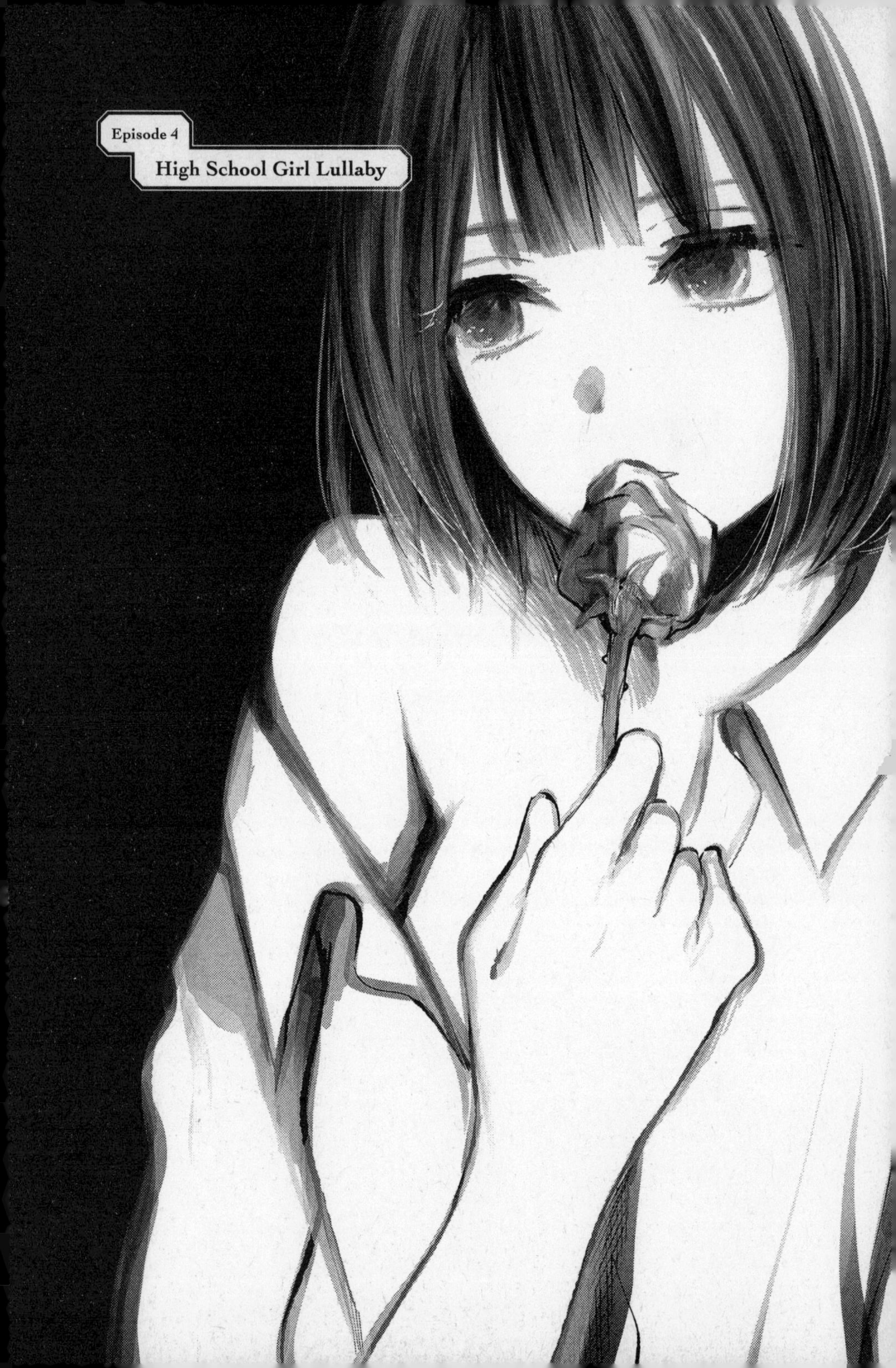

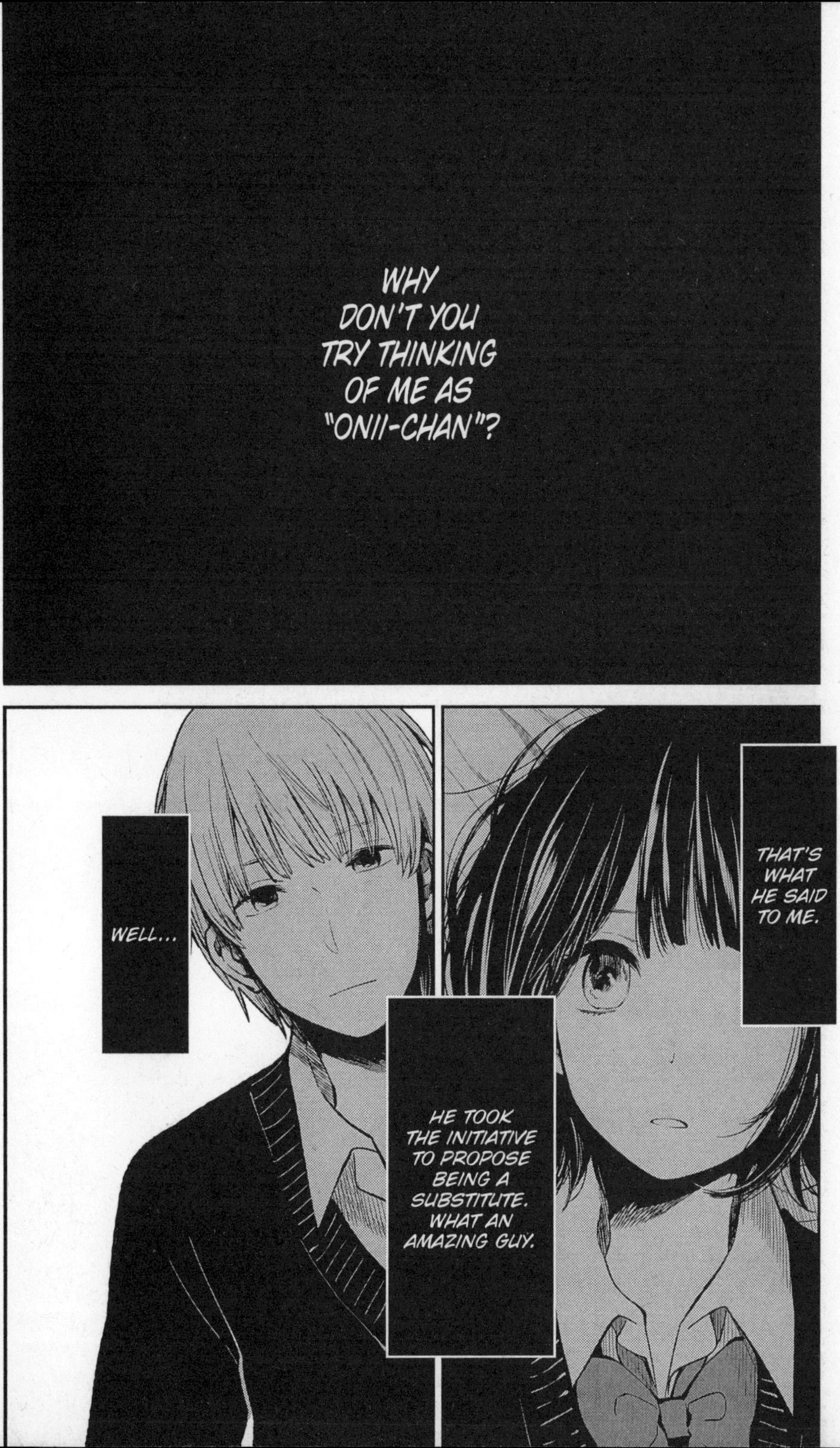
WHY DON'T YOU TRY THINKING OF ME AS "ONII-CHAN"?
THAT'S WHAT HE SAID TO ME.
HE TOOK THE INITIATIVE TO PROPOSE BEING A SUBSTITUTE. WHAT AN AMAZING GUY.
WELL...

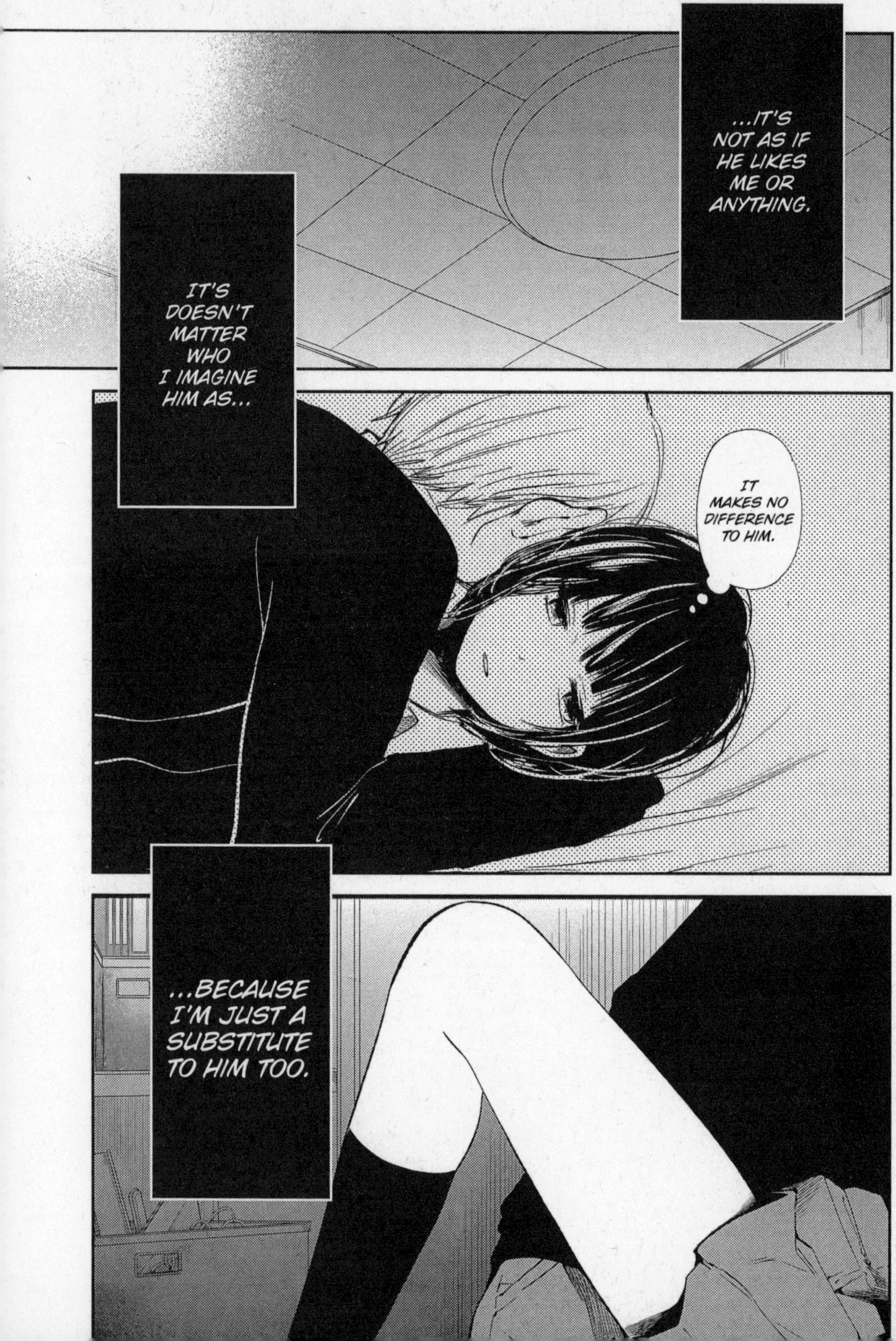
...IT'S NOT AS IF HE LIKES ME OR ANYTHING.
IT'S DOESN'T MATTER WHO I IMAGINE HIM AS...
IT MAKES NO DIFFERENCE TO HIM.
...BECAUSE I'M JUST A SUBSTITUTE TO HIM TOO.

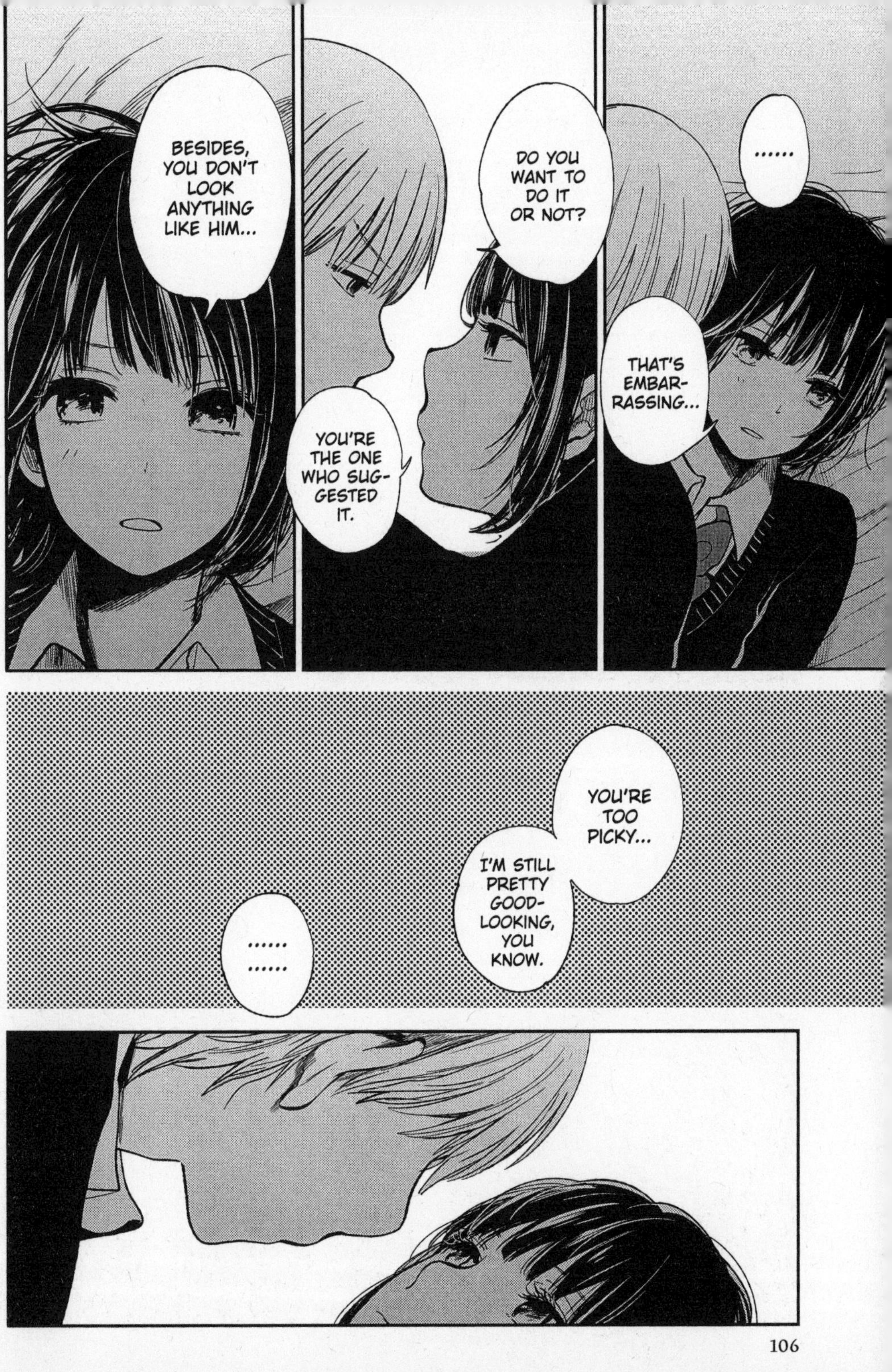
......
THAT'S EMBARRASSING...
DO YOU WANT TO DO IT OR NOT?
YOU'RE THE ONE WHO SUGGESTED IT.
BESIDES, YOU DON'T LOOK ANYTHING LIKE HIM...
YOU'RE TOO PICKY...
I'M STILL PRETTY GOOD-LOOKING, YOU KNOW.
......
......

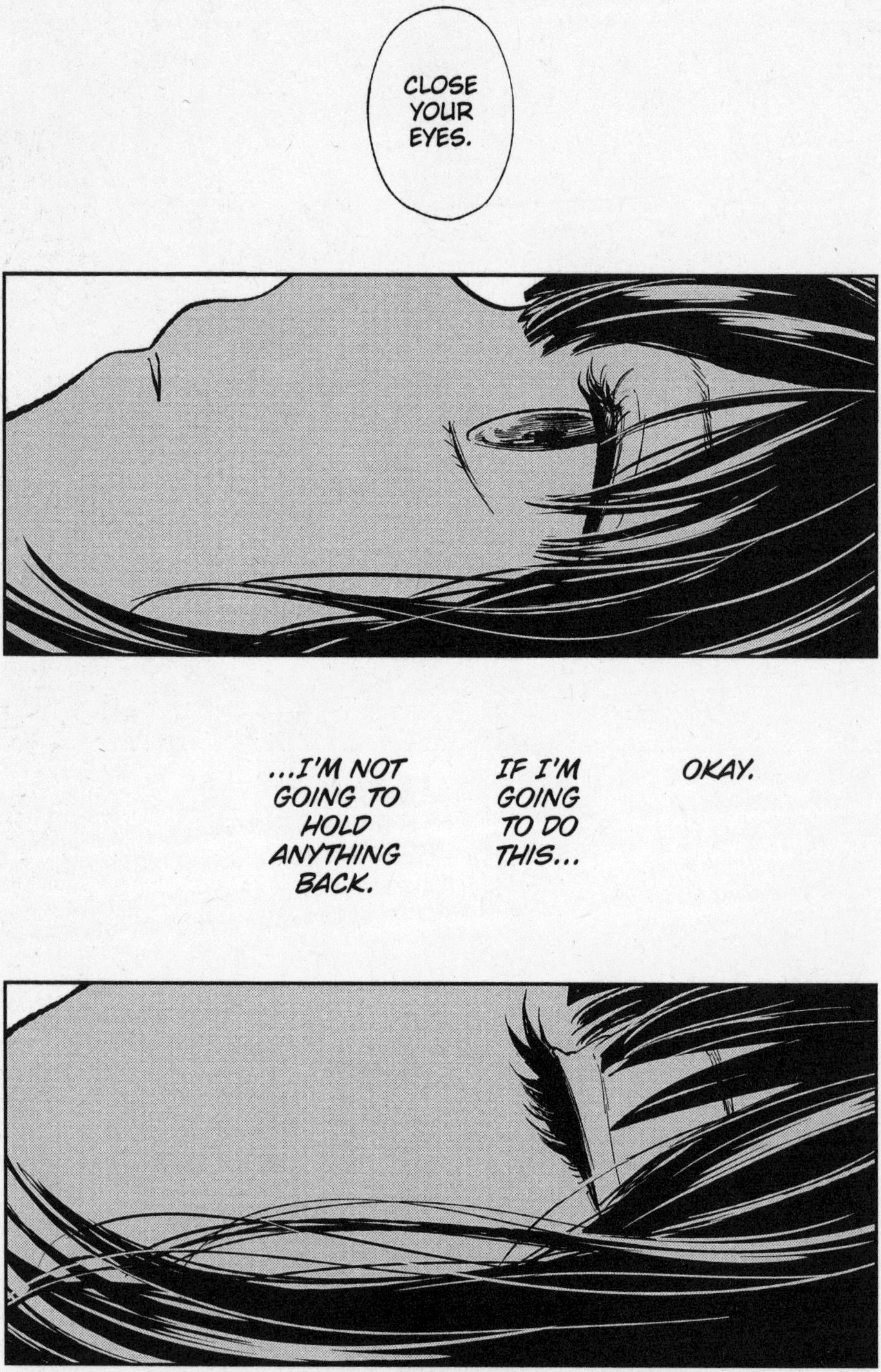
CLOSE YOUR EYES.
OKAY.
IF I'M GOING TO DO THIS...
...I'M NOT GOING TO HOLD ANYTHING BACK.

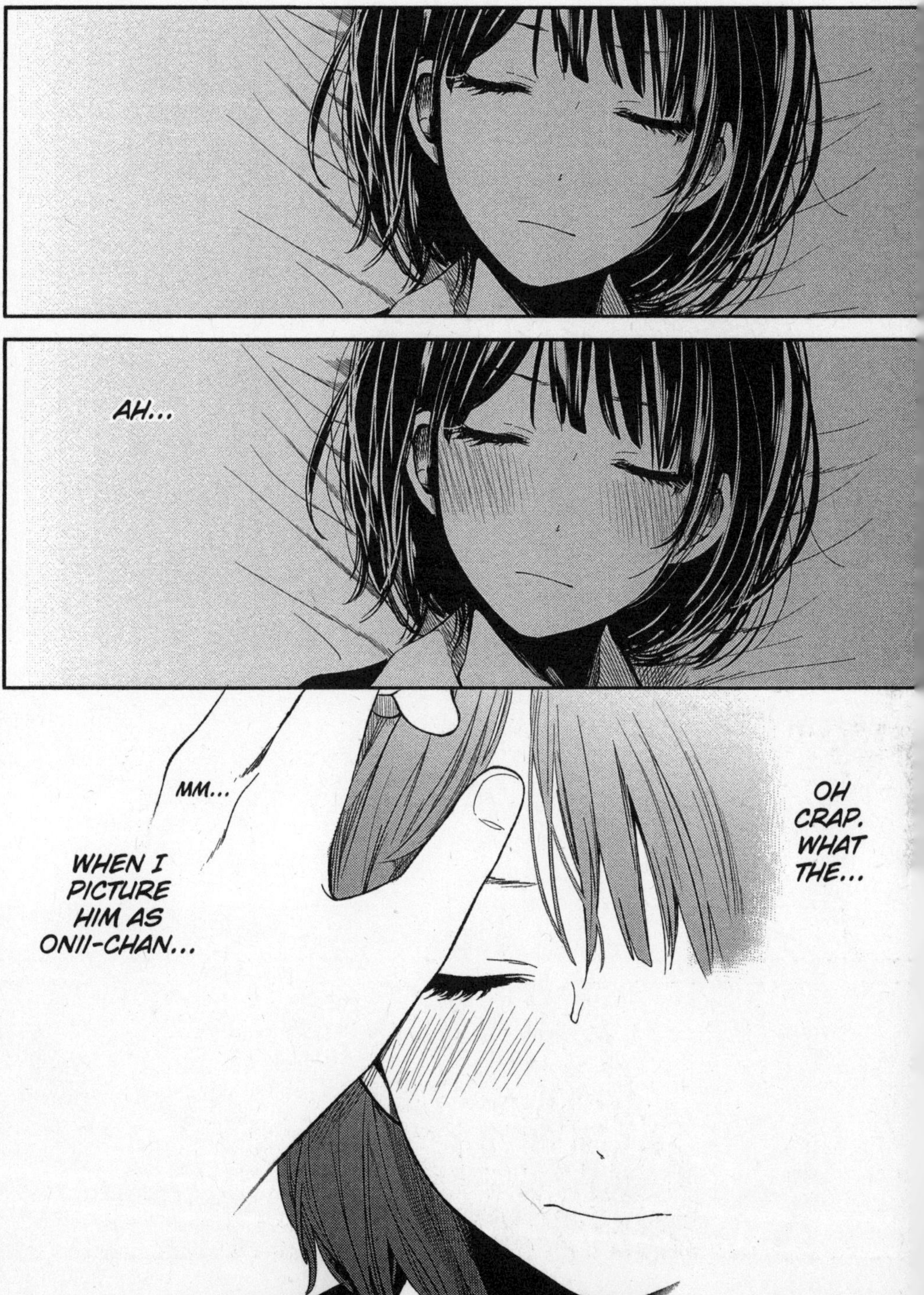
AH...
MM...
WHEN I PICTURE HIM AS ONII-CHAN...
OH CRAP. WHAT THE...

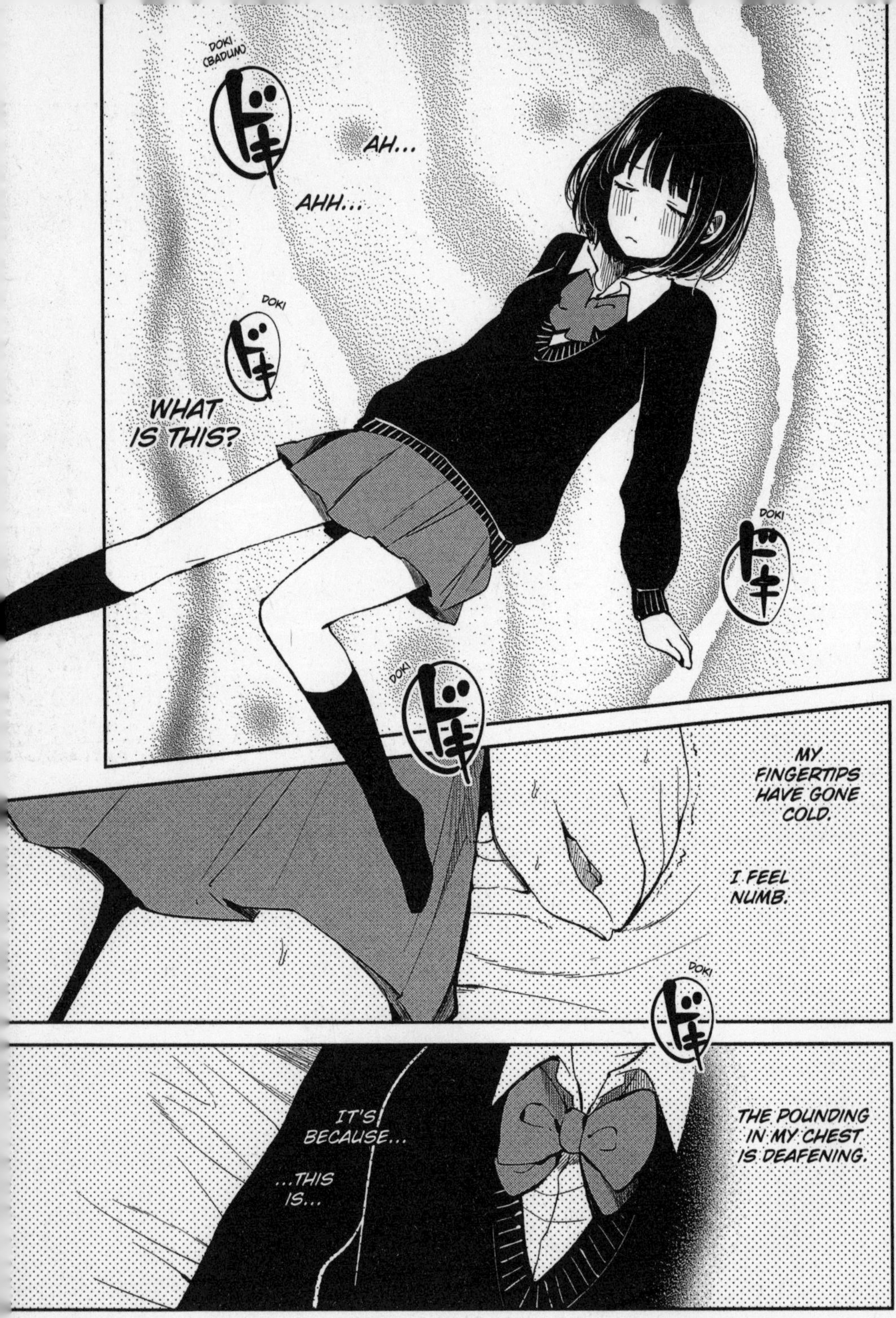
DOKI (BADUM)
AH...
AHH...
DOKI
WHAT IS THIS?
DOKI
DOKI
MY FINGERTIPS HAVE GONE COLD.
I FEEL NUMB.
DOKI
THE POUNDING IN MY CHEST IS DEAFENING.
IT'S BECAUSE...
...THIS IS...

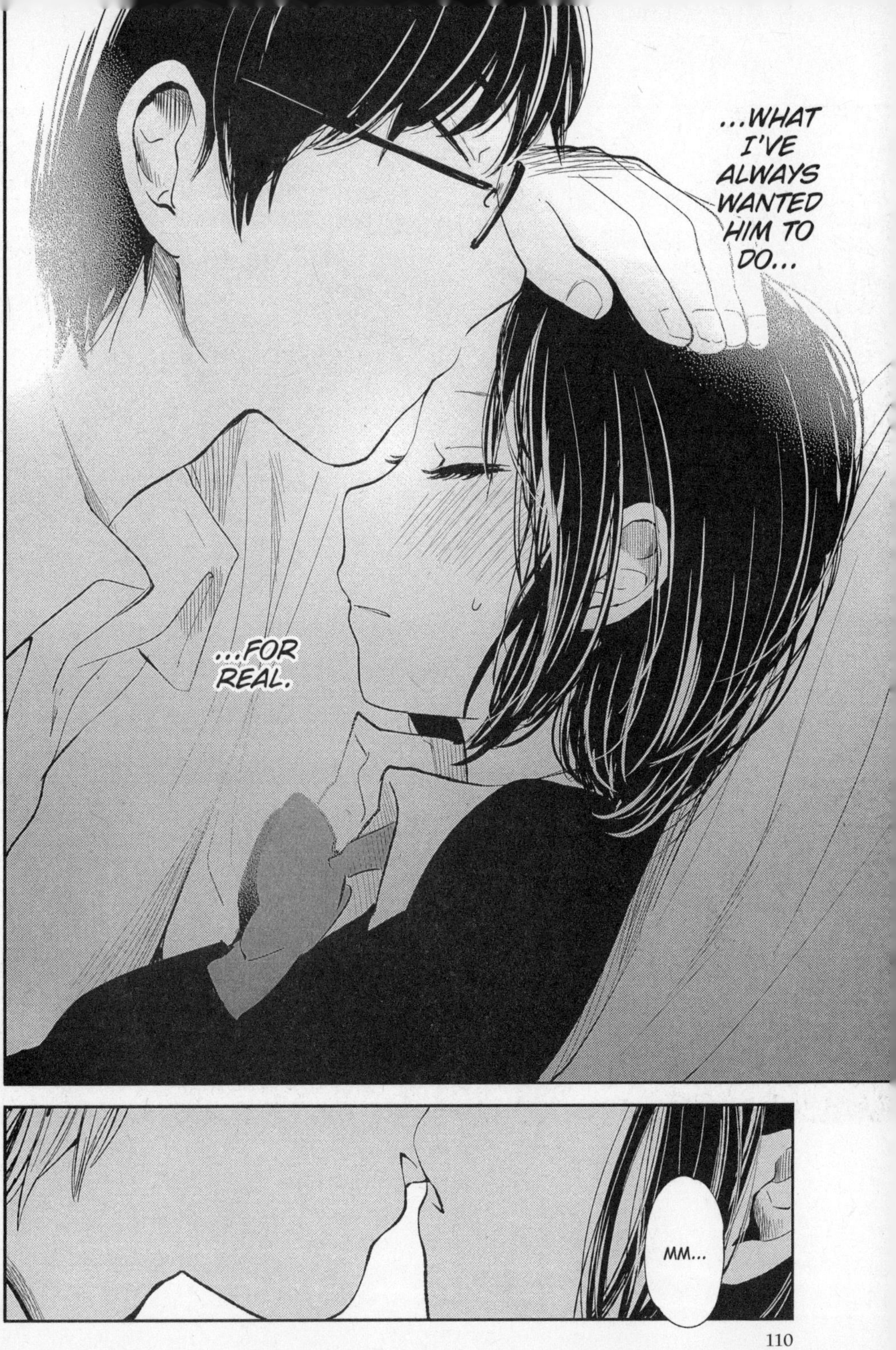
...WHAT I'VE ALWAYS WANTED HIM TO DO...
...FOR REAL.
MM...

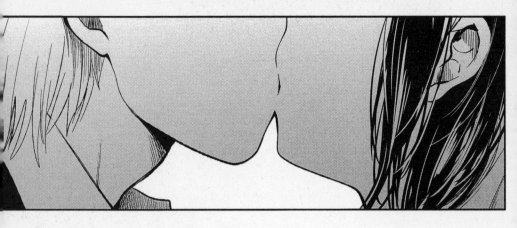

IT'S
ELECTRIFYING.

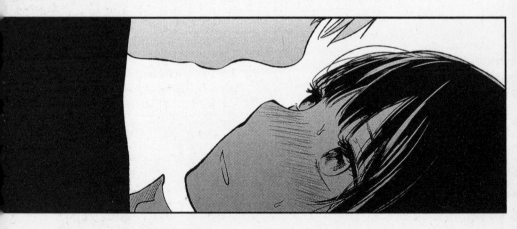

...FEELS
LIKE IT'S
ON FIRE.

MY
FACE...

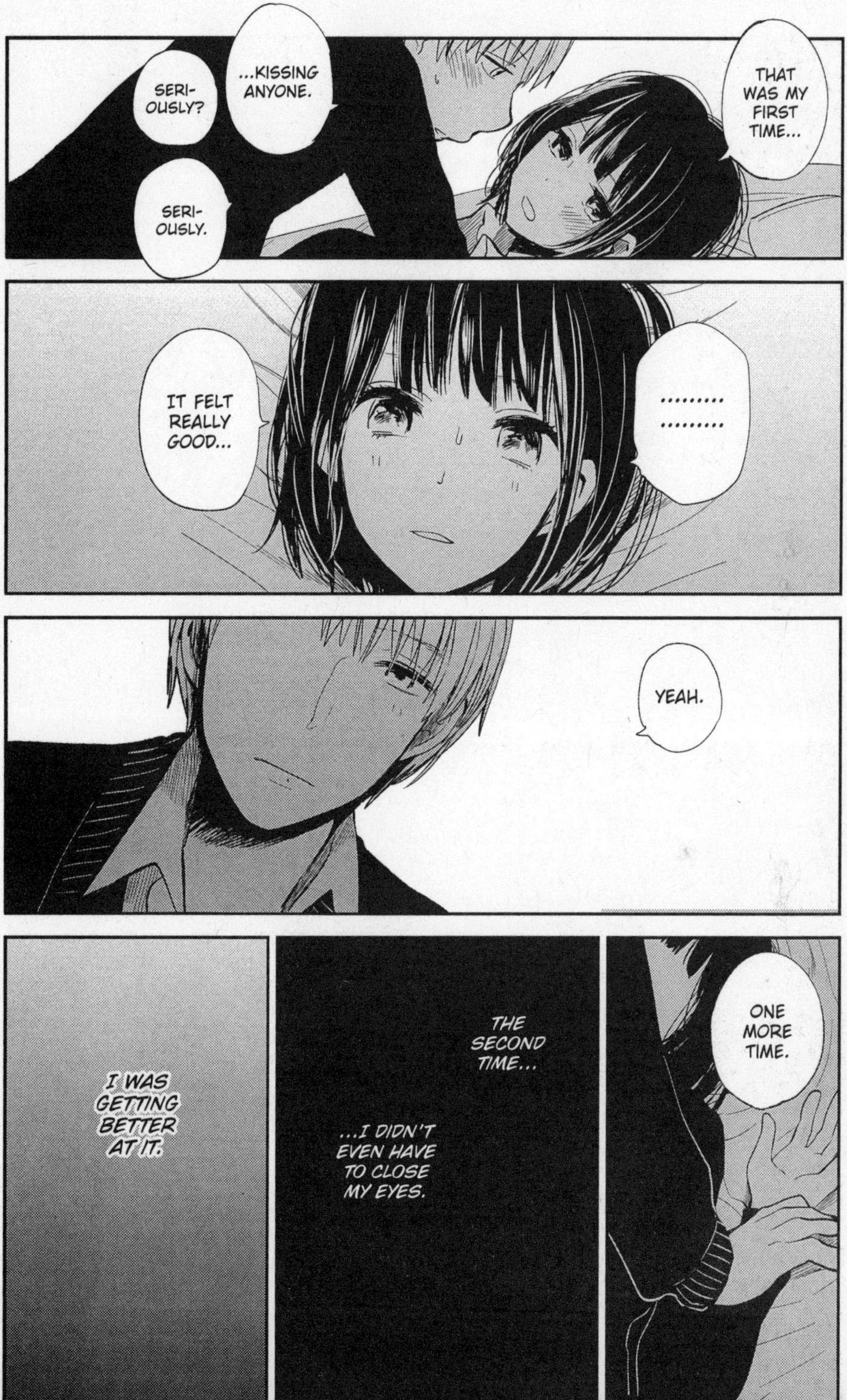
THAT WAS MY FIRST TIME...
...KISSING ANYONE.
SERI-OUSLY?
SERI-OUSLY.
....
....
IT FELT REALLY GOOD...
YEAH.
ONE MORE TIME.
THE SECOND TIME...
...I DIDN'T EVEN HAVE TO CLOSE MY EYES.
I WAS GETTING BETTER AT IT.

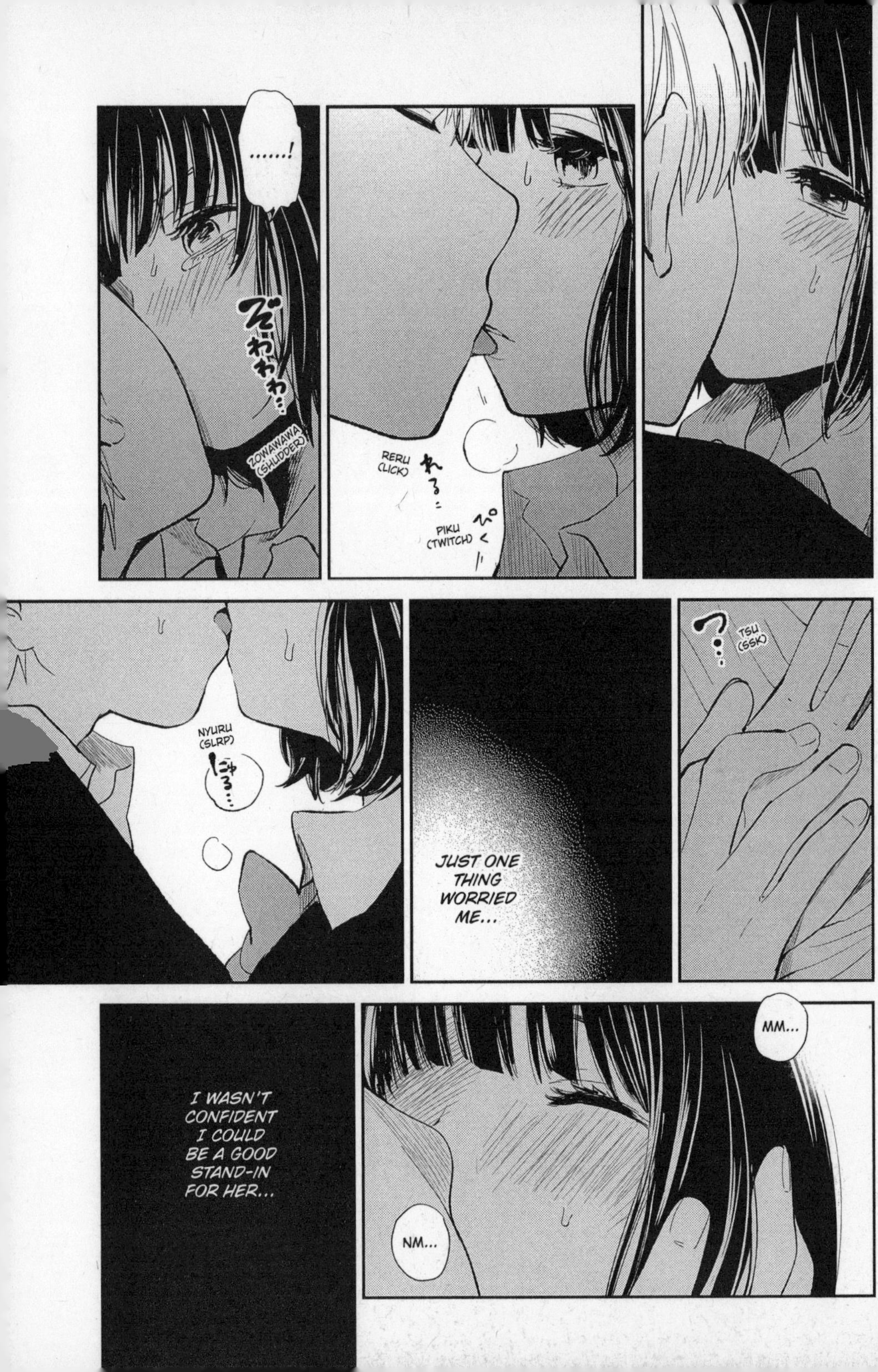

れる
RERU (LICK)
ぴく
PIKU (TWITCH)
......!
ぞわわわ...
ZOWAWAWA (SHUDDER)
っ...
TSU (SSK)
JUST ONE THING WORRIED ME...
NYURU (SLRP)
にゅる...
MM...
NM...
I WASN'T CONFIDENT I COULD BE A GOOD STAND-IN FOR HER...

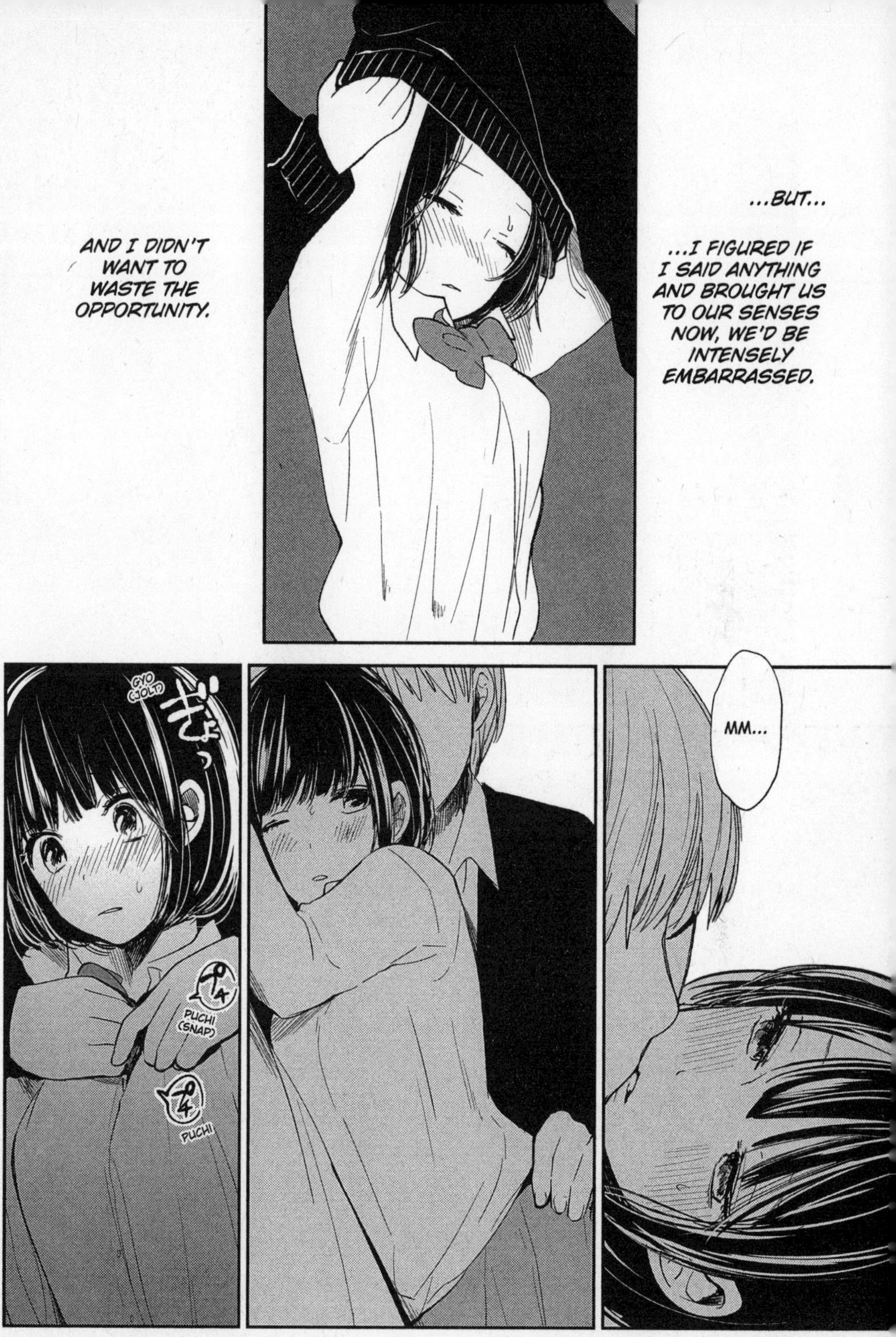
...BUT...
...I FIGURED IF I SAID ANYTHING AND BROUGHT US TO OUR SENSES NOW, WE'D BE INTENSELY EMBARRASSED.
AND I DIDN'T WANT TO WASTE THE OPPORTUNITY.
MM...
GYO (JOLT)
PUCHI (SNAP)
PUCHI

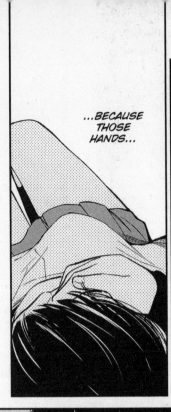

...BECAUSE THOSE HANDS...

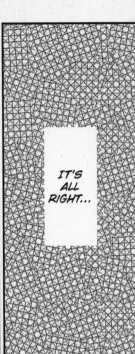

IT'S ALL RIGHT...

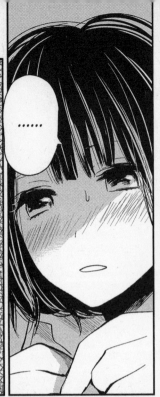

......

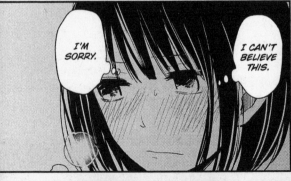

I'M SORRY.

I CAN'T BELIEVE THIS.

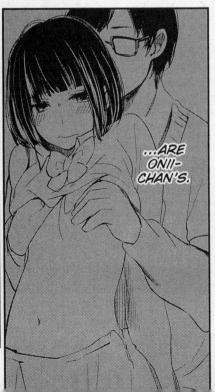

...ARE ONII-CHAN'S.

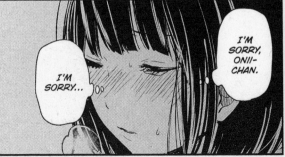

I'M SORRY...

I'M SORRY, ONII-CHAN.

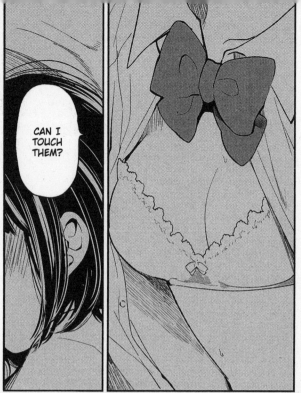

THINGS
ONII-CHAN
HAD NEVER
DONE...

CAN I
TOUCH
THEM?

THINGS
HE HAD
NEVER
DONE FOR
ME...

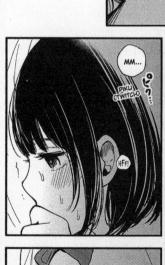

MM...

PIKU
(TWITCH)

HFF!

SURI
(STROKE)

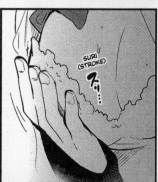

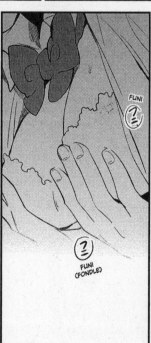

FUNI

FUNI
(FONDLE)

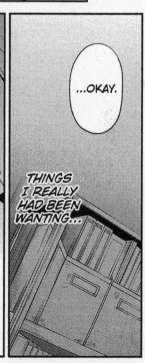

...OKAY.

THINGS
I REALLY
HAD BEEN
WANTING...

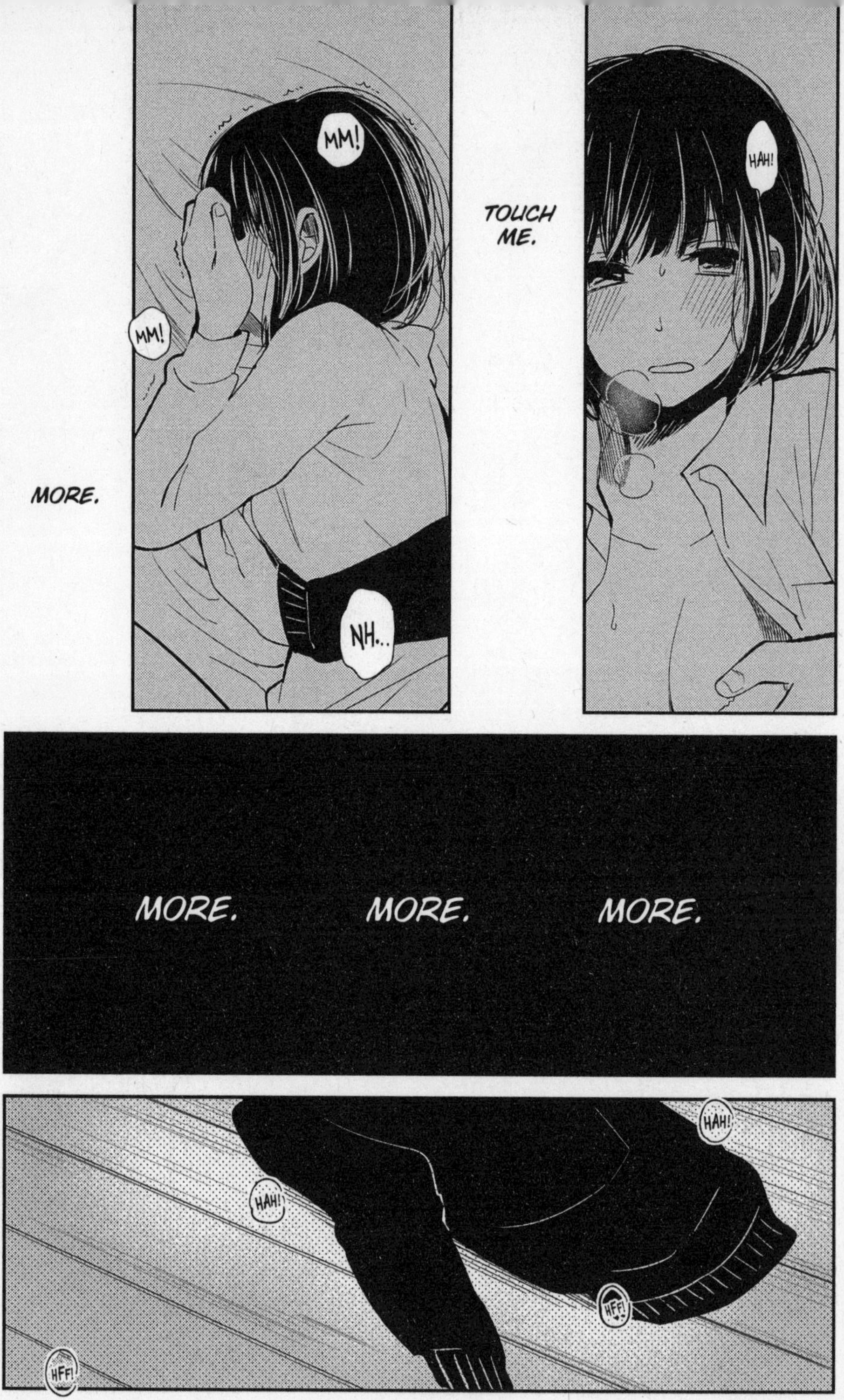

HAH!
TOUCH ME.
MM!
MM!
NH...
MORE.
MORE.
MORE.
MORE.
HAH!
HFF!
HAH!
HFF!

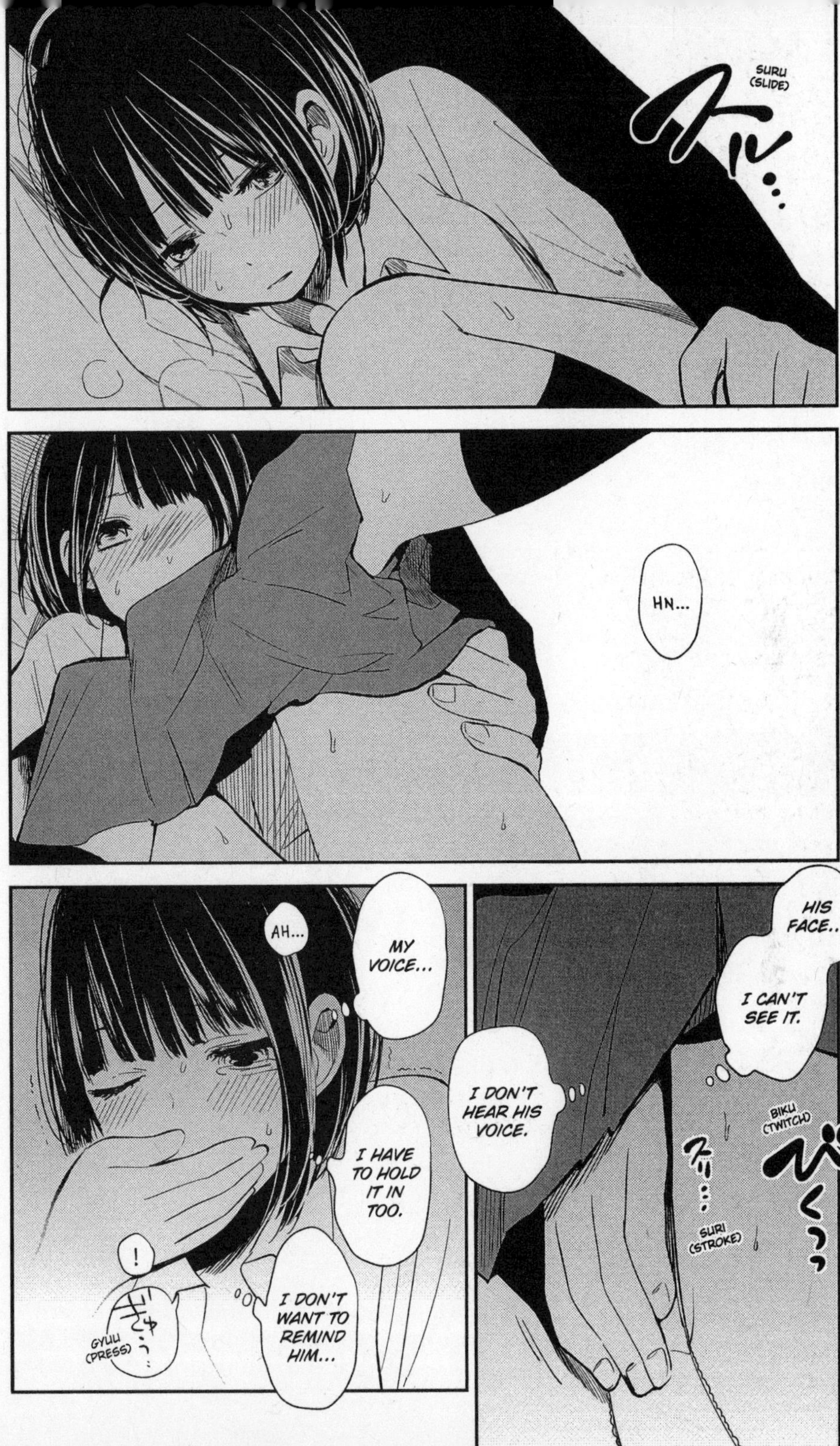
SURU (SLIDE)
HN...
HIS FACE...
I CAN'T SEE IT.
I DON'T HEAR HIS VOICE.
BIKU (TWITCH)
SURI (STROKE)
AH...
MY VOICE...
I HAVE TO HOLD IT IN TOO.
!
I DON'T WANT TO REMIND HIM...
GYUU (PRESS)

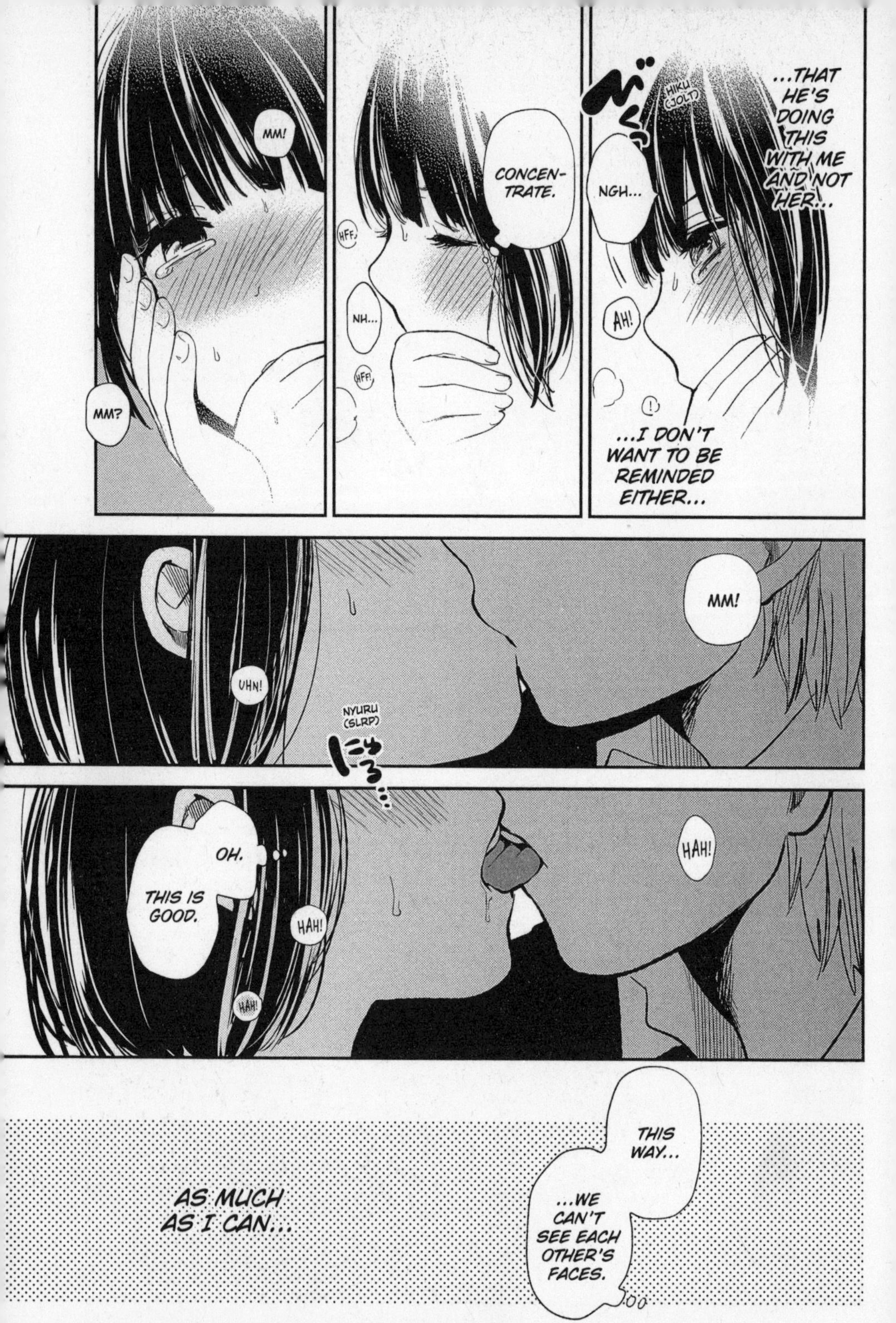
...THAT HE'S DOING THIS WITH ME AND NOT HER...
HIKU (JOLT)
NGH...
AH!
!
...I DON'T WANT TO BE REMINDED EITHER...
CONCENTRATE.
HFF,
NH...
HFF!
MM!
MM?
MM!
NYURU (SLRP)
UHN!
HAH!
OH.
THIS IS GOOD.
HAH!
HAH!
THIS WAY...
...WE CAN'T SEE EACH OTHER'S FACES.
AS MUCH AS I CAN...

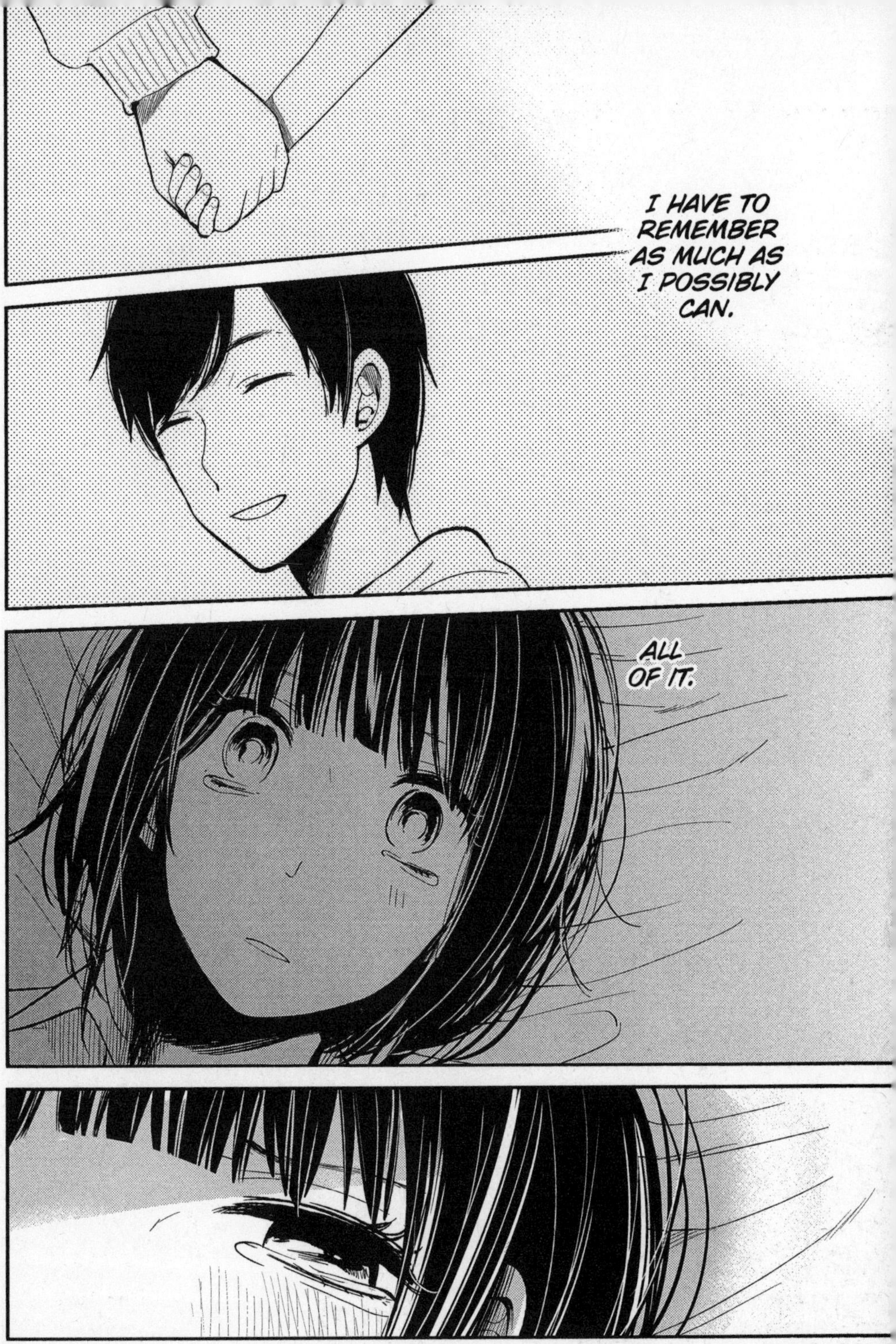
I HAVE TO REMEMBER AS MUCH AS I POSSIBLY CAN.
ALL OF IT.

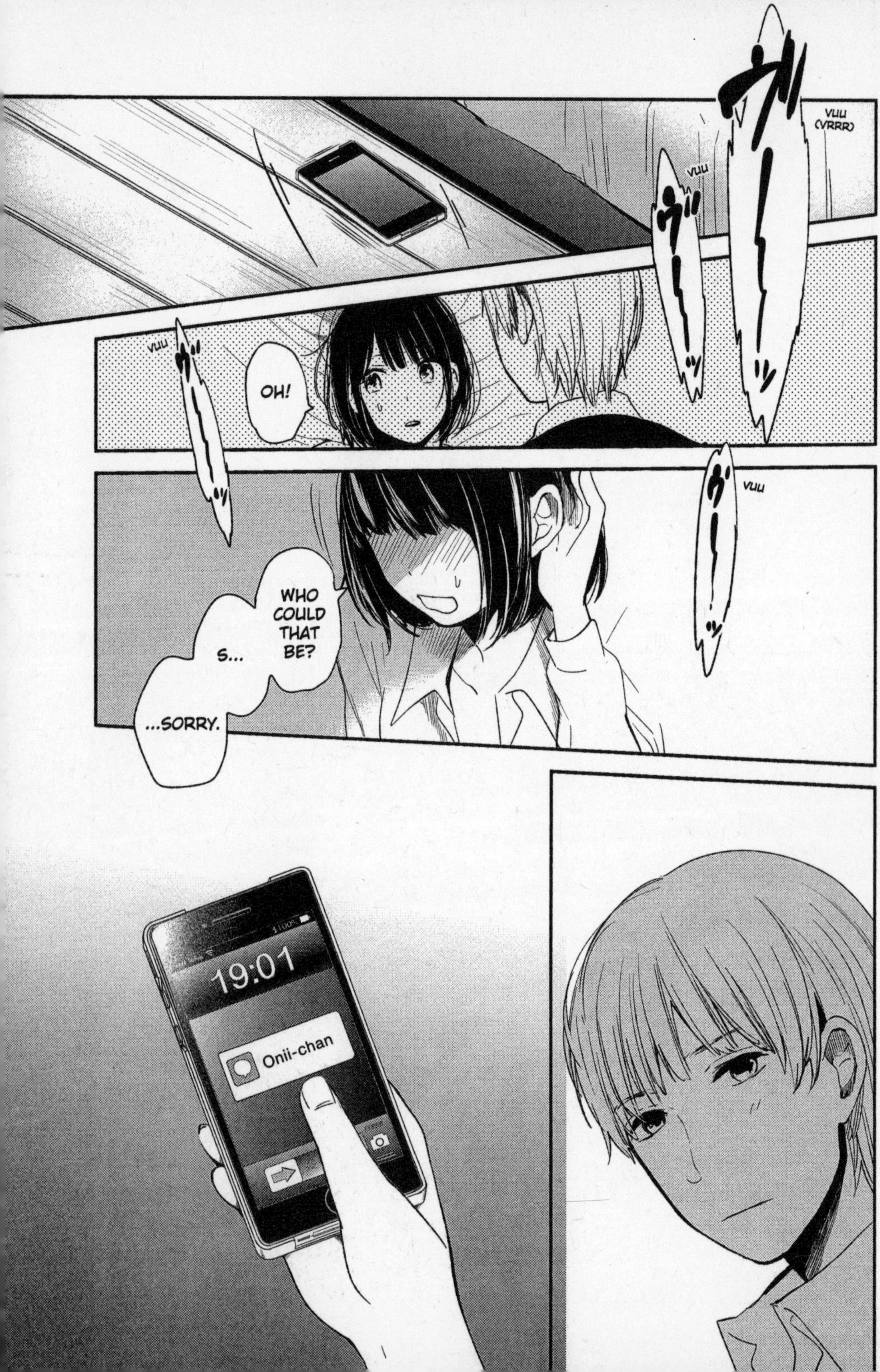
VUU (VRRR)
VUU
VUU
OH!
VUU
WHO COULD THAT BE?
S...
...SORRY.
19:01
Onii-chan

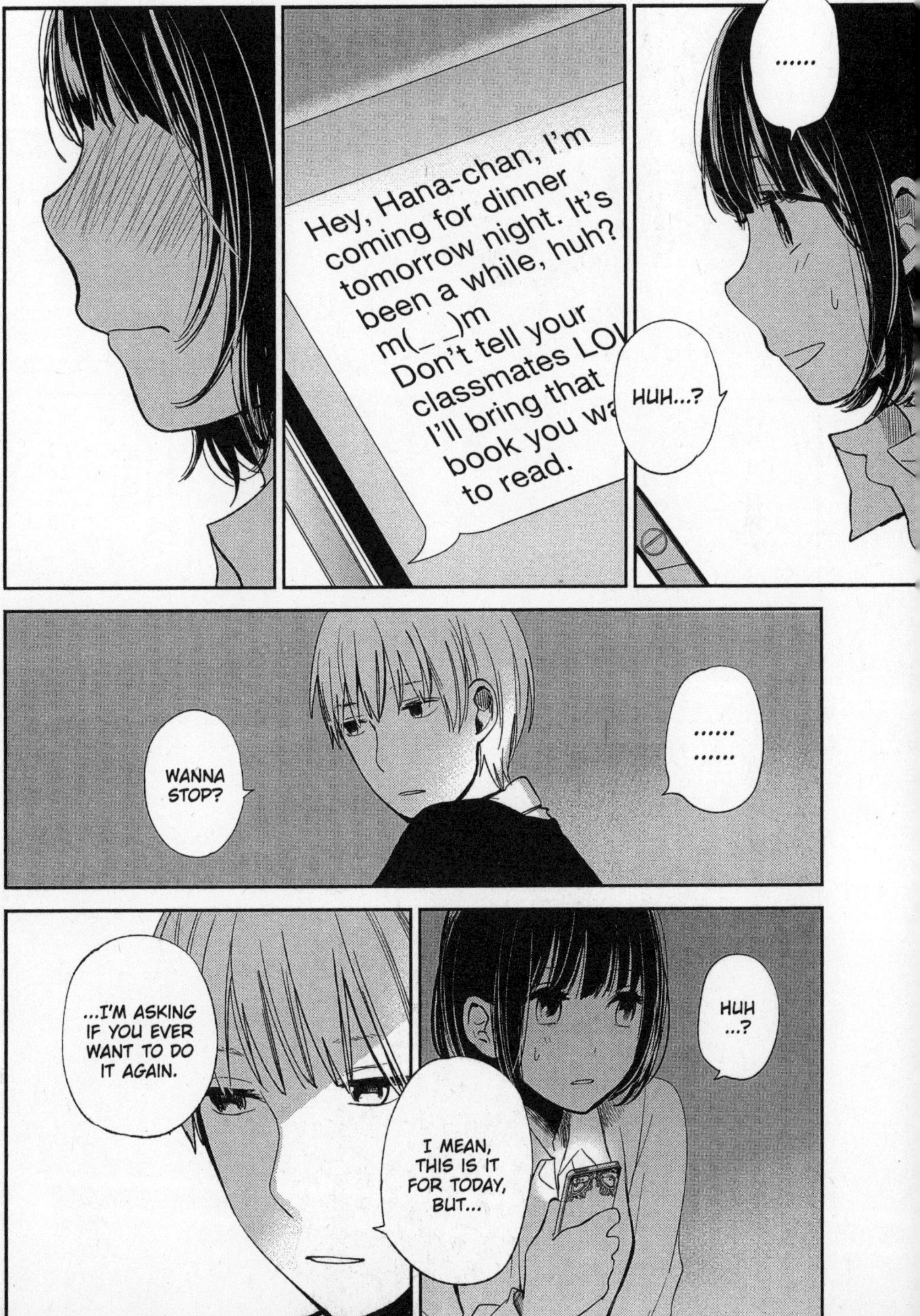
......
HUH...?
Hey, Hana-chan, I'm coming for dinner tomorrow night. It's been a while, huh? m(_ _)m Don't tell your classmates LO I'll bring that book you wa to read.
....
WANNA STOP?
HUH ...?
I MEAN, THIS IS IT FOR TODAY, BUT...
...I'M ASKING IF YOU EVER WANT TO DO IT AGAIN.

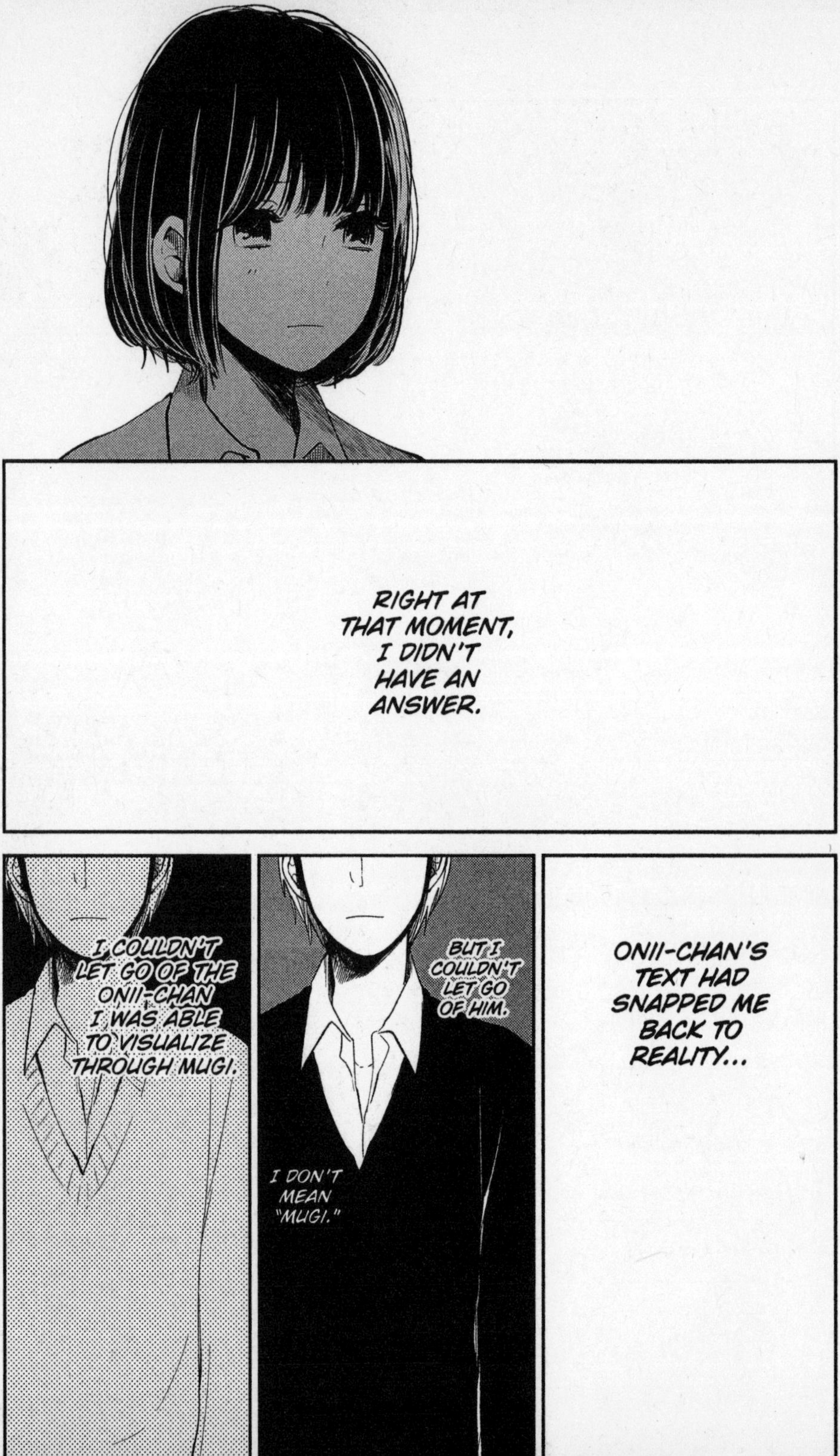
RIGHT AT THAT MOMENT, I DIDN'T HAVE AN ANSWER.
ONII-CHAN'S TEXT HAD SNAPPED ME BACK TO REALITY...
BUT I COULDN'T LET GO OF HIM.
I DON'T MEAN "MUGI."
I COULDN'T LET GO OF THE ONII-CHAN I WAS ABLE TO VISUALIZE THROUGH MUGI.

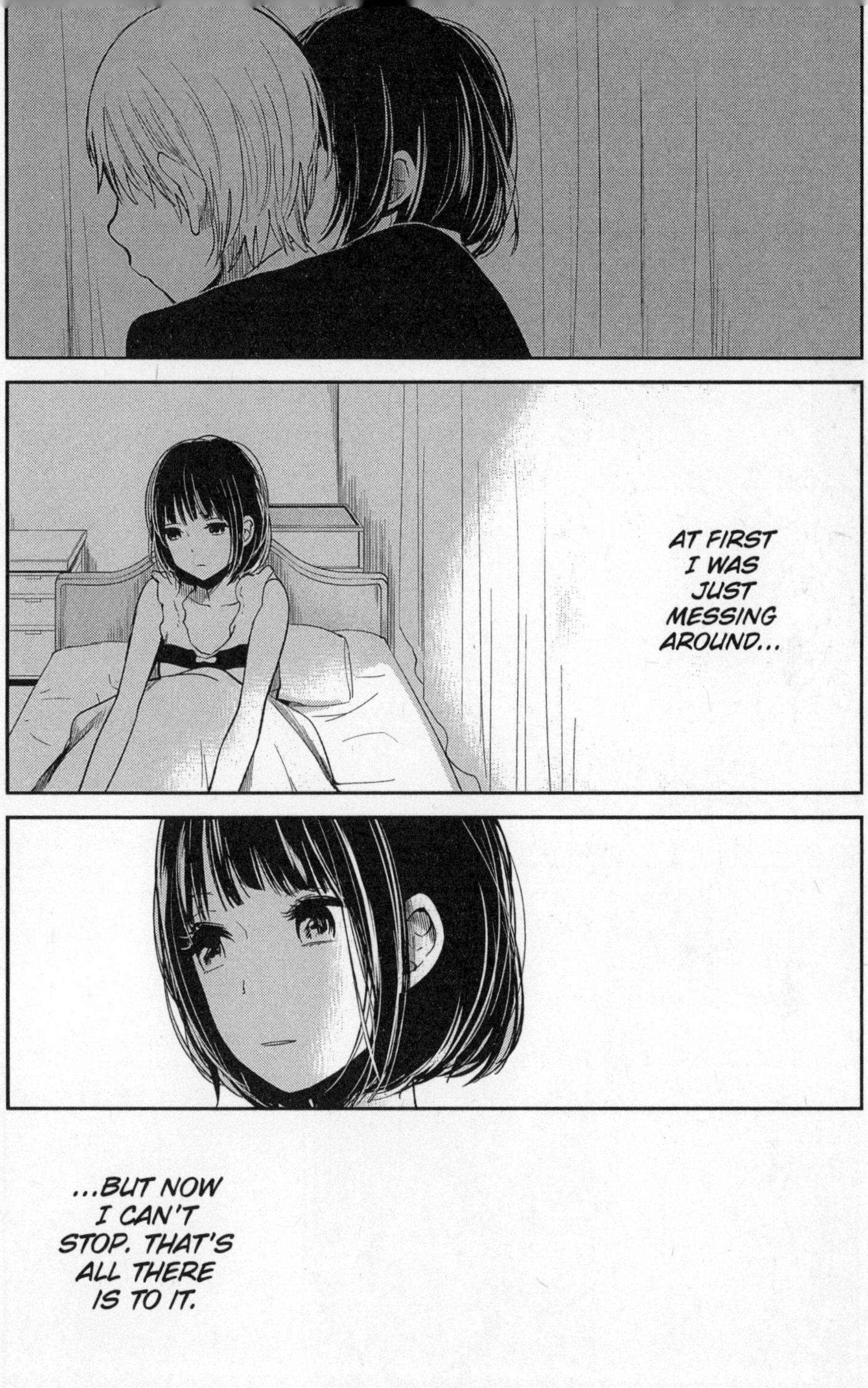
AT FIRST I WAS JUST MESSING AROUND...
...BUT NOW I CAN'T STOP. THAT'S ALL THERE IS TO IT.

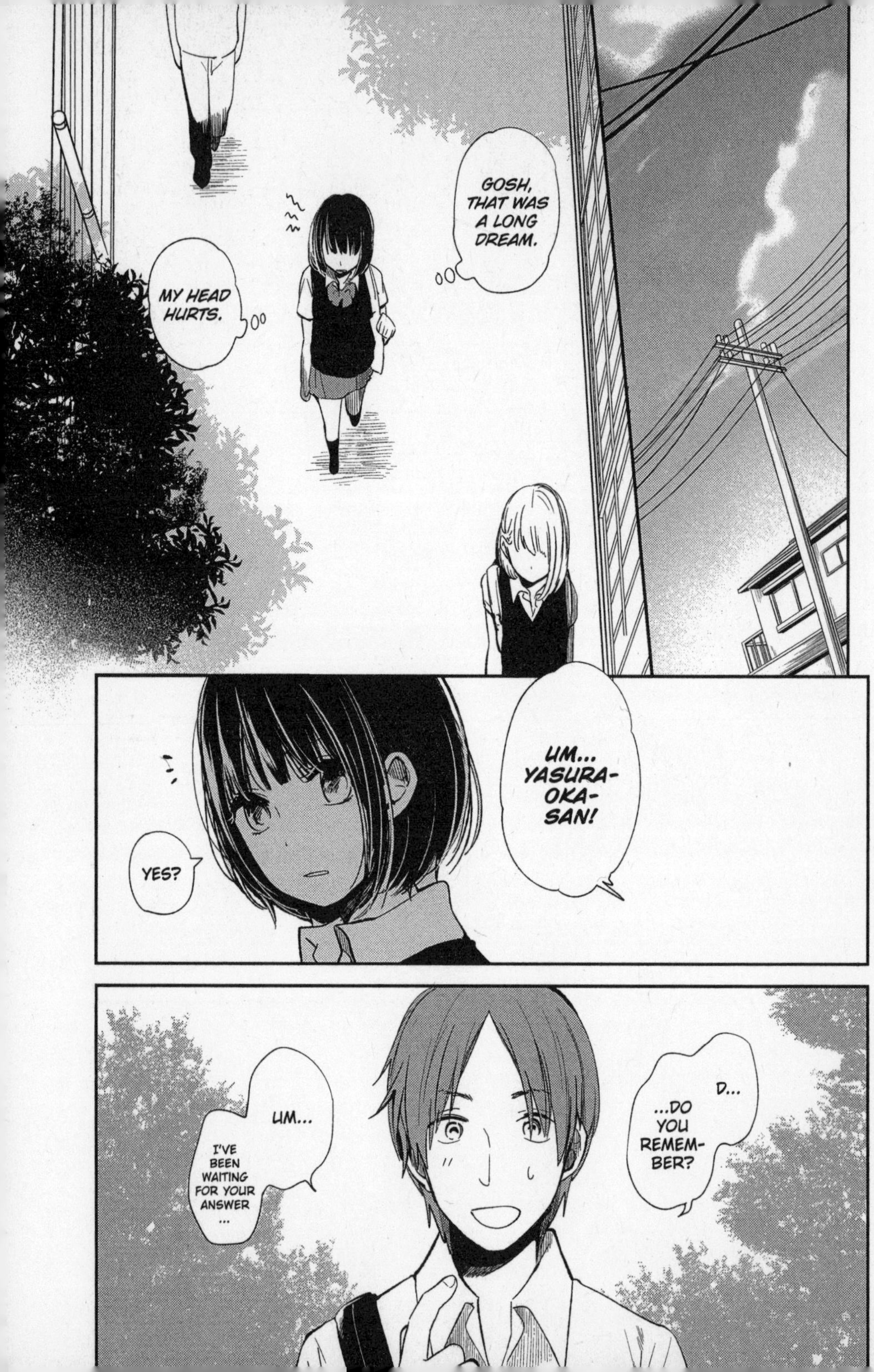
GOSH, THAT WAS A LONG DREAM.
MY HEAD HURTS.
UM... YASURA-OKA-SAN!
YES?
D... ...DO YOU REMEM-BER?
UM... I'VE BEEN WAITING FOR YOUR ANSWER ...

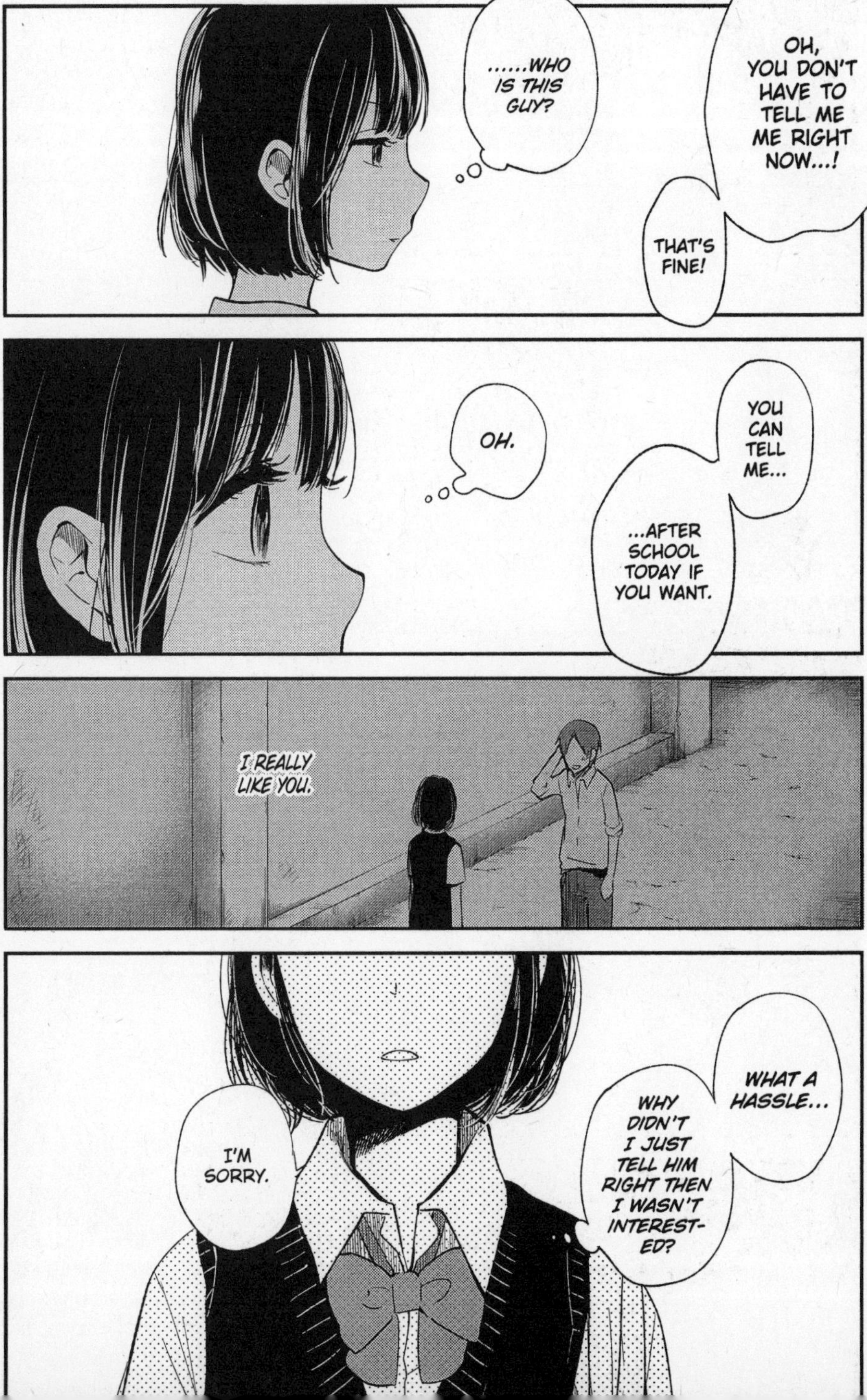
OH, YOU DON'T HAVE TO TELL ME ME RIGHT NOW...!
THAT'S FINE!
......WHO IS THIS GUY?
YOU CAN TELL ME...
...AFTER SCHOOL TODAY IF YOU WANT.
OH.
I REALLY LIKE YOU.
WHAT A HASSLE...
WHY DIDN'T I JUST TELL HIM RIGHT THEN I WASN'T INTEREST-ED?
I'M SORRY.

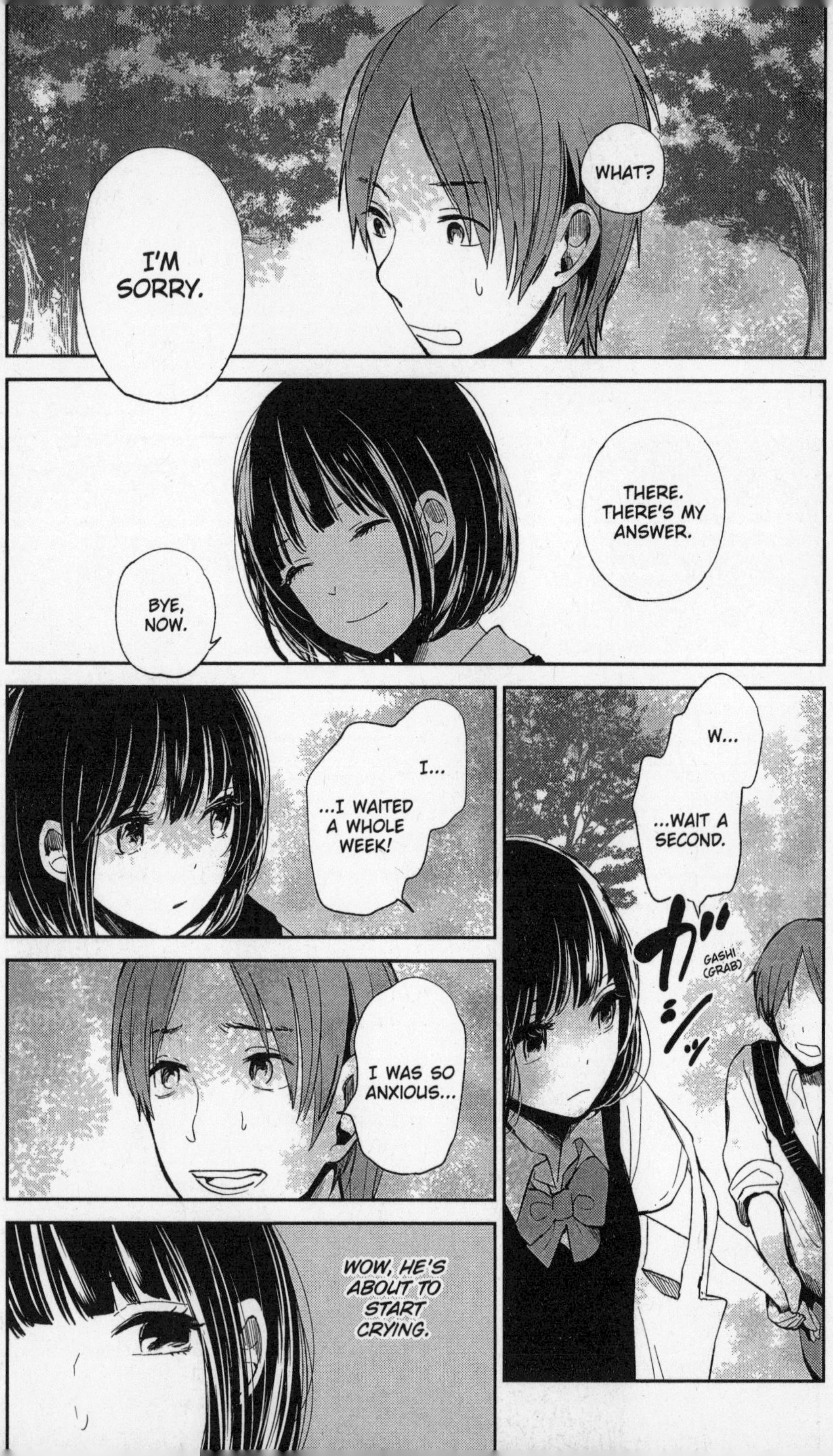
WHAT?
I'M SORRY.
THERE. THERE'S MY ANSWER.
BYE, NOW.
W...
...WAIT A SECOND.
GASHI (GRAB)
I...
...I WAITED A WHOLE WEEK!
I WAS SO ANXIOUS...
WOW, HE'S ABOUT TO START CRYING.

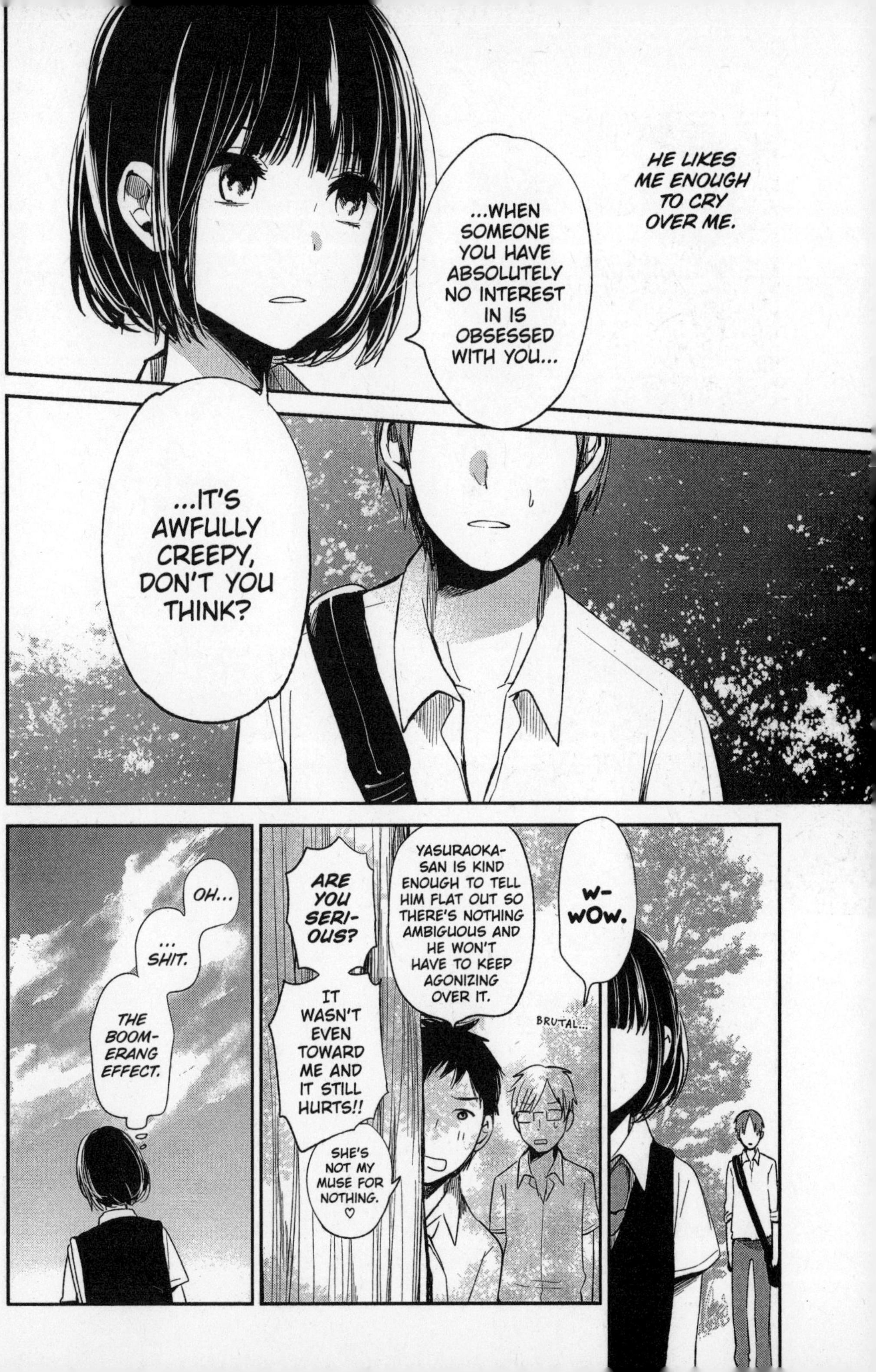
HE LIKES ME ENOUGH TO CRY OVER ME.
...WHEN SOMEONE YOU HAVE ABSOLUTELY NO INTEREST IN IS OBSESSED WITH YOU...
...IT'S AWFULLY CREEPY, DON'T YOU THINK?
W-WOW.
YASURAOKA-SAN IS KIND ENOUGH TO TELL HIM FLAT OUT SO THERE'S NOTHING AMBIGUOUS AND HE WON'T HAVE TO KEEP AGONIZING OVER IT.
BRUTAL...
ARE YOU SERI-OUS?
IT WASN'T EVEN TOWARD ME AND IT STILL HURTS!!
SHE'S NOT MY MUSE FOR NOTHING. ♡
OH...
...SHIT.
THE BOOM-ERANG EFFECT.

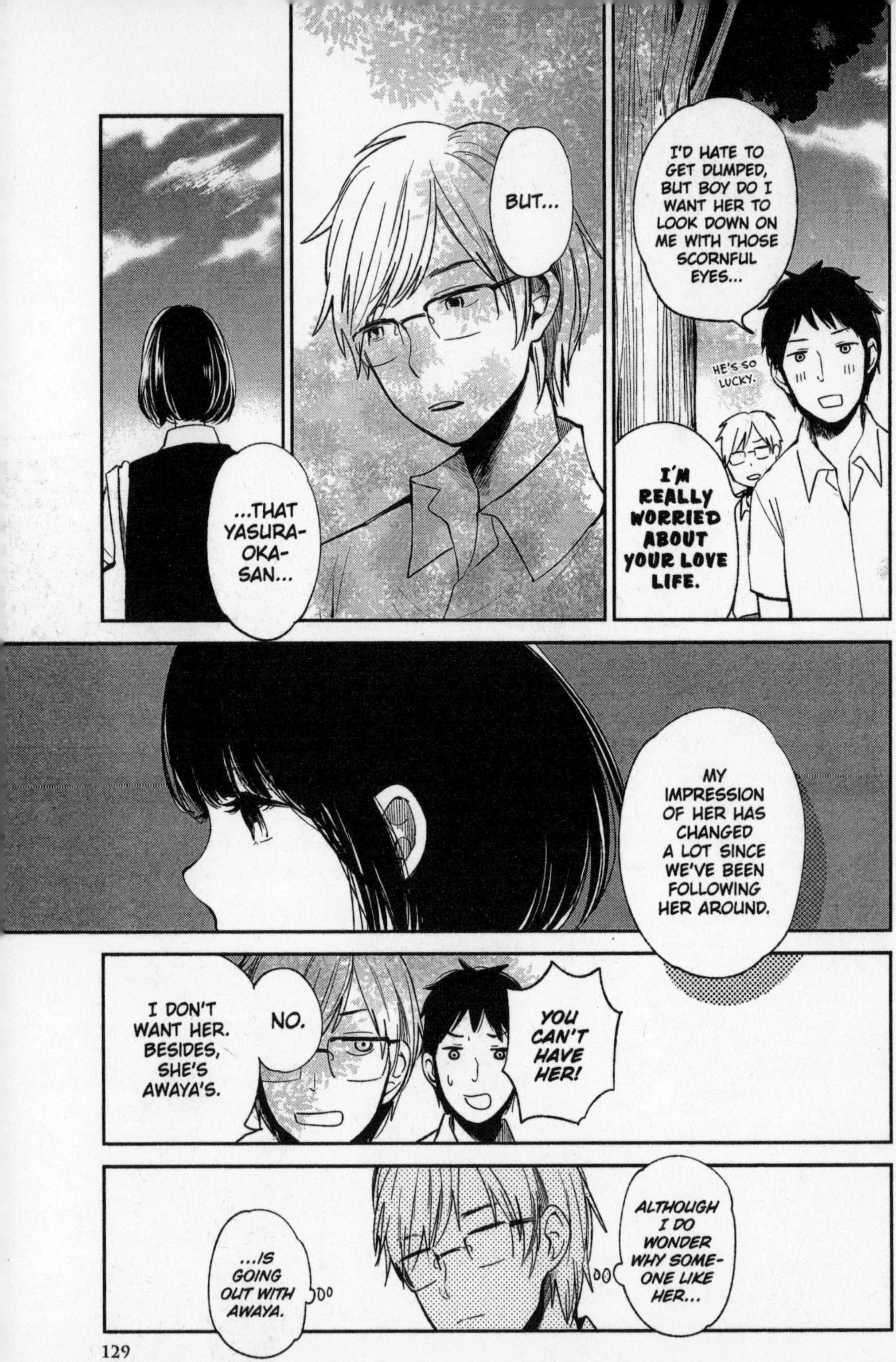
I'D HATE TO GET DUMPED, BUT BOY DO I WANT HER TO LOOK DOWN ON ME WITH THOSE SCORNFUL EYES...
HE'S SO LUCKY.
I'M REALLY WORRIED ABOUT YOUR LOVE LIFE.
BUT...
...THAT YASURA-OKA-SAN...
MY IMPRESSION OF HER HAS CHANGED A LOT SINCE WE'VE BEEN FOLLOWING HER AROUND.
YOU CAN'T HAVE HER!
NO.
I DON'T WANT HER. BESIDES, SHE'S AWAYA'S.
ALTHOUGH I DO WONDER WHY SOME-ONE LIKE HER...
...IS GOING OUT WITH AWAYA.

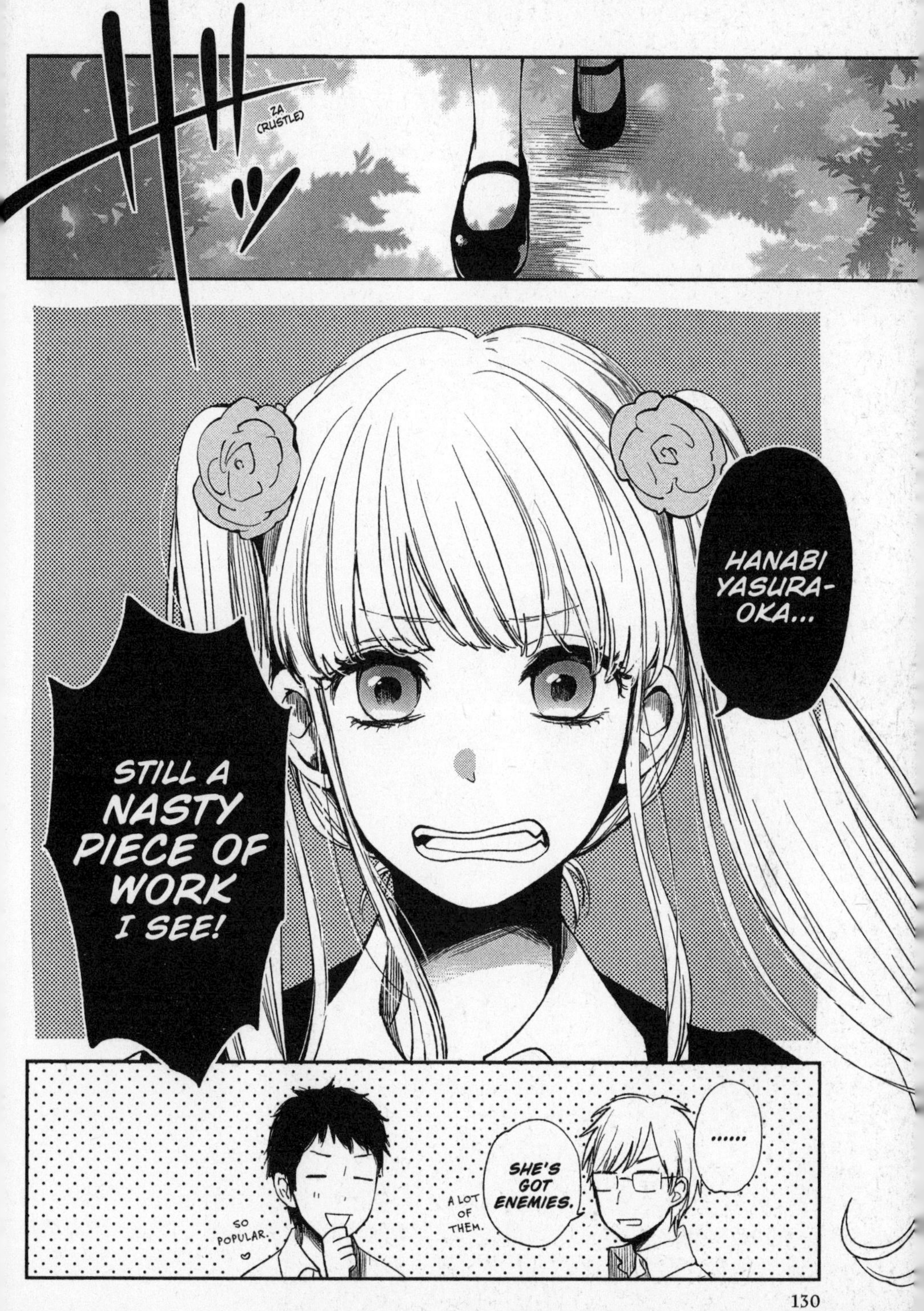
ZA (RUSTLE)
HANABI YASURA-OKA...
STILL A NASTY PIECE OF WORK I SEE!
......
SHE'S GOT ENEMIES.
A LOT OF THEM.
SO POPULAR.

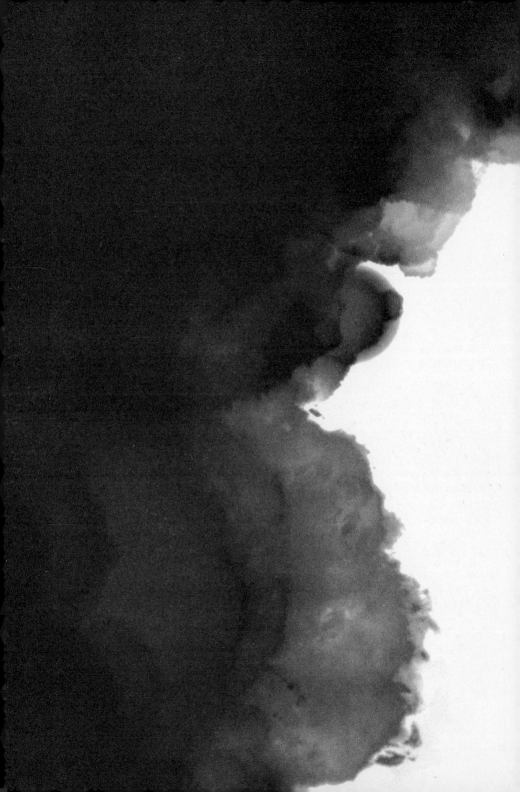

Scum's Wish

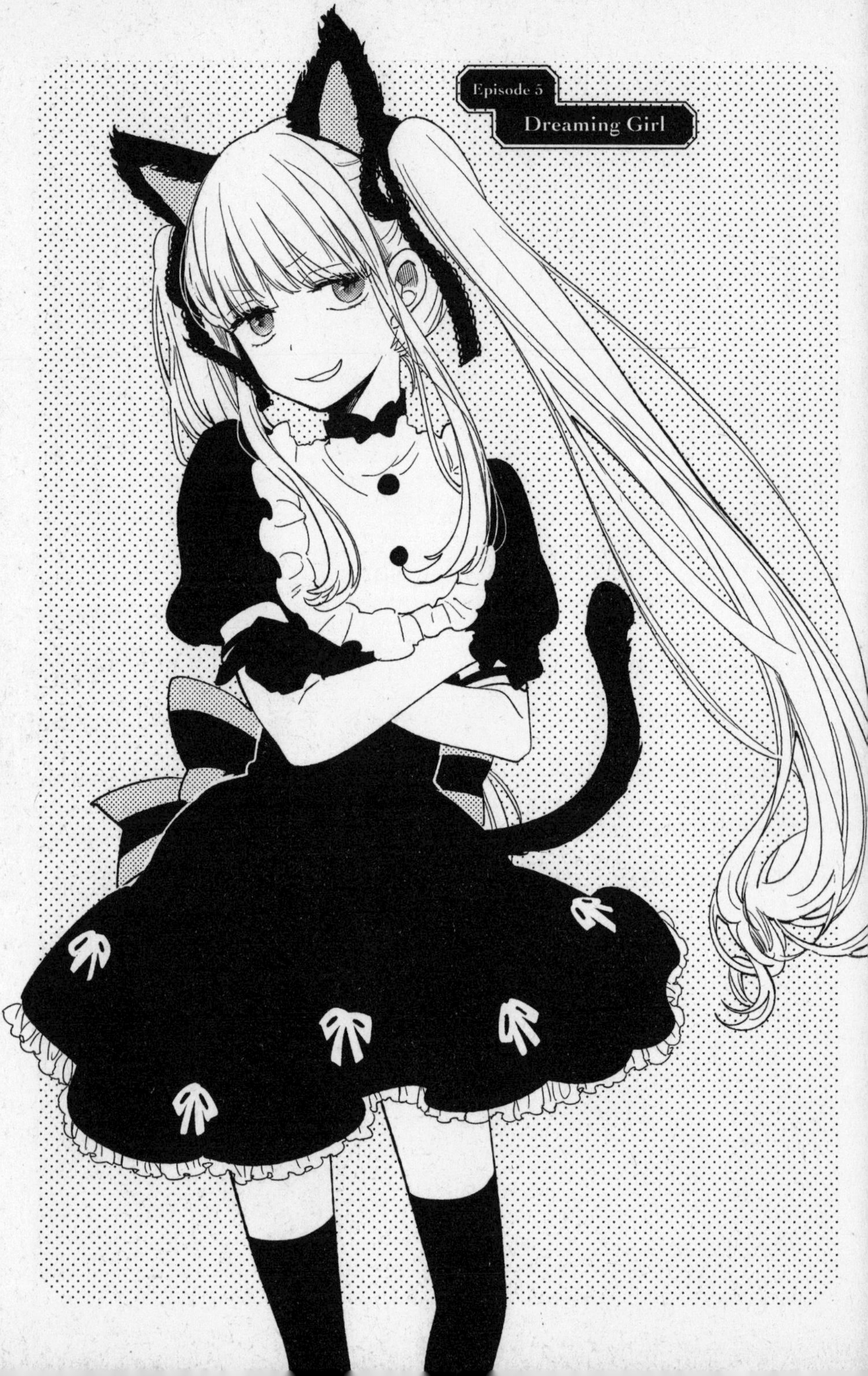
Episode 5
Dreaming Girl

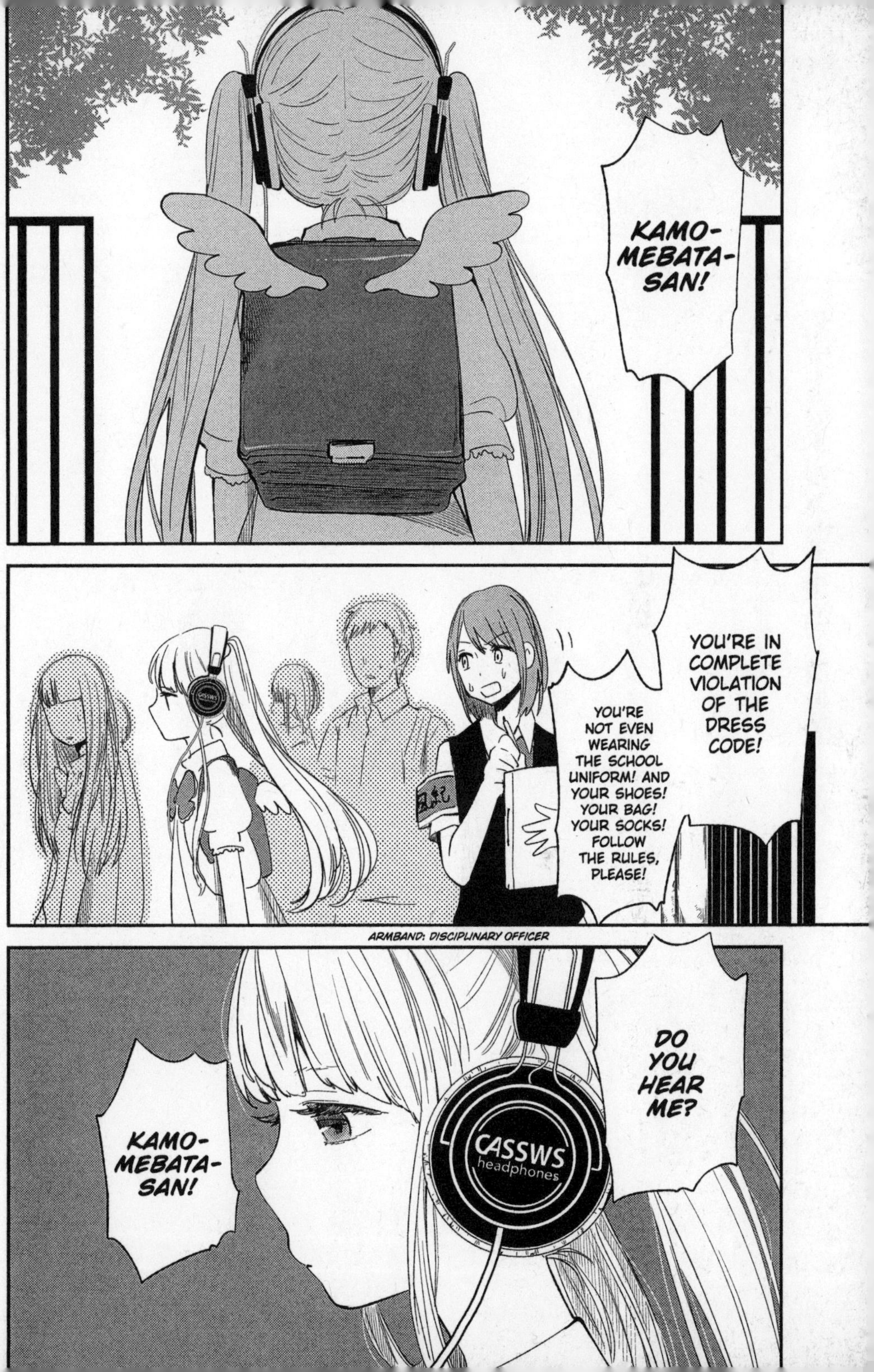
KAMO-MEBATA-SAN!
YOU'RE IN COMPLETE VIOLATION OF THE DRESS CODE!
YOU'RE NOT EVEN WEARING THE SCHOOL UNIFORM! AND YOUR SHOES! YOUR BAG! YOUR SOCKS! FOLLOW THE RULES, PLEASE!
CASSWS
ARMBAND: DISCIPLINARY OFFICER
DO YOU HEAR ME?
KAMO-MEBATA-SAN!
CASSWS headphones

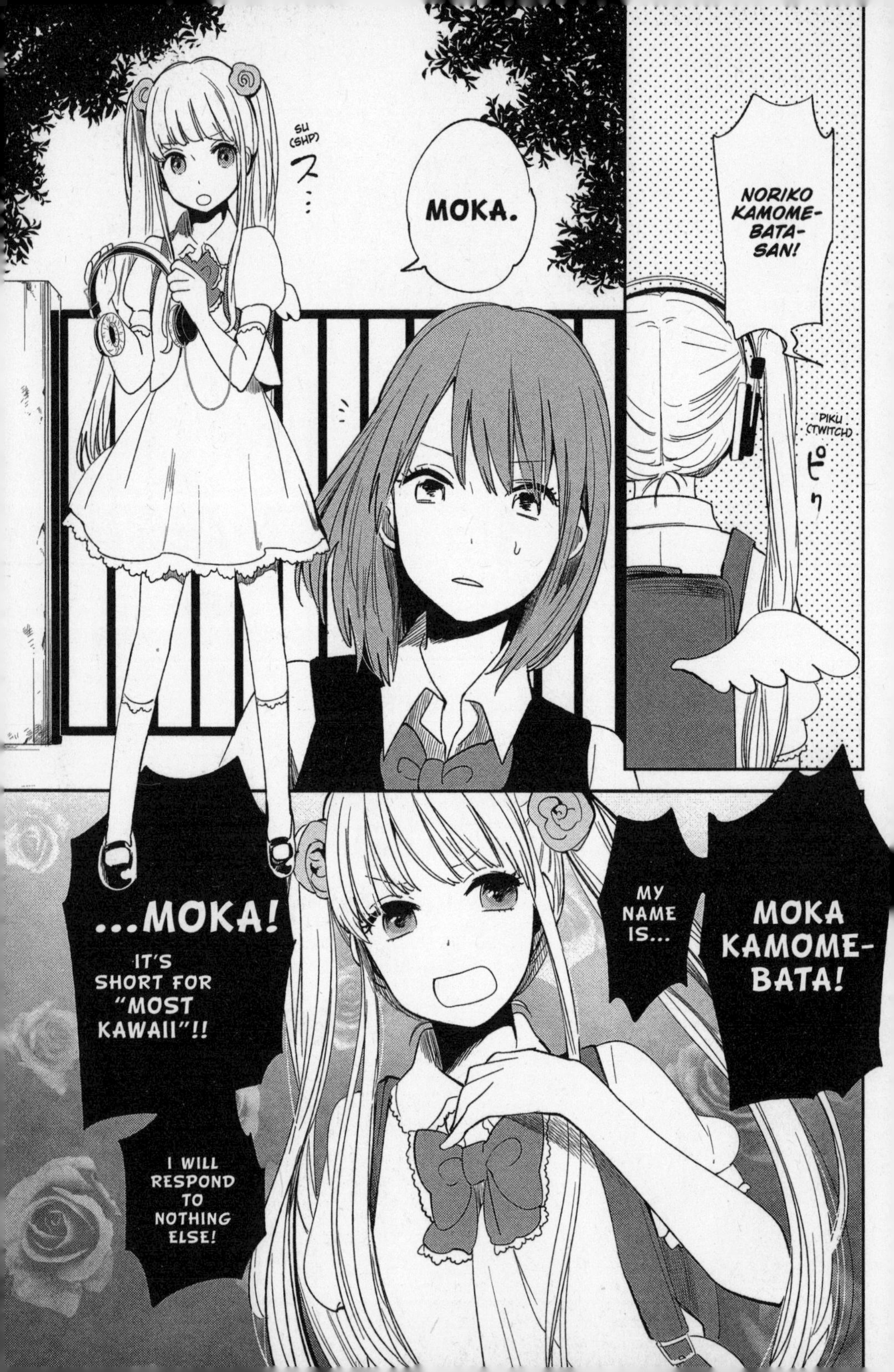

NORIKO KAMOME-BATA-SAN!
PIKU (TWITCH)
ピク
SU (SHP)
ス…
MOKA.
MY NAME IS...
MOKA KAMOME-BATA!
...MOKA!
IT'S SHORT FOR "MOST KAWAII"!!
I WILL RESPOND TO NOTHING ELSE!

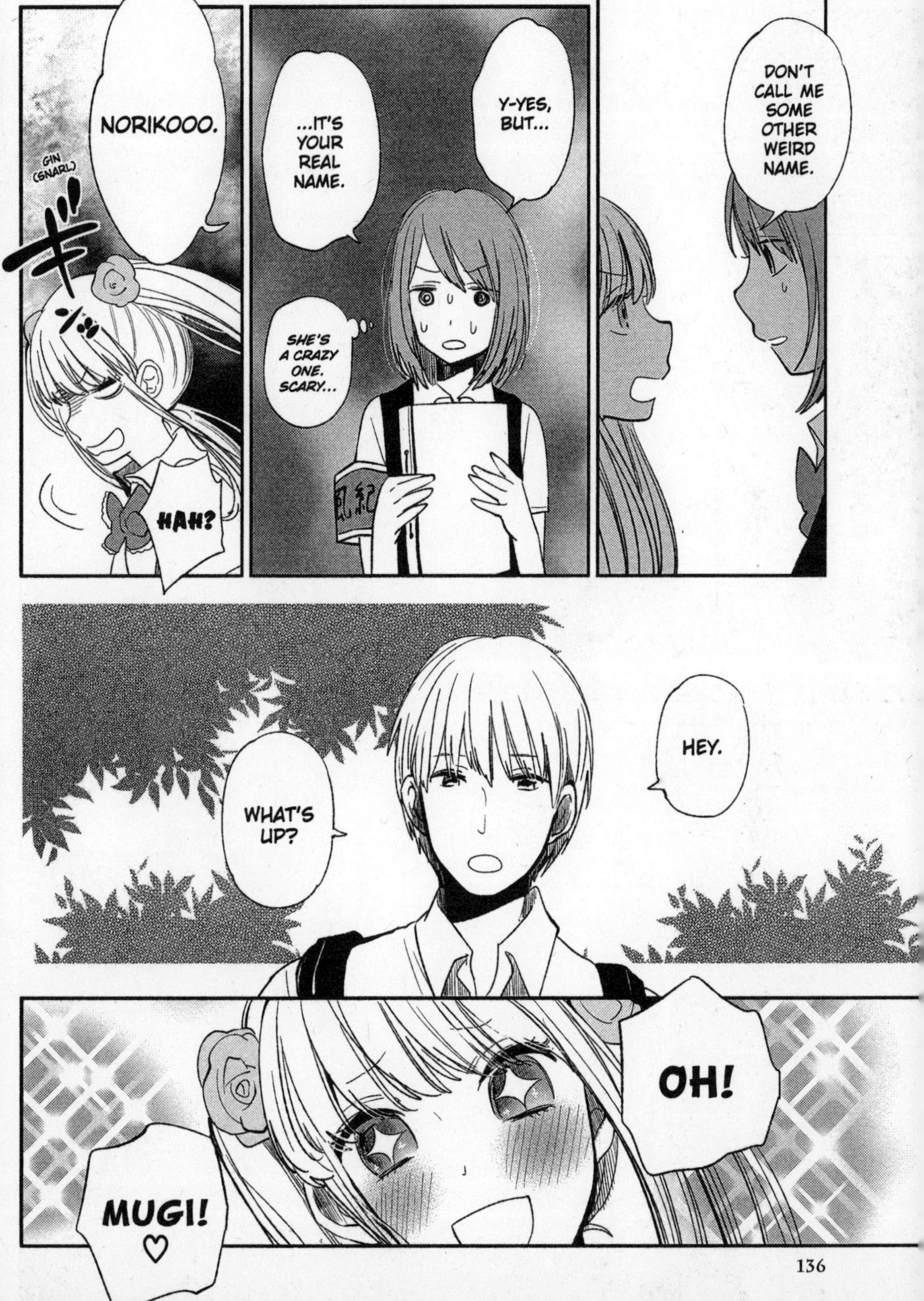

DON'T CALL ME SOME OTHER WEIRD NAME.
Y-YES, BUT...
...IT'S YOUR REAL NAME.
SHE'S A CRAZY ONE. SCARY...
NORIKOOO.
GIN (GNARL)
HAH?
HEY.
WHAT'S UP?
OH!
MUGI! ♡

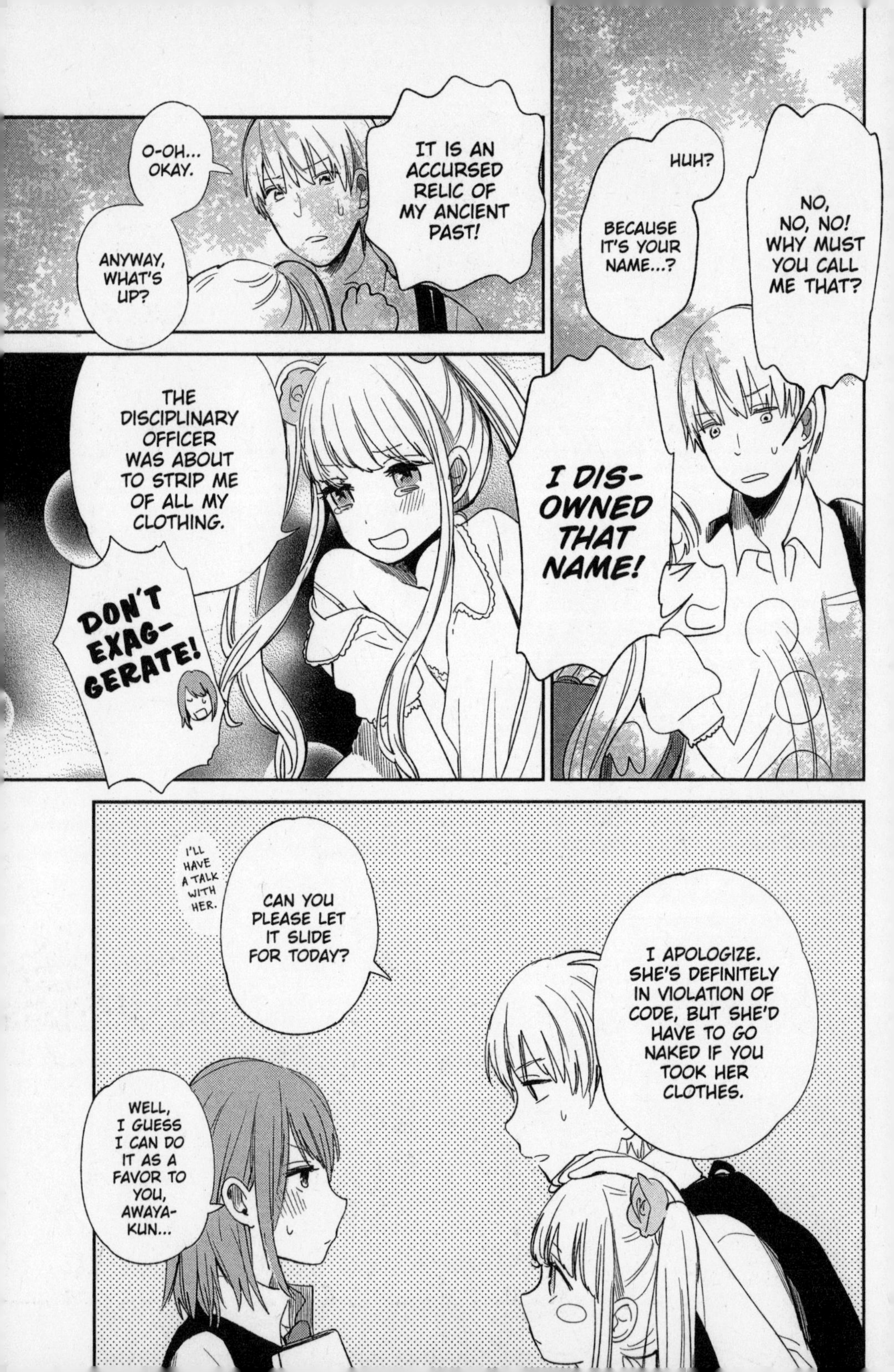
NO, NO, NO! WHY MUST YOU CALL ME THAT?
HUH?
BECAUSE IT'S YOUR NAME...?
I DIS-OWNED THAT NAME!
IT IS AN ACCURSED RELIC OF MY ANCIENT PAST!
O-OH... OKAY.
ANYWAY, WHAT'S UP?
THE DISCIPLINARY OFFICER WAS ABOUT TO STRIP ME OF ALL MY CLOTHING.
DON'T EXAG-GERATE!
I APOLOGIZE. SHE'S DEFINITELY IN VIOLATION OF CODE, BUT SHE'D HAVE TO GO NAKED IF YOU TOOK HER CLOTHES.
CAN YOU PLEASE LET IT SLIDE FOR TODAY?
I'LL HAVE A TALK WITH HER.
WELL, I GUESS I CAN DO IT AS A FAVOR TO YOU, AWAYA-KUN...

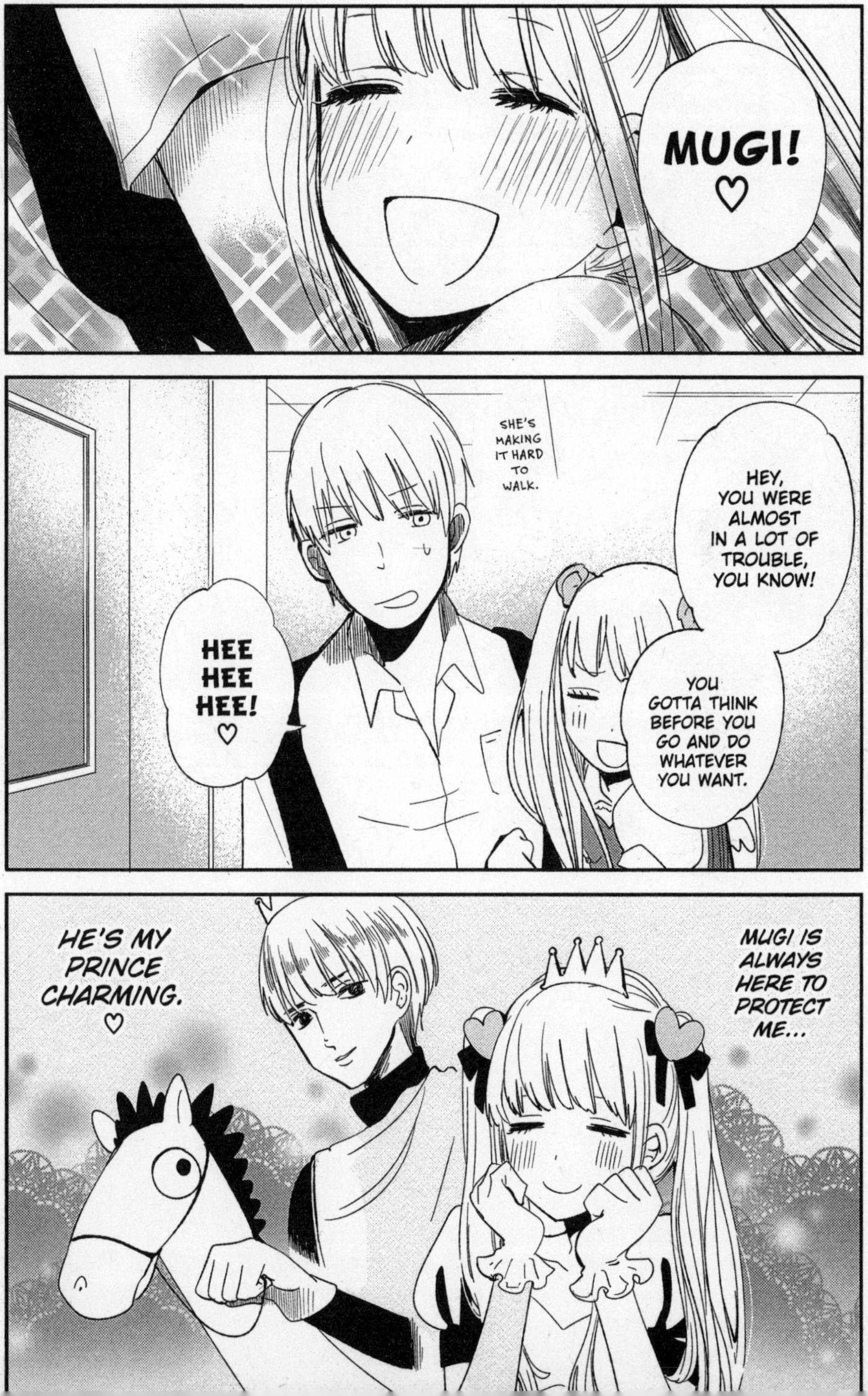
MUGI! ♡
HEY, YOU WERE ALMOST IN A LOT OF TROUBLE, YOU KNOW!
YOU GOTTA THINK BEFORE YOU GO AND DO WHATEVER YOU WANT.
SHE'S MAKING IT HARD TO WALK.
HEE HEE HEE! ♡
MUGI IS ALWAYS HERE TO PROTECT ME...
HE'S MY PRINCE CHARMING. ♡

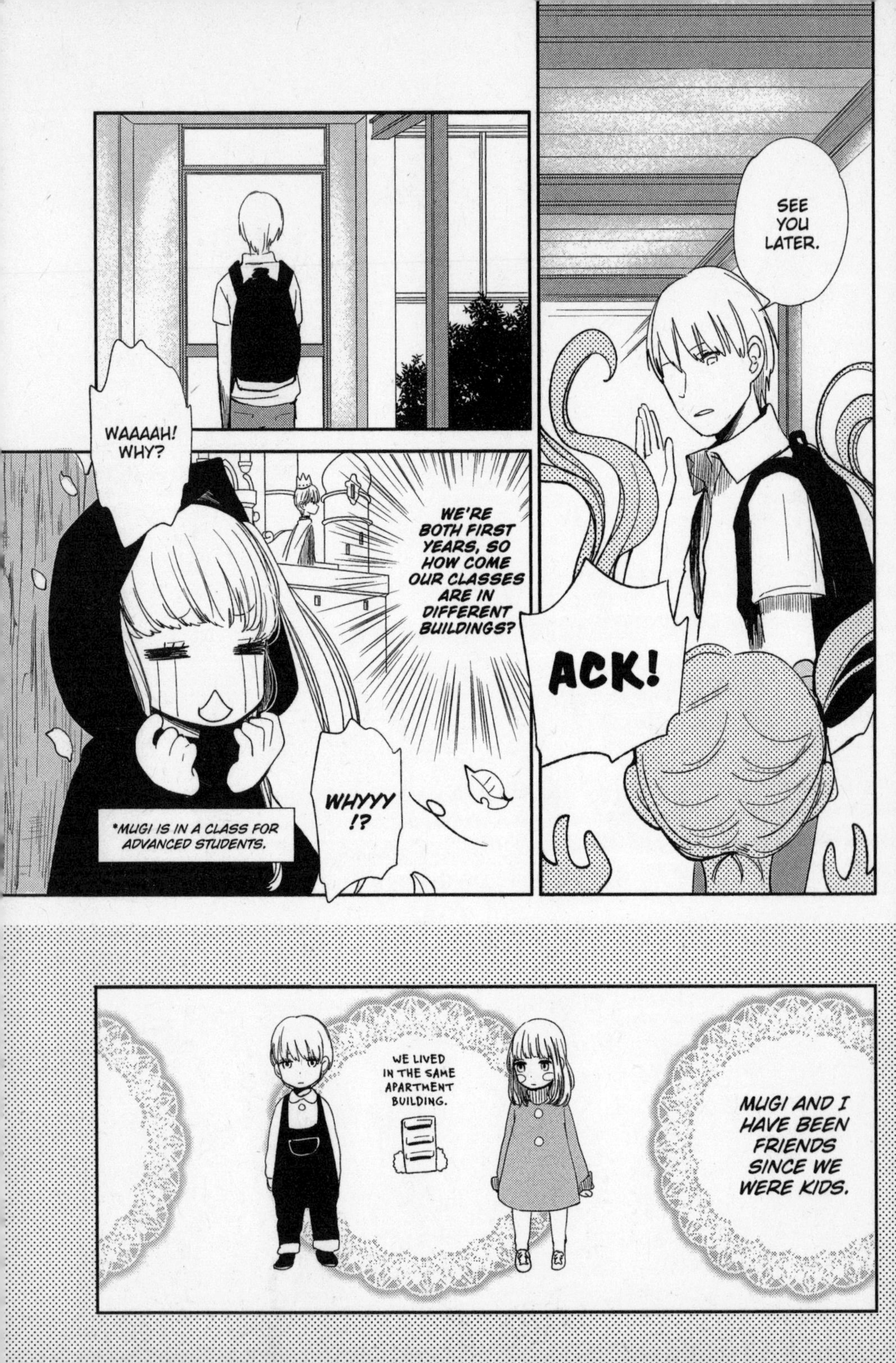
SEE YOU LATER.
ACK!
WAAAAH! WHY?
WE'RE BOTH FIRST YEARS, SO HOW COME OUR CLASSES ARE IN DIFFERENT BUILDINGS?
WHYYY!?
*MUGI IS IN A CLASS FOR ADVANCED STUDENTS.
MUGI AND I HAVE BEEN FRIENDS SINCE WE WERE KIDS.
WE LIVED IN THE SAME APARTMENT BUILDING.

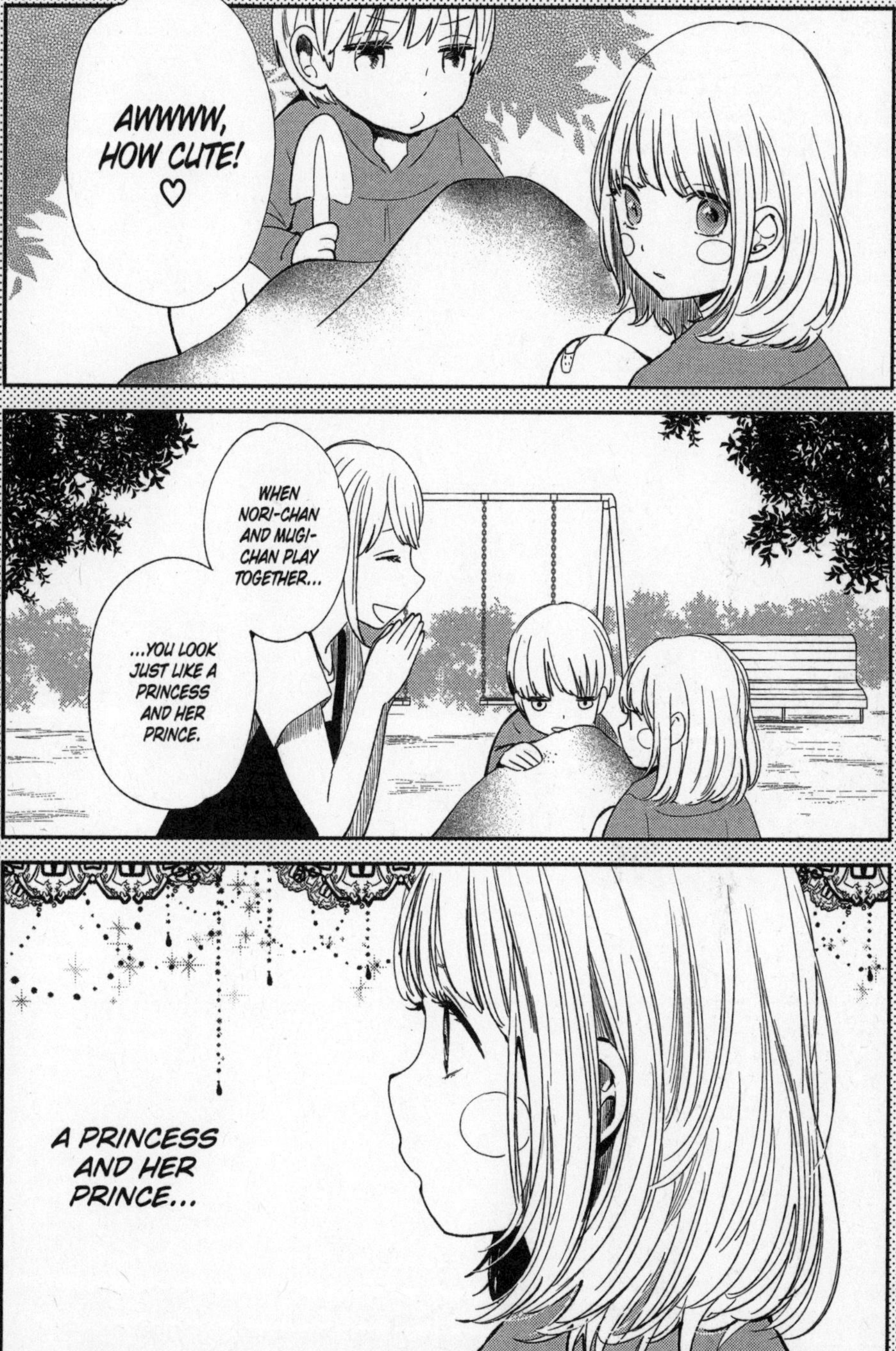
AWWWW, HOW CUTE! ♡
WHEN NORI-CHAN AND MUGI-CHAN PLAY TOGETHER...
...YOU LOOK JUST LIKE A PRINCESS AND HER PRINCE.
A PRINCESS AND HER PRINCE...

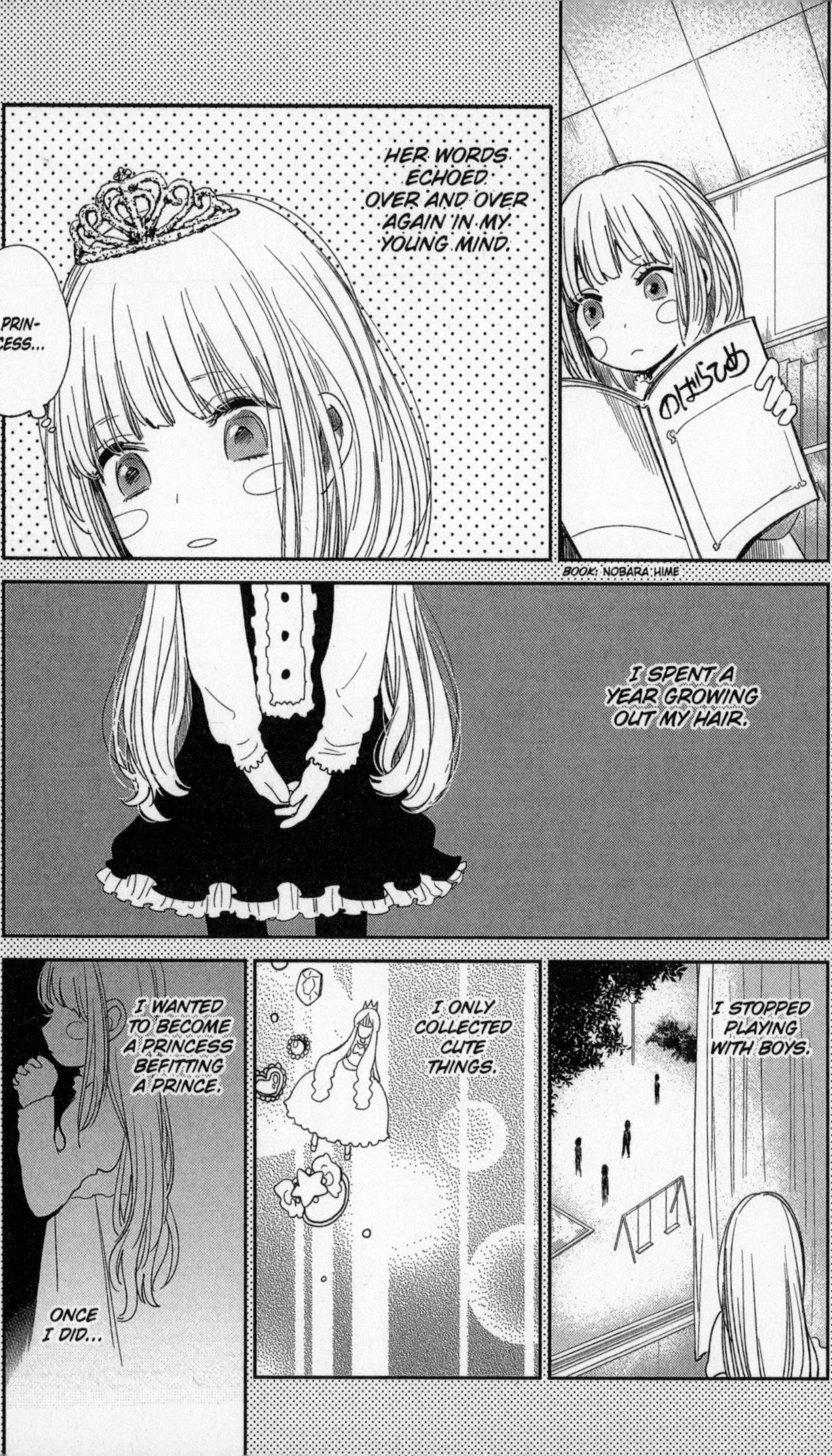
のばらひめ
BOOK: NOBARA HIME
HER WORDS ECHOED OVER AND OVER AGAIN IN MY YOUNG MIND.
PRIN-CESS...
I SPENT A YEAR GROWING OUT MY HAIR.
I STOPPED PLAYING WITH BOYS.
I ONLY COLLECTED CUTE THINGS.
I WANTED TO BECOME A PRINCESS BEFITTING A PRINCE.
ONCE I DID...

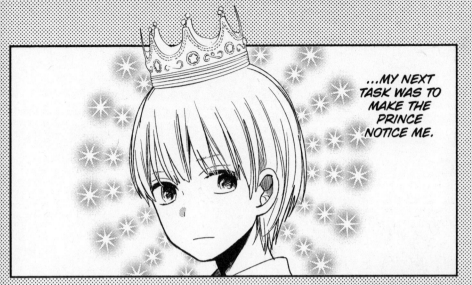

...MY NEXT TASK WAS TO MAKE THE PRINCE NOTICE ME.

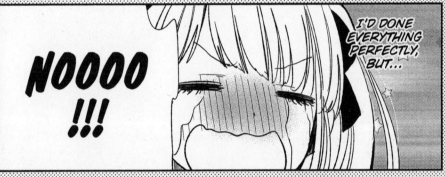

NOOOO !!!

I'D DONE EVERYTHING PERFECTLY, BUT...

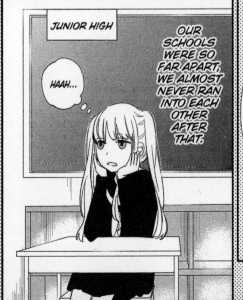

JUNIOR HIGH

HAAH...

OUR SCHOOLS WERE SO FAR APART, WE ALMOST NEVER RAN INTO EACH OTHER AFTER THAT.

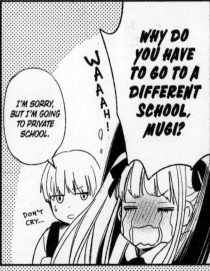

WHY DO YOU HAVE TO GO TO A DIFFERENT SCHOOL, MUGI?

WAAAH!

I'M SORRY, BUT I'M GOING TO PRIVATE SCHOOL.

DON'T CRY...

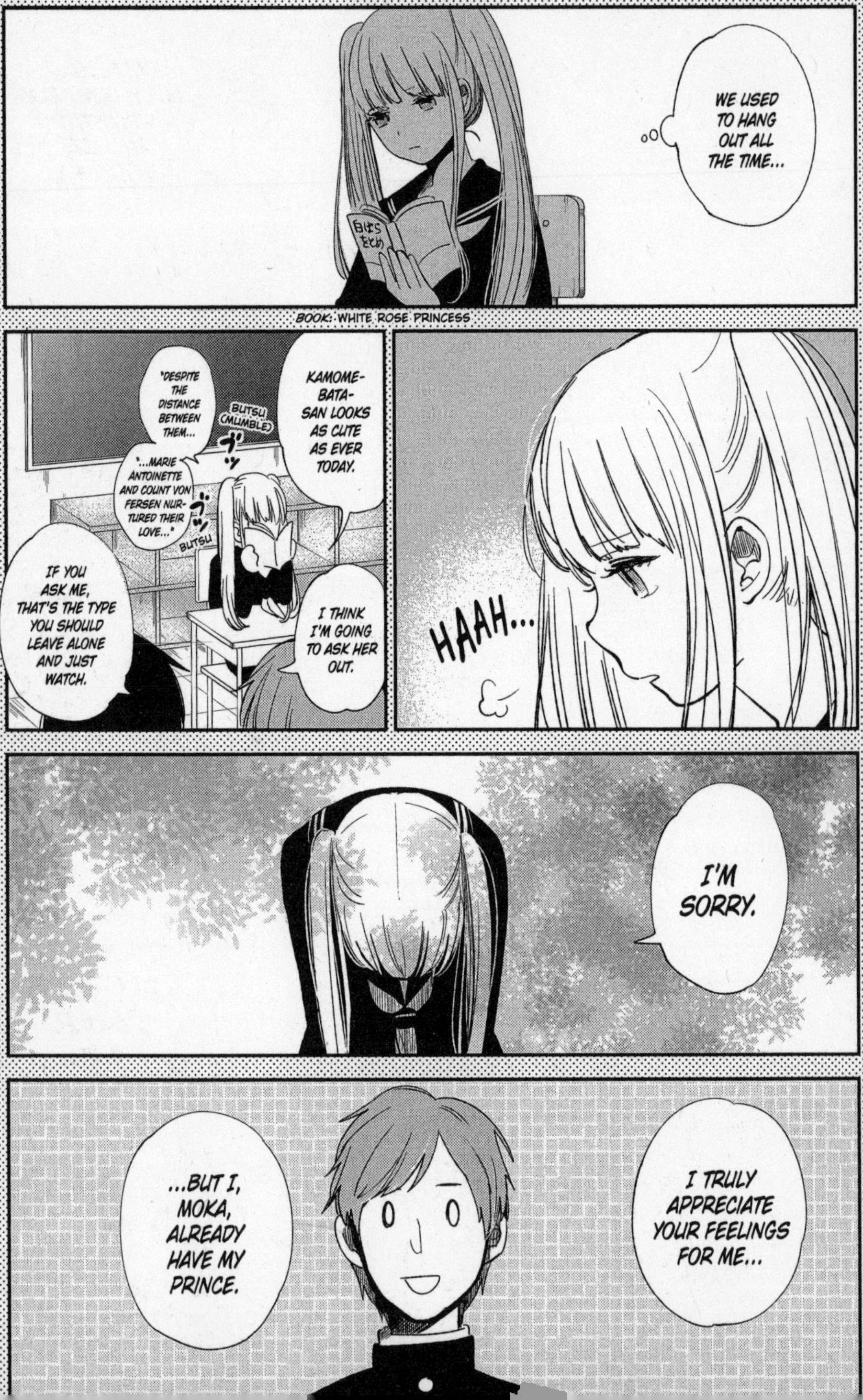
WE USED TO HANG OUT ALL THE TIME...
BOOK: WHITE ROSE PRINCESS
HAAH...
KAMOME-BATA-SAN LOOKS AS CUTE AS EVER TODAY.
"DESPITE THE DISTANCE BETWEEN THEM...
BUTSU (MUMBLE)
"...MARIE ANTOINETTE AND COUNT VON FERSEN NURTURED THEIR LOVE..."
BUTSU
I THINK I'M GOING TO ASK HER OUT.
IF YOU ASK ME, THAT'S THE TYPE YOU SHOULD LEAVE ALONE AND JUST WATCH.
I'M SORRY.
I TRULY APPRECIATE YOUR FEELINGS FOR ME...
...BUT I, MOKA, ALREADY HAVE MY PRINCE.

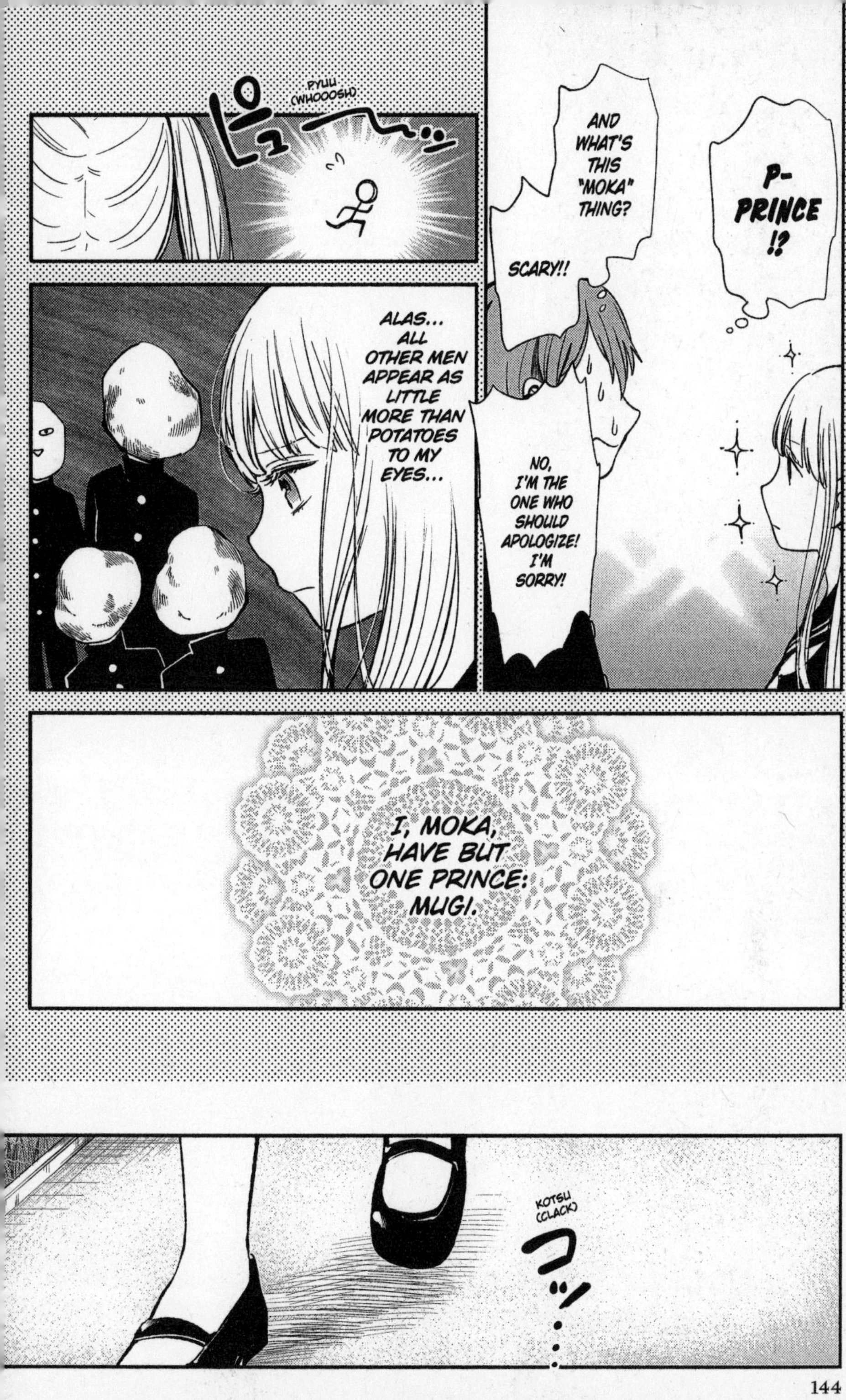
P-PRINCE!?
AND WHAT'S THIS "MOKA" THING?
SCARY!!
NO, I'M THE ONE WHO SHOULD APOLOGIZE! I'M SORRY!
PYUU (WHOOOSH)
ALAS... ALL OTHER MEN APPEAR AS LITTLE MORE THAN POTATOES TO MY EYES...
I, MOKA, HAVE BUT ONE PRINCE: MUGI.
KOTSU (CLACK)

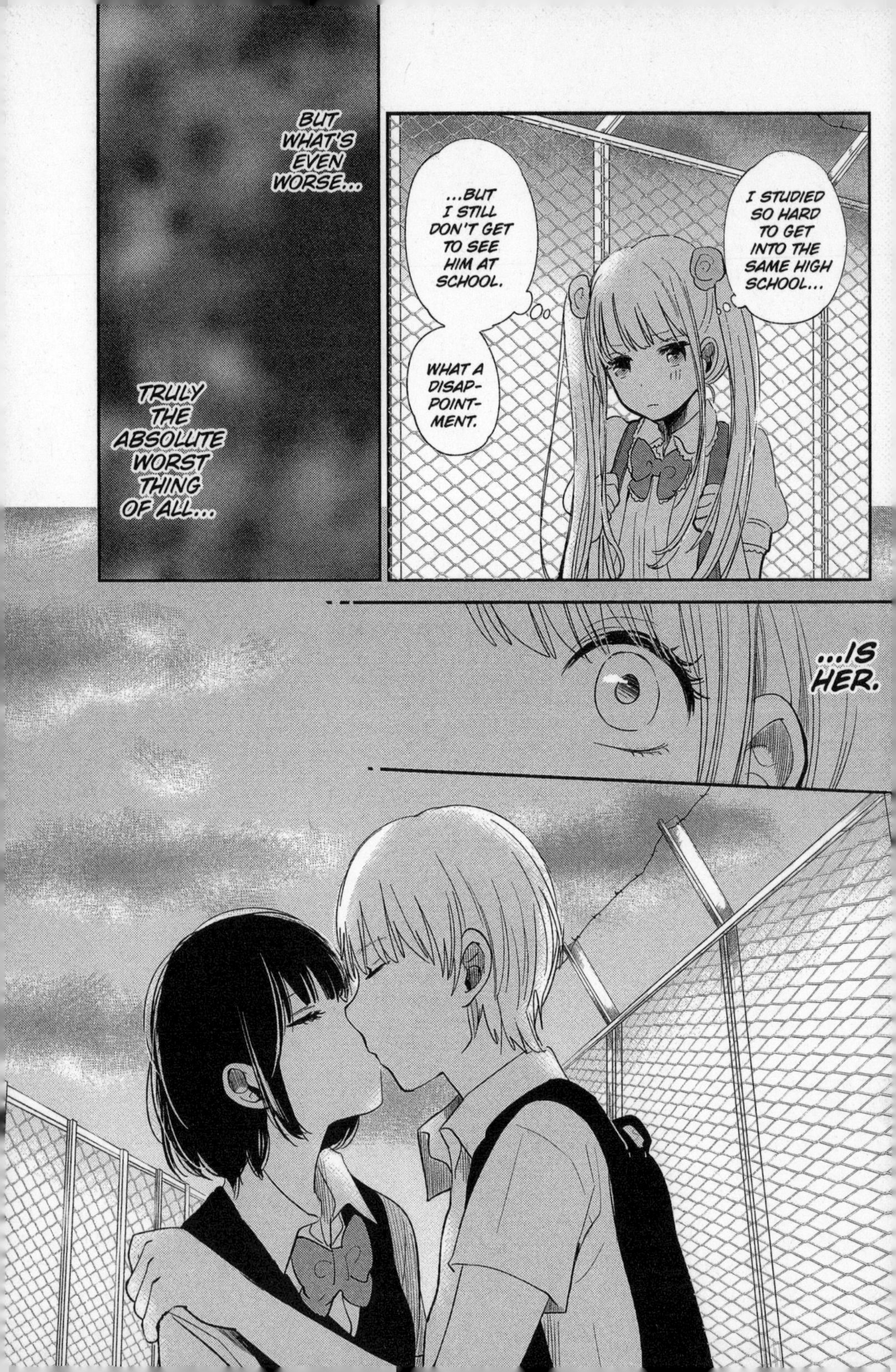
I STUDIED SO HARD TO GET INTO THE SAME HIGH SCHOOL...
...BUT I STILL DON'T GET TO SEE HIM AT SCHOOL.
WHAT A DISAPPOINTMENT.
BUT WHAT'S EVEN WORSE...
TRULY THE ABSOLUTE WORST THING OF ALL...
...IS HER.

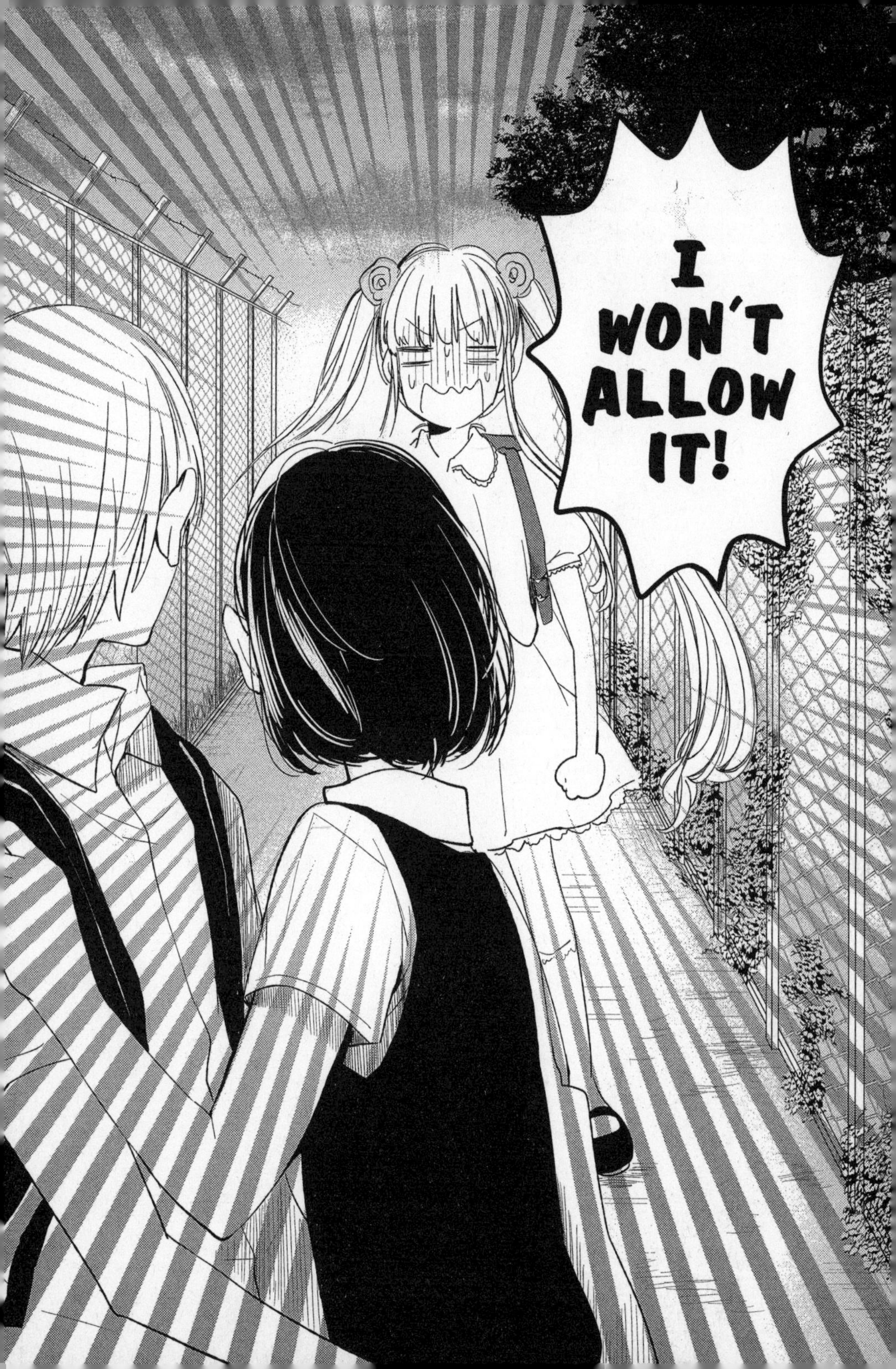
I WON'T ALLOW IT!

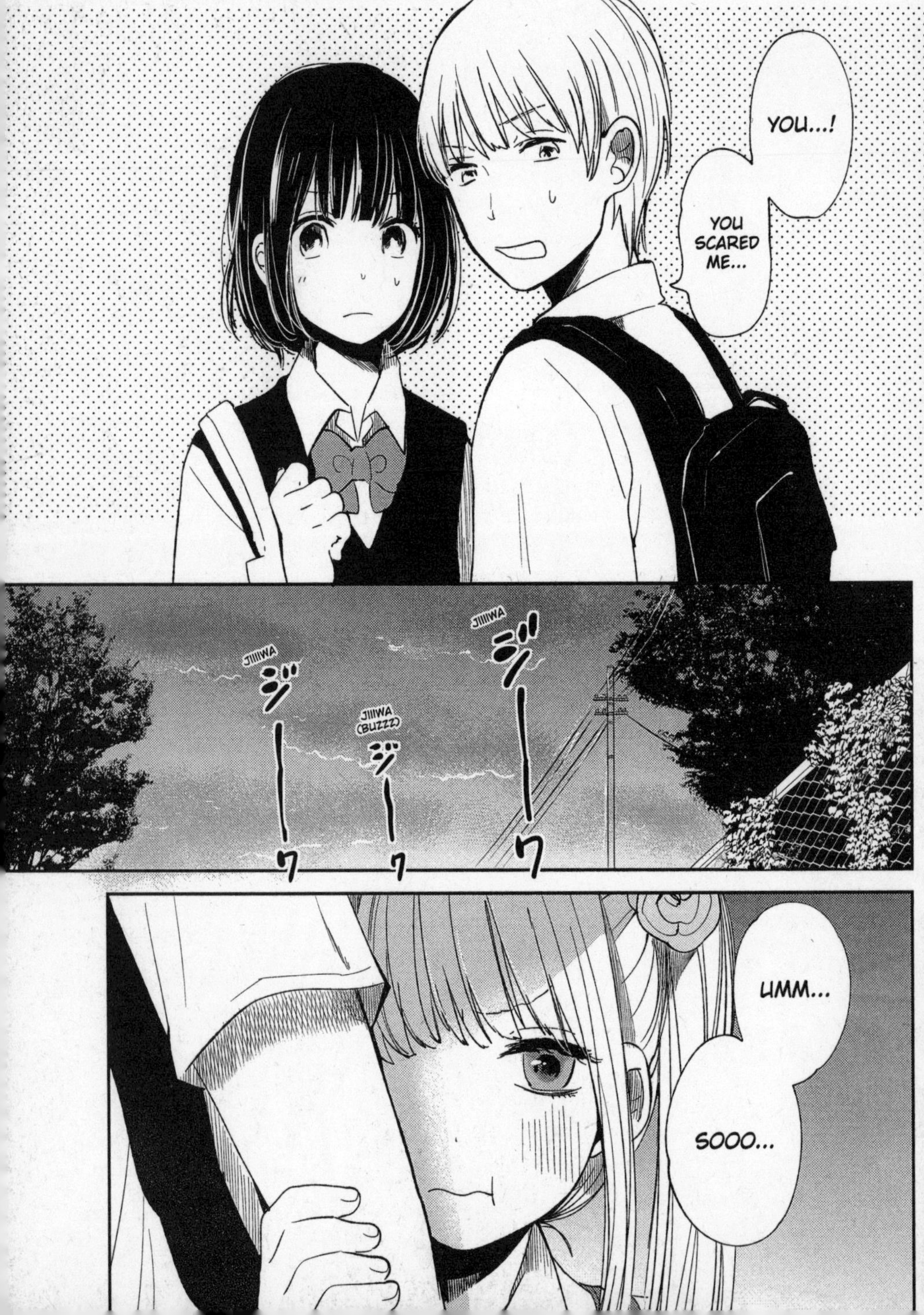
YOU...!
YOU SCARED ME...
JIIIWA
ジーワ
JIIIWA (BUZZZ)
ジーワ
JIIIWA
ジーワ
UMM...
SOOO...

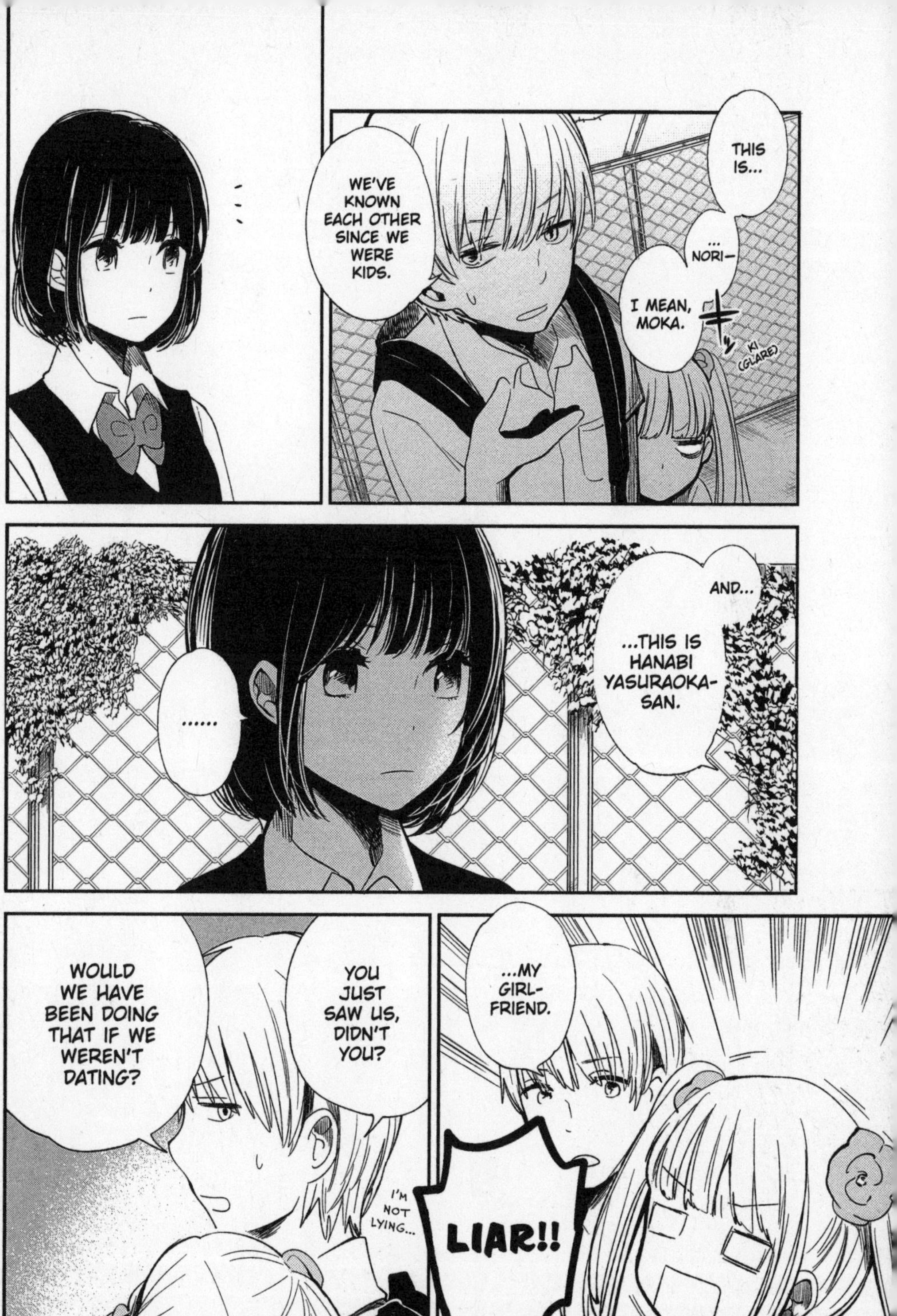
THIS IS...
... NORI—
I MEAN, MOKA.
KI (GLARE)
WE'VE KNOWN EACH OTHER SINCE WE WERE KIDS.
AND...
...THIS IS HANABI YASURAOKA-SAN.
......
...MY GIRL-FRIEND.
LIAR!!
YOU JUST SAW US, DIDN'T YOU?
WOULD WE HAVE BEEN DOING THAT IF WE WEREN'T DATING?
I'M NOT LYING...

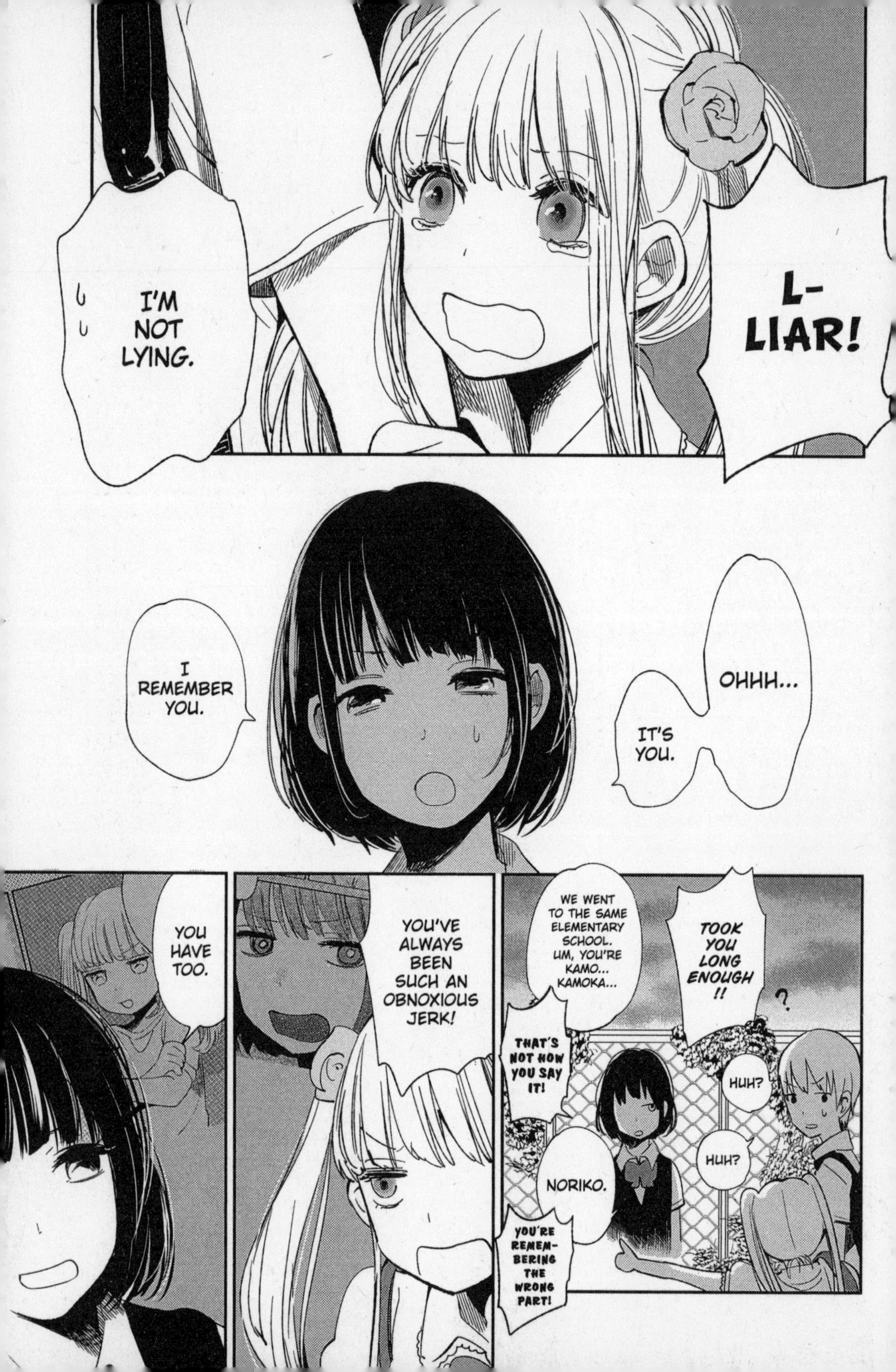
L-LIAR!
I'M NOT LYING.
OHHH... IT'S YOU.
I REMEMBER YOU.
TOOK YOU LONG ENOUGH!!
WE WENT TO THE SAME ELEMENTARY SCHOOL. UM, YOU'RE KAMO... KAMOKA...
?
HUH?
THAT'S NOT HOW YOU SAY IT!
HUH?
NORIKO.
YOU'RE REMEMBERING THE WRONG PART!
YOU'VE ALWAYS BEEN SUCH AN OBNOXIOUS JERK!
YOU HAVE TOO.

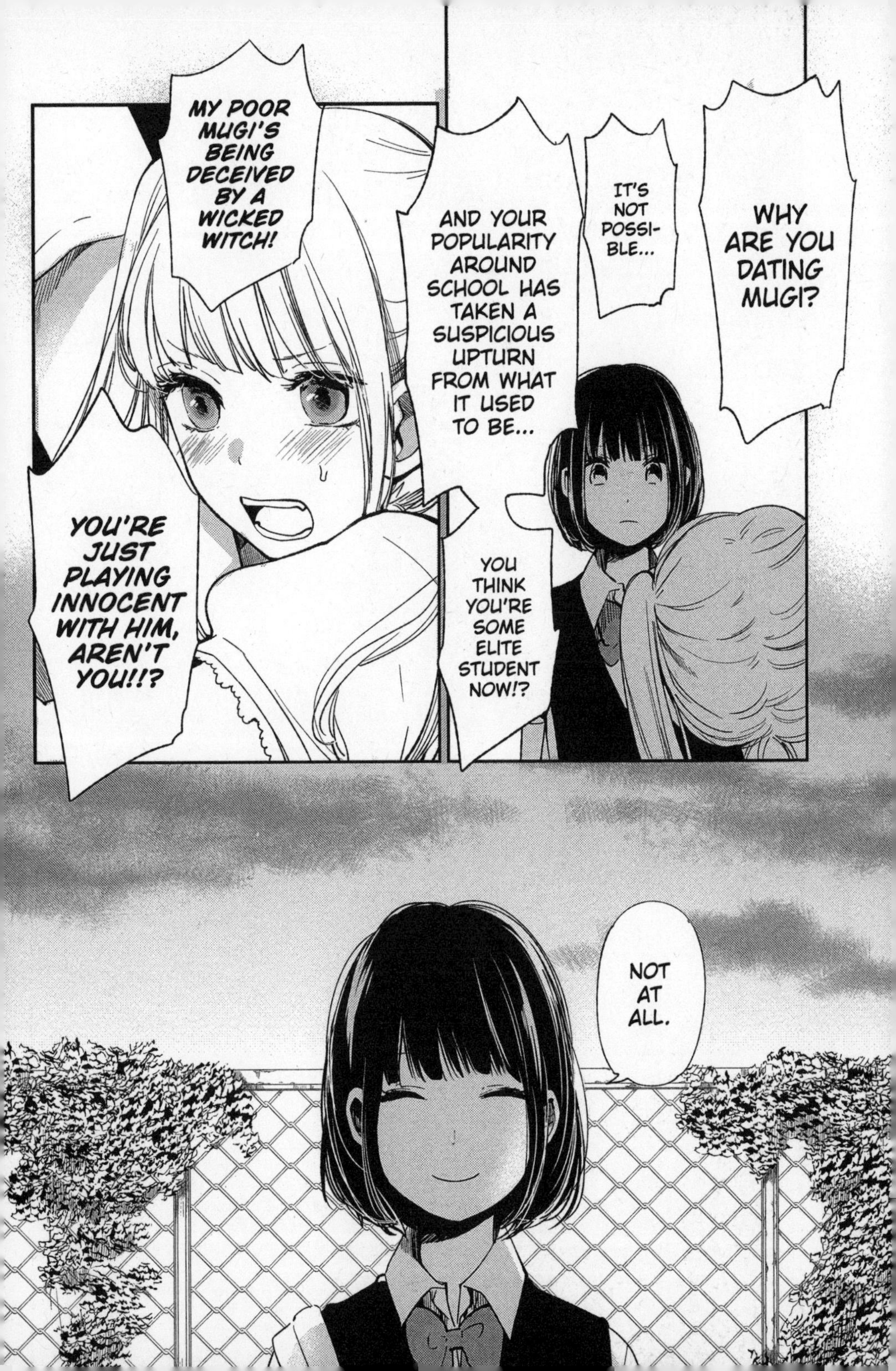
WHY ARE YOU DATING MUGI?
IT'S NOT POSSIBLE...
AND YOUR POPULARITY AROUND SCHOOL HAS TAKEN A SUSPICIOUS UPTURN FROM WHAT IT USED TO BE...
YOU THINK YOU'RE SOME ELITE STUDENT NOW!?
MY POOR MUGI'S BEING DECEIVED BY A WICKED WITCH!
YOU'RE JUST PLAYING INNOCENT WITH HIM, AREN'T YOU!!?
NOT AT ALL.

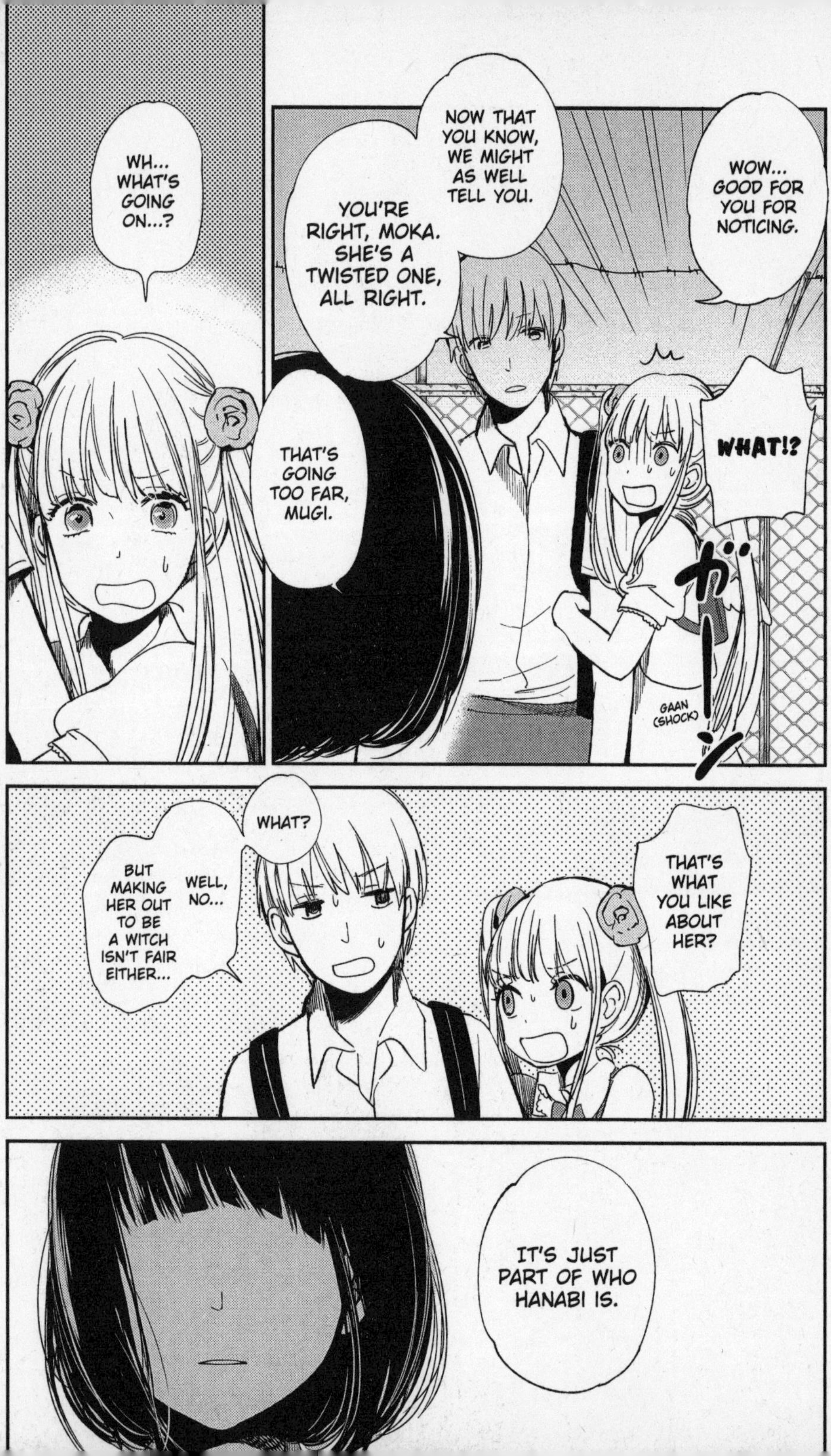
WOW... GOOD FOR YOU FOR NOTICING.
NOW THAT YOU KNOW, WE MIGHT AS WELL TELL YOU.
YOU'RE RIGHT, MOKA. SHE'S A TWISTED ONE, ALL RIGHT.
WHAT!?
GAAN (SHOCK)
THAT'S GOING TOO FAR, MUGI.
WH... WHAT'S GOING ON...?
THAT'S WHAT YOU LIKE ABOUT HER?
WHAT?
WELL, NO...
BUT MAKING HER OUT TO BE A WITCH ISN'T FAIR EITHER...
IT'S JUST PART OF WHO HANABI IS.

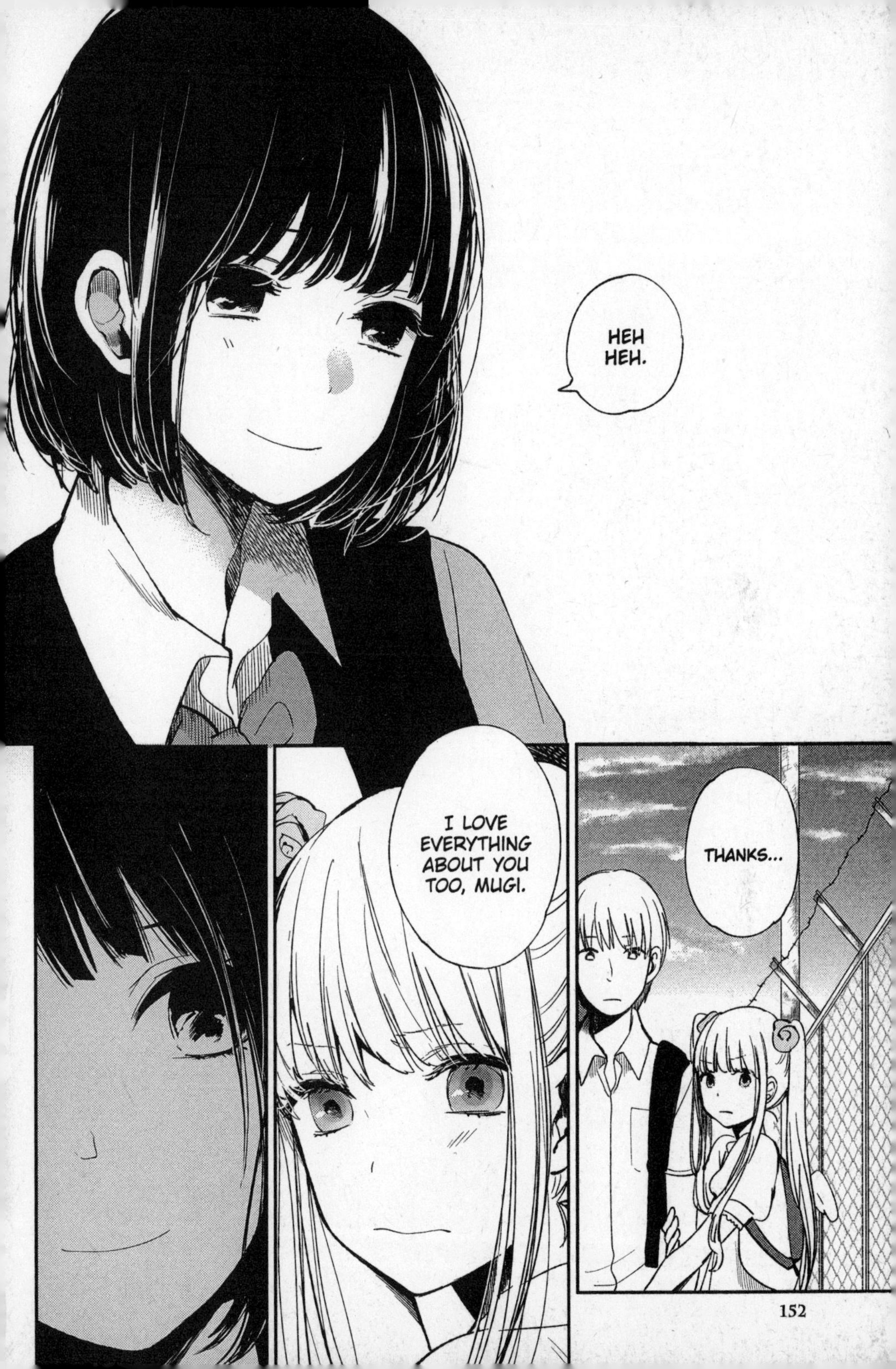
HEH HEH.
THANKS...
I LOVE EVERYTHING ABOUT YOU TOO, MUGI.

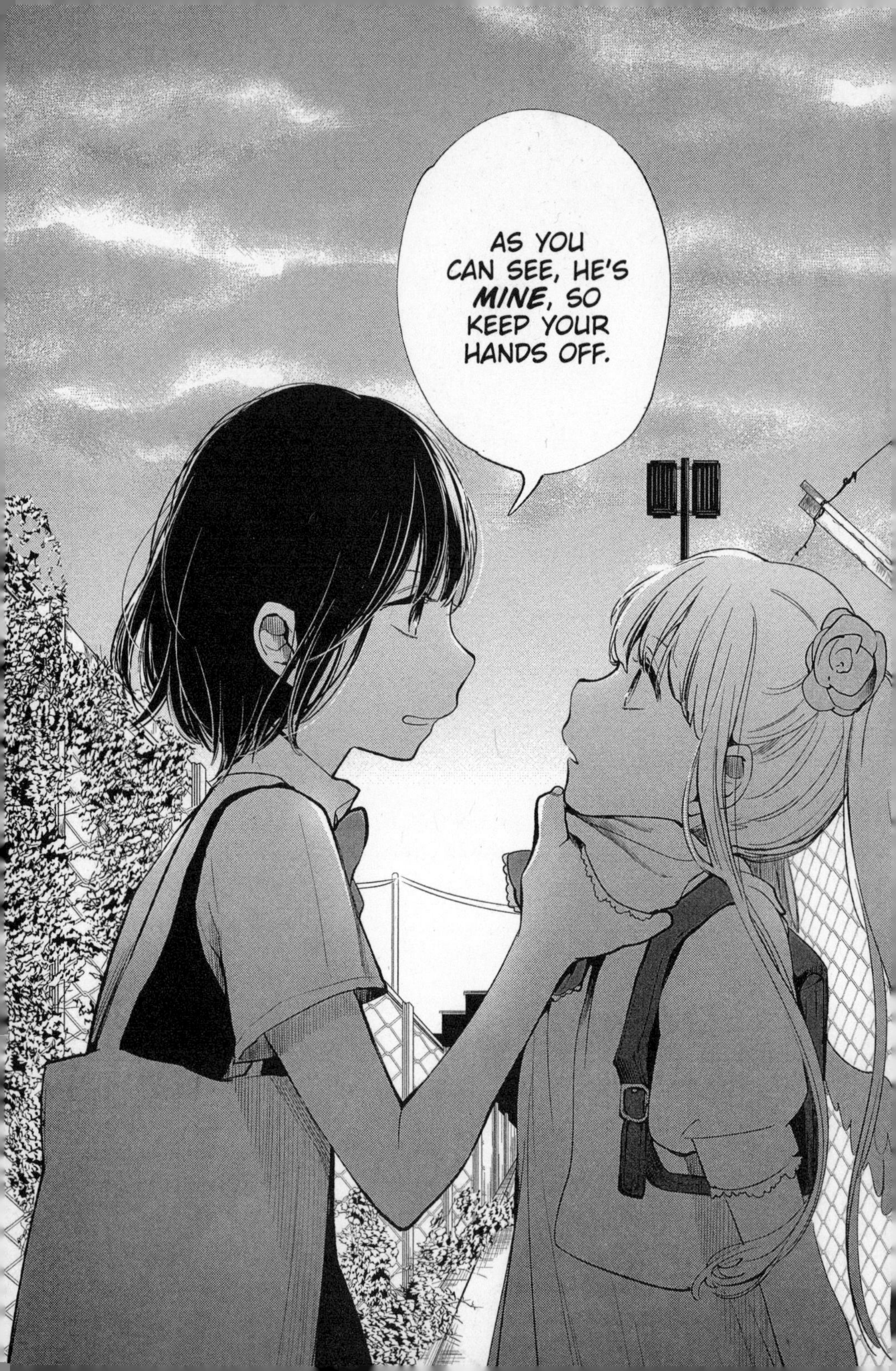
AS YOU CAN SEE, HE'S *MINE*, SO KEEP YOUR HANDS OFF.

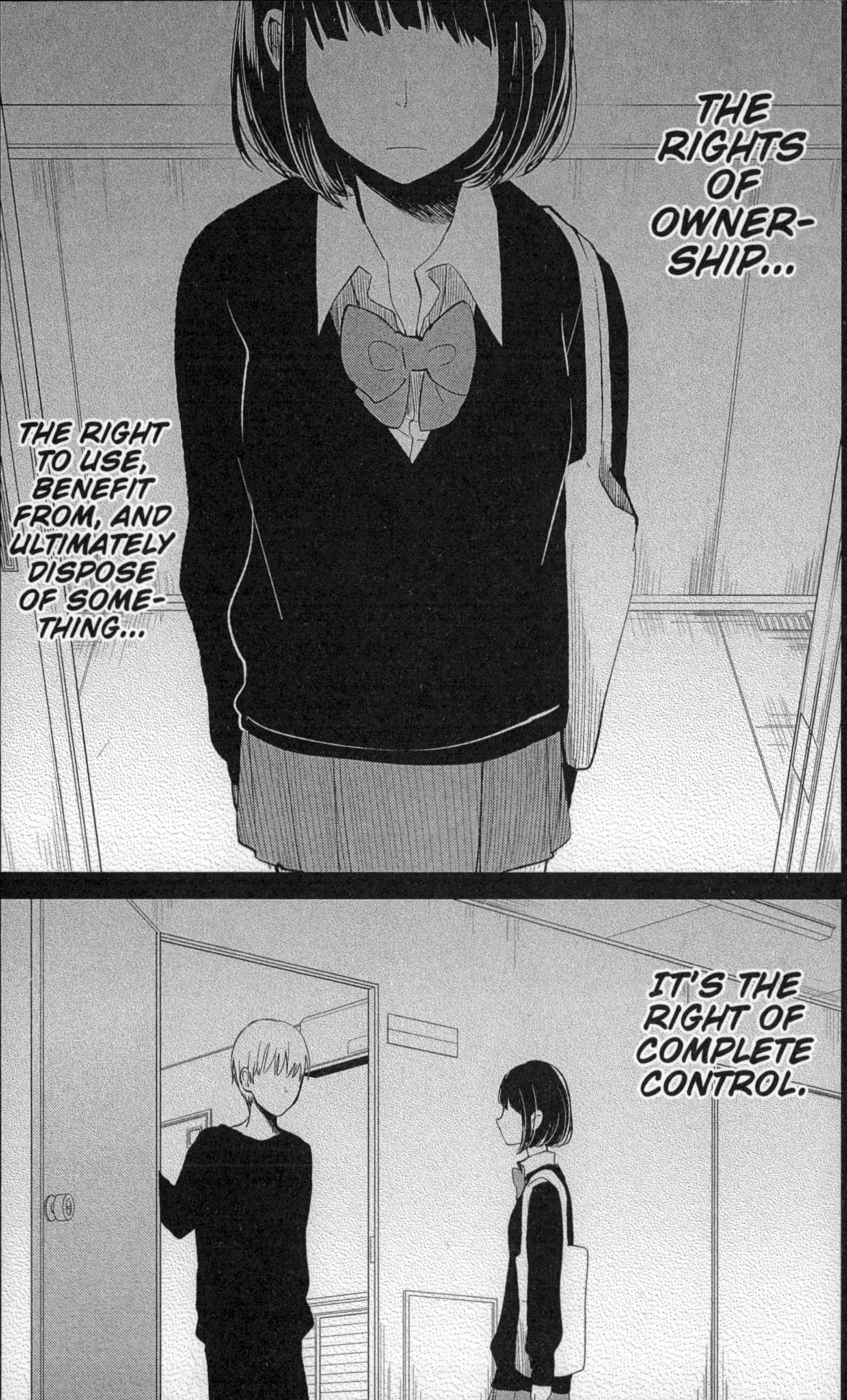
THE RIGHTS OF OWNER-SHIP...
THE RIGHT TO USE, BENEFIT FROM, AND ULTIMATELY DISPOSE OF SOME-THING...
IT'S THE RIGHT OF COMPLETE CONTROL.

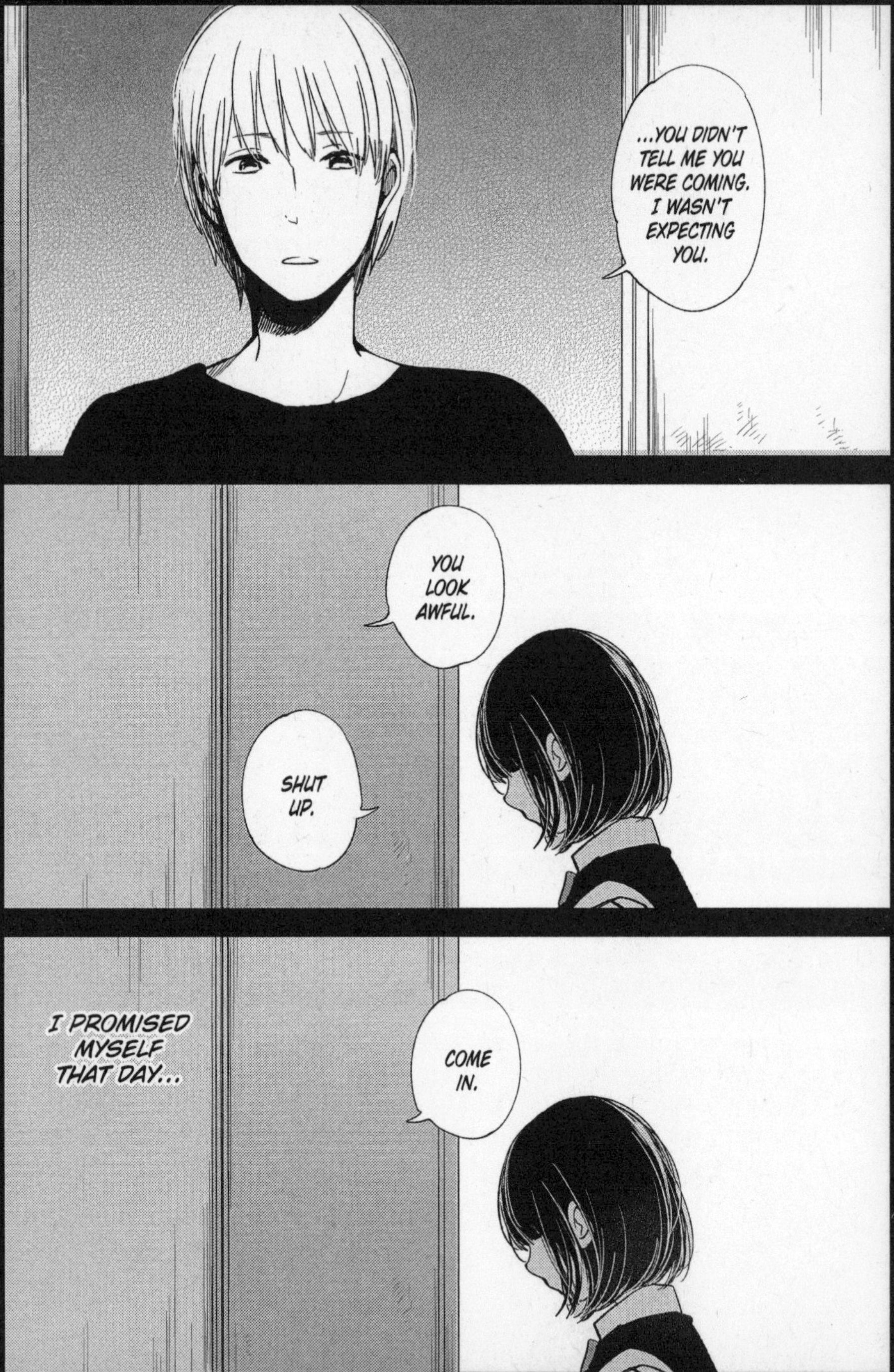
...YOU DIDN'T TELL ME YOU WERE COMING. I WASN'T EXPECTING YOU.
YOU LOOK AWFUL.
SHUT UP.
COME IN.
I PROMISED MYSELF THAT DAY...

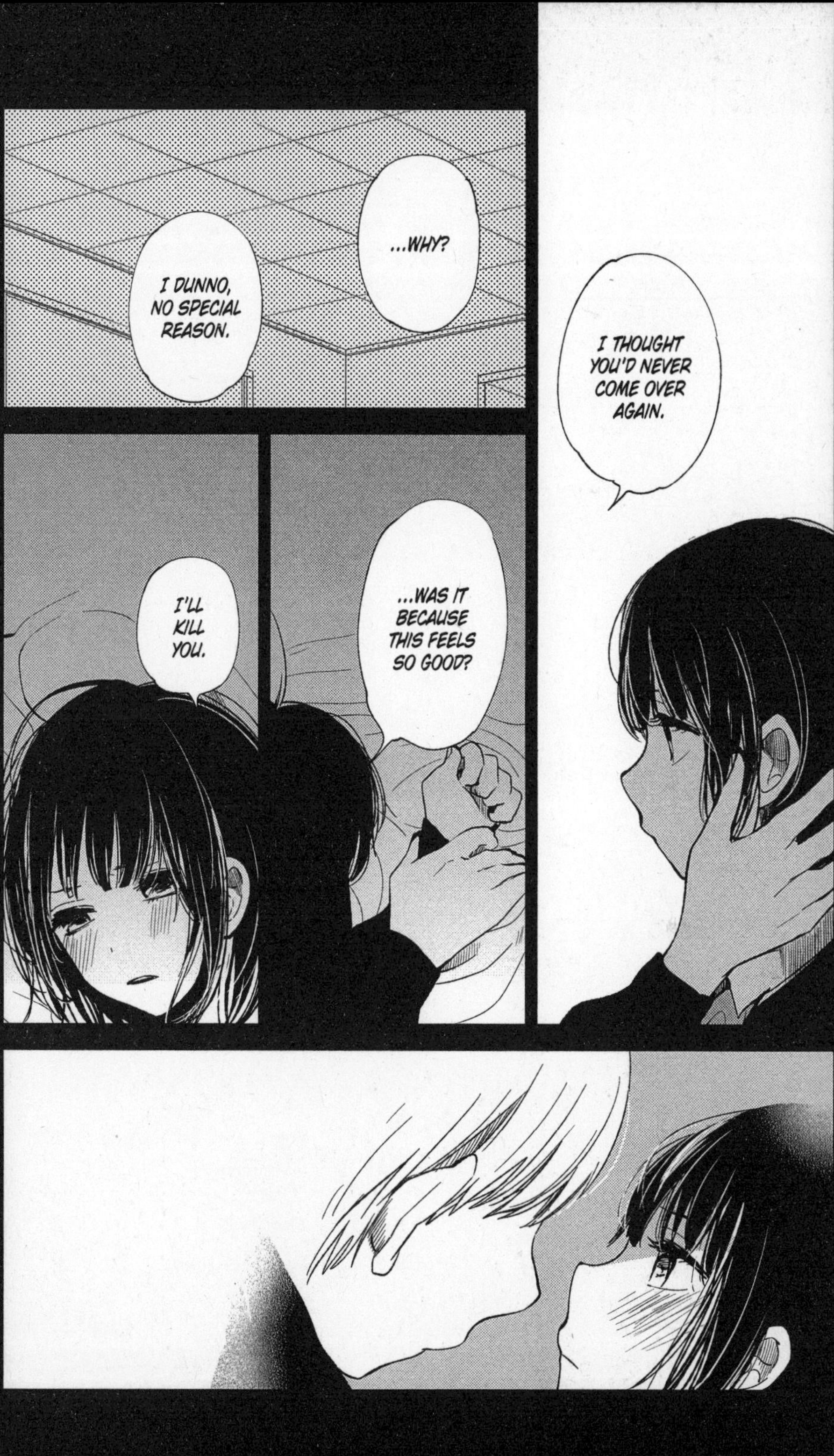
I THOUGHT YOU'D NEVER COME OVER AGAIN.
...WHY?
I DUNNO, NO SPECIAL REASON.
...WAS IT BECAUSE THIS FEELS SO GOOD?
I'LL KILL YOU.

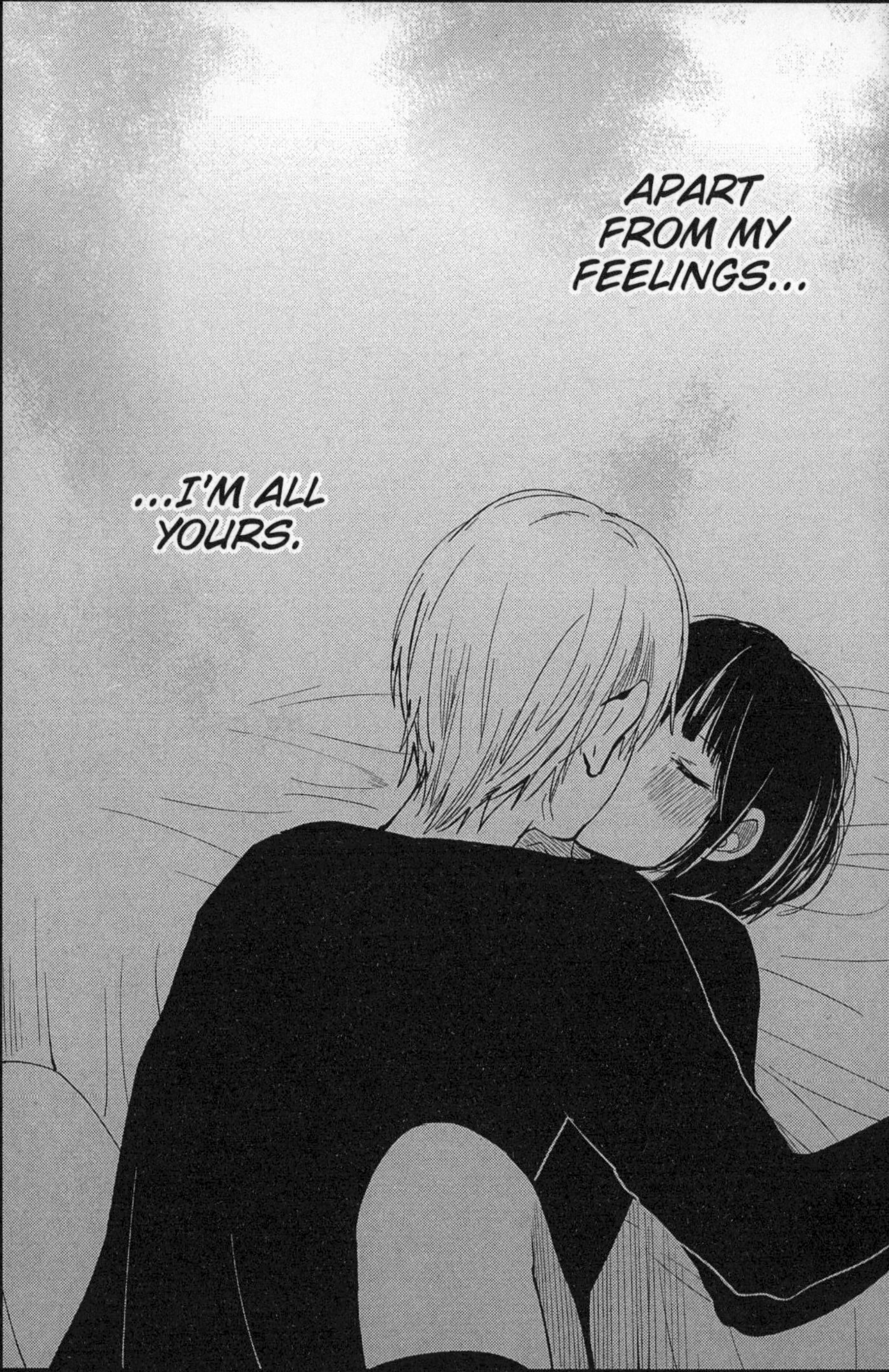
APART FROM MY FEELINGS...
...I'M ALL YOURS.

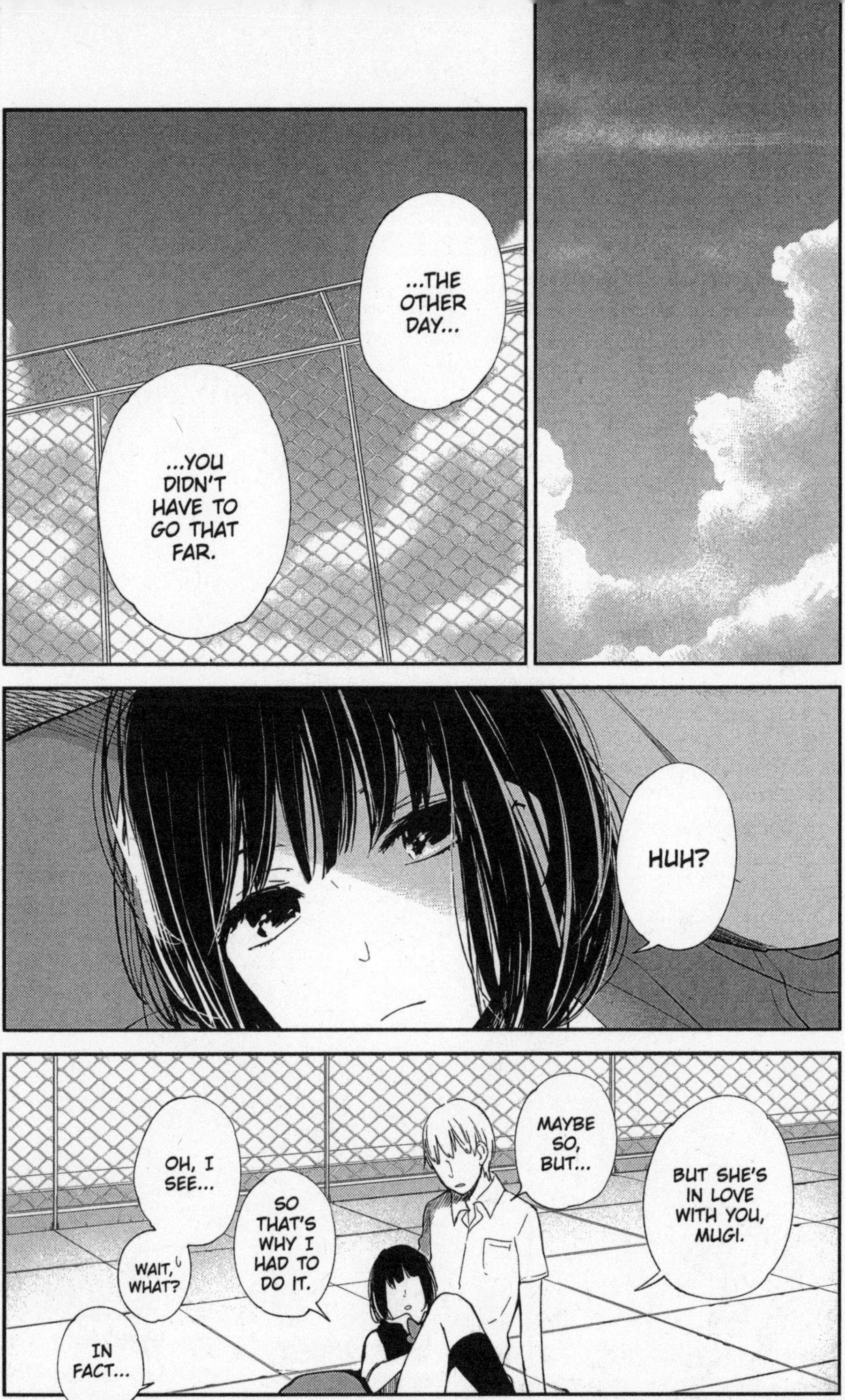
...THE OTHER DAY...
...YOU DIDN'T HAVE TO GO THAT FAR.
HUH?
MAYBE SO, BUT...
BUT SHE'S IN LOVE WITH YOU, MUGI.
SO THAT'S WHY I HAD TO DO IT.
OH, I SEE...
WAIT, WHAT?
IN FACT...

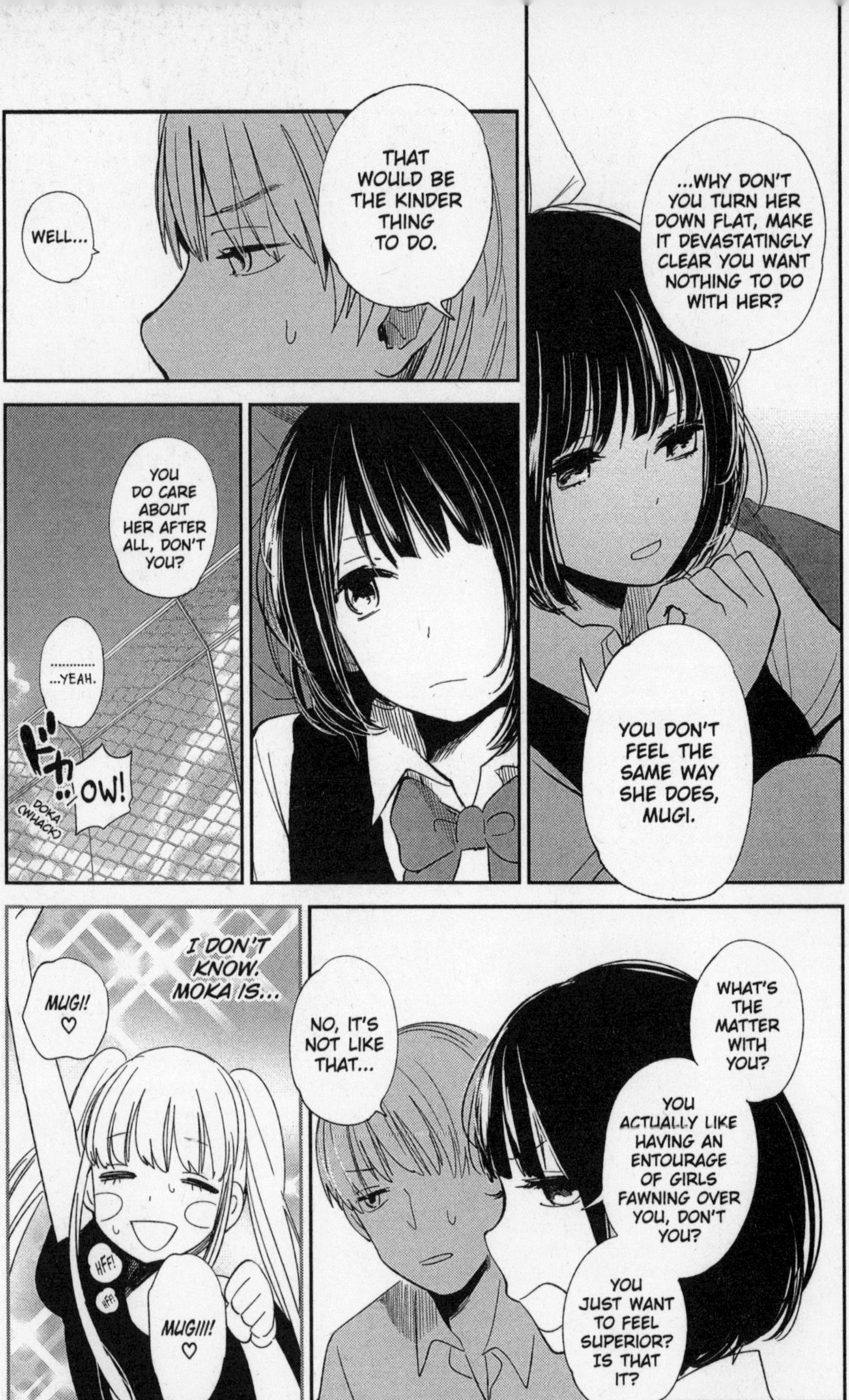
...WHY DON'T YOU TURN HER DOWN FLAT, MAKE IT DEVASTATINGLY CLEAR YOU WANT NOTHING TO DO WITH HER?
YOU DON'T FEEL THE SAME WAY SHE DOES, MUGI.
THAT WOULD BE THE KINDER THING TO DO.
WELL...
YOU DO CARE ABOUT HER AFTER ALL, DON'T YOU?
....YEAH.
ドカッ
DOKA (WHACK)
OW!
WHAT'S THE MATTER WITH YOU?
YOU ACTUALLY LIKE HAVING AN ENTOURAGE OF GIRLS FAWNING OVER YOU, DON'T YOU?
YOU JUST WANT TO FEEL SUPERIOR? IS THAT IT?
NO, IT'S NOT LIKE THAT...
I DON'T KNOW. MOKA IS...
MUGI! ♡
HFF!
HFF!
MUGIII! ♡

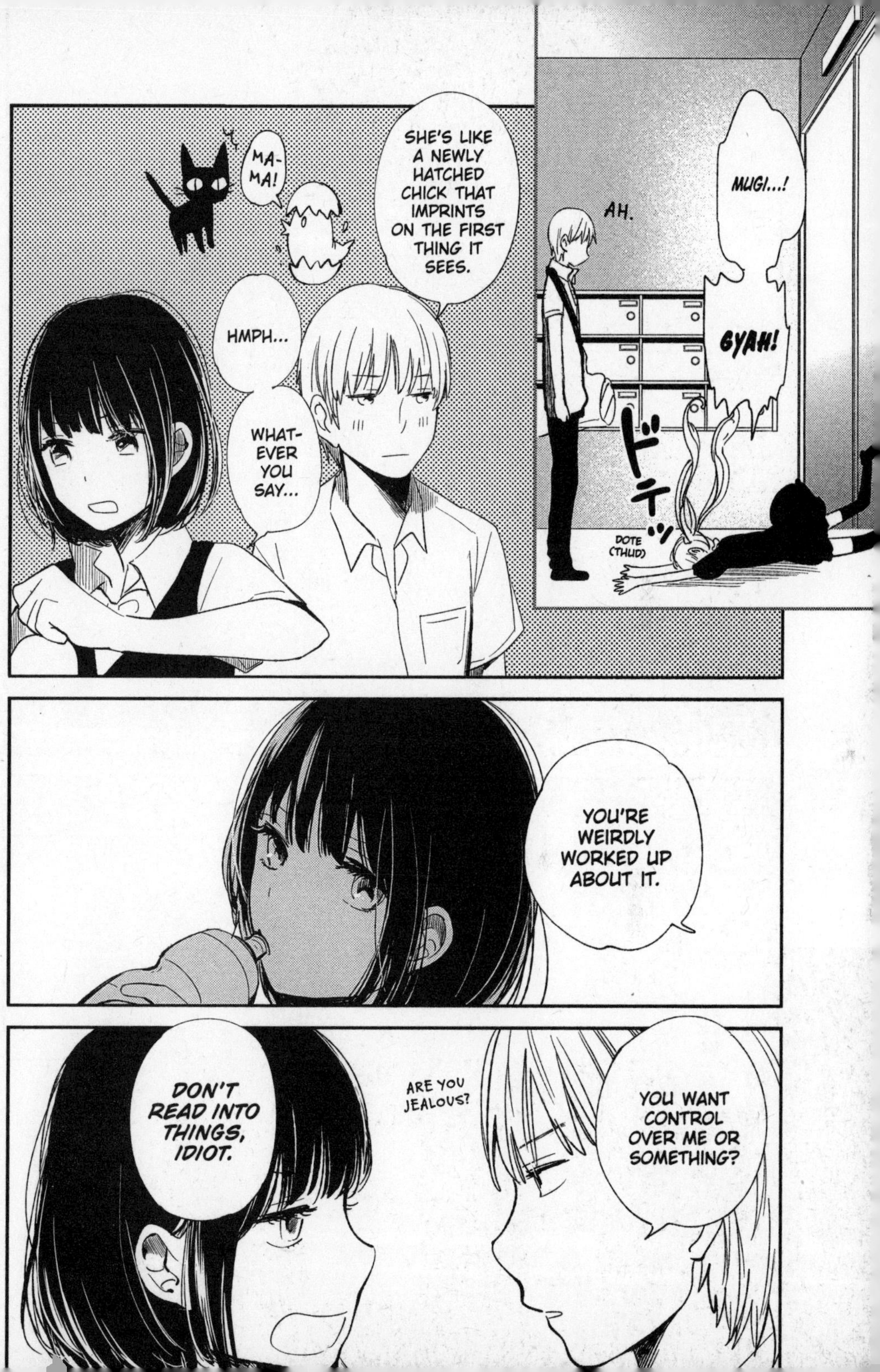
MUGI...!
AH.
GYAH!
ドテッ
DOTE (THUD)
SHE'S LIKE A NEWLY HATCHED CHICK THAT IMPRINTS ON THE FIRST THING IT SEES.
MA-MA!
HMPH...
WHATEVER YOU SAY...
YOU'RE WEIRDLY WORKED UP ABOUT IT.
YOU WANT CONTROL OVER ME OR SOMETHING?
ARE YOU JEALOUS?
DON'T READ INTO THINGS, IDIOT.

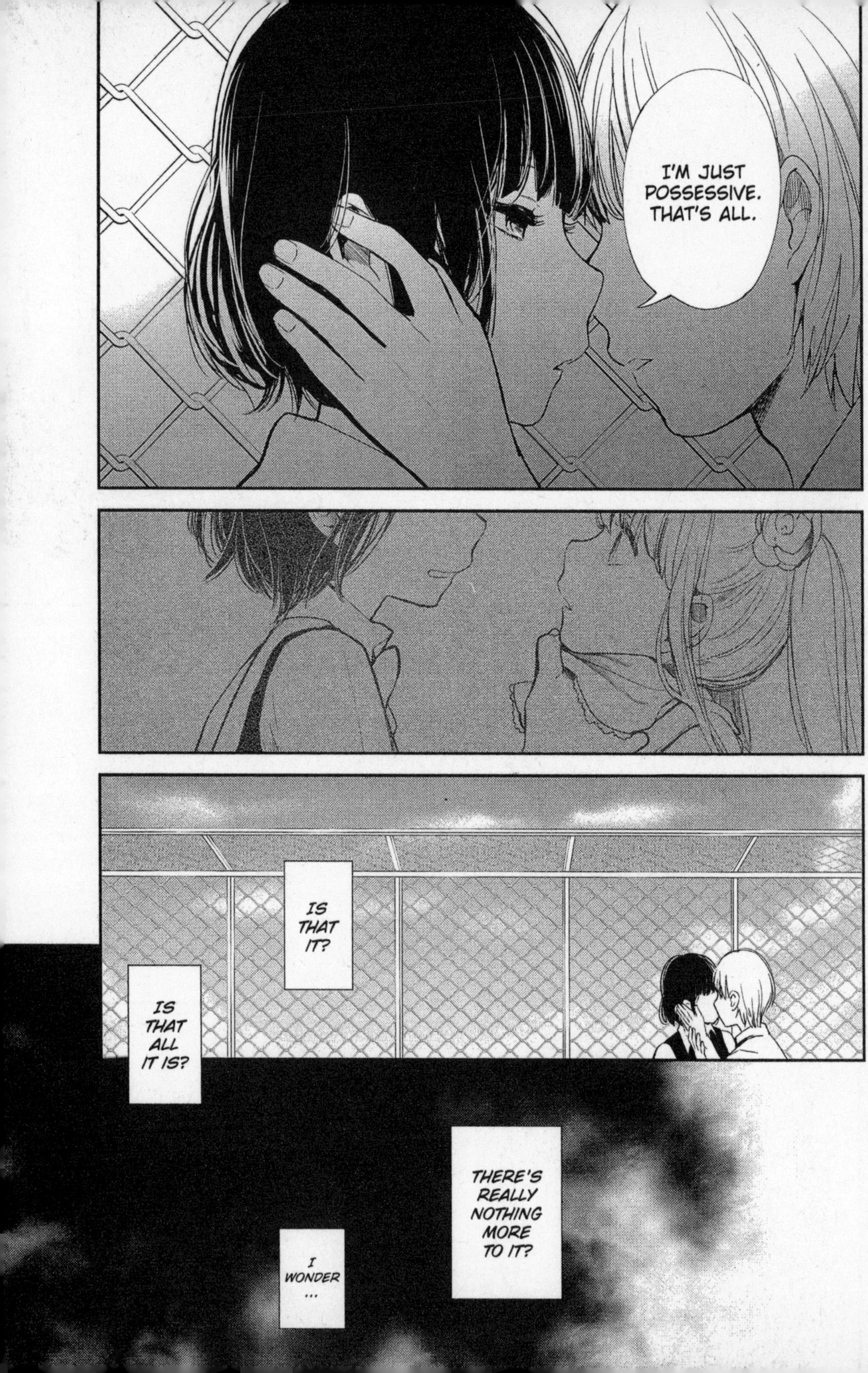
I'M JUST POSSESSIVE. THAT'S ALL.
IS THAT IT?
IS THAT ALL IT IS?
THERE'S REALLY NOTHING MORE TO IT?
I WONDER...

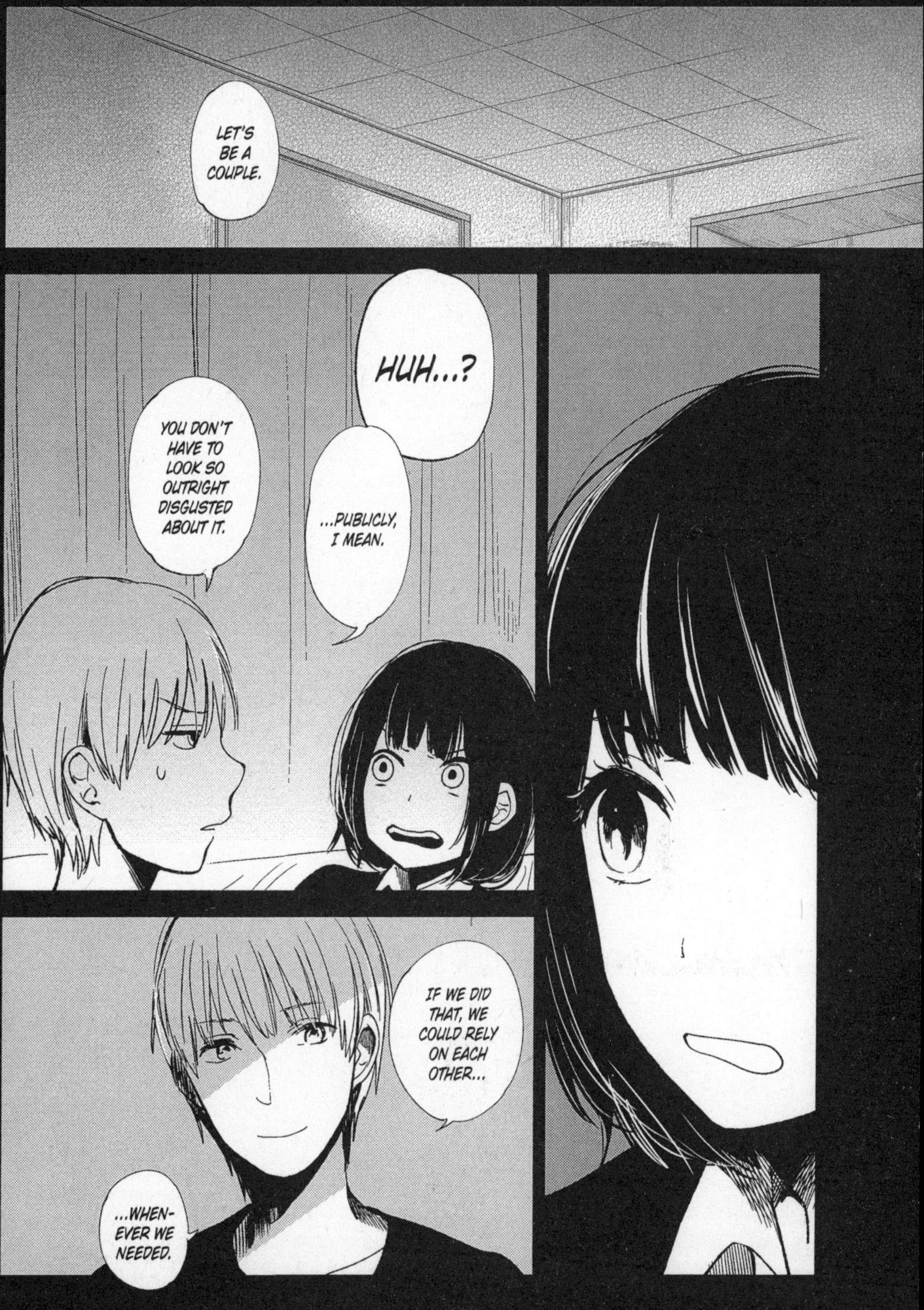
LET'S BE A COUPLE.
HUH...?
...PUBLICLY, I MEAN.
YOU DON'T HAVE TO LOOK SO OUTRIGHT DISGUSTED ABOUT IT.
IF WE DID THAT, WE COULD RELY ON EACH OTHER...
...WHEN-EVER WE NEEDED.

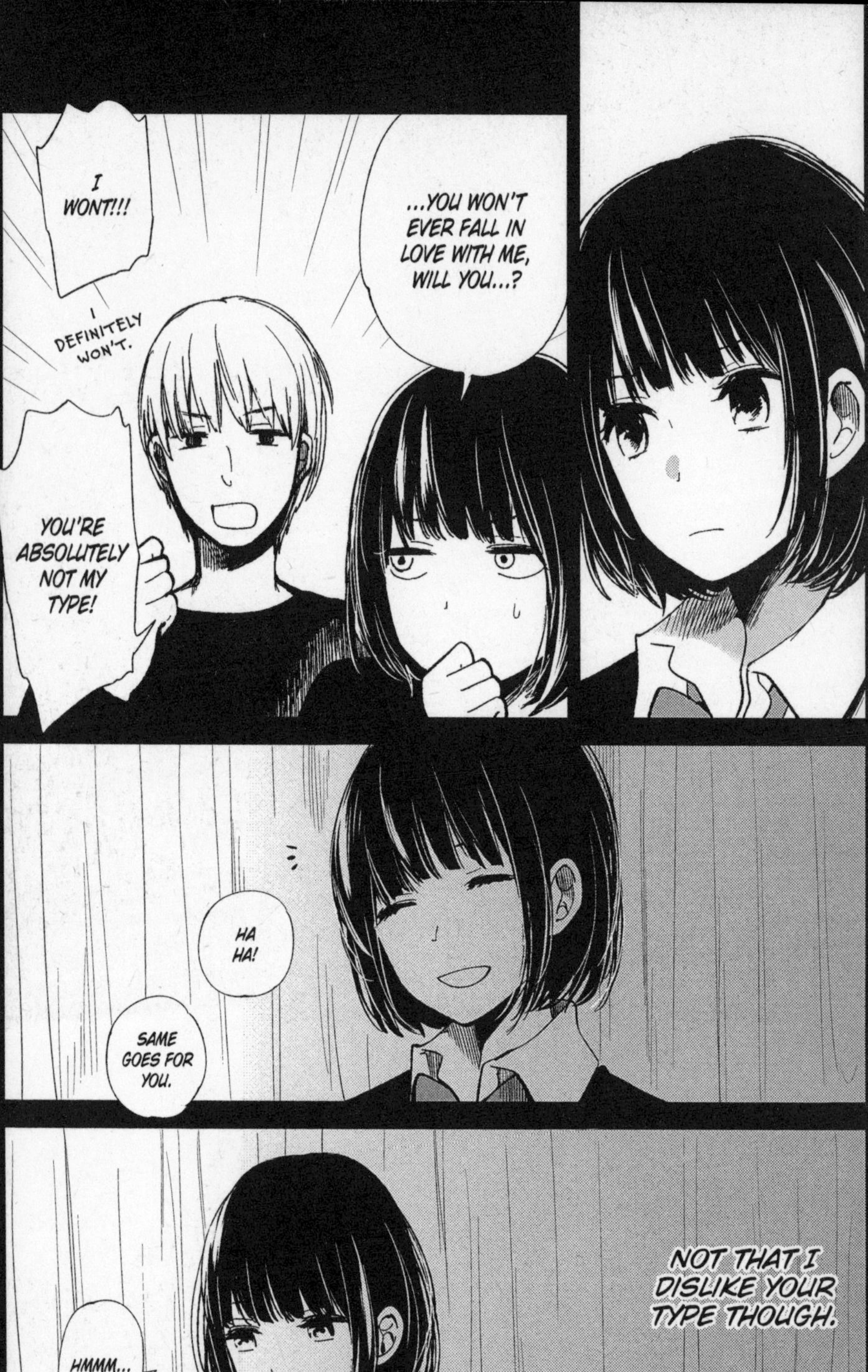
...YOU WON'T EVER FALL IN LOVE WITH ME, WILL YOU...?
I WONT!!!
I DEFINITELY WON'T.
YOU'RE ABSOLUTELY NOT MY TYPE!
HA HA!
SAME GOES FOR YOU.
NOT THAT I DISLIKE YOUR TYPE THOUGH.
HMMM...

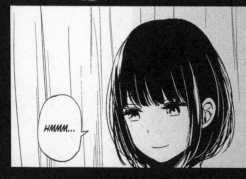

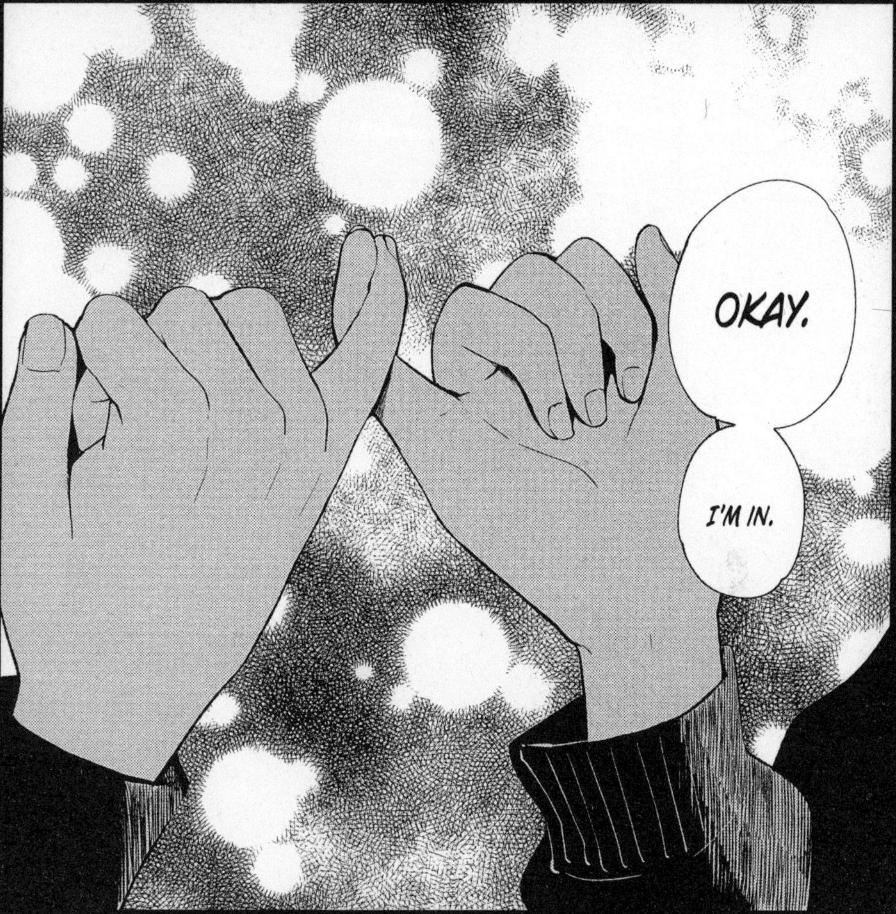
OKAY.
I'M IN.
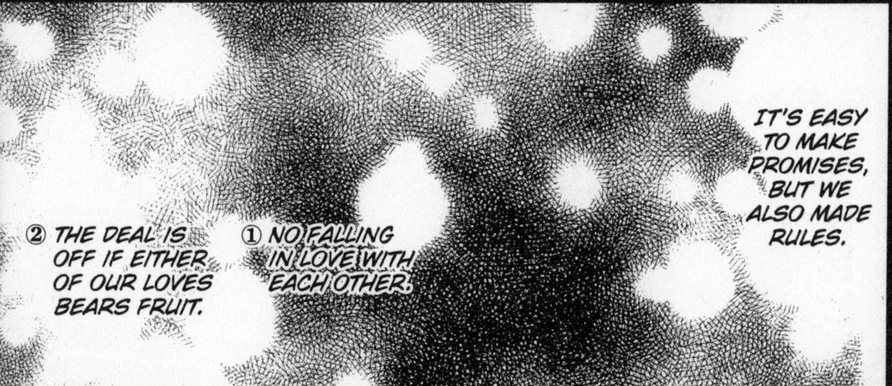
IT'S EASY TO MAKE PROMISES, BUT WE ALSO MADE RULES.
① NO FALLING IN LOVE WITH EACH OTHER.
② THE DEAL IS OFF IF EITHER OF OUR LOVES BEARS FRUIT.

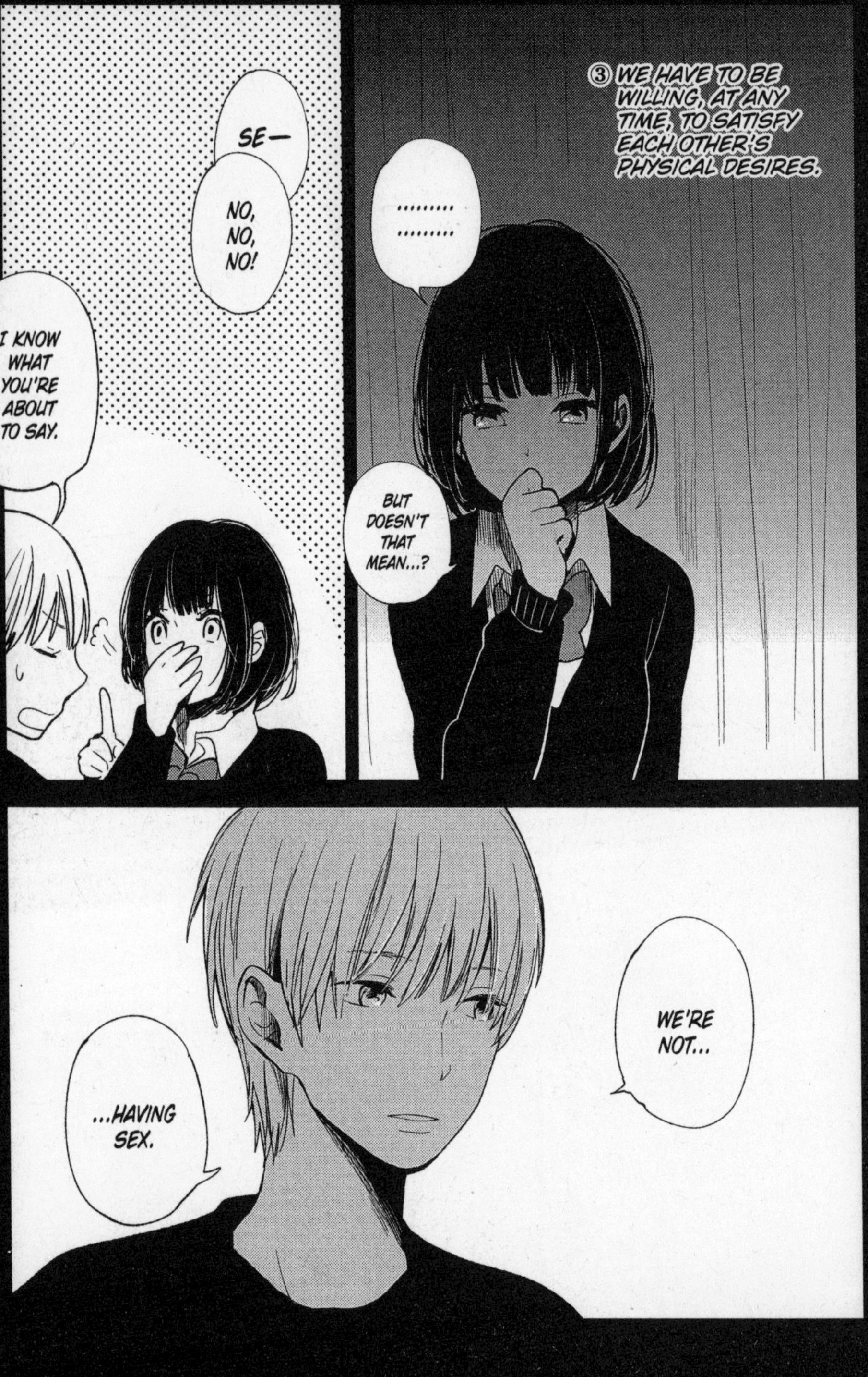
③ WE HAVE TO BE WILLING, AT ANY TIME, TO SATISFY EACH OTHER'S PHYSICAL DESIRES.
....
BUT DOESN'T THAT MEAN...?
SE—
NO, NO, NO!
I KNOW WHAT YOU'RE ABOUT TO SAY.
WE'RE NOT...
...HAVING SEX.

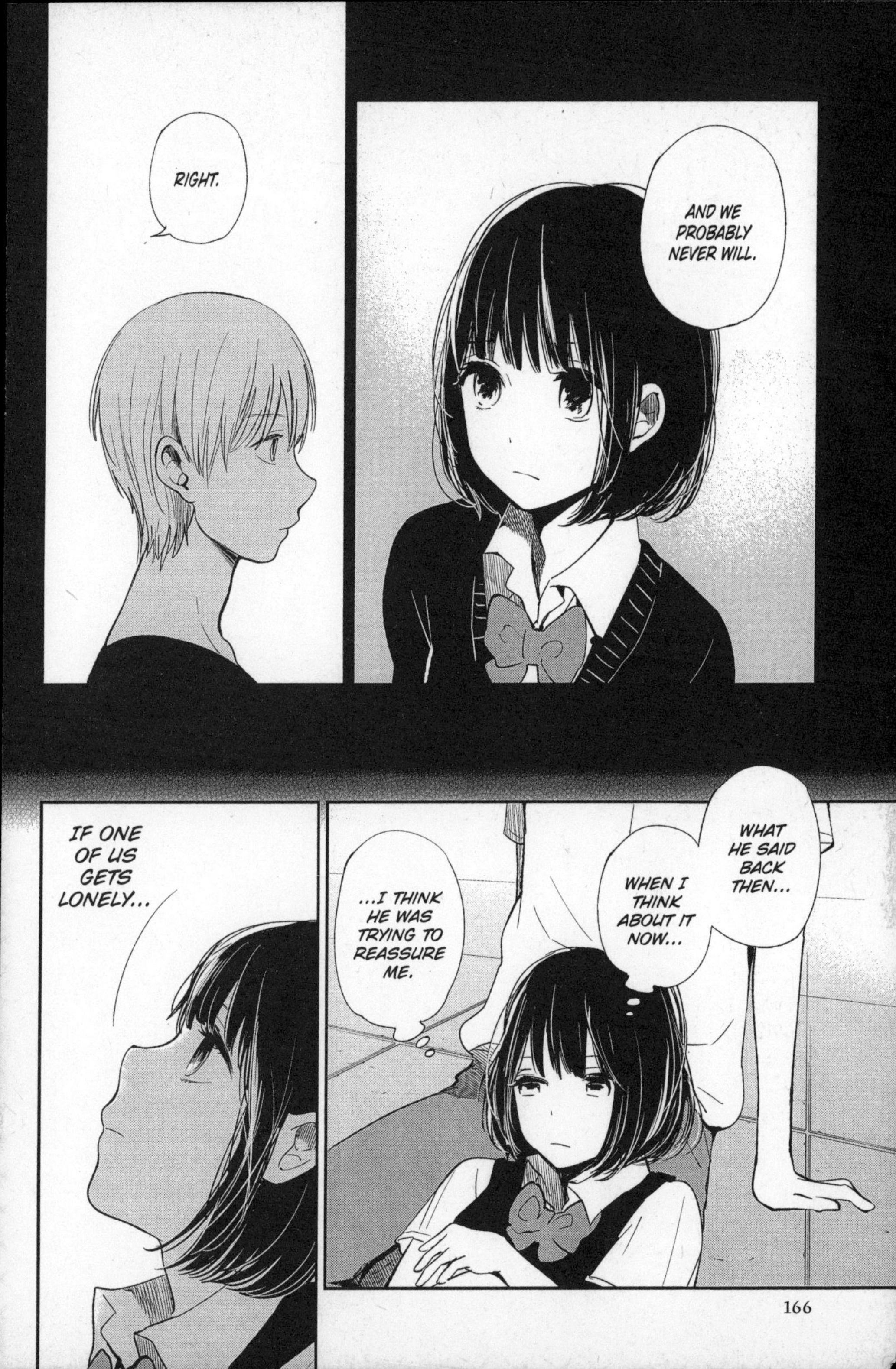
AND WE PROBABLY NEVER WILL.
RIGHT.
WHAT HE SAID BACK THEN...
WHEN I THINK ABOUT IT NOW...
...I THINK HE WAS TRYING TO REASSURE ME.
IF ONE OF US GETS LONELY...

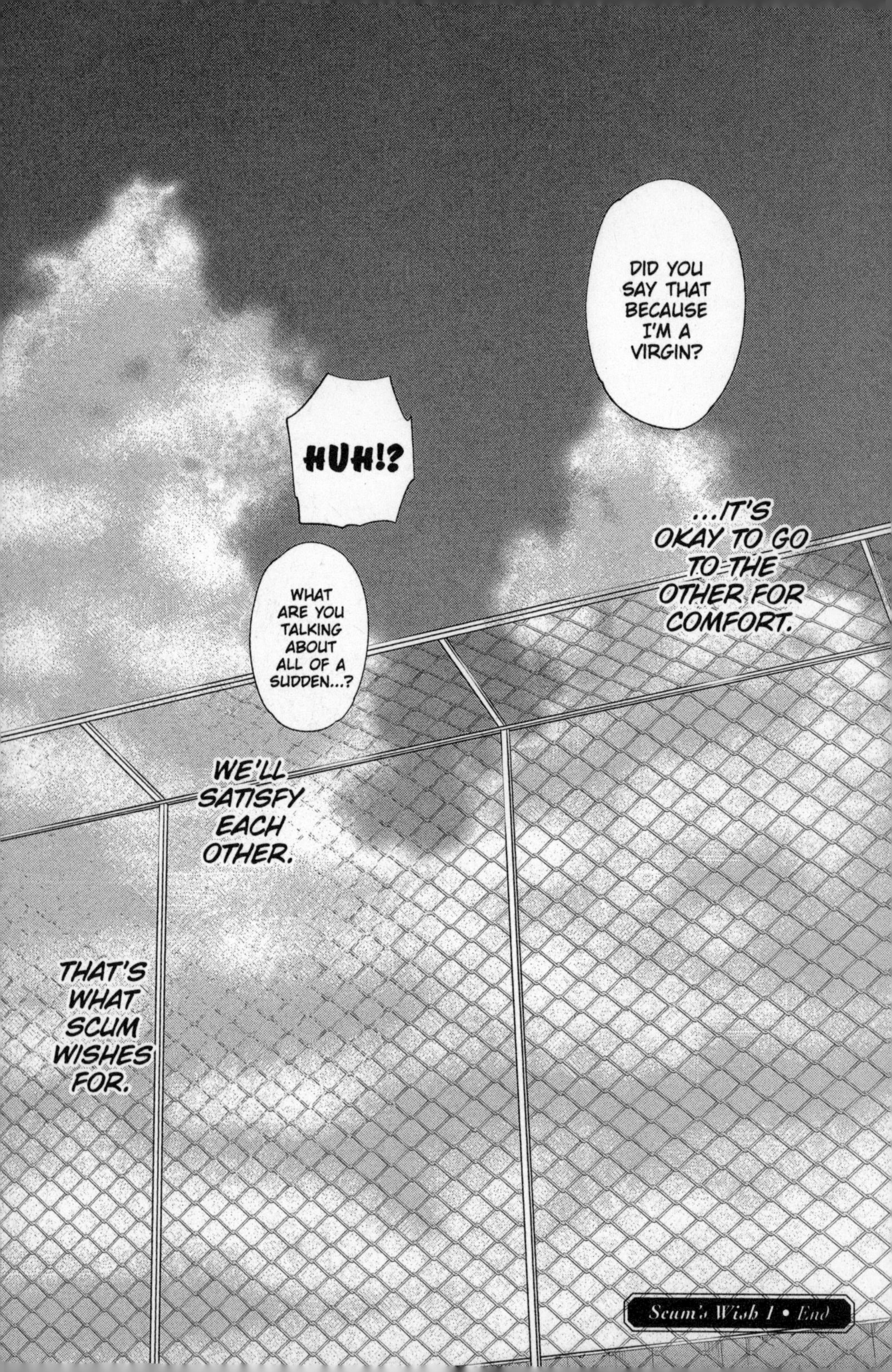
DID YOU SAY THAT BECAUSE I'M A VIRGIN?
HUH!?
...IT'S OKAY TO GO TO THE OTHER FOR COMFORT.
WHAT ARE YOU TALKING ABOUT ALL OF A SUDDEN...?
WE'LL SATISFY EACH OTHER.
THAT'S WHAT SCUM WISHES FOR.
Scum's Wish 1 • End

Scum's
Wish

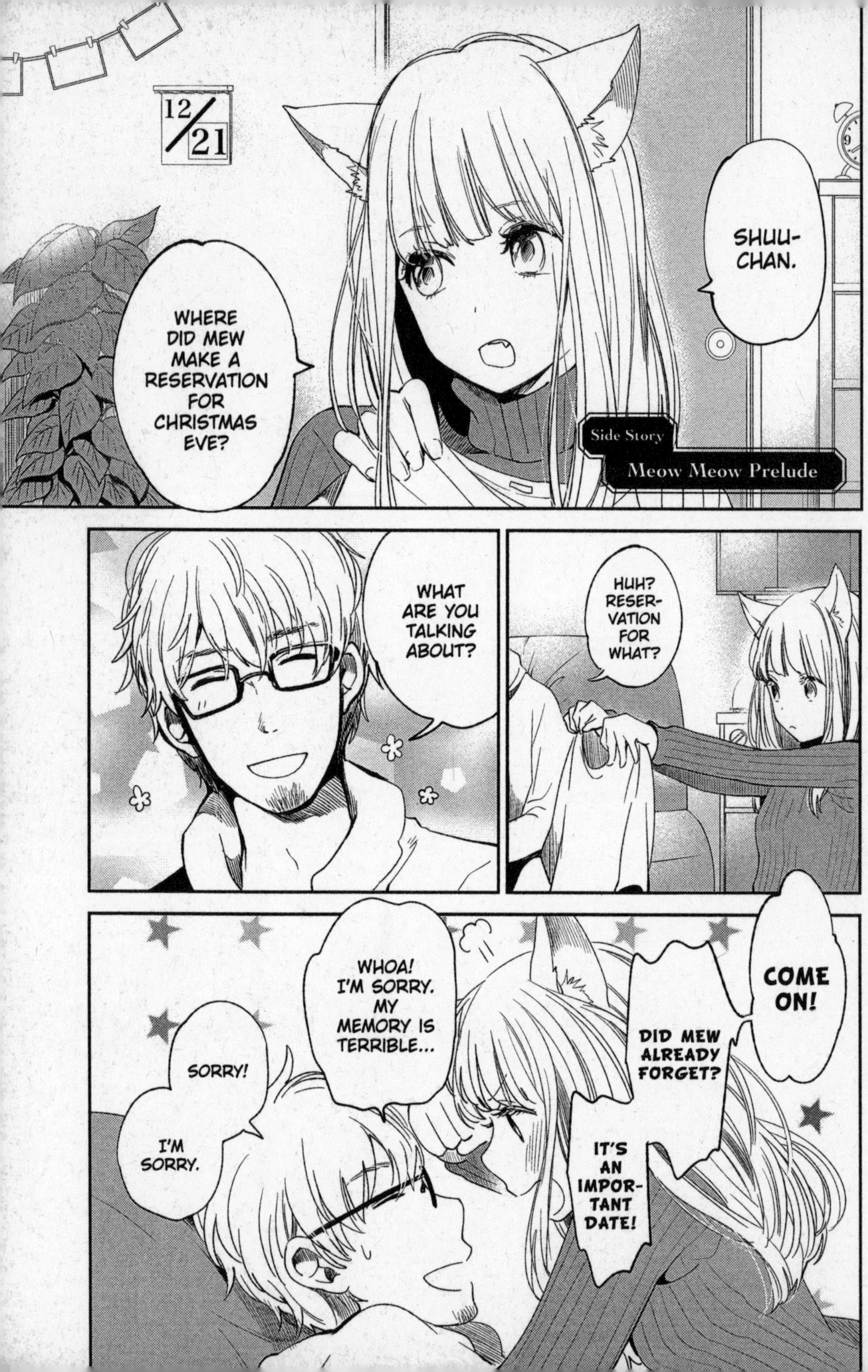
12/21
SHUU-CHAN.
WHERE DID MEW MAKE A RESERVATION FOR CHRISTMAS EVE?
Side Story
Meow Meow Prelude
HUH? RESERVATION FOR WHAT?
WHAT ARE YOU TALKING ABOUT?
COME ON!
DID MEW ALREADY FORGET?
IT'S AN IMPORTANT DATE!
WHOA! I'M SORRY. MY MEMORY IS TERRIBLE...
SORRY!
I'M SORRY.

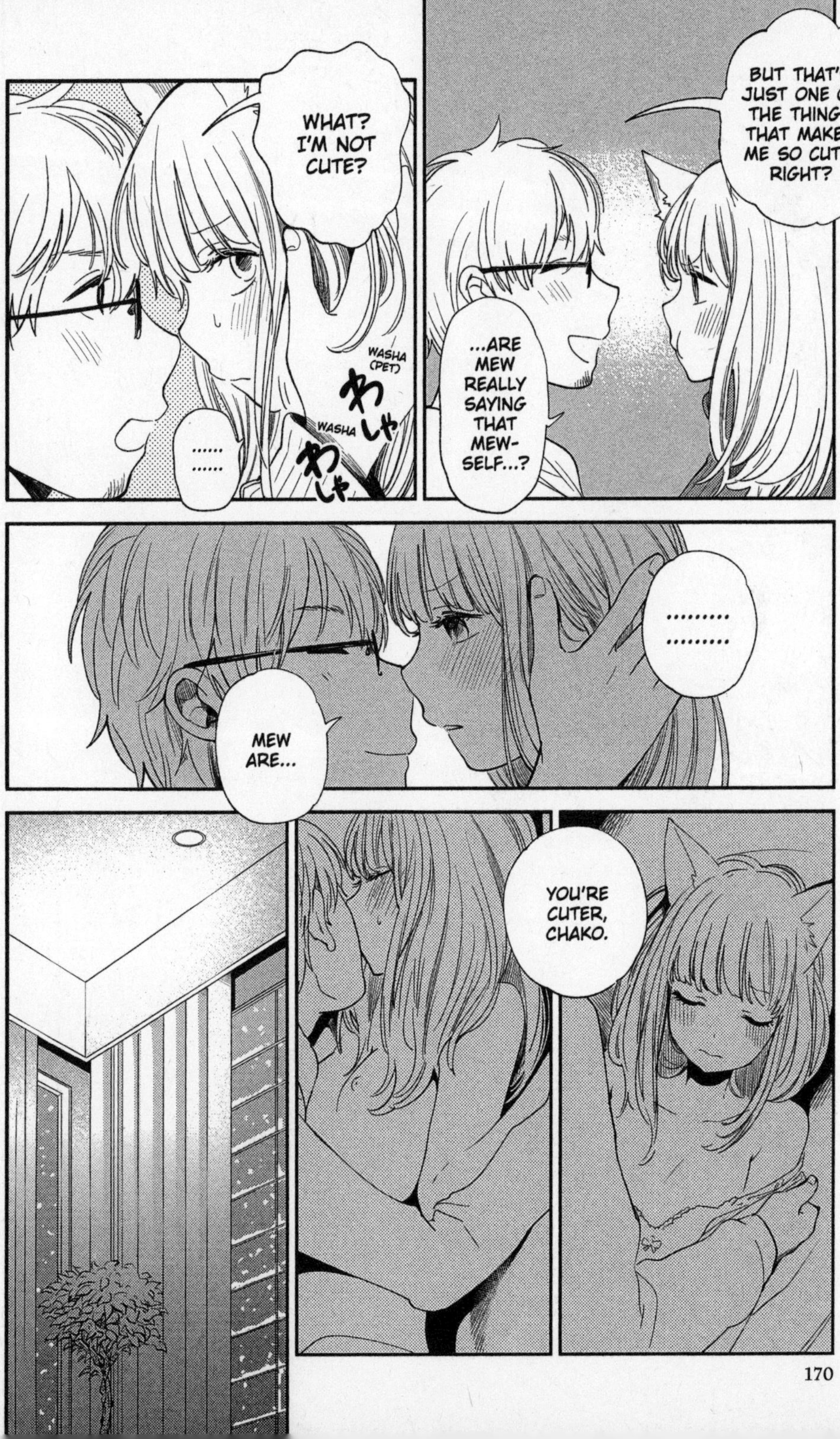
BUT THAT'S JUST ONE OF THE THINGS THAT MAKES ME SO CUTE, RIGHT?
...ARE MEW REALLY SAYING THAT MEW-SELF...?
WHAT? I'M NOT CUTE?
WASHA (PET)
わしゃ
WASHA
わしゃ
....
....
MEW ARE...
YOU'RE CUTER, CHAKO.

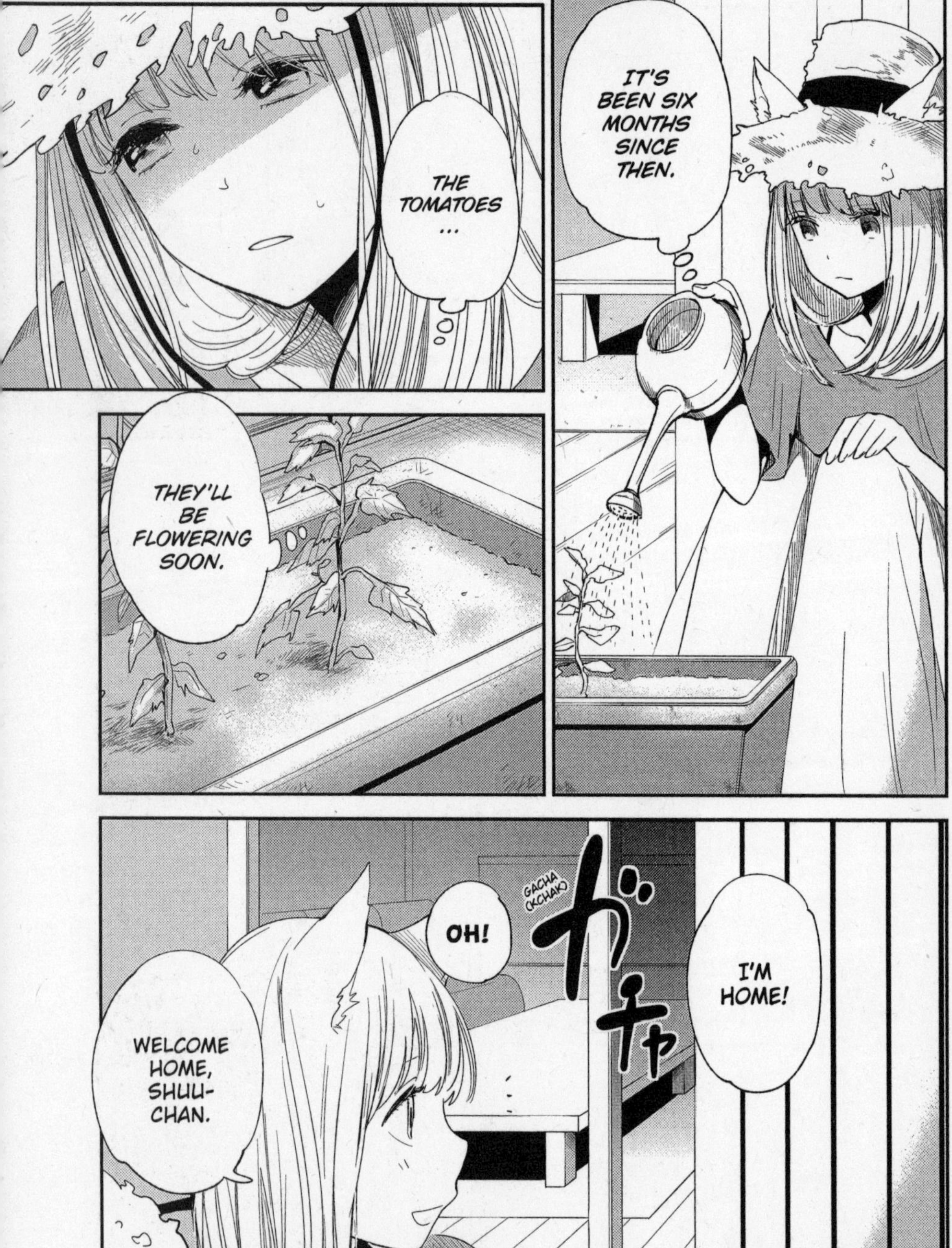
IT'S BEEN SIX MONTHS SINCE THEN.
THE TOMATOES ...
THEY'LL BE FLOWERING SOON.
I'M HOME!
ガチャ
GACHA (KCHAK)
OH!
WELCOME HOME, SHUU-CHAN.

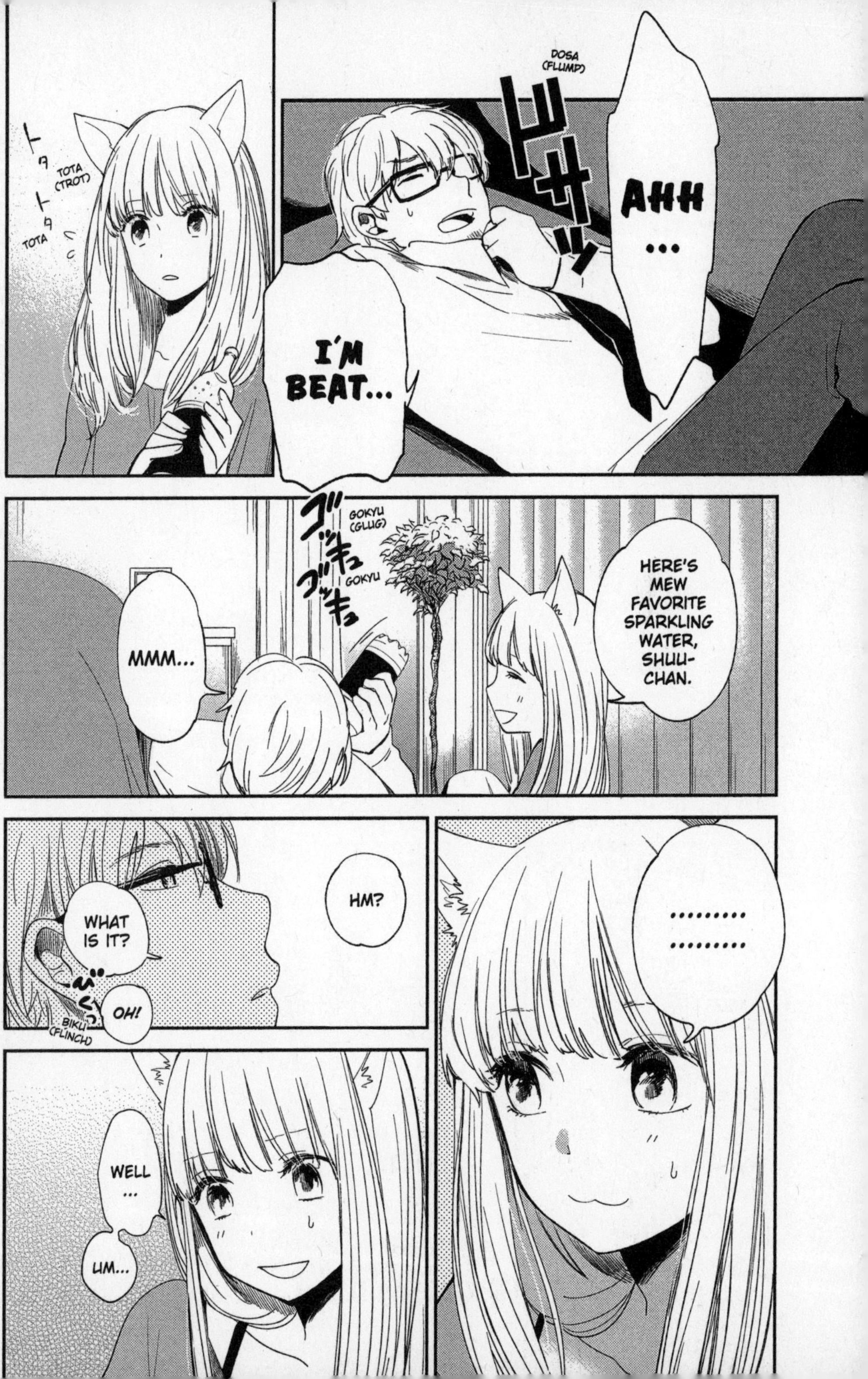
ドサッ
DOSA (FLUMP)
AHH ...
I'M BEAT...
トタトタ
TOTA (TROT)
TOTA
HERE'S MEW FAVORITE SPARKLING WATER, SHUU-CHAN.
ゴッキュ ゴッキュ
GOKYU (GLUG)
GOKYU
MMM...
....
HM?
WHAT IS IT?
ビクッ
OH!
BIKU (FLINCH)
WELL ...
UM...

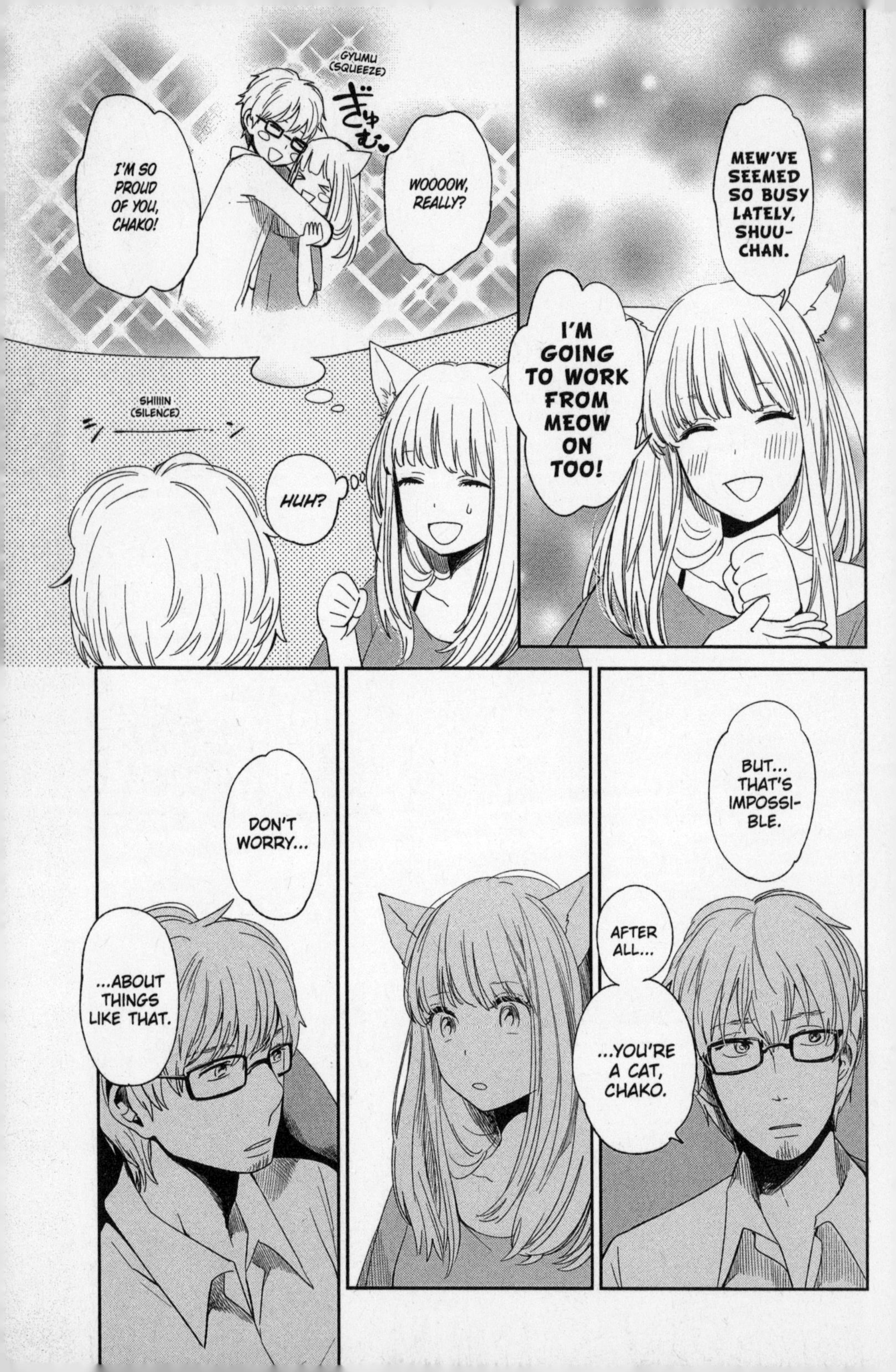
MEW'VE SEEMED SO BUSY LATELY, SHUU-CHAN.
I'M GOING TO WORK FROM MEOW ON TOO!
GYUMU (SQUEEZE)
ぎゅむ
WOOOOW, REALLY?
I'M SO PROUD OF YOU, CHAKO!
SHIIIIN (SILENCE)
HUH?
BUT... THAT'S IMPOSSIBLE.
AFTER ALL...
...YOU'RE A CAT, CHAKO.
DON'T WORRY...
...ABOUT THINGS LIKE THAT.

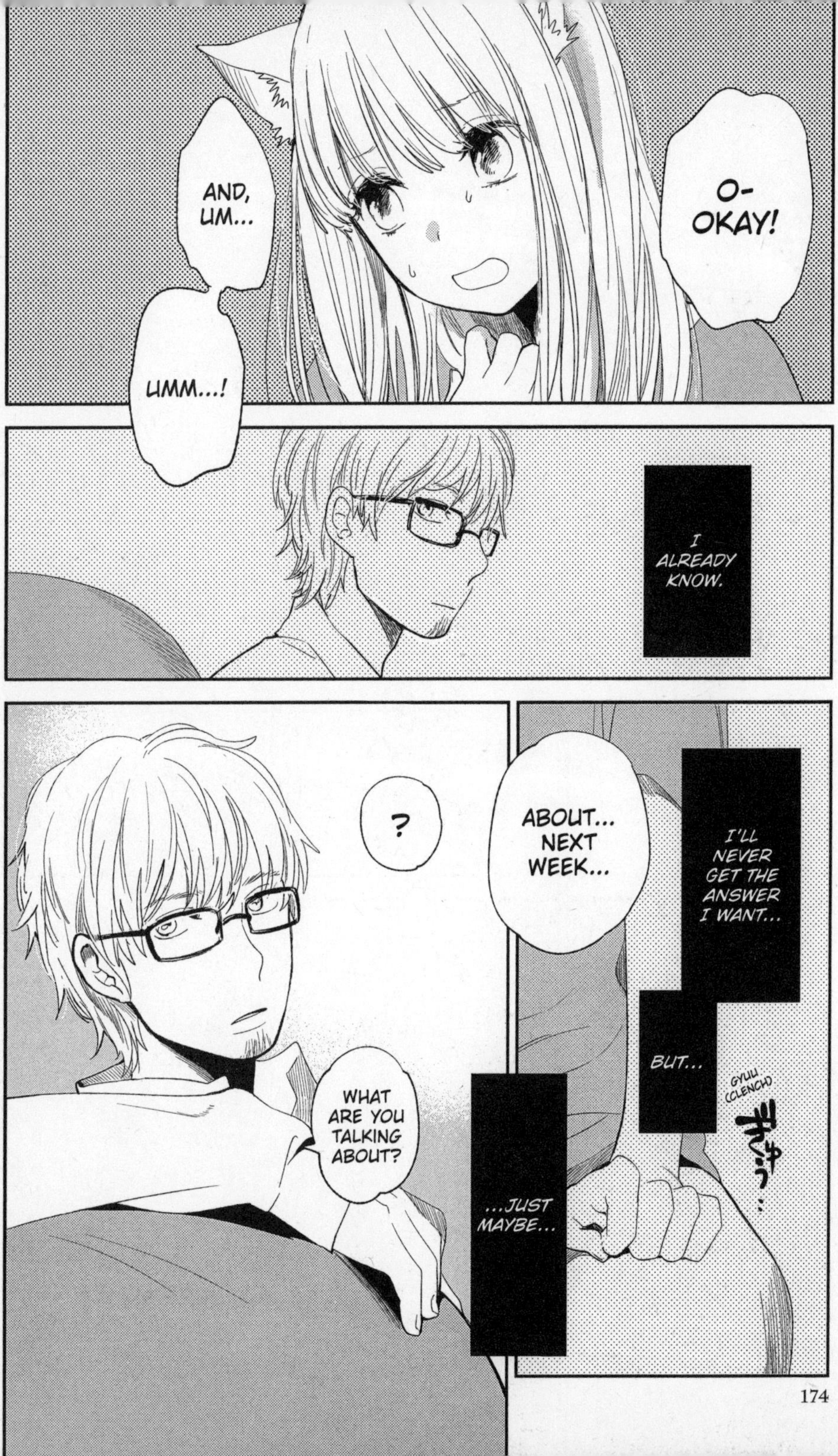
O-OKAY!
AND, UM...
UMM...!
I ALREADY KNOW.
I'LL NEVER GET THE ANSWER I WANT...
ABOUT... NEXT WEEK...
BUT...
GYUU (CLENCH)
...JUST MAYBE...
?
WHAT ARE YOU TALKING ABOUT?

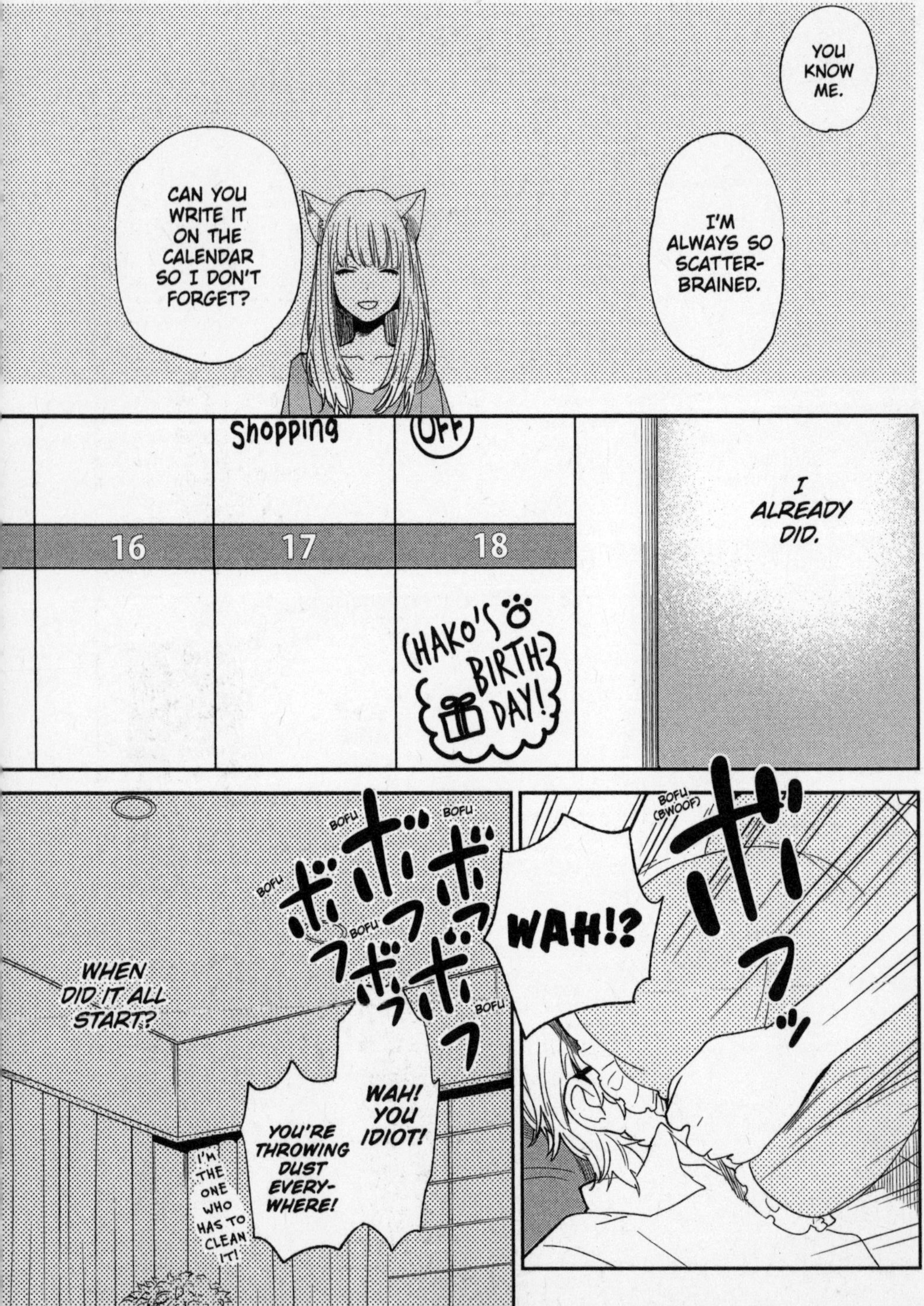
YOU KNOW ME.
I'M ALWAYS SO SCATTER-BRAINED.
CAN YOU WRITE IT ON THE CALENDAR SO I DON'T FORGET?
I ALREADY DID.
Shopping
OFF
16
17
18
HAKO'S BIRTHDAY!
ボフッ
BOFU (BWOOF)
WAH!?
BOFU
BOFU
BOFU
BOFU
BOFU
WAH! YOU IDIOT!
YOU'RE THROWING DUST EVERYWHERE!
I'M THE ONE WHO HAS TO CLEAN IT!
WHEN DID IT ALL START?

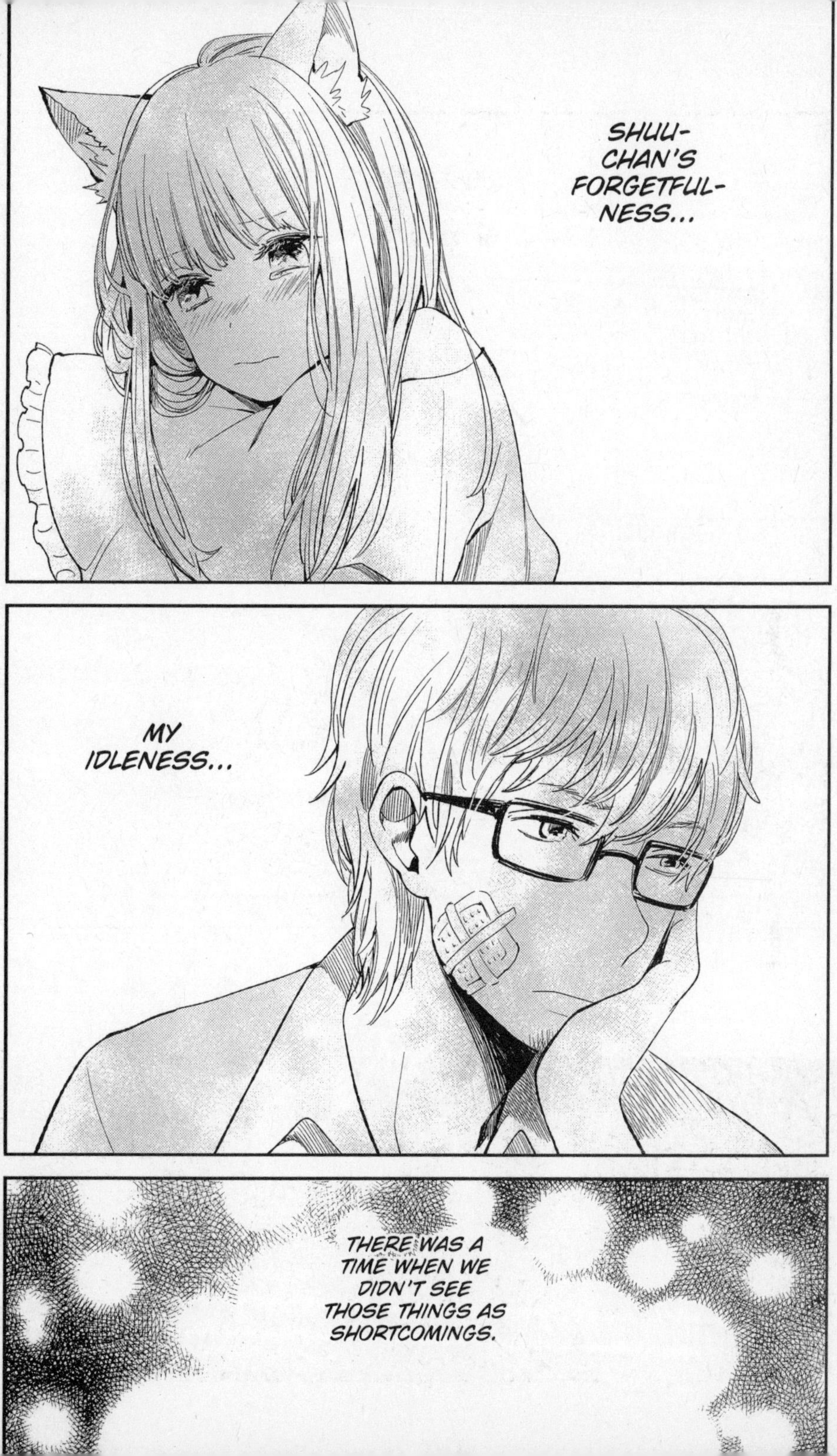
SHUU-CHAN'S FORGETFUL-NESS...
MY IDLENESS...
THERE WAS A TIME WHEN WE DIDN'T SEE THOSE THINGS AS SHORTCOMINGS.

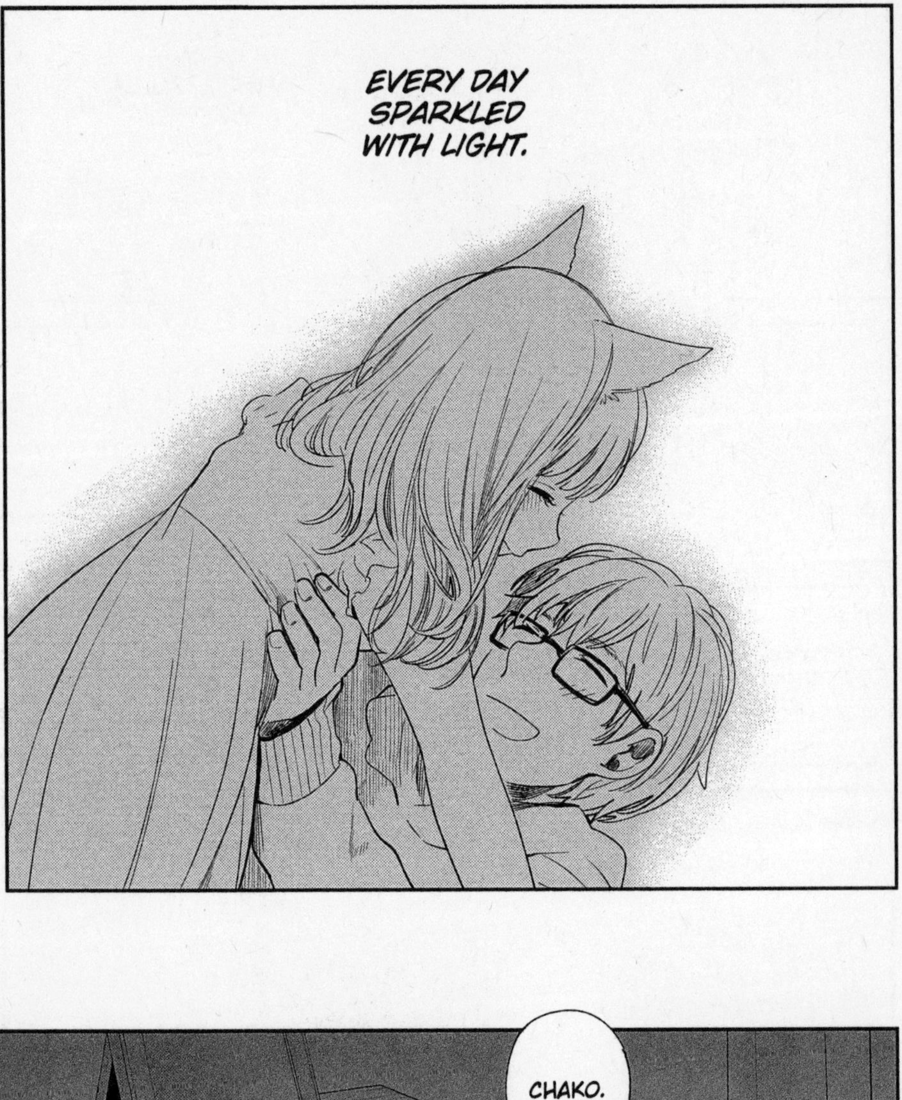
EVERY DAY SPARKLED WITH LIGHT.

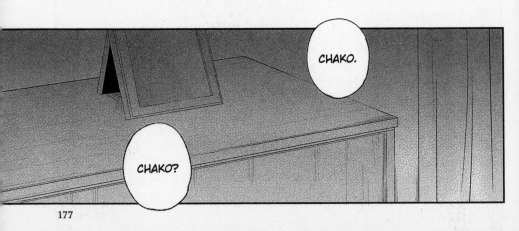

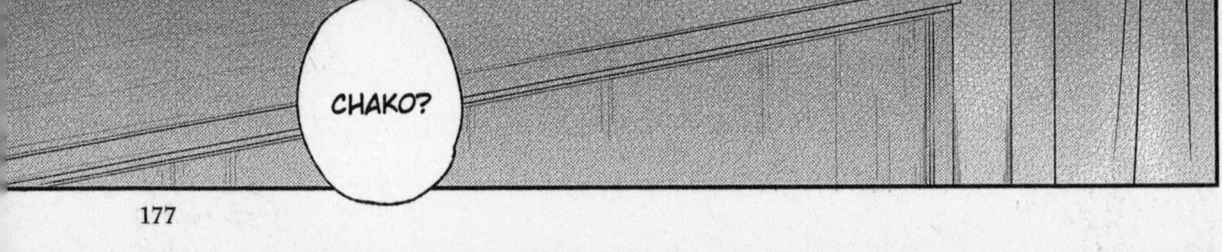
CHAKO.
CHAKO?

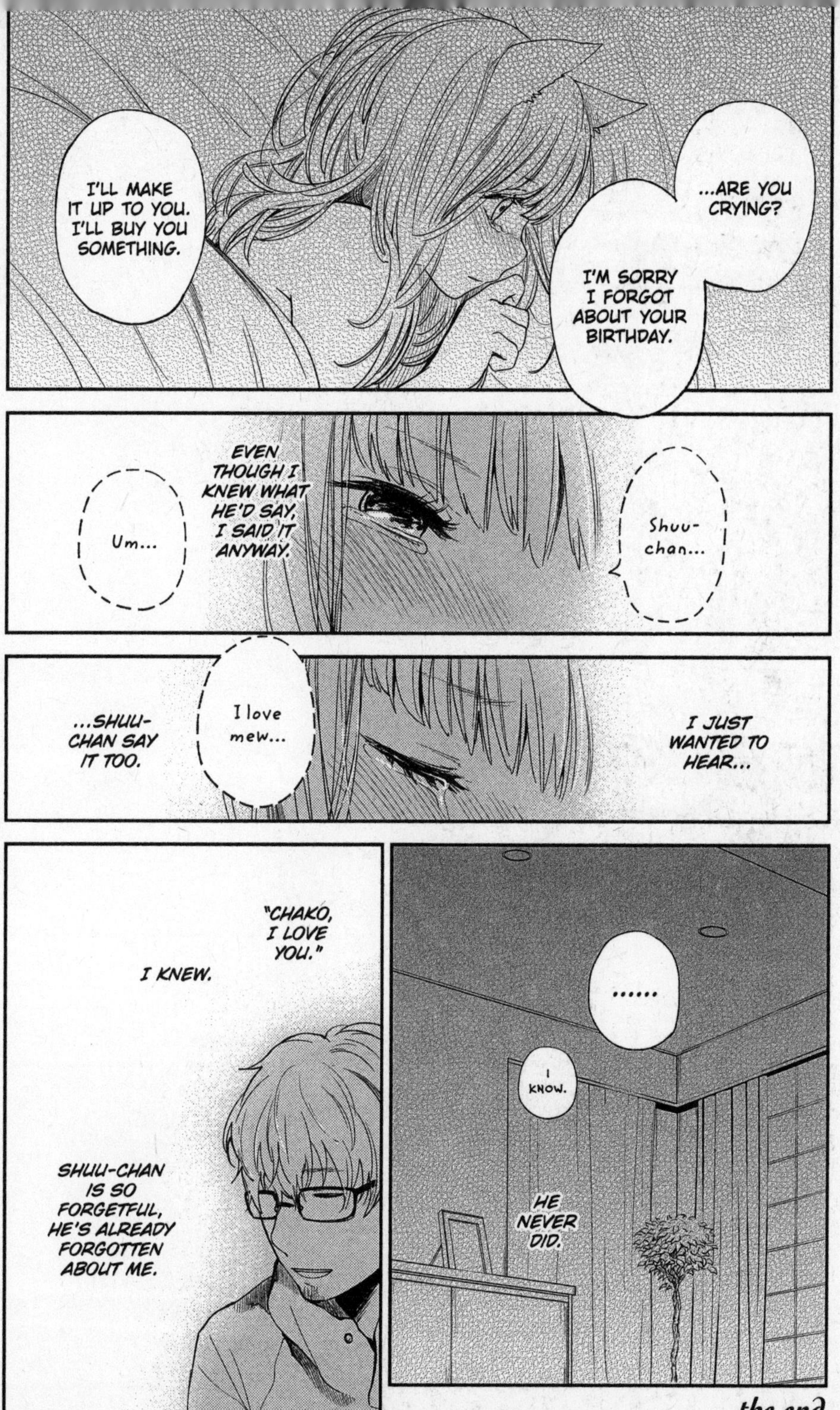
...ARE YOU CRYING?
I'M SORRY I FORGOT ABOUT YOUR BIRTHDAY.
I'LL MAKE IT UP TO YOU. I'LL BUY YOU SOMETHING.
Shuu-chan...
EVEN THOUGH I KNEW WHAT HE'D SAY, I SAID IT ANYWAY.
Um...
I JUST WANTED TO HEAR...
I love mew...
...SHUU-CHAN SAY IT TOO.
......
I KNOW.
HE NEVER DID.
"CHAKO, I LOVE YOU."
I KNEW.
SHUU-CHAN IS SO FORGETFUL, HE'S ALREADY FORGOTTEN ABOUT ME.

the end

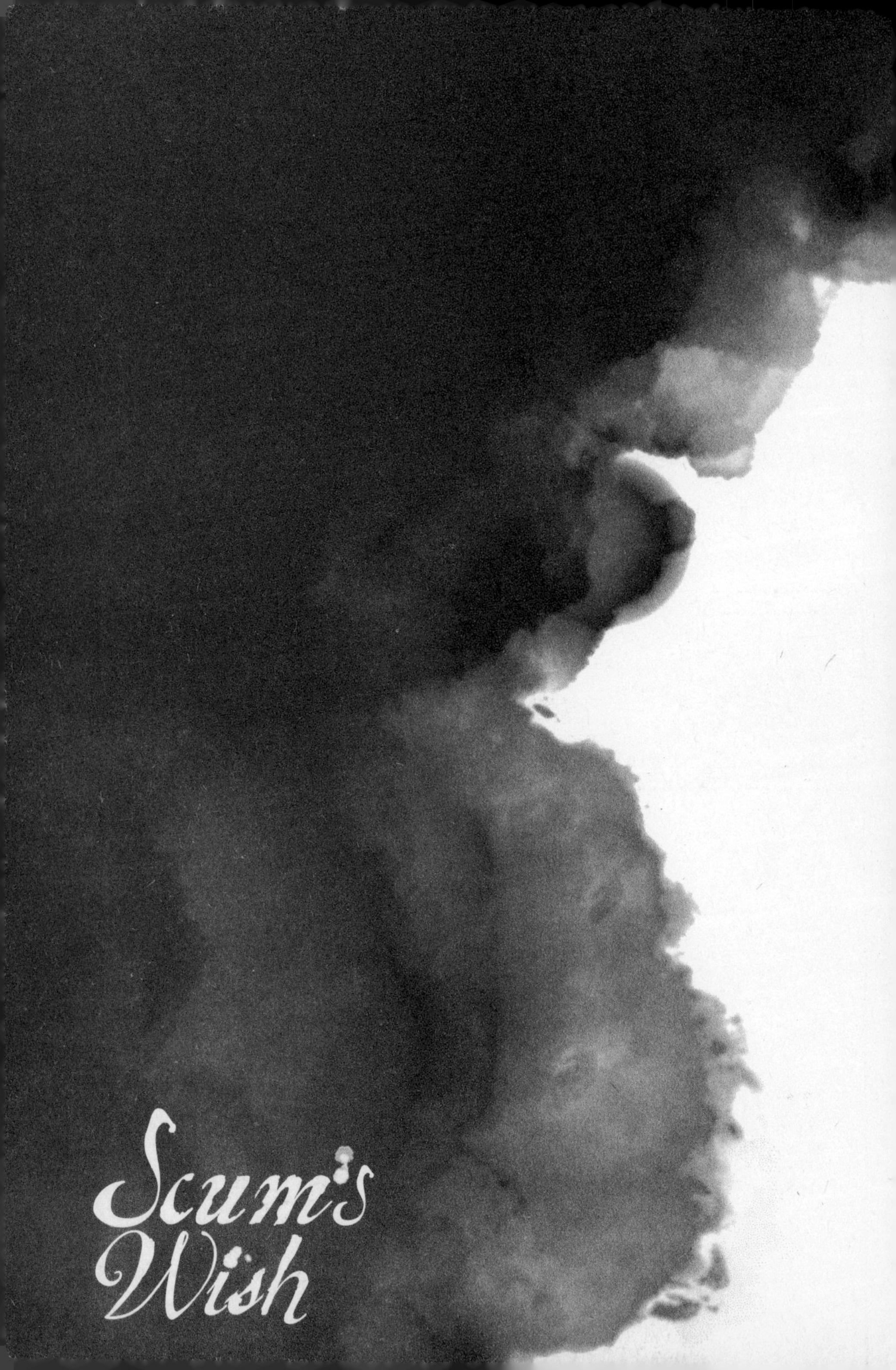
Scum's
Wish

W9-AJQ-974

SCUM'S WISH 1

mengo yokoyari

Original Translation Draft: David Rowe-Caplan, Megan Denton
Lettering: Erin Hickman

This book is a work of fiction. Names, characters, places, and incidents are the product of the author's imagination or are used fictitiously. Any resemblance to actual events, locales, or persons, living or dead, is coincidental.

KUZU NO HONKAI Vol. 1
© 2013 mengo yokoyari / SQUARE ENIX CO., LTD. First published in Japan in 2013 by SQUARE ENIX CO., LTD. English translation rights arranged with SQUARE ENIX CO., LTD. and Yen Press, LLC through Tuttle-Mori Agency, Inc., Tokyo.

English translation © 2016 by SQUARE ENIX CO., LTD.

Yen Press, LLC supports the right to free expression and the value of copyright. The purpose of copyright is to encourage writers and artists to produce the creative works that enrich our culture.

The scanning, uploading, and distribution of this book without permission is a theft of the author's intellectual property. If you would like permission to use material from the book (other than for review purposes), please contact the publisher. Thank you for your support of the author's rights.

Yen Press
1290 Avenue of the Americas
New York, NY 10104

Visit us at yenpress.com
facebook.com/yenpress
twitter.com/yenpress
yenpress.tumblr.com
instagram.com/yenpress

First Yen Press Edition: October 2016

Yen Press is an imprint of Yen Press, LLC.
The Yen Press name and logo are trademarks of Yen Press, LLC.

The publisher is not responsible for websites (or their content) that are not owned by the publisher.

Library of Congress Control Number: 2016946071

ISBNs: 978-0-316-46372-0 (paperback)
       978-0-316-50402-7 (ebook)

10 9 8 7 6 5 4 3 2 1

BVG

Printed in the United States of America